THE GUINNESS BOOK OF
BRITISH HIT ALBUMS
JO & TIM RICE
PAUL GAMBACCINI MIKE READ

THE GUINNESS BOOK OF BRITISH HIT ALBUMS

JO AND TIM RICE
PAUL GAMBACCINI
AND MIKE READ

Editorial Associate
Steve Smith

THE BRITISH HIT ALBUMS 1958-82
Alphabetically by Artist Pages 9-180
Album Facts & Feats Pages 181-216

GRRR BOOKS/**GUINNESS** BOOKS

ACKNOWLEDGEMENTS

Our grateful thanks to the following who supplied reference material for the cover design: Aubrey Powell of Hipgnosis; Capitol Records; Sian Davies of Virgin Records; Jonathan Morrish of CBS Records; Brian Southall of EMI; Patsy Johnson of WEA Records; Lionel Berge and Clive Fisher of Polydor Ltd; Decca Records; Sheila Sedgewick of RCA Records; Shelly Clarke of Charisma; Chris Poole of Chrysalis; Cherry Lill of DJM Records; A & M Records.

Thanks also to those who supplied photos, in particular John Beecher, Tony Barratt, Rex Features, Adrian Boot, S. K. R. Photos, Anabas Products, London Features International and Duffy.

Special thanks, too, to Eileen Heinink and Judy Craymer for their continuing support.

Editor: Alex E Reid

Design and Layout: David Roberts

Cover Design and Artwork: David Roberts, Brian Robins and Eddie Botchway.

Editorial Assistance: Maureen E Anderson, Sheila Goldsmith, Barbara Edwards and Melanie Georgi

First Edition
© **Grrr Books Ltd and Guinness Superlatives Ltd 1983**

Published in Great Britain by
Guinness Superlatives Ltd,
2 Cecil Court, London Road, Enfield, Middlesex
GRRR Books
196 Shaftesbury Avenue, London WC2

**Guinness is a registered trade mark of
Guinness Superlatives Ltd**

British Library Cataloguing in Publication Data

The Guinness book of British hit albums.
1. Music, Popular (Songs, etc.)–Great Britain–
Discography
I. Rice, Jo
016. 7899′1245   ML156.4.P6

ISBN 0-85112-246-9

Typeset by Bemrose Confidential and Information Products Ltd. and Hazell Watson & Viney Ltd.

Printed and bound in England by Hazell Watson & Viney Ltd, Aylesbury, Bucks

INTRODUCTION

'By Popular Demand' has become a much abused phrase, trotted out to justify television repeats, shallow but safe West End revivals, and repetitive encores from musicians who don't know any other material. *The Guinness Book of British Hit Albums* is genuinely presented, dare we say it, by popular demand.

When our first edition of *The Guinness Book of British Hit Singles* became a surprise success, we decided to make it a biennial affair, but dismissed the idea of compiling a companion volume on the LP charts. After all, we thought, people are more likely to remember an individual single than an entire album, and the very idea of 'our song' focusses attention on one side of one 45.

We underestimated the interest of our readers. For years letters arrived regularly asking us to provide a definitive reference book on the UK album charts. It seems that in the latter years of rock-and-roll history, the long-player has become just as important to collectors and chart watchers as the single, particularly since singles are now invariably taken from albums. This was not always the case, but in the seventies record companies learned that for marketing purposes the presence of one or two hits on an LP was invaluable. Gone are the days when the Beatles and the Rolling Stones would release singles and albums as separate events: "Don't You Want Me," the 1981 Christmas number one, was the fourth single from the Human League's 'Dare'.

It was the Beatles who changed the LP market. Before the Fab Four, the album lists were dominated by film soundtracks and original Broadway cast performances. Elvis Presley, Cliff Richard and the Shadows were the only rock artists who regularly did well in this form of recording. A mere glance at the list of number ones since the inception of charts in 1958 will provide the startling news that the soundtrack of 'South Pacific' topped the table for over 2 years. High spots were held for over a year by 'My Fair Lady' and 'West Side Story', to name but the two most prominent of a batch of stage and screen successes. When the Beatles issued 'Please Please Me' in 1963, the album chart changed irrevocably. Rock music became the major force in the field, and most of the

number ones since have come from artists whose greatest appeal is to the younger buyer. The historic success of 'The Sound of Music' soundtrack only points out how the packages from other major movies, from the James Bond films to 'Star Wars', have failed to perform in similar style.

In the early seventies another kind of long player began making the chart. Innocuous compilation albums shot to the top when supported by television advertising. This type of promotion had tremendous impact in its first years. After all, bringing a particular piece of plastic to the attention of millions of consumers at the same moment greatly enhanced the possibility the product would be bought. But by the mid-seventies, the novelty had worn off, and the songs had to be strong and the commercial catchy to attract enough purchasers to affect the chart.

Many of the records which scored with television touting are found in our Various Artists section, but it is sadly not possible to distinguish all those solo sets (for example, those of the heavily advertised Slim Whitman) whose numerical placings were doubtlessly improved by TV. The other hidden distortion in the chart came from mid-price or budget albums, which until 1972 were not segregated from their full price relations. Some boasted remarkable chart careers they might never have enjoyed at regular cost.

With these notable caveats, we invite our old friends and new chums keen on LP history to sample this very first edition of *The Guinness Book of British Hit Albums*. Should you enjoy it, we hope to present updated volumes on a regular basis. Should you not like it, we will flagellate ourselves with wet strands of spaghetti and find some other way to express our passion for the charts. These books are, after all, a socially approved form of madness, and they allow us to be crazy together.

PAUL GAMBACCINI
MIKE READ
JO RICE
TIM RICE
Directors, Grrr Books Ltd

EDITORIAL COMMENT

Here it is at last — the companion volume to *The Guinness Book of British Hit Singles,* currently in its fourth edition. Compiling *Hit Albums* turned out to be quite different from the preparation of the singles book, and we had to make one or two changes to our usual format.

The first problem stemmed from the longevity of an album compared to a single. Many albums return to the chart on numerous occasions and were we to list every re-entry separately this book would probably be thick enough to warrant an entry in our publisher's *Guinness Book of Records*. To simplify the proceedings and keep the book at a reasonable length (and price!) we decided to publish the highest position an album reached overall and the *total* amount of weeks it spent on the chart. Only re-issues of albums were listed separately. On occasions this method does not fully reflect chart developments; for instance, when Elvis Presley died nearly two dozen of his LPs flooded into the chart. However, many of these were old albums re-entering and so their runs in 1977 will have been added to their previous runs. Thankfully moments like this are few and far between.

A second problem was that the album chart wasn't as well-disciplined as the singles chart, especially in the late sixties and early seventies. At this time it seemed that no two consecutive charts had the same amount of LPs in them. An album floating around the lower reaches of the Top Forty could suddenly disappear as the chart contracted to a Top Thirty, only to reappear when the chart returned to normal size a few weeks later. Nonetheless, the task of this book is to report the charts, not to guess what they might have been.

A third problem was the difficulty we had in obtaining all the charts. In the end we got our hands on all but those for 28 April and 12 May 1960. Fortunately, we could work out these missing charts by back-tracking from the following weeks' lists. The only thing we may have missed is if an album happened to chart for one of those weeks and didn't appear again. Our humble apologies to any artist who may have been denied chart success in this way.

Please let us know what you think of this first *Hit Albums* and any improvements you can suggest for future editions.

STEVE SMITH : Editorial Associate

THE CHARTS

This is a brief section about the charts we used to compile this book and to explain how they changed over the years. If ever a week went by without a chart being compiled, the previous week's chart was used again for the purposes of all the information and statistics used in this book. When albums began to be produced in both mono and stereo (1966) we listed the stereo catalogue number only. The dates used in this book correspond to the Saturday of the week in which the chart was published. This does not necessarily coincide with the date given on the chart, but we have tried to create a consistent dating over a period in which the dates of compilation of each week's charts tended to vary.

A) MELODY MAKER
8 Nov 1958. First album chart published—Top Ten.
27 Jun–Aug 1959 inclusive: No charts published so 20 Jun chart repeated throughout.

B) RECORD RETAILER
26 Mar 1960   First Record Retailer chart published. Top twenty. We now take our information from this chart though the MM chart continued.

14 Apr 1966:	*Chart increases to Top Thirty.*
8 Dec 1966:	*Chart increases to Top Forty.*
12 Feb 1969:	*Chart drops to Top Fifteen.*
11 Jun 1969:	*Chart increases to Top Twenty.*
25 Jun 1969:	*Chart increases to Top Forty.*
9 Aug 1969:	*32 records in chart this week only.*
11 Oct 1969:	*Chart drops to Top Twenty-five.*
8 Nov 1969—	
24 Jan 1970:	*Chart varies between 20 and 24 records each week*
31 Jan 1970—	
9 Jan 1971:	*Chart varies between 47 and 77 records each week*

A Top 100 was compiled during this period but was only available to special subscribers.

9 Jan 1971:	*Record Retailer becomes RECORD AND TAPE RETAILER.*
16 Jan 1971:	*Chart stabilises at Top Fifty.*
6 Feb—	
27 Mar 1971:	*No charts published due to a postal strike. 30 Jan chart repeated throughout.*
7 Aug 1971:	*Record and Tape Retailer combine their Full Price (the one we have been using) and the previously separate Budget charts. This means there is a sudden influx of budget label albums into the chart.*
8 Jan 1972:	*The chart reverts to Full Price albums only so the budget albums exit as quickly as they appeared.*
18 Mar 1972:	*Record and Tape Retailer becomes MUSIC WEEK.*
13 Jan 1973:	*Top 24 only for this week.*
5 Jan 1974:	*Top 42 only for this week.*
5 Jul 1975:	*Chart increases to Top 60.*
14 Jan 1978:	*Top 30 only for this week.*
2 Dec 1978:	*Chart increases to Top 75.*
13 Oct 1979:	*Two consecutive weeks' charts published simultaneously as a result of a speedy new chart compilation system which enabled Music Week, hitherto publishing the album chart more than a week after the survey period, to catch up a week. Both charts of this date are included in our calculations.*
8 Aug 1981:	*Chart increases to Top 100.*

Part One: HIT ALBUMS
Alphabetically by Artist

The information given in this part of the book is as follows: Date LP first hit the chart, title, label, catalogue number, highest position reached on chart, total number of weeks on the chart. Number one albums are highlighted with a green star, other top ten albums by a black dot and a black dagger indicates hits still on chart at 31 December 1982, as follows:

> * **Number one album**
> ● **Top ten album**
> † **Album still on chart at 31 December 1982**

For the purposes of this book, an album is considered a re-issue if it hits the chart for a second time with a new catalogue number.

Describing a recording act in one sentence is often fraught with danger, but we have attempted to do so above each act's list of hits. Although we are aware that many of the 'vocalists' thus described also play an instrument, we have only mentioned this fact where the artist's instrumental skills were an important factor in the album's success.

Date	Title *Label Number*	Position		Date	Title *Label Number*	Position

ABBA

Sweden, male/female vocal instrumental group

8 Jun 74	**WATERLOO** *Epic EPC 80179*	28	2 wks
31 Jan 76	**ABBA** *Epic EPC 80835*	13	10 wks
10 Apr 76	★ **GREATEST HITS** *Epic EPC 69218*	1	130 wks
27 Nov 76	★ **ARRIVAL** *Epic EPC 86108*	1	92 wks
4 Feb 78	★ **THE ALBUM** *Epic EPC 86052*	1	61 wks
19 May 79	★ **VOULEZ-VOUS** *Epic EPC 86086*	1	43 wks
10 Nov 79	★ **GREATEST HITS VOL.2** *Epic EPC 10017*	1	63 wks
22 Nov 80	★ **SUPER TROUPER** *Epic EPC 10022*	1	43 wks
19 Dec 81	★ **THE VISITORS** *Epic EPC 10032*	1	21 wks
20 Nov 82	★ **THE SINGLES-THE FIRST TEN YEARS** *Epic ABBA 10*	1†	6 wks

ABC

UK, male vocal/instrumental group

3 Jul 82	★ **THE LEXICON OF LOVE** *Neutron/Phonogram NTRS 1*	1†	26 wks

Father ABRAHAM and the SMURFS

Holland, male vocalist as himself and Smurfs

25 Nov 78	**FATHER ABRAHAM IN SMURFLAND** *Decca Smurf 1*	19	11 wks

AC/DC

Australia/UK, male vocal/instrumental group

5 Nov 77	**LET THERE BE ROCK** *Atlantic K 50366*	17	5 wks
20 May 78	**POWERAGE** *Atlantic K 50483*	26	9 wks
28 Oct 78	**IF YOU WANT BLOOD YOU'VE GOT IT** *Atlantic K 50532*	13	58 wks
18 Aug 79	● **HIGHWAY TO HELL** *Atlantic K 50628*	8	32 wks
9 Aug 80	★ **BACK IN BLACK** *Atlantic K 50735*	1	40 wks
5 Dec 81	● **FOR THOSE ABOUT TO ROCK** *Atlantic K 50851*	3	29 wks

Australia only for first four hits.

ADAM and the ANTS

UK, male vocal/instrumental group

15 Nov 80	★ **KINGS OF THE WILD FRONTIER** *CBS 84549*	1	66 wks
17 Jan 81	**DIRK WEARS WHITE SOX** *Do It RIDE 3*	16	29 wks
14 Nov 81	● **PRINCE CHARMING** *CBS 85268*	2	21 wks
23 Oct 82	● **FRIEND OR FOE** *CBS 25040*	5†	10 wks

ADAMS SINGERS

UK, male/female vocal group

16 Apr 60	**SING SOMETHING SIMPLE** *Pye MPL 28013*	15	4 wks
24 Nov 62	**SING SOMETHING SIMPLE** *Pye Golden Guinea GGL 0150*	15	2 wks
20 Nov 76	**SING SOMETHING SIMPLE '76** *Warwick WW 5016/17*	23	8 wks
25 Dec 82	**SING SOMETHING SIMPLE** *Ronco RTD 2087*	74	1 wk

All these similarly titled albums are different.

ADICTS

US, male vocal/instrumental group

4 Dec 82	**SOUND OF MUSIC** *Razor RAZ 2*	99	1 wk

ADVERTS

UK, male/female vocal instrumental group

11 Mar 78	**CROSSING THE RED SEA WITH THE ADVERTS** *Bright BRL 201*	38	1 wk

AFTER THE FIRE

UK, male vocal/instrumental group

13 Oct 79	**LASER LOVE** *CBS 83795*	57	1 wk
1 Nov 80	**80 F** *Epic EPC 84545*	69	1 wk
3 Apr 82	**BATTERIES NOT INCLUDED** *CBS 85566*	82	2 wks

ALEXANDER BROTHERS

UK, male vocal duo

10 Dec 66	**THESE ARE MY MOUNTAINS** *Pye GGL 0375*	29	1 wk

Mose ALLISON

US, male vocalist/instrumentalist - piano

4 Jun 66	**MOSE ALIVE** *Atlantic 587-007*	30	1 wk

Date	Title Label Number	Position		Date	Title Label Number	Position	

ALLMAN BROTHERS BAND

US, male vocal/instrumental group

6 Oct 73	BROTHERS AND SISTERS	42	3 wks
	Warner Bros. K 47507		
6 Mar 76	THE ROAD GOES ON FOREVER	54	1 wk
	Capricorn 2637 101		

Herb ALPERT and the TIJUANA BRASS

US, male instrumentalist - trumpet

29 Jan 66	● GOING PLACES Pye NPL 28065	4	138 wks
23 Apr 66	● WHIPPED CREAM AND OTHER DELIGHTS	2	42 wks
	Pye NPL 28058		
28 May 66	WHAT NOW MY LOVE Pye NPL 28077	18	17 wks
11 Feb 67	● S.R.O. Pye NSPL 28088	5	26 wks
15 Jul 67	SOUNDS LIKE A&M AMLS 900	21	10 wks
3 Feb 68	NINTH A&M AMLS 905	26	9 wks
29 Jun 68	● BEST OF THE BRASS A&M AMLS 916	4	21 wks
9 Aug 69	WARM A&M AMLS 937	30	4 wks
14 Mar 70	THE BRASS ARE COMIN' A&M AMLS 962	40	1 wk
30 May 70	● GREATEST HITS A&M AMLS 980	8	27 wks
27 Jun 70	DOWN MEXICO WAY A&M AMLS 974	64	1 wk
13 Nov 71	AMERICA A&M AMLB 1000	45	1 wk
12 Nov 77	40 GREATEST K-Tel NE 1005	45	2 wks
17 Nov 79	RISE A&M AMLH 64790	37	7 wks

Rise credits only Herb Alpert. On 29 Jun 67 Going Places and What Now My Love changed labels and numbers to A&M AMLS 965 and AMLS 977 respectively.

ALTERED IMAGES

UK, male/female vocal instrumental group

19 Sep 81	HAPPY BIRTHDAY Epic EPC 84893	26	21 wks
15 May 82	PINKY BLUE Epic EPC 85665	12	10 wks

AMEN CORNER

UK, male vocal/instrumental group

30 Mar 68	ROUND AMEN CORNER Deram SML 1021	26	7 wks
1 Nov 69	EXPLOSIVE COMPANY Immediate IMSP 023	19	1 wk

AMERICA

US, male vocal/instrumental group

22 Jan 72	AMERICA Warner Bros. K 46093	14	13 wks
9 Dec 72	HOMECOMING Warner Bros. K 46180	21	5 wks
10 Nov 73	HAT TRICK Warner Bros. K 56016	41	3 wks
7 Feb 76	HISTORY - AMERICA'S GREATEST HITS	60	1 wk
	Warner Bros. K 56169		

Jon ANDERSON

UK, male vocalist

24 Jul 76	● OLIAS OF SUNHILLOW Atlantic K 50261	8	10 wks
15 Nov 80	SONG OF SEVEN Atlantic K 50756	38	3 wks
5 Jun 82	ANIMATION Polydor POLD 5044	43	6 wks

See also Jon and Vangelis

Laurie ANDERSON

US, female vocalist/multi-instrumentalist

1 May 82	BIG SCIENCE Warner Bros. K 57002	29	6 wks

Lynn ANDERSON

US, female vocalist

17 Apr 71	ROSE GARDEN CBS 64333	45	1 wk

Moira ANDERSON

UK, female vocalist

20 Jun 70	THESE ARE MY SONGS Decca SKL 5016	50	1 wk

See also Harry Secombe and Moira Anderson

ANGELIC UPSTARTS

UK, male vocal/instrumental group

18 Aug 79	TEENAGE WARNING Warner Bros. K 50634	29	7 wks
12 Apr 80	WE'VE GOTTA GET OUT OF THIS PLACE	54	3 wks
	Warner Bros. K 56806		
26 Sep 81	ANGELIC UPSTARTS Zonophone ZEM 102	27	7 wks

ANIMALS

UK, male vocal/instrumental group

14 Nov 64	● THE ANIMALS Columbia 33SX 1669	6	20 wks
22 May 65	● ANIMAL TRACKS Columbia 33SX 1708	6	26 wks
16 Apr 66	● MOST OF THE ANIMALS Columbia 33SX 6035	4	20 wks
28 May 66	● ANIMALISMS Decca LK 4797	4	17 wks
25 Sep 71	MOST OF THE ANIMALS MFP 5218	18	3 wks

ANTI - PASTI

UK, male vocal vocal/instrumental group

15 Aug 81	THE LAST CALL Rondelet ABOUT 5	31	7 wks

A.B.C. Initial success with their Dictionary of Romance.

Right **THE ANIMALS** 3 years of Animal Magic in the chart before the leader of the pack Eric Burdon made tracks in the opposite direction.

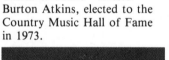

CHET ATKINS Chester Burton Atkins, elected to the Country Music Hall of Fame in 1973.

HERB ALBERT Prophetic title for their debut chart album.

BAD MANNERS
Rude Boys.

JOAN BAEZ A snap taken the same month that her eponymous album hit the chart—in folk circles she was the Baez Knaez.

Date	Title *Label Number*	Position		Date	Title *Label Number*	Position	

ANTI-NOWHERE LEAGUE

UK, male vocal/instrumental group

22 May 82	**WE ARE.....THE LEAGUE** *WXYZ LMNOP 1*	24	11 wks

ANTS — See *ADAM and the ANTS*

APRIL WINE

Canada, male vocal/instrumental group

15 Mar 80	**HARDER...FASTER** *Capitol EST 12013*	34	5 wks
24 Jan 81	**THE NATURE OF THE BEAST** *Capitol EST 12125*	48	3 wks

ARGENT

UK, male vocal/instrumental group

29 Apr 72	**ALL TOGETHER NOW** *Epic EPC 64962*	13	8 wks
31 Mar 73	**IN DEEP** *Epic EPC 65475*	49	1 wk

Joan ARMATRADING

UK, female vocalist

4 Sep 76	**JOAN ARMATRADING** *A & M AMLH 64588*	12	27 wks
1 Oct 77	● **SHOW SOME EMOTION** *A & M AMLH 68433*	6	11 wks
14 Oct 78	**TO THE LIMIT** *A & M AMLH 64732*	13	10 wks
24 May 80	● **ME MYSELF I** *A & M AMLH 64809*	5	23 wks
12 Sep 81	● **WALK UNDER LADDERS** *A & M AMLH 64876*	6	29 wks

Louis ARMSTRONG

US, male vocalist/instrumentalist - trumpet

28 Oct 61	**JAZZ CLASSICS** *Ace Of Hearts AH 7*	20	1 wk
22 Oct 60	**SATCHMO PLAYS KING OLIVER** *Audio Fidelity AFLP 1930*	20	1 wk
27 Jun 64	**HELLO DOLLY** *London HAR 8190*	11	6 wks
16 Nov 68	**WHAT A WONDERFUL WORLD** *Stateside SSL 10247*	37	3 wks
20 Feb 82	**THE VERY BEST OF LOUIS ARMSTRONG** *Warwick WW 5112*	30	3 wks

ASIA

UK, male vocal/instrumental group

10 Apr 82	**ASIA** *Geffen GEF 85577*	11	36 wks

ASSOCIATES

UK, male vocal/instrumental group

22 May 82	● **SULK** *Associates ASCL 1*	10	20 wks

ASWAD

UK, male vocal/instrumental group

24 Jul 82	**NOT SATISFIED** *CBS 85666*	50	6 wks

ATHLETICO SPIZZ 80

UK, male vocal/instrumental group

26 Jul 80	**DO A RUNNER** *A & M AMLE 68514*	27	5 wks

Chet ATKINS

US, male instrumentalist - guitar

18 Mar 61	**THE OTHER CHET ATKINS** *RCA RD 27194*	20	1 wk
17 Jun 61	**CHET ATKINS' WORKSHOP** *RCA RD 27214*	19	1 wk
30 Feb 63	**CARIBBEAN GUITAR** *RCA RD 7519*	17	3 wks

Rowan ATKINSON

UK, male comedian

7 Feb 81	**LIVE IN BELFAST** *Arista SPART 1150*	44	9 wks

ATOMIC ROOSTER

UK, male vocal/instrumental group

13 Jun 70	**ATOMIC ROOSTER** *B & C CAS 1010*	49	1 wk
16 Jan 71	**DEATH WALKS BEHIND YOU** *Charisma CAS 1026*	12	8 wks
21 Aug 71	**IN HEARING OF ATOMIC ROOSTER** *Pegasus PEG 1*	18	4 wks

ATTRACTIONS — See *Elvis COSTELLO and the ATTRACTIONS*

AU PAIRS

UK, female/male vocal/instrumental group

6 Jun 81	**PLAYING WITH A DIFFERENT SEX** *Human HUMAN 1*	33	7 wks
4 Sep 82	**SENSE AND SENSUALITY** *Kamera KAM 010*	79	3 wks

Brian AUGER TRINITY — See *Julie DRISCOLL and the Brian AUGER TRINITY*

Date	Title *Label Number*	Position

Patti AUSTIN

US, female vocalist

26 Sep 81	EVERY HOME SHOULD HAVE ONE *Quest K 56931*	99	1 wk

AVERAGE WHITE BAND

UK, male vocal/instrumental group

1 Mar 75	● AVERAGE WHITE BAND *Atlantic K 50058*	6	14 wks
5 Jul 75	CUT THE CAKE *Atlantic K 50146*	28	4 wks
31 Jul 76	SOUL SEARCHING TIME *Atlantic K 50272*	60	1 wk
10 Mar 79	I FEEL NO FRET *RCA XL 13063*	15	15 wks
31 May 80	SHINE *RCA XL 13123*	14	13 wks

Pam AYERS

UK, female vocalist

27 Mar 76	SOME OF ME POEMS AND SONGS *Galaxy GAL 6003*	13	14 wks
18 Dec 76	SOME MORE OF ME POEMS AND SONGS *Galaxy GAL 6010*	23	6 wks

Charles AZNAVOUR

France, male vocalist

29 Jun 74	AZNAVOUR SINGS AZNAVOUR VOL.3 *Barclay 80472*	23	7 wks
7 Sep 74	● A TAPESTRY OF DREAMS *Barclay 90003*	9	13 wks
2 Aug 80	HIS GREATEST LOVE SONGS *K-Tel NE 1078*	73	1 wk

BACCARA

Spain, female vocal duo

4 Mar 78	BACCARA *RCA PL 28316*	26	6 wks

Burt BACHARACH

US, orchestra and chorus

22 May 65	● HIT MAKER - BURT BACHARACH *London HAR 8233*	3	18 wks
28 Nov 70	REACH OUT *A & M AMLS 908*	52	3 wks
3 Apr 71	● PORTRAIT IN MUSIC *A & M AMLS 2010*	5	22 wks

BACHELORS

Ireland, male vocal group

27 Jun 64	● THE BACHELORS AND 16 GREAT SONGS *Decca LK 4614*	2	44 wks
9 Oct 65	MORE GREAT SONG HITS FROM THE BACHELORS *Decca LK 4721*	15	6 wks
9 Jul 66	HITS OF THE SIXTIES *Decca TXL 102*	12	9 wks
5 Nov 66	BACHELORS' GIRLS *Decca LK 4827*	24	8 wks
1 Jul 67	GOLDEN ALL TIME HITS *Decca SKL 4849*	19	7 wks
14 Jun 69	● WORLD OF THE BACHELORS *Decca SPA 2*	8	18 wks
23 Aug 69	WORLD OF THE BACHELORS VOL.2 *Decca SPA 22*	11	7 wks
22 Dec 79	25 GOLDEN GREATS *Warwick WW 5068*	38	4 wks

BACHMAN-TURNER OVERDRIVE

Canada, male vocal/instrumental group

14 Dec 74	NOT FRAGILE *Mercury 9100 007*	12	13 wks

BAD COMPANY

UK, male vocal/instrumental group

15 Jun 74	● BAD COMPANY *Island ILPS 9279*	3	25 wks
12 Apr 75	● STRAIGHT SHOOTER *Island ILPS 9304*	3	27 wks
21 Feb 76	● RUN WITH THE PACK *Island ILPS 9346*	4	12 wks
19 Mar 77	BURNIN' SKY *Island ILPS 9441*	17	8 wks
17 Mar 79	● DESOLATION ANGELS *Swansong SSK 59408*	10	9 wks
28 Aug 82	ROUGH DIAMONDS *Swansong SSK 59419*	15	6 wks

BAD MANNERS

UK, male vocal/instrumental group

26 Apr 80	SKA 'N' B *Magnet MAG 5033*	34	13 wks
29 Nov 80	LOONEY TUNES *Magnet MAG 5038*	36	12 wks
24 Oct 81	GOSH IT'S BAD MANNERS *Magnet MAGL 5043*	18	12 wks
27 Nov 82	FORGING AHEAD *Magnet MAGL 5050*	78	1 wk

Joan BAEZ

US, female vocalist

18 Jul 64	● JOAN BAEZ IN CONCERT VOL.2	8	19 wks
	Fontana TFL 6033		
15 May 65	● JOAN BAEZ NO.5 *Fontana TFL 6043*	3	27 wks
19 Jun 65	● JOAN BAEZ *Fontana TFL 6002*	9	13 wks
27 Nov 65	● FAREWELL ANGELINA *Fontana TFL 6058*	5	23 wks
19 Jul 69	JOAN BAEZ ON VANGUARD	15	5 wks
	Vanguard SVXL 100		
3 Apr 71	FIRST TEN YEARS *Vanguard 6635 003*	41	1 wk

BAKER-GURVITZ ARMY

UK, male vocal/instrumental group

22 Feb 75	BAKER-GURVITZ ARMY *Vertigo 9103 201*	22	5 wks

See also Ginger Baker's Air Force.

Ginger BAKER'S AIR FORCE

UK, male vocal/instrumental group

13 Jun 70	GINGER BAKER'S AIR FORCE *Polydor 2662-001*	37	1 wk

See also Baker-Gurvitz Army.

Kenny BALL

UK, male vocalist/instrumentalist - trumpet

7 Sep 63	● KENNY BALL'S GOLDEN HITS	4	26 wks
	Pye Golden Guinea GGL 0209		

See also Kenny Ball, Chris Barber and Acker Bilk.

Kenny BALL, Chris BARBER and Acker BILK

UK, All That Jazz

25 Aug 62	★ BEST OF BALL, BARBER AND BILK	1	24 wks
	Pye Golden Guinea GGL 0131		

See also Kenny Ball, and Chris Barber, and Chris Barber and Acker Bilk, and Mr Acker Bilk.

BAND

Canada, male vocal/instrumental group

31 Jan 70	THE BAND *Capitol EST 132*	25	11 wks
3 Oct 70	STAGE FRIGHT *Capitol EA SW 425*	15	6 wks
27 Nov 71	CAHOOTS *Capitol EA-ST 651*	41	1 wk
6 May 78	THE LAST WALTZ *Warner Bros. K 66076*	39	4 wks

The Last Waltz *also features various other artists.*

Tony BANKS

UK, male instrumentalist - keyboards

20 Oct 79	A CURIOUS FEELING *Charisma CAS 1148*	21	5 wks

BANSHEES — See *SIOUXSIE and the BANSHEES*

Chris BARBER

UK, male vocalist/instrumentalist - trombone

24 Sep 60	CHRIS BARBER BAND BOX NO.2	17	1 wk
	Columbia 33SCX 3277		
5 Nov 60	ELITE SYNCOPATIONS *Columbia 33SX 1245*	18	1 wk
12 Nov 60	BEST OF CHRIS BARBER	17	1 wk
	Ace Of Clubs ACL 1037		

See also Kenny Ball, Chris Barber and Acker Bilk, and Chris Barber and Acker Bilk.

Chris BARBER and Acker BILK

UK, jazzmen

27 May 61	● BEST OF BARBER AND BILK VOL.1	4	43 wks
	Pye GGL 0075		
11 Nov 61	● BEST OF BARBER AND BILK VOL.2	8	18 wks
	Pye GGL 0096		

See also Kenny Ball, Chris Barber and Acker Bilk, and Chris Barber, and Mr Acker Bilk.

BARCLAY JAMES HARVEST

UK, male vocal/instrumental group

14 Dec 74	BARCLAY JAMES HARVEST LIVE	40	2 wks
	Polydor 2683 052		
18 Oct 75	TIME HONOURED GHOST *Polydor 2383 361*	32	3 wks
23 Oct 76	OCTOBERON *Polydor 2442 144*	19	4 wks
1 Oct 77	GONE TO EARTH *Polydor 2442 148*	30	7 wks
21 Oct 78	BARCLAY JAMES HARVEST XII	31	2 wks
	Polydor POLD 5006		
23 May 81	TURN OF THE TIDE *Polydor POLD 5040*	55	2 wks
24 Jul 82	A CONCERT FOR THE PEOPLE (BERLIN)	15	11 wks
	Polydor POLD 5052		

Daniel BARENBOIM — See *John WILLIAMS and Daniel BARENBOIM*

Syd BARRETT

UK, male vocalist/instrumentalist - guitar

7 Feb 70	MADCAP LAUGHS *Harvest SHVL 765*	40	1 wk

BARRON-KNIGHTS

UK, male vocal/instrumental group

Date	Title *Label Number*	Position	
2 Dec 78	**NIGHT GALLERY** *Epic EPC 83221*	15	13 wks
1 Dec 79	**TEACH THE WORLD TO LAUGH** *Epic EPC 83891*	51	4 wks
13 Dec 80	**JUST A GIGGLE** *Epic EPC 84550*	62	5 wks

John BARRY

UK, male instrumental group/orchestra

Date	Title *Label Number*	Position	
29 Jan 72	**THE PERSUADERS** *CBS 64816*	18	9 wks

Count BASIE

US, male orchestra leader and instrumentalist - piano

Date	Title *Label Number*	Position	
16 Apr 60	**CHAIRMAN OF THE BOARD** *Columbia 33SX 1209*	17	1 wk

See also Frank Sinatra and Count Basie.

Toni BASIL

US, female vocalist

Date	Title *Label Number*	Position	
6 Feb 82	**WORD OF MOUTH** *Radialchoice BASIL 1*	15	16 wks

Shirley BASSEY

UK, female vocalist

Date	Title *Label Number*	Position	
28 Jan 61	**FABULOUS SHIRLEY BASSEY** *Columbia 33SX 1178*	12	2 wks
25 Feb 61	● **SHIRLEY** *Columbia 33SX 1286*	9	10 wks
17 Feb 62	**SHIRLEY BASSEY** *Columbia 33SX 1382*	14	11 wks
15 Dec 62	**LET'S FACE THE MUSIC** *Columbia 33SX 1454*	12	7 wks
4 Dec 65	**SHIRLEY BASSEY AT THE PIGALLE** *Columbia 33SX 1787*	16	7 wks
27 Aug 66	**I'VE GOT A SONG FOR YOU** *United Artists ULP 1142*	26	1 wk
17 Feb 68	**TWELVE OF THOSE SONGS** *Columbia SCX 6204*	38	3 wks
7 Dec 68	**GOLDEN HITS OF SHIRLEY BASSEY** *Columbia SCX 6294*	28	40 wks
11 Jul 70	**LIVE AT THE TALK OF THE TOWN** *United Artists UAS 29095*	38	6 wks
29 Aug 70	● **SOMETHING** *United Artists UAS 29100*	5	28 wks
15 May 71	● **SOMETHING ELSE** *United Artists UAG 29149*	7	9 wks
2 Oct 71	**BIG SPENDER** *Sunset SLS 50262*	27	8 wks
30 Oct 71	**IT'S MAGIC** *Starline SRS 5082*	32	1 wk
6 Nov 71	**THE FABULOUS SHIRLEY BASSEY** *MFP 1398*	48	1 wk
4 Dec 71	**WHAT NOW MY LOVE** *MFP 5230*	17	5 wks
8 Jan 72	**THE SHIRLEY BASSEY COLLECTION** *United Artists UAD 60013/4*	37	1 wk

Date	Title *Label Number*	Position	
19 Feb 72	**I CAPRICORN** *United Artists UAS 29246*	13	11 wks
29 Nov 72	**AND I LOVE YOU SO** *United artists UAS 29385*	24	9 wks
2 Jun 73	● **NEVER NEVER NEVER** *United Artists UAG 29471*	10	10 wks
15 Mar 75	● **THE SHIRLEY BASSEY SINGLES ALBUM** *United Artists UAS 29728*	2	23 wks
1 Nov 75	**GOOD, BAD BUT BEAUTIFUL** *United Artists UAS 29881*	13	7 wks
15 May 76	**LOVE, LIFE AND FEELINGS** *United Artists UAS 29944*	17	5 wks
4 Dec 76	**THOUGHTS OF LOVE** *United Artists UAS 30011*	15	9 wks
25 Jun 77	**YOU TAKE MY HEART AWAY** *United Artists UAS 30037*	34	5 wks
4 Nov 78	● **25TH ANNIVERSARY ALBUM** *United Artists SBTV 601 4748*	3	12 wks
12 May 79	**THE MAGIC IS YOU** *United Artists UATV 30230*	40	5 wks
17 Jul 82	**LOVE SONGS** *Applause APKL 1163*	48	5 wks

Let's Face The Music *has credit "with The Nelson Riddle Orchestra"*

BAUHAUS

UK, male vocal/instrumental group

Date	Title *Label Number*	Position	
15 Nov 80	**IN THE FLAT FIELD** *4AD CAD 13*	72	1 wk
24 Oct 81	**MASK** *Beggars Banquet BEGA 29*	30	5 wks
30 Oct 82	● **THE SKY'S GONE OUT** *Beggars Banquet BEGA 42*	4	6 wks

BAY CITY ROLLERS

UK, male vocal/instrumental group

Date	Title *Label Number*	Position	
12 Oct 74	★ **ROLLIN'** *Bell BELLS 244*	1	62 wks
3 May 75	★ **ONCE UPON A STAR** *Bell SYBEL 8001*	1	37 wks
13 Dec 75	● **WOULDN'T YOU LIKE IT** *Bell SYBEL 8002*	3	12 wks
25 Sep 76	● **DEDICATION** *Bell SYBEL 8005*	4	12 wks
13 Aug 77	**IT'S A GAME** *Arista SPARTY 1009*	18	4 wks

BBC SYMPHONY ORCHESTRA, SINGERS and CHORUS

UK, orchestra, singers with male/female vocal audience

Date	Title *Label Number*	Position	
11 Dec 82	**HIGHLIGHTS - LAST NIGHT OF THE PROMS '82** *K-Tel NE 1198*	69†	3 wks

See also Colin Davis/BBC Symphony Orchestra

BEACH BOYS

US, male vocal/instrumental group

Date	Title *Label Number*	Position	
25 Sep 65	**SURFIN' USA** *Capitol T 1890*	17	7 wks
19 Feb 66	● **BEACH BOYS PARTY** *Capitol T 2398*	3	14 wks
16 Apr 66	● **BEACH BOYS TODAY** *Capitol T 2269*	6	25 wks
9 Jul 66	● **PET SOUNDS** *Capitol T 2458*	2	39 wks
16 Jul 66	● **SUMMER DAYS** *Capitol T 2354*	4	22 wks

Left
BAUHAUS Unmasked!

Bottom Left **SYD BARRETT** Once Pink Floyd's guiding light, the madcap quit the group in 1968, flirted briefly with the album chart in 1970, fell short with another album 'Terrapin' and is now a totally uncommunicative and untraceable recluse.

Below **THE BAY CITY ROLLERS** The kilted sound brothers reveal assorted Celtic undergarments.

Date	Title Label Number	Position			Date	Title Label Number	Position	

Date	Title Label Number	Position	
12 Nov 66	● BEST OF THE BEACH BOYS *Capitol T 20865*	2	142 wks
11 Mar 67	SURFER GIRL *Capitol ST 1981*	13	14 wks
21 Oct 67	● BEST OF THE BEACH BOYS VOL.2 *Capitol ST 20956*	3	39 wks
18 Nov 67	● SMILEY SMILE *Capitol ST 9001*	9	8 wks
16 Mar 68	● WILD HONEY *Capitol ST 2859*	7	15 wks
21 Sep 68	FRIENDS *Capitol ST 2895*	13	8 wks
23 Nov 68	● BEST OF THE BEACH BOYS VOL. 3 *Capitol ST 21142*	9	12 wks
29 Mar 69	● 20/20 *Capitol EST 133*	3	10 wks
19 Sep 70	● GREATEST HITS *Capitol ST 21628*	5	30 wks
5 Dec 70	SUNFLOWER *Stateside SSL 8251*	29	6 wks
27 Nov 71	SURF'S UP *Stateside SLS 10313*	15	7 wks
24 Jun 72	CARL AND THE PASSIONS/SO TOUGH *Reprise K 44184*	25	1 wk
17 Feb 73	● HOLLAND *Reprise K 54008*	20	7 wks
10 Jul 76	★ 20 GOLDEN GREATS *Capitol EMTV 1*	1	86 wks
24 Jul 76	15 BIG ONES *Reprise K 54079*	31	3 wks
7 May 77	THE BEACH BOYS LOVE YOU *Brother/Reprise K 54087*	28	1 wk
21 Apr 79	LA (LIGHT ALBUM) *Caribou CRB 86081*	32	6 wks
12 Apr 80	KEEPING THE SUMMER ALIVE *Caribou CRB 86109*	54	3 wks

BEAKY — See *Dave DEE, DOZY, BEAKY, MICK and TICH*

The BEAT

UK, male vocal/instrumental group

Date	Title Label Number	Position	
31 May 80	● JUST CAN'T STOP IT *Go-Feet BEAT 001*	3	32 wks
16 May 81	● WHA'PPEN *Go-Feet BEAT 3*	3	18 wks
9 Oct 82	SPECIAL BEAT SERVICE *Go Feet BEAT 5*	21	6 wks

BEATLES

UK, male vocal/instrumental group

Date	Title Label Number	Position	
6 Apr 63	★ PLEASE PLEASE ME *Parlophone PMC 1202*	1	70 wks
30 Nov 63	★ WITH THE BEATLES *Parlophone PMC 1206*	1	51 wks
18 Jul 64	★ A HARD DAY'S NIGHT *Parlophone PMC 1230*	1	38 wks
12 Dec 64	★ BEATLES FOR SALE *Parlophone PMC 1240*	1	46 wks
14 Aug 65	★ HELP *Parlophone PMC 1255*	1	37 wks
11 Dec 65	★ RUBBER SOUL *Parlophone PMC 1267*	1	42 wks
13 Aug 66	★ REVOLVER *Parlophone PMC 7009*	1	34 wks
10 Dec 66	● A COLLECTION OF BEATLES OLDIES *Parlophone PMC 7016*	7	25 wks
3 Jun 67	★ SERGEANT PEPPER'S LONELY HEARTS CLUB BAND *Parlophone PCS 7027*	1	148 wks
13 Jan 68	MAGICAL MYSTERY TOUR (import) *Capitol SMAL 2835*	31	2 wks
7 Dec 68	★ THE BEATLES (THE WHITE ALBUM) *Apple PCS 7167/8*	1	22 wks
1 Feb 69	● YELLOW SUBMARINE *Apple PCS 7070*	4	10 wks
4 Oct 69	★ ABBEY ROAD *Apple PCS 7088*	1	76 wks
23 May 70	★ LET IT BE *Apple PXS 1*	1	59 wks
16 Jan 71	A HARD DAY'S NIGHT (re-issue) *Parlophone PCS 3058*	39	1 wk
24 Jul 71	HELP (re-issue) *Parlophone PCS 3071*	33	2 wks

Date	Title Label Number	Position	
5 May 73	● THE BEATLES 1967-1970 *Apple PCSP 718*	2	113 wks
5 May 73	● THE BEATLES 1962-1966 *Apple PCSP 717*	3	148 wks
25 Jun 76	ROCK 'N' ROLL MUSIC *Parlophone PCSP 719*	11	15 wks
21 Aug 76	THE BEATLES TAPES *Polydor 2683 068*	45	1 wk
21 May 77	★ THE BEATLES AT THE HOLLYWOOD BOWL *Parlophone EMTV 4*	1	17 wks
17 Dec 77	● LOVE SONGS *Parlophone PCSP 721*	7	17 wks
3 Nov 79	RARITIES *Parlophone PCM 1001*	71	1 wk
15 Nov 80	BEATLES BALLADS *Parlophone PCS 7214*	17	16 wks
30 Oct 82	● 20 GREATEST HITS *Parlophone PCTC 260*	10	9 wks

Yellow Submarine featured several tracks by the George Martin Orchestra.

BE-BOP DE LUXE

UK, male vocal/instrumental group

Date	Title Label Number	Position	
31 Jan 76	SUNBURST FINISH *Harvest SHSP 4053*	17	12 wks
25 Sep 76	MODERN MUSIC *Harvest SHSP 4058*	12	6 wks
6 Aug 77	● LIVE! IN THE AIR AGE *Harvest SHVL 816*	10	5 wks
25 Feb 78	DRASTIC PLASTIC *Harvest SHSP 4091*	22	5 wks

Jeff BECK

UK, male vocalist/instrumentalist - guitar

Date	Title Label Number	Position	
13 Sep 69	COSA NOSTRA BECK-OLA *Columbia SCX 6351*	39	1 wk
24 Jul 76	WIRED *CBS 86012*	38	5 wks
19 Jul 80	THERE AND BACK *Epic EPC 83288*	38	4 wks

See also Jeff Beck, Tim Bogert and Carmine Appice.

Jeff BECK, Tim BOGERT and Carmine APPICE

UK/US, male vocal/instrumental group

Date	Title Label Number	Position	
28 Apr 73	JEFF BECK, TIM BOGERT & CARMINE APPICE *Epic EPC 65455*	28	3 wks

See also Jeff Beck.

BEE GEES

UK/Australia, male vocal/instrumental group

Date	Title Label Number	Position	
12 Aug 67	● BEE GEES FIRST *Polydor 583-012*	8	26 wks
24 Feb 68	HORIZONTAL *Polydor 582-020*	16	15 wks
28 Sep 68	● IDEA *Polydor 583-036*	4	18 wks
5 Apr 69	● ODESSA *Polydor 583-049/50*	10	1 wk
8 Nov 69	● BEST OF THE BEE GEES *Polydor 583-063*	7	22 wks
9 May 70	CUCUMBER CASTLE *Polydor 583-063*	57	2 wks
17 Feb 79	★ SPIRITS HAVING FLOWN *RSO RSBG 001*	1	33 wks
10 Nov 79	● BEE GEES GREATEST *RSO RSDX 001*	6	25 wks
7 Nov 81	LIVING EYES *RSO RSBG 002*	73	8 wks

All albums from Cucumber Castle onwards group were UK only

Above **JEFF BECK**   Beck in the U.S.S.R.

Top Left **THE BEATLES**   John, Paul, George, Ringo & Harold.

Left **THE BEAT**   The Beat—looking anything but.

Sir Thomas BEECHAM

UK, conductor

26 Mar 60	**CARMEN** *HMV ALP 1762/4*	18	2 wks

Full credit on sleeve reads 'Orchestre National de la Radio Diffusion Francaise, conducted by Sir Thomas Beecham'.

Captain BEEFHEART and his MAGIC BAND

UK, male vocal/instrumental group

6 Dec 69	**TROUT MASK REPLICA** *Straight STS 1053*	21	1 wk
23 Jan 71	**LICK MY DECALS OFF BABY** *Straight STS 1063*	20	10 wks
29 May 71	**MIRROR MAN** *Buddah 2365 002*	49	1 wk
19 Feb 72	**THE SPOTLIGHT KID** *Reprise K 44162*	44	2 wks
18 Sep 82	**ICE CREAM FOR CROW** *Virgin V 2337*	90	2 wks

BELLAMY BROTHERS

US, male vocal duo

19 Jun 76	**BELLAMY BROTHERS** *Warner Bros. K 56242*	21	6 wks

Pierre BELMONDE

US, male instrumentalist - panpipes

7 Jun 80	**THEMES FOR DREAMS** *K-Tel ONE 1077*	13	10 wks

BELMONTS — See *DION and the BELMONTS*

Pat BENATAR

US, female vocalist

25 Jul 81	**PRECIOUS TIME** *Chrysalis CHR 1346*	30	7 wks
13 Nov 82	**GET NERVOUS** *Chrysalis CHR 1396*	90	2 wks

Cliff BENNETT and the REBELROUSERS

UK, male vocal/instrumental group

22 Oct 66	**DRIVIN' ME WILD** *MFP 1121*	25	3 wks

Tony BENNETT

US, male vocalist

29 May 65	**I LEFT MY HEART IN SAN FRANCISCO** *CBS BPG 62201*	13	14 wks
19 Feb 66	● **A STRING OF TONY'S HITS** *CBS DP 66010*	9	13 wks
10 Jun 67	**TONY'S GREATEST HITS** *CBS SBPG 62821*	14	24 wks
23 Sep 67	**TONY MAKES IT HAPPEN** *CBS SBPG 63055*	31	3 wks
23 Mar 68	**FOR ONCE IN MY LIFE** *CBS SBPG 63166*	29	5 wks
26 Feb 77	**THE VERY BEST OF TONY BENNETT - 20 GREATEST HITS** *Warwick PA 5021*	23	4 wks

George BENSON

US, male vocalist/instrumentalist - guitar

19 Mar 77	**IN FLIGHT** *Warner Bros. K 56237*	19	23 wks
18 Feb 78	**WEEKEND IN L.A.** *Warner Bros. K 66074*	47	1 wk
24 Mar 79	**LIVING INSIDE YOUR LOVE** *Warner Bros. K 66085*	24	14 wks
26 Jul 80	● **GIVE ME THE NIGHT** *Warner Bros. K 56823*	3	40 wks
14 Nov 81	**GEORGE BENSON COLLECTION** *Warner Bros. K 66107*	19	33 wks

BERLIN PHILHARMONIC ORCHESTRA conducted by HERBERT VON KARAJAN

Germany, orchestra

26 Sep 70	**BEETHOVEN TRIPLE CONCERTO** *HMV ASD 2582*	51	2 wks

Soloists: David Oistrakh (violin), Mstislav Rostropovich (cello) and Sviatoslau Richter (piano)

Shelley BERMAN

US, male vocalist - comedian

19 Nov 60	**INSIDE SHELLEY BERMAN** *Capitol CLP 1300*	12	4 wks

Chuck BERRY

US, male vocalist/instrumentalist - guitar

25 May 63	**CHUCK BERRY** *Pye International NPL 28024*	12	16 wks
5 Oct 63	● **CHUCK BERRY ON STAGE** *Pye International NPL 28027*	6	11 wks
7 Dec 63	● **MORE CHUCK BERRY** *Pye International NPL 28028*	9	8 wks
30 May 64	● **HIS LATEST AND GREATEST** *Pye NPL 28037*	8	7 wks
3 Oct 64	**YOU NEVER CAN TELL** *Pye NPL 29039*	18	2 wks
12 Feb 77	● **MOTORVATIN'** *Chess 9288 690*	7	9 wks

Date	Title *Label Number*	Position	Date	Title *Label Number*	Position

Mike BERRY

UK, male vocalist

24 Jan 81	**THE SUNSHINE OF YOUR SMILE** *Polydor 2383 592*	**63**	3 wks

BEVERLEY-PHILLIPS ORCHESTRA

UK, orchestra

9 Oct 76	**GOLD ON SILVER** *Warwick WW 5018*	**22**	9 wks

BIG BEN BANJO BAND

UK, male instrumental group

17 Dec 60	**MORE MINSTREL MELODIES** *Columbia 33SX 1254*	**20**	1 wk

BIG ROLL BAND — See *Zoot MONEY and the BIG ROLL BAND*

BIG SOUND — See *Simon DUPREE and BIG SOUND*

Mr. Acker BILK

UK, male band leader, vocalist/instrumentalist - clarinet

19 Mar 60	● **SEVEN AGES OF ACKER** *Columbia 33SX 1205*	**6**	6 wks
9 Apr 60	**ACKER BILK'S OMNIBUS** *Pye NJL 22*	**14**	3 wks
4 Mar 61	**ACKER** *Columbia 33SX 1248*	**17**	1 wk
1 Apr 61	**GOLDEN TREASURY OF BILK** *Columbia 33SX 1304*	**11**	6 wks
26 May 62	● **STRANGER ON THE SHORE** *Columbia 33SX 1407*	**6**	28 wks
4 May 63	**A TASTE OF HONEY** *Columbia 33SX 1493*	**17**	4 wks
9 Oct 76	**THE ONE FOR ME** *Pye NSPX 41052*	**38**	6 wks
4 Jun 77	● **SHEER MAGIC** *Warwick WW 5028*	**5**	8 wks
11 Nov 78	**EVERGREEN** *Warwick PW 5045*	**17**	14 wks

See also Kenny Ball, Chris Barber and Acker Bilk, and Chris Barber and Acker Bilk.

BIRTHDAY PARTY

UK, male vocal/instrumental group

24 Jul 82	**JUNKYARD** *4AD CAD 207*	**73**	3 wks

Stephen BISHOP

US, male instrumentalist - piano

1 Apr 72	**GREIG AND SCHUMANN PIANO CONCERTOS** *Philips 6500 166*	**34**	3 wks

Cilla BLACK

UK, female vocalist

13 Feb 65	● **CILLA** *Parlophone PMC 1243*	**5**	11 wks
14 May 66	● **CILLA SINGS A RAINBOW** *Parlophone PMC 7004*	**4**	15 wks
13 Apr 68	● **SHER-OO** *Parlophone PCS 7041*	**7**	11 wks
30 Nov 68	**BEST OF CILLA BLACK** *Parlophone PCS 7065*	**21**	11 wks
25 Jul 70	**SWEET INSPIRATION** *Parlophone PCS 7103*	**42**	4 wks

BLACK AND WHITE MINSTRELS with the Joe LOSS ORCHESTRA

UK, male/female vocal group and UK orchestra

19 Nov 77	● **30 GOLDEN GREATS** *EMI EMTV 7*	**10**	10 wks

See also the George Mitchell Minstrels.

BLACK SABBATH

UK/US, male vocal/instrumental group

7 Mar 70	● **BLACK SABBATH** *Vertigo VO 6*	**8**	42 wks
26 Sep 70	★ **PARANOID** *Vertigo 6360 011*	**1**	27 wks
21 Aug 71	● **MASTER OF REALITY** *Vertigo 6360 050*	**5**	13 wks
30 Sep 72	● **BLACK SABBATH VOL.4** *Vertigo 6360 071*	**8**	10 wks
8 Dec 73	● **SABBATH BLOODY SABBATH** *WWA WWA 005*	**4**	11 wks
27 Sep 75	● **SABOTAGE** *NEMS 9119 001*	**7**	7 wks
7 Feb 76	**WE SOLD OUR SOUL FOR ROCK 'N' ROLL** *NEMS 6641 335*	**35**	5 wks
6 Nov 76	**TECHNICAL ECSTASY** *Vertigo 9102 750*	**13**	6 wks
14 Oct 78	**NEVER SAY DIE** *Vertigo 9102 751*	**12**	6 wks
26 Apr 80	● **HEAVEN AND HELL** *Vertigo 9102 752*	**9**	22 wks
5 Jul 80	● **BLACK SABBATH LIVE AT LAST** *NEMS BS 001*	**5**	15 wks
27 Sep 80	**PARANOID** (re-issue) *NEMS NEL 6003*	**54**	2 wks
14 Nov 81	**MOB RULES** *Mercury 6V02119*	**12**	14 wks

BLACK UHURU

Jamaica, male/female vocal instrumental group

13 Jun 81	**RED** *Island ILPS 9625*	**28**	13 wks
22 Aug 81	**BLACK UHURU** *Virgin VX 1004*	**81**	2 wks
19 Jun 82	**CHILL OUT** *Island ILPS 9701*	**38**	6 wks

Band Of The BLACK WATCH

UK, military band

7 Feb 76	**SCOTCH ON THE ROCKS** *Spark SRLM 503*	**11**	13 wks

Left **GEORGE BENSON** Weekend in L.A. stretched to an extra five days in the U.K. chart.

Above **CAPTAIN BEEFHEART** Though surprisingly he did not chart with his album 'Safe As Milk', the Captain (Don Van Vliet) and his outfit made the best selling lists with their blues-orientated 3rd LP, the delightfully titled 'Trout Mask Replica'.

BEE GEES The Bee Gees—Vertical.

23

Left **JACKSON BROWNE** With his 12 inch platter he became a Great Pretender in 1976.

Right **JOE BROWN** A picture of Joe Brown—live.

Below **BOOKER T & THE MGs** Donald 'Duck' Dunn, Booker T. Jones, Steve Cropper and Al Jackson.

Above **CILLA BLACK** Changed her name from White to Black but neither colour featured in her 1966 album.

BLACK WIDOW

UK, male vocal/instrumental group

4 Apr 70	**SACRIFICE** *CBS 63948*	32	2 wks

BLACKFOOT

US, male vocal/instrumental group

18 Jul 81	**MARAUDER** *Atco K 50799*	38	12 wks
11 Sep 82	**HIGHWAY SONG-BLACKFOOT LIVE** *Atco K 50910*	14	6 wks

BLANCMANGE

UK, male vocal/instrumental group

9 Oct 82	**HAPPY FAMILIES** *London SH 8552*	30†	12 wks

BLIND FAITH

UK, male vocal/instrumental group

13 Sep 69	★ **BLIND FAITH** *Polydor 583-059*	1	10 wks

BLITZ

UK, male vocal/instrumental group

6 Nov 82	**VOICE OF A GENERATION** *No Future PUNK 1*	27	3 wks

BLIZZARD OF OZ — See *Ozzy OSBOURNE'S BLIZZARD OF OZ*

BLOCKHEADS — See *Ian DURY and the BLOCKHEADS*

BLODWYN PIG

UK, male vocal/instrumental group

16 Aug 69	● **AHEAD RINGS OUT** *Island ILPS 9101*	9	4 wks
23 Apr 70	● **GETTING TO THIS** *Island ILPS 9122*	8	7 wks

BLONDIE

US/UK, female/male vocal/instrumental group

4 Mar 78	● **PLASTIC LETTERS** *Chrysalis CHR 1166*	10	54 wks
23 Sep 78	★ **PARALLEL LINES** *Chrysalis CDL 1992*	1	105 wks
10 Mar 79	**BLONDIE** *Chrysalis CHR 1165*	75	1 wk
13 Oct 79	★ **EAT TO THE BEAT** *Chrysalis CDL 1225*	1	38 wks
29 Nov 80	● **AUTOAMERICAN** *Chrysalis CDL 1290*	3	16 wks
31 Oct 81	● **BEST OF BLONDIE** *Chrysalis CDLTV 1*	4	23 wks
5 Jun 82	● **THE HUNTER** *Chrysalis CDL 1384*	9	12 wks

BLOOD SWEAT AND TEARS

US, male vocal/instrumental group

13 Jul 68	**CHILD IS FATHER TO THE MAN** *CBS 63296*	40	1 wk
12 Apr 69	**BLOOD SWEAT AND TEARS** *CBS 63504*	15	8 wks
8 Aug 70	**BLOOD SWEAT AND TEARS 3** *CBS 64024*	14	12 wks

BLUE OYSTER CULT

US, male vocal/instrumental group

3 Jul 76	**AGENTS OF FORTUNE** *CBS 81385*	26	10 wks
4 Feb 78	**SPECTRES** *CBS 86050*	60	1 wk
28 Oct 78	**SOME ENCHANTED EVENING** *CBS 86074*	18	4 wks
18 Aug 79	**MIRRORS** *CBS 86087*	46	5 wks
19 Jul 80	**CULTOSAURUS ERECTUS** *CBS 86120*	12	7 wks
25 Jul 81	**FIRE OF UNKNOWN ORIGIN** *CBS 85137*	29	7 wks
22 May 82	**EXTRATERRESTRIAL LIVE** *CBS 22203*	39	5 wks

BLUE RONDO A LA TURK

UK, male vocal/instrumental group

6 Nov 82	**CHEWING THE FAT** *Diable Noir/Virgin V 2240*	80	2 wks

BLUES BAND

UK, male vocal/instrumental group

8 Mar 80	**OFFICIAL BOOTLEG ALBUM** *Arista BBBP 101*	40	9 wks
18 Oct 80	**READY** *Arista BB 2*	36	6 wks
17 Oct 81	**ITCHY FEET** *Arista BB 3*	60	3 wks

Graham BOND

UK, male instrumentalist - keyboards

20 Jun 70	**SOLID BOND** *Warner Bros. WS 3001*	40	2 wks

Gary U.S. BONDS

US, male vocalist

22 Aug 81	**DEDICATION** *EMI-America AML 3017*	43	3 wks
10 Jul 82	**ON THE LINE** *EMI America AML 3022*	55	5 wks

BONEY M.

Various West Indian Islands, male/female vocal group

23 Apr 77	**TAKE THE HEAT OFF ME** *Atlantic K 50314*	40	15 wks
6 Aug 77	**LOVE FOR SALE** *Atlantic K 50385*	60	1 wk
29 Jul 78	★ **NIGHT FLIGHT TO VENUS** *Atlantic/Hansa K 50498*	1	65 wks
29 Sep 79	★ **OCEANS OF FANTASY** *Atmatic/Hansa K 50610*	1	18 wks
12 Apr 80	★ **THE MAGIC OF BONEY M.** *Atlantic/Hansa BMTV 1*	1	26 wks

Graham BONNET

UK, male vocalist

7 Nov 81	**LINE UP** *Mercury 6302151*	62	3 wks

BONZO DOG DOO-DAH BAND

UK, male vocal/instrumental group

18 Jan 69	**DOUGHNUT IN GRANNY'S GREENHOUSE** *Liberty LBS 83158*	40	1 wk
30 Aug 69	**TADPOLES** *Liberty LBS 83257*	36	1 wk
22 Jun 74	**THE HISTORY OF THE BONZOS** *United Artists UAD 60071*	41	2 wks

BOOKER T. and the MG'S

US, male instrumental group

25 Jul 64	**GREEN ONIONS** *London HAK 8182*	11	4 wks
11 Jul 70	**MCLEMORE AVENUE** *Stax SXATS 1031*	70	1 wk

BOOMTOWN RATS

Ireland, male vocal/instrumental group

17 Sep 77	**BOOMTOWN RATS** *Ensign ENVY 1*	18	11 wks
8 Jul 78	● **TONIC FOR THE TROOPS** *Ensign ENVY 3*	8	44 wks
3 Nov 79	● **THE FINE ART OF SURFACING** *Ensign ENROX 11*	7	26 wks
24 Jan 81	● **MONDO BONGO** *Mercury 6359 042*	6	7 wks
3 Apr 82	**V DEEP** *Mercury/Phonogram 6359 082*	64	5 wks

Pat BOONE

US, male vocalist

22 Nov 58	● **STARDUST** *London HAD 2127*	10	1 wk
28 May 60	**HYMNS WE HAVE LOVED** *London HAD 2228*	12	2 wks
25 Jun 60	**HYMNS WE LOVE** *London HAD 2092*	14	1 wk
24 Apr 76	**PAT BOONE ORIGINALS** *ABC ABSD 301*	16	8 wks

BOSTON

US, male vocal/instrumental group

5 Feb 77	**BOSTON** *Epic EPC 81611*	11	20 wks
9 Sep 78	● **DON'T LOOK BACK** *Epic EPC 86057*	9	10 wks
4 Apr 81	**BOSTON** *Epic EPC 32038*	58	2 wks

BOW WOW WOW

UK, female/male vocal/instrumental group

24 Oct 81	**SEE JUNGLE! SEE JUNGLE! GO JOIN YOUR GANG YEAH CITY ALL OVER! GO APE CRAZY!** *RCA RCALP 3000*	31	7 wks
7 Aug 82	**I WANT CANDY** *EMI EMC 3416*	26	6 wks

David BOWIE

UK, male vocalist

1 Jul 72	● **THE RISE AND FALL OF ZIGGY STARDUST AND THE SPIDERS FROM MARS** *RCA Victor SF 8287*	5	106 wks
23 Sep 72	● **HUNKY DORY** *RCA Victor SF 8244*	3	69 wks
29 Nov 72	**SPACE ODDITY** *RCA Victor LSP 4813*	17	37 wks
29 Nov 72	**THE MAN WHO SOLD THE WORLD** *RCA Victor LSP 4816*	26	22 wks
5 May 73	★ **ALADDIN SANE** *RCA Victor RS 1001*	1	47 wks
3 Nov 73	★ **PIN-UPS** *RCA Victor RS 1003*	1	21 wks
8 Jun 74	★ **DIAMOND DOGS** *RCA Victor APLI 0576*	1	17 wks
16 Nov 74	● **DAVID LIVE** *RCA Victor APL 2 0771*	2	12 wks
5 Apr 75	● **YOUNG AMERICANS** *RCA Victor RS 1006*	2	12 wks
7 Feb 76	● **STATION TO STATION** *RCA Victor APLI 1327*	5	16 wks
12 Jun 76	● **CHANGESONEBOWIE** *RCA Victor RS 1055*	2	23 wks
29 Jan 77	● **LOW** *RCA Victor PL 12030*	2	18 wks
29 Oct 77	● **HEROES** *RCA Victor PL 12522*	3	18 wks
14 Oct 78	● **STAGE** *RCA Victor PL 02913*	5	10 wks
9 Jun 79	● **LODGER** *RCA Bow LP1*	4	17 wks
27 Sep 80	★ **SCARY MONSTERS AND SUPER CREEPS** *RCA Bow LP2*	1	32 wks
10 Jan 81	● **VERY BEST OF DAVID BOWIE** *K-Tel NE 1111*	3	20 wks
17 Jan 81	**HUNKY DORY** (re-issue) *RCA Ints 5064*	68	17 wks
31 Jan 81	**....ZIGGY STARDUST....** (re-issue) *RCA Ints 5063*	63	21 wks
28 Nov 81	**CHANGESTWOBOWIE** *RCA Bow LP*	24	17 wks
6 Mar 82	**ALADDIN SANE** (re-issue) *RCA Ints 5067*	98	2 wks

BOXCAR WILLIE

US, male vocalist

31 May 80	● **KING OF THE ROAD** *Warwick WW 5084*	5	12 wks

Date	Title Label Number	Position		Date	Title Label Number	Position	

Max BOYCE

UK, male vocalist - comedian

5 Jul 75	**LIVE AT TREORCHY** *One Up OU 2033*	21	32 wks
1 Nov 75	★ **WE ALL HAD DOCTORS' PAPERS** *EMI MB 101*	1	17 wks
20 Nov 76	● **THE INCREDIBLE PLAN** *EMI MB 102*	9	12 wks
7 Jan 78	**THE ROAD AND THE MILES** *EMI MB 103*	50	3 wks
11 Mar 78	**LIVE AT TREORCHY** (re-issue) *One Up OU 54043*	42	6 wks
27 May 78	● **I KNOW COS I WAS THERE** *EMI MAX 1001*	6	14 wks
13 Oct 79	**NOT THAT I'M BIASED** *EMI MAX 1002*	27	13 wks
15 Nov 80	**ME AND BILLY WILLIAMS** *EMI MAX 1003*	37	8 wks

BOYS

UK, male vocal/instrumental group

1 Oct 77	**THE BOYS** *NEMS NEL 6001*	50	1 wk

Wilfred BRAMBELL — See *Harry H. CORBETT and Wilfred BRAMBELL*

BRAND X

UK, male vocal/instrumental group

21 May 77	**MOROCCAN ROLL** *Charisma CAS 1126*	37	5 wks
11 Sep 82	**IS THERE ANYTHING ABOUT?** *CBS 85967*	93	1 wk

BRASS CONSTRUCTION

US, male vocal/instrumental group

20 Mar 76	● **BRASS CONSTRUCTION** *United Artists UAS 29923*	9	11 wks

Los BRAVOS

Spain/Germany, male vocal/instrumental group

8 Oct 66	**BLACK IS BLACK** *Decca LK 4822*	29	1 wk

BREAD

US, male vocal/instrumental group

26 Sep 70	**ON THE WATERS** *Elektra 2469-005*	34	5 wks
18 Mar 72	● **BABY I'M A WANT-YOU** *Elektra K 42100*	9	19 wks
28 Oct 72	● **BEST OF BREAD** *Elektra K 42115*	7	100 wks
27 Jul 74	**THE BEST OF BREAD VOL.2** *Elektra K 42161*	48	1 wk
29 Jan 77	**LOST WITHOUT YOUR LOVE** *Elektra K 52044*	17	6 wks
5 Nov 77	★ **THE SOUND OF BREAD** *Elektra K 52062*	1	45 wks

Adrian BRETT

UK, male instrumentalist - flute

10 Nov 79	**ECHOES OF GOLD** *Warwick WW 5062*	19	11 wks

Paul BRETT

UK, male instrumentalist - guitar

19 Jul 80	**ROMANTIC GUITAR** *K-Tel ONE 1079*	24	7 wks

BRIGHOUSE AND RASTRICK BRASS BAND

UK, male brass band

28 Jan 78	● **FLORAL DANCE** *Logo 1001*	10	11 wks

Johnny BRISTOL

US, male vocalist

5 Oct 74	**HANG ON IN THERE BABY** *MGM 2315 303*	12	7 wks

June BRONHILL and Thomas ROUND

Australia/UK, female/male vocal duo

18 Jun 60	**LILAC TIME** *HMV CLP 1248*	17	1 wk

Elkie BROOKS

UK, female vocalist

18 Jun 77	**TWO DAYS AWAY** *A & M AMLH 68409*	16	20 wks
13 May 78	**SHOOTING STAR** *A & M AMLH 64695*	20	13 wks
13 Oct 79	**LIVE AND LEARN** *A & M AMLH 68509*	34	6 wks
14 Nov 81	● **PEARLS** *A & M ELK 1981*	2†	59 wks
13 Nov 82	● **PEARLS II** *A & M ELK 1982*	5†	7 wks

Nigel BROOKS SINGERS

UK, male/female vocal group

29 Nov 75	● **SONGS OF JOY** *K-Tel NE 706*	5	16 wks
5 Jun 76	**20 ALL TIME EUROVISION FAVOURITES** *K-Tel NE 712*	44	1 wk

BROTHERHOOD OF MAN

UK, male/female vocal group

24 Apr 76	**LOVE AND KISSES FROM** *Pye NSPL 18490*	20	8 wks
12 Aug 78	**B FOR BROTHERHOOD** *Pye NSPL 18567*	18	9 wks
7 Oct 78	● **BROTHERHOOD OF MAN** *K-Tel BML 7980*	6	15 wks
29 Nov 80	**SING 20 NUMBER ONE HITS** *Warwick WW 5087*	14	8 wks

BROTHERS JOHNSON

US, male vocal/instrumental duo

19 Aug 78	**BLAM!!** *A & M AMLH 64714*	48	8 wks
23 Feb 80	**LIGHT UP THE NIGHT** *A & M AMLK 63716*	22	12 wks
18 Jul 81	**WINNERS** *A & M AMLK 63724*	42	2 wks

Edgar BROUGHTON BAND

UK, male vocal/instrumental group

20 Jun 70	**SING BROTHER SING** *Harvest SHVL 772*	18	4 wks
5 Jun 71	**THE EDGAR BROUGHTON BAND** *Harvest SHVL 791*	28	2 wks

Crazy World Of Arthur BROWN

UK, male vocal/instrumental group

6 Jul 68	● **CRAZY WORLD OF ARTHUR BROWN** *Track 612005*	2	16 wks

Dennis BROWN

Jamaica, male vocalist

26 Jun 82	**LOVE HAS FOUND ITS WAY** *A&M AMLH 64886*	72	6 wks

Joe BROWN

UK, male vocalist/instrumentalist - guitar

1 Sep 62	● **A PICTURE OF YOU** *Pye Golden Guinea GGL 0146*	3	39 wks
25 May 63	**JOE BROWN - LIVE** *Piccadilly NPL 38006*	14	8 wks

Jackson BROWNE

US, male vocalist

4 Dec 76	**THE PRETENDER** *Asylum K 53048*	26	5 wks
21 Jan 78	**RUNNING ON EMPTY** *Asylum K 53070*	28	7 wks
12 Jul 80	**HOLD OUT** *Asylum K 52226*	44	5 wks

Dave BRUBECK QUARTET

US, male instrumental group

25 Jun 60	**TIME OUT** *Fontana TFL 5085*	11	1 wk
7 Apr 62	**TIME FURTHER OUT** *Fontana TFL 5161*	12	16 wks

Second album just credited to Dave Brubeck.

Jack BRUCE

UK, male vocalist/instrumentalist - bass

27 Sep 69	● **SONGS FOR A TAILOR** *Polydor 583-058*	6	9 wks

BUCKS FIZZ

UK, male/female vocal group

8 Aug 81	**BUCKS FIZZ** *RCA RCALP 5050*	14	28 wks
18 May 82	● **ARE YOU READY?** *RCA RCALP 8000*	10	21 wks

BUDGIE

UK, male vocal/instrumental group

8 Jun 74	**IN FOR THE KILL** *MCA MCF 2546*	29	3 wks
27 Sep 75	**BANDOLIER** *MCA MCF 2723*	36	4 wks
31 Oct 81	**NIGHT FLIGHT** *RCA RCALP 6003*	68	2 wks
23 Oct 82	**DELIVER US FROM EVIL** *RCA RCALP 6054*	62	1 wk

BUGGLES

UK, male vocal/instrumental duo

16 Feb 80	**THE AGE OF PLASTIC** *Island ILPS 9585*	27	6 wks

BUNNYMEN — See *ECHO and the BUNNYMEN*

Eric BURDON and WAR

UK, male vocalist and US, male instrumental group

3 Oct 70	**ERIC BURDON DECLARES WAR** *Polydor 2310-041*	50	2 wks

DAVE BRUBECK Pianist Dave Brubeck (Dave Warren) took time out twice in the early '60s to chart with his quartet which comprised Dave, Paul Desmond (alto sax) Joe Morello (drums) and Eugene Wright (bass).

BYRDS Early Byrds: Clark, McGuinn, Clark, Hillman and Crosby.

VIKKI CARR Her 'Way Of Today' included versions of the Beatles' 'Nowhere Man', Cilla Black's 'Anyone Who Had A Heart' and Dusty Springfield's 'You Don't Have To Say You Love Me.'

Jean-Jacques BURNEL

UK, male vocalist/instrumentalist - bass guitar

21 Apr 79	**EUROMAN COMETH** *United Artists UAG 30214*	40	5 wks

Kate BUSH

UK, female vocalist

11 Mar 78	● **THE KICK INSIDE** *EMI EMC 3223*	3	70 wks
25 Nov 78	● **LIONHEART** *EMI EMA 787*	6	36 wks
20 Sep 80	★ **NEVER FOR EVER** *EMI EMA 796*	1	23 wks
25 Sep 82	● **THE DREAMING** *EMI EMC 3419*	3	9 wks

BUZZCOCKS

UK, male vocal/instrumental group

25 Mar 78	**ANOTHER MUSIC IN A DIFFERENT KITCHEN** *United Artists UAG 30159*	15	11 wks
7 Oct 78	**LOVE BITES** *United Artists UAG 30184*	13	9 wks
6 Oct 79	**A DIFFERENT KIND OF TENSION** *United Artists UAG 30260*	26	3 wks

Max BYGRAVES

UK, male vocalist

23 Sep 72	● **SING ALONG WITH MAX** *Pye NSPL 18361*	4	44 wks
2 Dec 72	**SING ALONG WITH MAX VOL.2** *Pye NSPL 18383*	11	23 wks
5 May 73	● **SINGALONGAMAX VOL.3** *Pye NSPL 18401*	5	30 wks
29 Sep 73	● **SINGALONGAMAX VOL.4** *Pye NSPL 18410*	7	12 wks
15 Dec 73	**SINGALONGPARTY SONG** *Pye NSPL 18419*	15	6 wks
12 Oct 74	**YOU MAKE ME FEEL LIKE SINGING A SONG** *Pye NSPL 18436*	39	3 wks
7 Dec 74	**SINGALONGAXMAS** *Pye NSPL 18439*	21	6 wks
13 Nov 76	● **100 GOLDEN GREATS** *Ronco RTDX 2019*	3	21 wks
28 Oct 78	**LINGALONGAMAX** *Ronco RPL 2033*	39	5 wks
16 Dec 78	**THE SONG AND DANCE MEN** *Pye NSPL 18574*	67	1 wk

Charlie BYRD — See *Stan GETZ and Charlie BYRD*

Donald BYRD

US, male instrumentalist - trumpet

10 Oct 81	**LOVE BYRD** *Elektra K 52301*	70	3 wks

BYRDS

US, male vocal/instrumental group

28 Aug 65	● **MR. TAMBOURINE MAN** *CBS BPG 62571*	7	12 wks
9 Apr 66	**TURN, TURN, TURN** *CBS BPG 62652*	11	5 wks
1 Oct 66	**5TH DIMENSION** *CBS BPG 62783*	27	2 wks
22 Apr 67	**YOUNGER THAN YESTERDAY** *CBS SBPG 62988*	37	4 wks
4 May 68	**THE NOTORIOUS BYRD BROTHERS** *CBS 63169*	12	11 wks
24 May 69	**DR. BYRDS AND MR. HYDE** *CBS 63545*	15	1 wk
14 Feb 70	**BALLAD OF EASY RIDER** *CBS 63795*	41	1 wk
28 Nov 70	**UNTITLED** *CBS 66253*	11	4 wks
14 Apr 73	**BYRDS** *Asylum SYLA 8754*	31	1 wk
19 May 73	**HISTORY OF THE BYRDS** *CBS 68242*	47	1 wk

David BYRNE — See *Brian ENO and David BYRNE*

B-52S

US, male/female vocal instrumental group

4 Aug 79	**B-52S** *Island ILPS 9580*	22	9 wks
13 Sep 80	**WILD PLANET** *Island ILPS 9622*	18	4 wks
11 Jul 81	**THE PARTY MIX ALBUM** *Island IPM 1001*	36	5 wks
27 Feb 82	**MESOPOTAMIA** *EMI ISSP 4006*	18	6 wks

CABARET VOLTAIRE

UK, male vocal/instrumental group

26 Jun 82	**2 X 45** *Rough Trade ROUGH 42*	98	1 wk

J.J. CALE

US, male vocalist/instrumentalist - guitar

2 Oct 76	**TROUBADOUR** *Island ISA 5011*	53	1 wk
25 Aug 79	**5** *Shelter ISA 5018*	40	6 wks
21 Feb 81	**SHADES** *Shelter ISA 5021*	44	7 wks
20 Mar 82	**GRASSHOPPER** *Shelter/Island IFA 5022*	36	5 wks

CAMEL

UK, male vocal/instrumental group

24 May 75	**THE SNOW GOOSE** *Decca SKL 5207*	22	13 wks
17 Apr 76	**MOON MADNESS** *Decca TXS 115*	15	6 wks
17 Sep 77	**RAIN DANCES** *Decca TXS 124*	20	8 wks

Date	Title Label Number	Position		Date	Title Label Number	Position	
14 Oct 78	**BREATHLESS** Decca TXS 132	26	1 wk				
27 Oct 79	**I CAN SEE YOUR HOUSE FROM HERE** Decca TXS 137	45	3 wks				
31 Jan 81	**NUDE** Decca SKL 5323	34	7 wks				
15 May 82	**THE SINGLE FACTOR** Decca FKL 5328	57	5 wks				

Glen CAMPBELL

US, male vocalist/instrumentalist - guitar

Date	Title Label Number	Position	
31 Jan 70	**GLEN CAMPBELL LIVE** Capitol SB 21444	16	14 wks
30 May 70	**TRY A LITTLE KINDNESS** Capitol ESW 389	37	10 wks
12 Dec 70	**THE GLEN CAMPBELL ALBUM** Capitol ST 22493	16	5 wks
27 Nov 71	● **GREATEST HITS** Capitol ST 21885	8	113 wks
25 Oct 75	**RHINESTONE COWBOY** Capitol E-SW 11430	38	9 wks
20 Nov 76	★ **20 GOLDEN GREATS** Capitol EMTV 2	1	27 wks
23 Apr 77	**SOUTHERN NIGHTS** Capitol E-ST 11601	51	1 wk

CANNED HEAT

US, vocal instrumental group

Date	Title Label Number	Position	
29 Jun 68	● **BOOGIE WITH CANNED HEAT** Liberty LBL 83103	5	21 wks
14 Feb 70	● **CANNED HEAT COOKBOOK** Liberty LBS 83303	8	12 wks
4 Jul 70	**CANNED HEAT '70 CONCERT** Liberty LBS 83333	15	3 wks
10 Oct 70	**FUTURE BLUES** Liberty LBS 83364	27	4 wks

Freddy CANNON

US, male vocalist

Date	Title Label Number	Position	
27 Feb 60	★ **THE EXPLOSIVE FREDDY CANNON** Top Rank 25/108	1	11 wks

CAPTAIN and TENNILLE

US, male instrumentalist - keyboards/female vocalist

Date	Title Label Number	Position	
22 Mar 80	**MAKE YOUR MOVE** Casablanca CAL 2060	33	6 wks

CARAVAN

UK, male vocal/instrumental group

Date	Title Label Number	Position	
30 Aug 75	**CUNNING STUNTS** Decca SKL 5210	50	1 wk
15 May 76	**BLIND DOG AT ST.DUNSTAN'S** BTM BTM 1007	53	1 wk

Eric CARMEN

US, male vocalist

Date	Title Label Number	Position	
15 May 76	**ERIC CARMEN** Arista ARTY 120	58	1 wk

Kim CARNES

UK, female vocalist

Date	Title Label Number	Position	
20 Jun 81	**MISTAKEN IDENTITY** EMI-America AML 3018	26	16 wks

CARPENTERS

US, male/female, vocal/instrumental duo

Date	Title Label Number	Position	
23 Jan 71	**CLOSE TO YOU** A & M AMLS 998	23	82 wks
30 Oct 71	**THE CARPENTERS** A & M AMLS 63502	12	36 wks
15 Apr 72	**TICKET TO RIDE** A & M AMLS 64342	20	3 wks
23 Sep 72	**A SONG FOR YOU** A & M AMLS 63511	13	37 wks
7 Jul 73	● **NOW AND THEN** A & M AMLH 63519	2	65 wks
26 Jan 74	● **THE SINGLES 1969-1973** A & M AMLH 63601	1	115 wks
28 Jun 75	★ **HORIZON** A & M AMLK 64530	1	27 wks
23 Aug 75	**TICKET TO RIDE** (re-issue) Hamlet AMLP 8001	35	2 wks
3 Jul 76	● **A KIND OF HUSH** A & M AMLK 64581	3	15 wks
8 Jan 77	**LIVE AT THE PALLADIUM** A & M AMLS 68403	28	3 wks
8 Oct 77	**PASSAGE** A & M AMLK 64703	12	12 wks
2 Dec 78	● **SINGLES 1974-78** A & M AMLT 19748	2	20 wks
27 Jun 81	**MADE IN AMERICA** A & M AMLK 63723	12	10 wks

Vikki CARR

US, female vocalist

Date	Title Label Number	Position	
22 Jul 67	**WAY OF TODAY** Liberty SLBY 1331	31	2 wks
12 Aug 67	**IT MUST BE HIM** Liberty LBS 83037	12	10 wks

Jasper CARROTT

UK, male vocalist

Date	Title Label Number	Position	
18 Oct 75	● **RABBITS ON AND ON** DJM DJLPS 462	10	7 wks
6 Nov 76	**CARROTT IN NOTTS** DJM DJF 20482	56	1 wk
25 Nov 78	**THE BEST OF JASPER CARROTT** DJM	38	13 wks
20 Oct 79	**THE UNRECORDED JASPER CARROTT** DJM DJF 20560	19	15 wks
19 Sep 81	**BEAT THE CARROTT** DJM DJF 20575	13	16 wks
25 Dec 82	**CARROTT'S LIB** DJM DJF 20580	80†	1 wk

CARS

US, male vocal/instrumental group

Date	Title Label Number	Position	
2 Dec 78	**CARS** Elektra K 52088	29	15 wks
7 Jul 79	**CANDY-O** Elektra K 52148	30	6 wks

Date	Title Label Number	Position		Date	Title Label Number	Position	

Johnny CASH

US, male vocalist

23 Jul 66	EVERYBODY LOVES A NUT CBS BPG 62717	28	1 wk
4 May 68	FROM SEA TO SHINING SEA CBS 62972	40	1 wk
6 Jul 68	OLD GOLDEN THROAT CBS 63316	37	2 wks
24 Aug 68	● FOLSOM PRISON CBS 63308	8	53 wks
23 Aug 69	● JOHNNY CASH AT SAN QUENTIN CBS 63629	2	114 wks
4 Oct 69	GREATEST HITS VOL.1 CBS 63062	23	25 wks
7 Mar 70	● HELLO I'M JOHNNY CASH CBS 63796	6	16 wks
15 Aug 70	● WORLD OF JOHNNY CASH CBS 66237	5	31 wks
12 Dec 70	THE JOHNNY CASH SHOW CBS 64089	18	6 wks
18 Sep 71	MAN IN BLACK CBS 64331	18	7 wks
13 Nov 71	JOHNNY CASH Hallmark SHM 739	43	2 wks
20 May 72	● A THING CALLED LOVE CBS 64898	8	11 wks
14 Oct 72	STAR PORTRAIT CBS 67201	16	7 wks
10 Jul 76	ONE PIECE AT A TIME CBS 81416	49	3 wks
9 Oct 76	THE BEST OF JOHNNY CASH CBS 10000	48	2 wks
2 Sep 78	ITCHY FEET CBS 10009	36	4 wks

David CASSIDY

US, male vocalist

20 May 72	● CHERISH Bell BELLS 210	2	43 wks
24 Feb 73	● ROCK ME BABY Bell BELLS 218	2	20 wks
24 Nov 73	★ DREAMS ARE NOTHIN' MORE THAN WISHES Bell BELLS 231	1	13 wks
3 Aug 74	● CASSIDY LIVE Bell BELLS 243	9	7 wks
9 Aug 75	THE HIGHER THEY CLIMB RCA Victor RS 1012	22	5 wks

C.C.S.

UK, male vocal/instrumental group

8 Apr 72	C.C.S. RAK SRAK 503	23	5 wks

CENTRAL LINE

UK, male vocal/instrumental group

13 Feb 82	BREAKING POINT Mercury/Phonogram MERA 001	64	5 wks

CERRONE

France, male producer and multi instrumentalist

30 Sep 78	SUPERNATURE Atlantic K 50431	60	1 wk

A CERTAIN RATIO

UK, male vocal/instrumental group

30 Jan 82	SEXTET Factory FACT 55	53	3 wks

Richard CHAMBERLAIN

US, male vocalist

16 Mar 63	● RICHARD CHAMBERLAIN SINGS MGM MGM C 923	8	8 wks

CHAMPAGNE

US, male/female vocal instrumental group

27 Jun 81	HOW 'BOUT US CBS 84927	38	4 wks

Michael CHAPMAN

UK, male vocalist

21 Mar 70	FULLY QUALIFIED SURVIVOR Harvest SHVL 764	45	1 wk

CHAQUITO and QUEDO BRASS

UK, male arranger/conductor Johnny Gregory under false name and UK, orchestra

24 Feb 68	THIS CHAQUITO Fontana SFXL 50	36	1 wk

See also Chaquito Orchestra.

CHAQUITO ORCHESTRA

UK, orchestra

4 Mar 72	THRILLER THEMES Philips 6308 087	48	1 wk

See also Chaquito and Quedo Brass.

CHARGE GBH

UK, male vocal/instrumental group

14 Aug 82	CITY BABY ATTACKED BY RATS Clay CLA YLP 4	17	6 wks

CHARLENE

US, female vocalist

17 Jul 82	I'VE NEVER BEEN TO ME *Motown STML 12171*	43	4 wks

Ray CHARLES

US, male vocalist/instrumentalist - piano

28 Jul 62	● MODERN SOUNDS IN COUNTRY & WESTERN MUSIC *HMV CLP 1580*	6	16 wks
23 Feb 63	MODERN SOUNDS IN COUNTRY AND WESTERN MUSIC VOL.2 *HMV CLP 1613*	15	5 wks
20 Jul 63	GREATEST HITS *HMV CLP 1626*	16	5 wks
5 Oct 68	GREATEST HITS VOL.2 *Stateside SSL 10241*	24	8 wks
19 Jul 80	HEART TO HEART - 20 HOT HITS *London RAY TV 1*	29	5 wks

Tina CHARLES

UK, female vocalist

3 Dec 77	HEART 'N' SOUL *CBS 82180*	35	7 wks

CHAS and DAVE

UK, male vocal/instrumental duo

5 Dec 81	CHAS AND DAVE'S CHRISTMAS JAMBOREE BAG *Warwick WW 5166*	25	8 wks
17 Apr 82	MUSN'T GRUMBLE *Rockney 909*	35	11 wks

CHEAP TRICK

US, male vocal/instrumental group

24 Feb 79	CHEAP TRICK AT BUDOKAN *Epic EPC 86083*	29	9 wks
6 Oct 79	DREAM POLICE *Epic EPC 83522*	41	5 wks
5 Jun 82	ONE ON ONE *Epic EPC 85740*	95	1 wk

Chubby CHECKER

US, male vocalist

27 Jan 62	TWIST WITH CHUBBY CHECKER *Columbia 33SX 1315*	13	4 wks
3 Mar 62	FOR TWISTERS ONLY *Columbia 33SX 1341*	17	3 wks

CHER

US, female vocalist

2 Oct 65	● ALL I REALLY WANT TO DO *Liberty LBY 3058*	7	9 wks
7 May 66	SONNY SIDE OF CHER *Liberty LBY 3072*	11	11 wks

See also Sonny and Cher.

CHIC

US, male/female vocal instrumental group

3 Feb 79	● C'EST CHIC *Atlantic K 50565*	2	24 wks
18 Aug 79	RISQUE *Atlantic K 50634*	29	12 wks
15 Dec 79	THE BEST OF CHIC *Atlantic K 50686*	30	8 wks

CHICAGO

US, male vocal/instrumental group

27 Sep 69	● CHICAGO TRANSIT AUTHORITY *CBS 66221*	9	14 wks
4 Apr 70	● CHICAGO *CBS 66233*	6	27 wks
3 Apr 71	CHICAGO 3 *CBS 66260*	31	1 wk
30 Sep 72	CHICAGO 5 *CBS 69108*	24	2 wks
23 Oct 76	CHICAGO X *CBS 86010*	21	11 wks
2 Oct 82	16 *Full Moon K 99235*	44	9 wks
4 Dec 82	LOVE SONGS *TV Records TVA 6*	42	4 wks

First album credited to Chicago Transit Authority.

CHICKEN SHACK

UK, male/female vocal/instrumental group

22 Jul 68	40 BLUE FINGERS FRESHLY PACKED *Blue Horizon 7-63203*	12	8 wks
15 Feb 69	● OK KEN? *Blue Horizon 7-63209*	9	1 wk

CHINA CRISIS

UK, male vocal/instrumental group

20 Nov 82	DIFFICULT SHAPES AND PASSIVE RHYTHMS *Virgin V 2243*	68	3 wks

CHORDS

UK, male vocal/instrumental group

24 May 80	SO FAR AWAY *Polydor POLS 1019*	30	3 wks

KID CREOLE "He goes by the name of Kid Creole".

BING CROSBY Singing with Hope.

Above **CROSBY, STILLS & NASH** In their post-Young days of the late 70's. Feelings of déjà vu for earlier success as a trio (pre-Young) in the late 60's.

Left **CREAM** Their 'Disraeli Gears' album was not named after Benjamin the Prime Minister, but through Ginger Baker's confusion over derailleur gears used on a racing bicycle.

35

Tony CHRISTIE

UK, male vocalist

Date	Title Label Number	Position	
24 Jul 71	I DID WHAT I DID FOR MARIA MCA MKPS 2016	37	1 wk
17 Feb 73	WITH LOVING FEELING *MCA MUPS 468*	19	2 wks
31 May 75	TONY CHRISTIE - LIVE *MCA MCF 2703*	33	3 wks
6 Nov 76	BEST OF TONY CHRISTIE *MCA MCF 2769*	28	4 wks

CHRON GEN

UK, male vocal/instrumental group

Date	Title Label Number	Position	
3 Apr 82	CHRONIC GENERATION *Secret SEC 3*	53	3 wks

Sir Winston CHURCHILL

UK, male statesman

Date	Title Label Number	Position	
13 Feb 65	● THE VOICE OF CHURCHILL *Decca LXT 6200*	6	8 wks

CLANCY BROTHERS and TOMMY MAKEM

Ireland, male vocal/instrumental group and male vocalist

Date	Title Label Number	Position	
16 Apr 66	ISN'T IT GRAND BOYS *CBS BPG 62674*	22	5 wks

Eric CLAPTON

UK, male vocalist/instrumentalist - guitar

Date	Title Label Number	Position	
5 Sep 70	ERIC CLAPTON *Polydor 2383-021*	17	8 wks
26 Aug 72	HISTORY OF ERIC CLAPTON *Polydor 2659 2478 027*	20	6 wks
24 Aug 74	● 461 OCEAN BOULEVARD *RSO 2479 118*	3	19 wks
12 Apr 75	THERE'S ONE IN EVERY CROWD *RSO 2479 132*	15	8 wks
13 Sep 75	E.C. WAS HERE *RSO 2394 160*	14	6 wks
11 Sep 76	● NO REASON TO CRY *RSO 2479 179*	8	7 wks
26 Nov 77	SLOWHAND *RSO 2479 201*	23	13 wks
9 Dec 78	BACKLESS *RSO RSD 5001*	18	12 wks
10 May 80	● JUST ONE NIGHT *RSO RSDX 2*	3	12 wks
7 Mar 81	ANOTHER TICKET *RSO RSD 5008*	18	8 wks
24 Apr 82	TIME PIECES - THE BEST OF ERIC CLAPTON *RSO RSD 5010*	20	13 wks

Petula CLARK

UK, female vocalist

Date	Title Label Number	Position	
30 Jul 66	I COULDN'T LIVE WITHOUT YOUR LOVE *Pye NPL 18148*	11	10 wks
4 Feb 67	HIT PARADE *Pye NPL 18159*	18	13 wks
18 Feb 67	COLOUR MY WORLD *Pye NSPL 18171*	16	9 wks
7 Oct 67	THESE ARE MY SONGS *Pye NSPL 18197*	38	3 wks
6 Apr 68	THE OTHER MAN'S GRASS IS ALWAYS GREENER *Pye NSPL 18211*	37	1 wk
5 Feb 77	20 ALL TIME GREATEST *K-Tel NE 945*	18	7 wks

Dave CLARK FIVE

UK, male vocal/instrumental group

Date	Title Label Number	Position	
18 Apr 64	● A SESSION WITH THE DAVE CLARK FIVE *Columbia 33SX 1598*	3	8 wks
14 Aug 65	● CATCH US IF YOU CAN *Columbia 33SX 1756*	8	8 wks
4 Mar 78	● 25 THUMPING GREAT HITS *Polydor POLTV 7*	7	10 wks

John Cooper CLARKE

UK, male vocalist

Date	Title Label Number	Position	
19 Apr 80	SNAP CRACKLE AND BOP *Epic EPC 84083*	26	7 wks
5 Jun 82	ZIP STYLE METHOD *Epic EPC 85667*	97	2 wks

Stanley CLARKE

UK, male vocalist/instrumentalist - bass

Date	Title Label Number	Position	
12 Jul 80	ROCKS PEBBLES AND SAND *Epic EPC 84342*	42	2 wks

Louis CLARK/ROYAL PHILHARMONIC ORCHESTRA

UK, conductor/arranger and orchestra

Date	Title Label Number	Position	
19 Sep 81	● HOOKED ON CLASSICS *K-Tel ONE 1146*	4	37 wks
31 Jul 82	CAN'T STOP THE CLASSICS *K-Tel ONE 1173*	13	21 wks
27 Nov 82	THE BEST OF CLASSIC ROCK *K-Tel ONE 1080*	35	5 wks

See also Royal Philharmonic Orchestra.

CLASH

UK, male vocal/instrumental group

Date	Title Label Number	Position	
30 Apr 77	CLASH *CBS 82000*	12	16 wks
25 Nov 78	● GIVE 'EM ENOUGH ROPE *CBS 82431*	2	14 wks
22 Dec 79	● LONDON CALLING *CBS CLASH 3*	9	20 wks
20 Dec 80	SANDINISTA *CBS FSLM 1*	19	9 wks
22 May 82	● COMBAT ROCK *CBS FMLN 2*	2	22 wks

Above **EDDIE COCHRAN** Signing pictures which are to become cherished memories after his death in a car crash in April 1960.

Right **ELVIS COSTELLO** His Aim Is True and Armed Forces were just two of his shots at the chart.

Left **RAY CHARLES** The Genius on stage.

Above **CHICKEN SHACK**   Finger lickin' good.

Left **CANNED HEAT**   Formed in 1965 as an electric country blues outfit.

Below **CLASH**   Had enough rope to hang in the charts until the big drop.

CLASSIX NOUVEAUX

UK, male vocal/instrumental group

Date	Title	Position	
30 May 81	**NIGHT PEOPLE** *Liberty LBG 30325*	66	2 wks
24 Apr 82	**LA VERITE** *Liberty LBG 30346*	44	4 wks

Richard CLAYDERMAN

France, male instrumentalist - piano

Date	Title	Position	
13 Nov 82	**RICHARD CLAYDERMAN** *Delphine/Decca SKL 5329*	12†	7 wks

John CLEESE

UK, male comedian

Date	Title	Position	
7 Feb 81	**FAWLTY TOWERS VOL.2** *BBC REB 405*	26	7 wks

CLIMAX BLUES BAND

UK, male vocal/instrumental group

Date	Title	Position	
13 Nov 76	**GOLD PLATED** *BTM 1009*	56	1 wk

Eddie COCHRAN

US, male vocalist/instrumentalist - guitar

Date	Title	Position	
30 Jul 60	**SINGING TO MY BABY** *London HAU 2093*	19	1 wk
1 Oct 60	● **EDDIE COCHRAN MEMORIAL ALBUM** *London HAG 2267*	9	12 wks
12 Jan 63	**CHERISHED MEMORIES** *Liberty LBY 1109*	15	3 wks
20 Apr 63	**EDDIE COCHRAN MEMORIAL ALBUM** (re-issue) *Liberty LBY 1127*	11	18 wks
19 Oct 63	**SINGING TO MY BABY** (re-issue) *Liberty LBY 1158*	20	1 wk
9 May 70	**VERY BEST OF EDDIE COCHRAN** *Liberty LBS 83337*	34	3 wks
18 Aug 79	**THE EDDIE COCHRAN SINGLES ALBUM** *United Artists UAK 30244*	39	6 wks

Joe COCKER

UK, male vocalist

Date	Title	Position	
26 Sep 70	**MAD DOGS AND ENGLISHMEN** *A & M AMLS 6002*	16	8 wks
6 May 72	**JOE COCKER/WITH A LITTLE HELP FROM MY FRIENDS** *Double Back TOOFA 1/2*	29	4 wks

Joe Cocker/With A Little Help From My Friends was a double re-issue although neither album had previously been a hit.

COCKNEY REBEL — See *Steve HARLEY and COCKNEY REBEL*

COCKNEY REJECTS

UK, male vocal/instrumental group

Date	Title	Position	
15 Mar 80	**GREATEST HITS VOL.1** *Zonophone ZONO 101*	22	11 wks
25 Oct 80	**GREATEST HITS VOL.2** *Zonophone ZONO 102*	23	3 wks
18 Apr 81	**GREATEST HITS VOL.3 (LIVE AND LOUD)** *Zonophone ZEM 101*	27	3 wks

Leonard COHEN

Canada, male vocalist

Date	Title	Position	
31 Aug 68	**SONGS OF LEONARD COHEN** *CBS 63241*	13	71 wks
3 May 69	● **SONGS FROM A ROOM** *CBS 63587*	2	26 wks
24 Apr 71	● **SONGS OF LOVE AND HATE** *CBS 69004*	4	18 wks
28 Sep 74	**NEW SKIN FOR THE OLD CEREMONY** *CBS 69087*	24	3 wks
10 Dec 77	**DEATH OF A LADIES' MAN** *CBS 86042*	35	5 wks

Nat "King" COLE

US, male vocalist

Date	Title	Position	
19 Aug 61	**STRING ALONG WITH NAT KING COLE** *Encore ENC 102*	12	9 wks
27 Mar 65	**UNFORGETTABLE NAT KING COLE** *Capitol W 20664*	19	8 wks
7 Dec 68	● **BEST OF NAT KING COLE** *Capitol ST 21139*	5	18 wks
5 Dec 70	**BEST OF NAT KING COLE VOL.2** *Capitol ST 21687*	39	2 wks
8 Apr 78	★ **20 GOLDEN GREATS** *Capitol EMTV 9*	1	30 wks
20 Nov 82	● **GREATEST LOVE SONGS** *Capitol EMTV 35*	7†	6 wks

See also Nat "King" Cole and Dean Martin, and Nat "King" Cole and the George Shearing Quintet.

Nat "King" COLE and Dean MARTIN

US, male vocal duo

Date	Title	Position	
27 Nov 71	**WHITE CHRISTMAS** *MFP 5224*	45	1 wk

See also Nat "King" Cole, and Nat "King" Cole and the George Shearing Quintet.

Nat "King" COLE and the George SHEARING QUINTET

US, male vocalist and instrumental group

Date	Title	Position	
20 Oct 62	● **NAT KING COLE SINGS AND THE GEORGE SHEARING QUINTET PLAYS** *Capitol W 1675*	8	7 wks

See also Nat "King" Cole, and Nat "King" Cole and Dean Martin.

Dave and Ansil COLLINS

Jamaica, male vocal duo

Date	Title *Label Number*	Position	
7 Aug 71	**DOUBLE BARRELL** *Trojan TBL 162*	41	2 wks

Judy COLLINS

US, female vocalist

Date	Title *Label Number*	Position	
10 Apr 71	**WHALES AND NIGHTINGALES** *Elektra EKS 75010*	37	2 wks
31 May 75	● **JUDITH** *Elektra K 52019*	7	12 wks

Phil COLLINS

UK, male vocalist

Date	Title *Label Number*	Position	
21 Feb 81	★ **FACE VALUE** *Virgin V 2185*	1	69 wks
13 Nov 82	● **HELLO I MUST BE GOING** *Virgin V 2252*	2†	7 wks

COLOSSEUM

UK, male vocal/instrumental group

Date	Title *Label Number*	Position	
17 May 69	**COLOSSEUM** *Fontana S 5510*	15	1 wk
22 Nov 69	**VALENTYNE SUITE** *Vertigo VO 1*	15	2 wks
5 Dec 70	**DAUGHTER OF TIME** *Vertigo 6360 017*	23	5 wks
26 Jun 71	**COLOSSEUM LIVE** *Bronze ICD 1*	17	6 wks

Alice COLTRANE — See *Carlos SANTANA and Alice COLTRANE*

COMETS — See *Bill HALEY and his COMETS*

COMMODORES

US, male vocal/instrumental group

Date	Title *Label Number*	Position	
13 May 78	**LIVE** *Motown TMSP 6007*	60	1 wk
10 Jun 78	● **NATURAL HIGH** *Motown STML 12087*	8	23 wks
2 Dec 78	**GREATEST HITS** *Motown STML 12100*	19	16 wks
18 Aug 79	**MIDNIGHT MAGIC** *Motown STMA 8032*	15	25 wks
28 Jun 80	**HEROES** *Motown STMA 8034*	50	5 wks
18 Jul 81	**IN THE POCKET** *Motown STML 12156*	69	5 wks
14 Aug 82	● **LOVE SONGS** *K-Tel NE 1171*	5	20 wks

Perry COMO

US, male vocalist

Date	Title *Label Number*	Position	
8 Nov 58	● **DEAR PERRY** *RCA RD 27078*	6	5 wks
31 Jan 59	● **COMO'S GOLDEN RECORDS** *RCA RD 27100*	4	5 wks
10 Apr 71	**IT'S IMPOSSIBLE** *RCA Victor SF 8175*	13	13 wks
7 Jul 73	★ **AND I LOVE YOU SO** *RCA Victor SF 8360*	1	109 wks

Date	Title *Label Number*	Position	
24 Aug 74	**PERRY** *RCA Victor APL1 0585*	26	3 wks
19 Apr 75	**MEMORIES ARE MADE OF HITS** *RCA Victor RS 1005*	14	16 wks
25 Oct 75	★ **40 GREATEST HITS** *K-Tel NE 700*	1	34 wks

COMPILATION ALBUMS — See *VARIOUS ARTISTS*

COMSAT ANGELS

UK, male vocal/instrumental group

Date	Title *Label Number*	Position	
5 Sep 81	**SLEEP NO MORE** *Polydor POLS 1038*	51	5 wks
18 Sep 82	**FICTION** *Polydor POLS 1075*	94	2 wks

Ray CONNIFF

UK, male orchestra leader

Date	Title *Label Number*	Position	
28 May 60	**IT'S THE TALK OF THE TOWN** *Philips 7354*	15	1 wk
25 Jun 60	**S'AWFUL NICE** *Philips BBL 7281*	13	1 wk
26 Nov 60	● **HI-FI COMPANION ALBUM** *Philips BET 101*	3	44 wks
20 May 61	**MEMORIES ARE MADE OF THIS** *Philips BBL 7439*	14	4 wks
29 Dec 62	**WE WISH YOU A MERRY CHRISTMAS** *CBS BPG 62092*	12	1 wk
29 Dec 62	**'S WONDERFUL 'S MARVELLOUS** *CBS DPG 66001*	18	3 wks
16 Apr 66	**HI-FI COMPANION** (re-issue) *CBS DP 66011*	24	4 wks
9 Sep 67	**SOMEWHERE MY LOVE** *CBS SBPG 62740*	34	3 wks
21 Jun 69	★ **HIS ORCHESTRA, HIS CHORUS, HIS SINGERS, HIS SOUND** *CBS SPR 27*	1	16 wks
23 May 70	**BRIDGE OVER TROUBLED WATER** *CBS 64020*	30	14 wks
12 Jun 71	**LOVE STORY** *CBS 64294*	34	1 wk
19 Feb 72	**I'D LIKE TO TEACH THE WORLD TO SING** *CBS 64449*	17	4 wks

Billy CONNOLLY

UK, male vocalist

Date	Title *Label Number*	Position	
20 Jul 74	● **SOLO CONCERT** *Transatlantic TRA 279*	8	33 wks
18 Jan 75	● **COP YER WHACK OF THIS** *Polydor 2383 310*	10	29 wks
20 Sep 75	**WORDS AND MUSIC** *Transatlantic TRA SAM 32*	34	10 wks
6 Dec 75	● **GET RIGHT INTAE HIM** *Polydor 2383 368*	6	14 wks
11 Dec 76	**ATLANTIC BRIDGE** *Polydor 2383 419*	20	9 wks
28 Jan 78	**RAW MEAT FOR THE BALCONY** *Polydor 2383 463*	57	3 wks
5 Dec 81	**PICK OF BILLY CONNOLLY** *Polydor POLTV 15*	23	8 wks

Date	Title *Label Number*	Position		Date	Title *Label Number*	Position	
				23 Dec 78	**FROM THE INSIDE** *Warner Bros. K 56577*	68	3 wks
				17 May 80	**FLUSH THE FASHION** *Warner Bros. K 56805*	56	3 wks
				12 Sep 81	**SPECIAL FORCES** *Warner Bros. K 56927*	96	1 wk

uss CONWAY

UK, male instrumentalist - piano

2 Nov 58	● **PACK UP YOUR TROUBLES**	9	5 wks
	Columbia 33SX 1120		
2 May 59	● **SONGS TO SING IN YOUR BATH**	8	10 wks
	Columbia 33SX 1149		
9 Sep 59	● **FAMILY FAVOURITES** *Columbia 33SX 1169*	3	16 wks
9 Dec 59	● **TIME TO CELEBRATE** *Columbia 33SX 1197*	3	7 wks
6 Mar 60	● **MY CONCERTO FOR YOU** *Columbia 33SX 1214*	5	17 wks
7 Dec 60	● **PARTY TIME** *Columbia 33SX 1279*	7	11 wks
3 Apr 77	**RUSS CONWAY PRESENTS 24 PIANO GREATS**	25	3 wks
	Ronco RTL 2022		

y COODER

US, male vocalist/instrumentalist - guitar

1 Aug 79	**BOP TILL YOU DROP** *Warner Bros. K 56691*	36	9 wks
8 Oct 80	**BORDER LINE** *Warner Bros. K 56864*	35	6 wks
4 Apr 82	**THE SLIDE AREA** *Warner Bros K 56976*	18	12 wks

eter COOK and Dudley MOORE

UK, male vocal duo

1 May 66	**ONCE MOORE WITH COOK** *Decca LK 4785*	25	1 wk
8 Sep 76	**DEREK AND CLIVE LIVE** *Island ILPS 9434*	12	25 wks
4 Dec 77	**COME AGAIN** *Virgin V 2094*	18	8 wks

e also Dudley Moore.

ita COOLIDGE

US, female vocalist

6 Aug 77	● **ANYTIME ANYWHERE** *A & M AMLH 64616*	6	28 wks
8 Jul 78	**LOVE ME AGAIN** *A & M AMLH 64699*	51	1 wk
4 Mar 81	● **VERY BEST OF** *A & M AMLH 68520*	6	11 wks

e also Kris Kristofferson and Rita Coolidge.

lice COOPER

US, male vocalist

5 Feb 72	**KILLER** *Warner Bros. K 56005*	27	18 wks
2 Jul 72	● **SCHOOL'S OUT** *Warner Bros. K 56007*	4	20 wks
9 Sep 72	**LOVE IT TO DEATH** *Warner Bros. K 46177*	28	7 wks
2 Jan 74	**MUSCLE OF LOVE** *Warner Bros. K 56018*	34	4 wks
5 Mar 75	**WELCOME TO MY NIGHTMARE**	19	8 wks
	Anchor ANCL 2011		
4 Jul 76	**ALICE COOPER GOES TO HELL**	23	7 wks
	Warner Bros. K 56171		
8 May 77	**LACE AND WHISKY** *Warner Bros. K 56365*	33	3 wks

Harry H. CORBETT and Wilfred BRAMBELL

UK, male comic duo

23 Mar 63	● **STEPTOE AND SON** *Pye NPL 18081*	4	28 wks
11 Jan 64	**STEPTOE & SON** *Pye GGL 0217*	14	5 wks
14 Mar 64	**MORE JUNK** *Pye NPL 18090*	19	1 wk

CORRIES

UK, male vocal/instrumental duo

9 May 70	**SCOTTISH LOVE SONGS** *Fontana 6309-004*	46	4 wks
16 Sep 72	**SOUND OF PIBROCH** *Columbia SCX 6511*	39	1 wk

Elvis COSTELLO and the ATTRACTIONS

UK, male vocalist and male vocal/instrumental group

6 Aug 77	**MY AIM IS TRUE** *Stiff SEEZ 3*	14	12 wks
1 Apr 78	● **THIS YEAR'S MODEL** *Radar RAD 3*	4	14 wks
20 Jan 79	● **ARMED FORCES** *Radar RAD 14*	2	28 wks
23 Feb 80	● **GET HAPPY** *F-Beat XXLP 1*	2	14 wks
31 Jan 81	● **TRUST** *F-Beat XXLP 11*	9	7 wks
31 Oct 81	● **ALMOST BLUE** *F-Beat XXLP 13*	7	18 wks
10 Jul 82	● **IMPERIAL BEDROOM** *F-Beat XXLP 17*	6	12 wks

My Aim Is True, This Year's Model, Trust *are credited to Elvis Costello only.*

John COUGAR

US, male vocalist

6 Nov 82	**AMERICAN FOOL** *Riva RVLP 16*	37	6 wks

David COVERDALE

UK, male vocalist

27 Feb 82	**NORTHWINDS** *Purple TTS 3513*	78	1 wk

CRASS

UK, male vocal/instrumental group

28 Aug 82	**CHRIST THE ALBUM** *Crass BOLLOX 2U2*	26	2 wks

Randy CRAWFORD

US, female vocalist

28 Jun 80	● **NOW WE MAY BEGIN** *Warner Bros. K 56791*	10	16 wks
16 May 81	● **SECRET COMBINATION** *Warner Bros. K 56904*	2	60 wks
12 Jun 82	● **WINDSONG** *Warner Bros. K 57011*	7	15 wks

CRAZY HORSE — See *Neil YOUNG*

CRAZY WORLD — See *Crazy World of Arthur BROWN*

CREAM

UK, male vocal/instrumental group

24 Dec 66	● **FRESH CREAM** *Reaction 593-001*	6	17 wks
18 Nov 67	● **DISRAELI GEARS** *Reaction 594-003*	5	42 wks
17 Aug 68	● **WHEELS OF FIRE (double)(live)** *Polydor 583-031/2*	3	26 wks
17 Aug 68	● **WHEELS OF FIRE (single)(studio)** *Polydor 583-033*	7	13 wks
8 Feb 69	● **FRESH CREAM** (re-issue) *Reaction 594-001*	7	2 wks
15 Mar 69	☆ **GOODBYE** *Polydor 583-053*	1	28 wks
8 Nov 69	● **BEST OF CREAM** *Polydor 583-060*	6	34 wks
4 Jul 70	● **LIVE CREAM** *Polydor 2383-016*	4	15 wks
24 Jun 72	**LIVE CREAM VOL.2** *Polydor 2383 119*	15	5 wks

CREEDENCE CLEARWATER REVIVAL

US, male vocal/instrumental group

24 Jan 70	**GREEN RIVER** *Liberty LBS 83273*	20	6 wks
28 Mar 70	● **WILLY AND THE POOR BOYS** *Liberty LBS 83338*	10	24 wks
2 May 70	**BAYOU COUNTRY** *Liberty LBS 83261*	62	1 wk
12 Sep 70	☆ **COSMO'S FACTORY** *Liberty LBS 83388*	1	15 wks
23 Jan 71	**PENDULUM** *Liberty LBG 83400*	23	12 wks
30 Jun 79	**GREATEST HITS** *Fantasy FT 558*	35	5 wks

CREME — See *Godley and CREME*

Kid CREOLE and the COCONUTS

US, male/female vocal instrumental group

22 May 82	● **TROPICAL GANGSTERS** *Ze/Island ILPS 7016*	3†	32 wks
26 Jun 82	**FRESH FRUIT IN FOREIGN PLACES** *Ze/Island ILPS 7014*	99	1 wk

CRICKETS

US, male vocal/instrumental group

25 Mar 61	**IN STYLE WITH THE CRICKETS** *Coral LVA 9142*	13	7 wks

See also Buddy Holly and the Crickets, Bobby Vee and the Crickets.

Bing CROSBY

US, male vocalist

8 Oct 60	**JOIN BING AND SING ALONG** *Warner Bros. NM4021*	7	11 wks
21 Dec 74	**WHITE CHRISTMAS** *MCA MCF 2568*	45	3 wks
20 Sep 75	**THAT'S WHAT LIFE IS ALL ABOUT** *United Artists UAG 2973*	28	6 wks
5 Nov 77	**THE BEST OF BING** *MCA MCF 2540*	41	7 wks
5 Nov 77	● **LIVE AT THE LONDON PALLADIUM** *K-Tel NE 951*	9	2 wks
17 Dec 77	**SEASONS** *Polydor 2442 151*	25	7 wks
5 May 79	**SONGS OF A LIFETIME** *Philips 6641 923*	29	3 wks

Dave CROSBY

US, male vocalist

24 Apr 71	**IF ONLY I COULD REMEMBER MY NAME** *Atlantic 2401-005*	12	7 wks

See also Crosby, Stills and Nash, and Crosby, Stills, Nash and Young, and, Graham Nash and David Crosby.

CROSBY, STILLS and NASH

US/UK/Canada, male vocal/instrumental group

23 Aug 69	**CROSBY STILLS AND NASH** *Atlantic 588-189*	25	5 wks
9 Jul 77	**CSN** *Atlantic K 50369*	23	9 wks

See also Dave Crosby, and Crosby, Stills, Nash and Young, and Graham Nash, and Graham Nash and David Crosby, and Stephen Stills, and Stills-Young Band, and Stephen Stills' Manassas.

CROSBY, STILLS, NASH and YOUNG

US/UK, male vocal/instrumental group

30 May 70	● **DEJA VU** *Atlantic 2401-001*	5	61 wks
22 May 71	● **FOUR-WAY STREET** *Atlantic 2956 004*	5	12 wks
21 Sep 74	**SO FAR** *Atlantic K 50023*	25	6 wks

See also Dave Crosby, and Crosby, Stills and Nash, and Graham Nash, and Graham Nash and David Crosby, and Stephen Stills, and Stills-Young Band, and Stephen Stills' Manassas, and Neil Young.

Date	Title *Label Number*	Position		Date	Title *Label Number*	Position	

Christopher CROSS

US, male vocalist

21 Feb 81	**CHRISTOPHER CROSS** *Warner Bros. K 56789*	14	76 wks

CROWN HEIGHTS AFFAIR

US, male vocal/instrumental group

23 Sep 78	**DREAM WORLD** *Philips 6372 754*	40	3 wks

CRUSADERS

US, male vocal/instrumental group

21 Jul 79	● **STREET LIFE** *MCA MCF 3008*	10	16 wks
19 Jul 80	**RHAPSODY AND BLUE** *MCA MCG 4010*	40	5 wks
12 Sep 81	**STANDING TALL** *MCA MCF 3122*	47	5 wks

Bobby CRUSH

UK, male instrumentalist - piano

29 Nov 72	**BOBBY CRUSH** *Philips 6308 135*	15	7 wks
18 Dec 82	**THE BOBBY CRUSH INCREDIBLE DOUBLE DECKER PARTY** *Warwick WW 5126/7*	53†	2 wks

CULTURE

Jamaica, male vocal/instrumental group

1 Apr 78	**TWO SEVENS CLASH** *Lightning LIP 1*	60	1 wk

CULTURE CLUB

UK, male vocal/instrumental group

16 Oct 82	● **KISSING TO BE CLEVER** *Virgin V 2232*	5†	11 wks

CURE

UK, male vocal/instrumental group

2 Jun 79	**THREE IMAGINARY BOYS** *Fiction FIX 001*	44	3 wks
3 May 80	**17 SECONDS** *Fiction FIX 004*	20	10 wks
25 Apr 81	**FAITH** *Fiction FIX 6*	14	8 wks
15 May 82	● **PORNOGRAPHY** *Fiction FIX D*	8	9 wks

CURVED AIR

UK, male/female vocal instrumental group

5 Dec 70	● **AIR CONDITIONING** *Warner Bros. WSX 3012*	8	21 wks
9 Oct 71	**CURVED AIR** *Warner Bros. K 46092*	11	6 wks
13 May 72	**PHANTASMAGORIA** *Reprise K 46158*	20	5 wks

Adge CUTLER and the WURZELS

UK, male vocal/instrumental group

11 Mar 67	**ADGE CUTLER AND THE WURZELS** *Columbia SX 6126*	38	4 wks

DAKOTAS — See *Billy J. KRAMER and the DAKOTAS*

DALEK I

UK, male vocal/instrumental group

9 Aug 80	**COMPASS KUMPAS** *Backdoor OPEN 1*	54	2 wks

Roger DALTREY

UK, male vocalist

26 Jul 75	**RIDE A ROCK HORSE** *Polydor 2660 111*	14	10 wks
4 Jun 77	**ONE OF THE BOYS** *Polydor 2442 146*	45	1 wk
23 Aug 80	**MCVICAR (film soundtrack)** *Polydor POLD 5034*	39	11 wks

Glen DALY

UK, male vocalist

20 Nov 71	**GLASGOW NIGHT OUT** *Golden Guinea GGL 0479*	28	2 wks

Above **SAMMY DAVIS JR.** 'Hey man, somebody stole my coconut!'

Right **DEREK & CLIVE** Pete and 'Dud put the 'bum' in album when they charted with their unbroadcastable blue sketches.

NEIL DIAMOND His previous efforts hadn't been rough cuts, but Diamond didn't show albumwise until 1971.

THE DOORS 5 hit albums, but their million selling disc 'The Doors' released in Britain in September 1967 failed to make the chart.

BO DIDDLEY The legendary Bo Diddley only pipped Richard Dimbleby by 11 weeks in the Album Charts.

Left **DOOBIE BROS.** A happy snap of the Doobies during a break in recording 'One Step Closer'.

45

DAMNED

UK, male vocal/instrumental group

Date	Title Label Number	Position	
12 Mar 77	**DAMNED DAMNED DAMNED** *Stiff SEEZ 1*	36	10 wks
17 Nov 79	**MACHINE GUN ETIQUETTE** *Chiswick CWK 3011*	31	5 wks
29 Nov 80	**THE BLACK ALBUM** *Chiswick CWK 3015*	29	3 wks
28 Nov 81	**BEST OF** *Chiswick DAM 1*	43	12 wks
23 Oct 82	**STRAWBERRIES** *Bronze BRON 542*	15	4 wks

Vic DAMONE

US, male vocalist

25 Apr 81	**NOW!** *RCA INTS 5080*	44	3 wks

Charlie DANIELS BAND

US, male vocal/instrumental group

10 Nov 79	**MILLION MILE REFLECTIONS** *Epic EPC 83446*	74	1 wk

Bobby DARIN

US, male vocalist

19 Mar 60	● **THIS IS DARIN** *London HA 2235*	4	8 wks
9 Apr 60	**THAT'S ALL** *London HAE 2172*	15	1 wk

DARTS

UK, male/female vocal instrumental group

3 Dec 77	● **DARTS** *Magnet MAG 5020*	9	22 wks
3 Jun 78	**EVERYONE PLAYS DARTS** *Magnet MAG 5022*	12	18 wks
18 Nov 78	● **AMAZING DARTS** *K-Tel/Magnet DLP 7981*	8	13 wks
6 Oct 79	**DART ATTACK** *Magnet MAG 5030*	38	4 wks

DAVE — See *CHAS and DAVE*

Miles DAVIS

US, male instrumentalist - trumpet

11 Jul 70	**BITCHES BREW** *CBS 66236*	71	1 wk

Windsor DAVIS — See *Don ESTELLE and Windsor DAVIS*

Spencer DAVIS GROUP

UK, male vocal/instrumental group

8 Jan 66	● **THEIR 1ST LP** *Fontana TL 5242*	6	9 wks
22 Jan 66	● **THE 2ND LP** *Fontana TL 5295*	3	18 wks
11 Sep 66	● **AUTUMN '66** *Fontana TL 5359*	4	20 wks

Sammy DAVIS JR.

US, male vocalist

13 Apr 63	**SAMMY DAVIS JR. AT THE COCONUT GROVE** *Reprise R 6063/2*	19	1 wk

Colin DAVIS/BBC SYMPHONY ORCHESTRA

UK, male conductor and orchestra

4 Oct 69	**LAST NIGHT OF THE PROMS** *Philips SFM 23033*	36	1 wk

See also BBC Symphony Orchestra, Singers and Chorus.

DAWN

US, male/female vocal group

4 May 74	**GOLDEN RIBBONS** *Bell BELLS 236*	46	2 wks

Doris DAY

US, female vocalist

6 Jan 79	**20 GOLDEN GREATS** *Warwick PR 5053*	12	11 wks

Chris DE BURGH

Ireland, male vocalist

12 Sep 81	**BEST MOVES** *A & M AMLH 68532*	65	4 wks
9 Oct 82	**THE GETAWAY** *A & M AMLH 68549*	30†	12 wks

Waldo DE LOS RIOS

Argentina, male orchestra

1 May 71	● **SYMPHONIES FOR THE SEVENTIES** *A & M AMLS 2014*	6	26 wks

Date	Title *Label Number*	Position		Date	Title *Label Number*	Position	

Manitas DE PLATA

Spanish, male instrumentalist - guitar

| 29 Jul 67 | **FLAMENCO GUITAR** *Philips SBL 7786* | 40 | 1 wk |

DEAD KENNEDYS

US, male vocal/instrumental group

| 13 Sep 80 | **FRESH FRUIT FOR ROTTING VEGETABLES** *Cherry Red BRED 10* | 33 | 6 wks |

DEAN — See *JAN and DEAN*

Kiki DEE

UK, female vocalist

| 26 Mar 77 | **KIKI DEE** *Rocket ROLA 3* | 24 | 5 wks |
| 18 Jul 81 | **PERFECT TIMING** *Ariola ARL 5050* | 47 | 4 wks |

Dave DEE, DOZY, BEAKY, MICK and TICH

UK, male vocal/instrumental group

| 2 Jul 66 | **DAVE DEE, DOZY, BEAKY, MICK AND TICH** *Fontana STL 5350* | 11 | 10 wks |
| 7 Jan 67 | **IF MUSIC BE THE FOOD OF LOVE...PREPARE FOR INDIGESTION** *Fontana STL 5388* | 27 | 5 wks |

DEEP PURPLE

UK, male vocal/instrumental group

24 Jan 70	**CONCERTO FOR GROUP AND ORCHESTRA** *Harvest SHVL 767*	26	4 wks
20 Jun 70	● **DEEP PURPLE IN ROCK** *Harvest SHVL 777*	4	68 wks
18 Sep 71	★ **FIREBALL** *Harvest SHVL 793*	1	25 wks
15 Apr 72	★ **MACHINE HEAD** *Purple TPSA 7504*	1	24 wks
6 Jan 73	★ **MADE IN JAPAN** *Purple TPSP 351*	16	14 wks
17 Feb 73	● **WHO DO WE THINK WE ARE** *Purple TPSA 7508*	4	11 wks
2 Mar 74	● **BURN** *Purple TPA 3505*	3	21 wks
23 Nov 74	● **STORM BRINGER** *Purple TPS 3508*	6	12 wks
5 Jul 75	**24 CARAT PURPLE** *Purple TPSM 2002*	14	17 wks
22 Nov 75	**COME TASTE THE BAND** *Purple TPSA 7515*	19	4 wks
27 Nov 76	**DEEP PURPLE LIVE** *Purple TPSA 7517*	12	6 wks
21 Apr 79	**THE MARK II PURPLE SINGLES** *Purple TPS 3514*	24	6 wks
19 Jul 80	★ **DEEPEST PURPLE** *Harvest EMTV 25*	1	15 wks
13 Dec 80	**IN CONCERT** *Harvest SHOW 4121/4122*	30	8 wks
4 Sep 82	**DEEP PURPLE LIVE IN LONDON** *Harvest SHSP 4124*	23	5 wks

DEF LEPPARD

UK, male vocal/instrumental group

| 22 Mar 80 | **ON THROUGH THE NIGHT** *Vertigo 9102 040* | 15 | 8 wks |
| 25 Jul 81 | **HIGH AND DRY** *Vertigo 6359 045* | 26 | 8 wks |

Desmond DEKKER

Jamaica, male vocalist

| 5 Jul 69 | **THIS IS DESMOND DEKKER** *Trojan TTL 4* | 27 | 4 wks |

DELANEY and BONNIE and FRIENDS

US, male/female vocal instrumental group

| 6 Jun 70 | **ON TOUR** *Atlantic 2400-013* | 39 | 3 wks |

DEMON

UK, male vocal/instrumental group

| 14 Aug 82 | **THE UNEXPECTED GUEST** *Carrere CAL 139* | 47 | 3 wks |

Sandy DENNY

UK, male vocalist

| 2 Oct 71 | **THE NORTH STAR GRASSMAN AND THE RAVENS** *Island ILPS 9165* | 31 | 2 wks |

John DENVER

US, male vocalist

30 Mar 74	● **THE BEST OF JOHN DENVER** *RCA Victor APL1 0374*	7	69 wks
7 Sep 74	● **BACK HOME AGAIN** *RCA Victor APL1 0548*	3	29 wks
22 Mar 75	**AN EVENING WITH JOHN DENVER** *RCA Victor LSA 3211/12*	31	4 wks
11 Oct 75	**WIND SONG** *RCA Victor APL1 1183*	14	21 wks
15 May 76	● **LIVE IN LONDON** *RCA Victor RS 1050*	2	29 wks
4 Sep 76	● **SPIRIT** *RCA Victor APL1 1694*	9	11 wks
19 Mar 77	● **BEST OF JOHN DENVER VOL.2** *RCA Victor PL 42120*	9	9 wks
11 Feb 78	**I WANT TO LIVE** *RCA PL 12561*	25	5 wks
21 Apr 79	**JOHN DENVER** *RCA Victor PL 13075*	68	1 wk

See also *Placido Domingo and John Denver.*

Karl DENVER

UK, male vocalist

23 Dec 61	● WIMOWEH *Ace Of Clubs ACL 1098*	7	27 wks

DEPECHE MODE

UK, male vocal/instrumental group

14 Nov 81	● SPEAK AND SPELL *Mute STUMM 5*	10	32 wks
9 Oct 82	● A BROKEN FRAME *Mute STUMM 9*	8	10 wks

DEREK AND CLIVE — See *Peter COOK and Dudley MOORE*

DESTROYERS — See *George THOROGOOD and the DESTROYERS*

DETROIT SPINNERS

US, male vocal group

14 May 77	DETROIT SPINNERS' SMASH HITS *Atlantic K 50363*	37	3 wks

Sydney DEVINE

UK, male vocalist

10 Apr 76	DOUBLY DEVINE *Philips 6625 019*	14	10 wks
11 Dec 76	DEVINE TIME *Philips 6308 283*	49	1 wk

DEVO

US, male vocal/instrumental group

23 Jun 79	DUTY NOW FOR THE FUTURE *Virgin V 2125*	49	6 wks
16 Sep 78	Q: ARE WE NOT MEN? A: NO WE ARE DEVO! *Virgin V 2106*	12	7 wks
24 May 80	FREEDOM OF CHOICE *Virgin V 2162*	47	5 wks
5 Sep 81	NEW TRADITIONALISTS *Virgin V 2191*	50	4 wks

DEXY'S MIDNIGHT RUNNERS

UK, male vocal/instrumental group

26 Jul 80	● SEARCHING FOR THE YOUNG SOUL REBELS *Parlophone PCS 7213*	6	10 wks
7 Aug 82	● TOO-RYE-AY *Mercury/Phonogram MERS 5*	2	21 wks

Neil DIAMOND

US, male vocalist

3 Apr 71	TAP ROOT MANUSCRIPT *Uni UNLS 117*	19	12 wks
3 Apr 71	GOLD *Uni UNLS 116*	23	11 wks
11 Dec 71	STONES *Uni UNLS 121*	18	14 wks
5 Aug 72	● MOODS *Uni UNLS 128*	7	19 wks
12 Jan 74	HOT AUGUST NIGHT *Uni ULD 1*	32	2 wks
16 Feb 74	JONATHAN LIVINGSTONE SEAGULL *CBS 69047*	35	1 wk
9 Mar 74	RAINBOW *MCA MCF 2529*	39	5 wks
29 Jul 74	HIS 12 GREATEST HITS *MCA MCF 2550*	13	78 wks
9 Nov 74	SERENADE *CBS 69067*	11	14 wks
10 Jul 76	● BEAUTIFUL NOISE *CBS 86004*	10	26 wks
12 Mar 77	● LOVE AT THE GREEK *CBS 95001*	3	32 wks
6 Aug 77	HOT AUGUST NIGHT (re-issue) *MCA MCSP 255*	60	1 wk
17 Dec 77	I'M GLAD YOU'RE HERE WITH ME TONIGHT *CBS 86044*	16	12 wks
25 Nov 78	● 20 GOLDEN GREATS *MCA EMTV 14*	2	26 wks
6 Jan 79	YOU DON'T BRING ME FLOWERS *CBS 86077*	15	23 wks
19 Jan 80	SEPTEMBER MORN *CBS 86096*	14	11 wks
22 Nov 80	THE JAZZ SINGER *Capitol EAST 12120*	14	73 wks
28 Feb 81	LOVE SONGS *MCA MCF 3092*	43	6 wks
5 Dec 81	THE WAY TO THE SKY *CBS 85343*	39	13 wks
19 Jun 82	12 GREATEST HITS VOL 2 *CBS 85844*	32	8 wks
13 Nov 82	HEARTLIGHT *CBS 25073*	43†	7 wks

DIAMOND HEAD

UK, male vocal/instrumental group

23 Oct 82	BORROWED TIME *MCA DH 1001*	24	5 wks

DICKIES

US, male vocal/instrumental group

17 Feb 79	THE INCREDIBLE SHRINKING DICKIES *A & M AMLE 64742*	18	17 wks
24 Nov 79	DAWN OF THE DICKIES *A & M AMLE 68510*	60	2 wks

Barbara DICKSON

UK, female vocalist

18 Jun 77	MORNING COMES QUICKLY *RSO 2394 188*	58	1 wk
12 Apr 80	● THE BARBARA DICKSON ALBUM *Epic EPC 84088*	7	12 wks
16 May 81	YOU KNOW IT'S ME *Epic EPC 84551*	39	6 wks
6 Feb 82	● ALL FOR A SONG *Epic 10030*	3	35 wks

Date	Title Label Number	Position	

Bo DIDDLEY

US, male vocalist/instrumentalist - guitar

5 Oct 63	**BO DIDDLEY** *Pye International NPL 28026*	11	8 wks
9 Nov 63	**BO DIDDLEY IS A GUNSLINGER** *Pye NJL 33*	20	1 wk
30 Nov 63	**BO DIDDLEY RIDES AGAIN** *Pye International NPL 28029*	19	1 wk
15 Feb 64	**BO DIDDLEY'S BEACH PARTY** *Pye NPL 28032*	13	6 wks

Richard DIMBLEBY

UK, male broadcaster

| 4 Jun 66 | **VOICE OF RICHARD DIMBLEBY** *MFP 1087* | 14 | 5 wks |

DION and the BELMONTS

US, male vocal group

| 12 Apr 80 | **20 GOLDEN GREATS** *K-Tel NE 1057* | 31 | 5 wks |

DIRE STRAITS

UK, male vocal/instrumental group

22 Jul 78	● **DIRE STRAITS** *Vertigo 9102 021*	5	79 wks
23 Jun 79	● **COMMUNIQUE** *Vertigo 9102 031*	5	18 wks
25 Oct 80	● **MAKIN' MOVIES** *Vertigo 6359 034*	4†	108 wks
2 Oct 82	★ **LOVE OVER GOLD** *Vertigo/Phonogram 6359 109*	1†	13 wks

DISCHARGE

UK, male vocal/instrumental group

| 15 May 82 | **HEAR NOTHING, SEE NOTHING, SAY NOTHING** *Clay CLAYLP 3* | 40 | 5 wks |

Sacha DISTEL

France, male vocalist

| 2 May 70 | **SACHA DISTEL** *Warner Bros. WS 3003* | 21 | 14 wks |

DR. FEELGOOD

UK, male vocal/instrumental group

18 Oct 75	**MALPRACTICE** *United Artists UAS 29880*	17	6 wks
2 Oct 76	★ **STUPIDITY** *United Artists UAS 29990*	1	9 wks
4 Jun 77	● **SNEAKIN' SUSPICION** *United Artists UAS 30075*	10	6 wks
8 Oct 77	**BE SEEING YOU** *United Artists UAS 30123*	55	3 wks
7 Oct 78	**PRIVATE PRACTICE** *United Artists UAG 30184*	41	5 wks
2 Jun 79	**AS IT HAPPENS** *United Artists UAK 30239*	42	4 wks

DR. HOOK

US, male vocal/instrumental group

25 Jun 76	● **A LITTLE BIT MORE** *Capitol E-St 23795*	5	42 wks
29 Oct 77	**MAKING LOVE AND MUSIC** *Capitol EST 11632*	39	4 wks
27 Oct 79	**PLEASURE AND PAIN** *Capitol EA-ST 11859*	47	6 wks
17 Nov 79	**SOMETIMES YOU WIN** *Capitol EST 12018*	14	44 wks
29 Nov 80	**RISING** *Mercury 6302 076*	44	5 wks
6 Dec 80	● **DR. HOOK'S GREATEST HITS** *Capitol EST 26037*	2	28 wks
14 Nov 81	**DR. HOOK LIVE IN THE UK** *Capitol EST 26706*	90	1 wk

Ken DODD

UK, male vocalist

25 Dec 65	● **TEARS OF HAPPINESS** *Columbia 33SX 1793*	6	12 wks
23 Jul 66	**HITS FOR NOW AND ALWAYS** *Columbia SX 6060*	14	11 wks
14 Jan 67	**FOR SOMEONE SPECIAL** *Columbia SCX 6224*	40	1 wk
29 Nov 80	● **20 GOLDEN GREATS OF KEN DODD** *Warwick WW 5098*	10	12 wks

Thomas DOLBY

UK, male vocalist/instrumentalist - keyboards

| 22 May 82 | **THE GOLDEN AGE OF WIRELESS** *Venice In Peril VIP 1001* | 65 | 10 wks |

DOLLAR

UK, male/female vocal duo

15 Sep 79	**SHOOTING STARS** *Carrere CAL 111*	36	8 wks
24 Apr 82	**THE VERY BEST OF DOLLAR** *Carrere CAL 3001*	31	9 wks
30 Oct 82	**THE DOLLAR ALBUM** *WEA DTV 1*	18	9 wks

Placido DOMINGO and John DENVER

Spain/US male vocal duo

| 28 Nov 81 | **PERHAPS LOVE** *CBS 73592* | 26 | 21 wks |

See also John Denver.

Below **BOB DYLAN** Charted his first fo̶
albums during 1964 and the following year
out as Album Champion, spending 112 we̶
in the chart with 6 different LPs.

Above **DURAN DURAN** 'Rio'
produced no less than four hit
singles for Duran Duran. 'My
Own Way', 'Hungry Like The
Wolf', 'Save A Prayer' and the
title track.

Right **DUBLINERS** Two drops
of the hard stuff topped up with
some of the best, meant that their
number of weeks in the 1967 lists
totted up to the same as the
Beatles.

Top Left **EAGLES**   Looking Eyrie in the hotel foyer.

Top Right **FAMILY**   The Family affair first blossomed in 1969.

Left **FAIRPORT CONVENTION**   In 1970 they built on the success of Unhalfbricking.

Above **SHEENA EASTON**   Pre-war trainspotters would have called her 'The Great Easton'.

51

Date	Title Label Number	Position

Fats DOMINO

US, male vocalist/instrumentalist - piano

Date	Title Label Number	Position	
16 May 70	**VERY BEST OF FATS DOMINO** *Liberty LBS 83331*	56	1 wk

Lonnie DONEGAN

UK, male vocalist

Date	Title Label Number	Position	
1 Sep 62	● **GOLDEN AGE OF DONEGAN** *Pye Golden Guinea GGL 0135*	3	23 wks
9 Feb 63	**GOLDEN AGE OF DONEGAN VOL.2** *Pye Golden Guinea GGL 0170*	15	3 wks
25 Feb 78	**PUTTING ON THE STYLE** *Chrysalis CHR 1158*	51	3 wks

DONOVAN

UK, male vocalist

Date	Title Label Number	Position	
5 Jun 65	● **WHAT'S BIN DID AND WHAT'S BIN HID** *Pye NPL 18117*	3	16 wks
6 Nov 65	**FAIRY TALE** *Pye NPL 18128*	20	2 wks
8 Jul 67	**SUNSHINE SUPERMAN** *Pye NPL 18181*	25	7 wks
14 Oct 67	● **UNIVERSAL SOLDIER** *Marble Arch MAL 718*	5	18 wks
11 May 68	**A GIFT FROM A FLOWER TO A GARDEN** *Pye NSPL 20000*	13	14 wks
12 Sep 70	**OPEN ROAD** *Dawn DNLS 3009*	30	4 wks
24 Mar 73	**COSMIC WHEELS** *Epic EPC 65450*	15	12 wks

DOOBIE BROTHERS

US, male vocal/instrumental group

Date	Title Label Number	Position	
30 Mar 74	**WHAT WERE ONCE VICES ARE NOW HABITS** *Warner Bros. K 56206*	19	10 wks
17 May 75	**STAMPEDE** *Warner Bros. K 56094*	14	11 wks
10 Apr 76	**TAKIN' IT TO THE STREETS** *Warner Bros. K 56196*	42	2 wks
17 Sep 77	**LIVING ON THE FAULT LINE** *Warner Bros. K 56383*	25	5 wks
11 Oct 80	**ONE STEP CLOSER** *Warner Bros. K 56824*	53	2 wks

DOOLEYS

UK, male/female vocal instrumental group

Date	Title Label Number	Position	
30 Jun 79	● **THE BEST OF THE DOOLEYS** *GTO GTTV 038*	6	21 wks
3 Nov 79	**THE CHOSEN FEW** *GTO GTLP 040*	56	4 wks
25 Oct 80	**FULL HOUSE** *GTO GTTV 050*	54	2 wks

Val DOONICAN

Ireland, male vocalist

Date	Title Label Number	Position	
12 Dec 64	● **LUCKY 13 SHADES OF VAL DOONICAN** *Decca LK 4648*	2	27 wks
3 Dec 66	● **GENTLE SHADES OF VAL DOONICAN** *Decca LK 4831*	5	52 wks
2 Dec 67	★ **VAL DOONICAN ROCKS BUT GENTLY** *Pye NSPL 18204*	1	23 wks
30 Nov 68	● **VAL** *Pye NSPL 18236*	6	11 wks
14 Jun 69	● **WORLD OF VAL DOONICAN** *Decca SPA 3*	2	31 wks
13 Dec 69	**SOUNDS GENTLE** *Pye NSPL 18321*	22	9 wks
19 Dec 70	**THE MAGIC OF VAL DOONICAN** *Philips 6642 003*	34	3 wks
27 Nov 71	**THIS IS VAL DOONICAN** *Philips 6382 017*	40	1 wk
22 Feb 75	**I LOVE COUNTRY MUSIC** *Philips 9299261*	37	2 wks
21 May 77	**SOME OF MY BEST FRIENDS ARE SONGS** *Philips 6641 607*	29	5 wks

DOORS

US, male vocal/instrumental group

Date	Title Label Number	Position	
28 Sep 68	**WAITING FOR THE SUN** *Elektra EKS7 4024*	16	10 wks
11 Apr 70	**MORRISON HOTEL** *Elektra EKS 75007*	12	8 wks
26 Sep 70	**ABSOLUTELY LIVE** *Elektra 2665 002*	69	1 wk
31 Jul 71	**L.A. WOMAN** *Elektra K42090*	28	3 wks
1 Apr 72	**WEIRD SCENES INSIDE A GOLDMINE** *Elektra K 62009*	50	1 wk

Lee DORSEY

US, male vocalist

Date	Title Label Number	Position	
17 Dec 66	**NEW LEE DORSEY** *Stateside SSL 10192*	34	4 wks

Craig DOUGLAS

US, male vocalist

Date	Title Label Number	Position	
6 Aug 60	**CRAIG DOUGLAS** *Top Rank BUY 049*	17	2 wks

DOZY — See *Dave DEE, DOZY, BEAKY, MICK and TICH*

DREAMERS — See *FREDDIE and the DREAMERS*

DRIFTERS

US, male vocal group

Date	Title Label Number	Position	
18 May 68	**GOLDEN HITS** *Atlantic 588-103*	27	7 wks
10 Jun 72	**GOLDEN HITS** *Atlantic K 40018*	26	8 wks
8 Nov 75	● **24 ORIGINAL HITS** *Atlantic K 60106*	2	34 wks
13 Dec 75	**LOVE GAMES** *Bell BELLS 246*	51	1 wk

Julie DRISCOLL and The Brian AUGER TRINITY

UK, female vocalist/male instrumental group

8 Jun 68	**OPEN** *Marmalade 608-002*	12	13 wks

D-TRAIN

US, male vocalist/multi-instrumentalist

8 May 82	**D-TRAIN** *Epic EPC 85683*	72	4 wks

D-Train is a pseudonym for Hubert Eaves.

DUBLINERS

Ireland, male vocal/instrumental group

13 May 67	● **A DROP OF THE HARD STUFF** *Major Minor MMLP 3*	5	41 wks
9 Sep 67	**BEST OF THE DUBLINERS** *Transatlantic TRA 158*	25	11 wks
7 Oct 67	● **MORE OF THE HARD STUFF** *Major Minor MMLP 5*	8	23 wks
2 Mar 68	**DRINKIN' AND COURTIN'** *Major Minor SMLP 14*	31	3 wks

George DUKE

US, male vocalist/instrumentalist

26 Jul 80	**BRAZILIAN LOVE AFFAIR** *Epic EPC 84311*	33	4 wks

Simon DUPREE and BIG SOUND

UK, male vocal/instrumental group

13 Aug 67	**WITHOUT RESERVATIONS** *Parlophone PCS 7029*	39	1 wk

DURAN DURAN

UK, male vocal/instrumental group

27 Jun 81	● **DURAN DURAN** *EMI EMC 3372*	3†	70 wks
22 May 82	● **RIO** *EMI EMC 3411*	2†	32 wks

Deanna DURBIN

US, female vocalist

30 Jan 82	**THE BEST OF DEANNA DURBIN** *MCA Int MCL 1634*	84	4 wks

Ian DURY and The BLOCKHEADS

UK, male vocal/instrumental group

22 Oct 77	● **NEW BOOTS AND PANTIES!!** *Stiff SEEZ 4*	5	90 wks
2 Jun 79	● **DO IT YOURSELF** *Stiff SEEZ 14*	2	18 wks
6 Dec 80	**LAUGHTER** *Stiff SEEZ 30*	48	4 wks
10 Oct 81	**LORD UPMINSTER** *Polydor POLD 5042*	53	4 wks

Bob DYLAN

US, male vocalist

23 May 64	☆ **THE FREEWHEELIN' BOB DYLAN** *CBS BPG 62193*	1	49 wks
11 Jul 64	● **THE TIMES THEY ARE A-CHANGIN'** *CBS BPG 62251*	4	20 wks
21 Nov 64	● **ANOTHER SIDE OF BOB DYLAN** *CBS BPG 62429*	8	19 wks
8 May 65	**BOB DYLAN** *CBS BPG 62022*	13	6 wks
15 May 65	**BRINGING IT ALL BACK HOME** ☆ *CBS BPG 62515*	1	29 wks
9 Oct 65	● **HIGHWAY 61 REVISITED** *CBS BPG 62572*	4	15 wks
20 Aug 66	● **BLONDE ON BLONDE** *CBS DDP 66012*	3	15 wks
14 Jan 67	● **GREATEST HITS** *CBS SBPG 62847*	6	82 wks
2 Mar 68	**JOHN WESLEY HARDING** *CBS SBPG 63252*	1	29 wks
17 May 69	☆ **NASHVILLE SKYLINE** *CBS 63601*	1	42 wks
11 Jul 70	☆ **SELF PORTRAIT** *CBS 66250*	1	15 wks
28 Nov 70	☆ **NEW MORNING** *CBS 69001*	1	18 wks
25 Dec 71	☆ **MORE BOB DYLAN GREATEST HITS** *CBS 67238/9*	12	15 wks
29 Sep 73	**PAT GARRETT & BILLY THE KID (FILM SOUNDTRACK)** *CBS 69042*	29	11 wks
23 Feb 74	● **PLANET WAVES** *Island ILPS 9261*	7	8 wks
13 Jul 74	● **BEFORE THE FLOOD** *Asylum IDBD 1*	8	7 wks
15 Feb 75	● **BLOOD ON THE TRACKS** *CBS 69097*	4	16 wks
26 Jul 75	● **THE BASEMENT TAPES** *CBS 88147*	8	10 wks
31 Jan 76	● **DESIRE** *CBS 86003*	3	35 wks
9 Oct 76	● **HARD RAIN** *CBS 86016*	3	7 wks
1 Jul 78	● **STREET LEGAL** *CBS 86067*	2	20 wks
26 May 79	● **BOB DYLAN AT BUDOKAN** *CBS 96004*	4	19 wks
8 Sep 79	● **SLOW TRAIN COMING** *CBS 86095*	2	13 wks
28 Jun 80	● **SAVED** *CBS 86113*	3	8 wks
29 Aug 81	● **SHOT OF LOVE** *CBS 85178*	6	8 wks

E

EAGLES

US, male vocal/instrumental group

Date	Title *Label Number*	Position	
27 Apr 74	**ON THE BORDER** *Asylum SYL 9016*	28	9 wks
12 Jul 75	● **ONE OF THESE NIGHTS** *Asylum SYLA 8759*	8	40 wks
12 Jul 75	**DESPERADO** *Asylum SYLL 9011*	39	9 wks
6 Mar 76	● **THEIR GREATEST HITS 1971-1975** *Asylum K 53017*	2	77 wks
25 Dec 76	● **HOTEL CALIFORNIA** *Asylum K 53051*	2	61 wks
13 Oct 79	● **THE LONG RUN** *Asylum K 52181*	4	16 wks
22 Nov 80	**LIVE** *Asylum K 62032*	24	4 wks

EARTH WIND AND FIRE

US, male vocal/instrumental group

Date	Title *Label Number*	Position	
21 Jan 78	**ALL 'N' ALL** *CBS 86051*	13	23 wks
16 Dec 78	● **THE BEST OF EARTH WIND AND FIRE VOL.1** *CBS 83284*	6	42 wks
23 Jun 79	● **I AM** *CBS 86084*	5	41 wks
1 Nov 80	● **FACES** *CBS 88498*	10	6 wks
14 Nov 81	**RAISE** *CBS 85272*	14	22 wks

EAST OF EDEN

UK, male instrumental group

Date	Title *Label Number*	Position	
14 Mar 70	**SNAFU** *Deram SML 1050*	29	2 wks

Sheena EASTON

UK, female vocalist

Date	Title *Label Number*	Position	
31 Jan 81	**TAKE MY TIME** *EMI EMC 3354*	17	9 wks
3 Oct 81	**YOU COULD HAVE BEEN WITH ME** *EMI EMC 3378*	33	6 wks
25 Sep 82	**MADNESS, MONEY AND MUSIC** *EMI EMC 3414*	44	4 wks

Clint EASTWOOD and General SAINT

Jamaica, male vocal duo

Date	Title *Label Number*	Position	
6 Feb 82	**TOO BAD DJ** *Greensleeves GREL 24*	99	2 wks

ECHO and the BUNNYMEN

UK, male vocal/instrumental group

Date	Title *Label Number*	Position	
26 Jul 80	**CROCODILES** *Korova KODE 1*	17	6 wks
6 Jun 81	● **HEAVEN UP HERE** *Korova KODE 3*	10	16 wks

EDDIE and the HOT RODS

UK, male vocal/instrumental group

Date	Title *Label Number*	Position	
18 Dec 76	**TEENAGE DEPRESSION** *Island ILPS 9457*	43	1 wk
3 Dec 77	**LIFE ON THE LINE** *Island ILPS 9509*	27	3 wks
24 Mar 79	**THRILLER** *Island ILPS 9563*	50	1 wk

Duane EDDY

US, male instrumentalist - guitar

Date	Title *Label Number*	Position	
6 Jun 59	● **HAVE TWANGY GUITAR WILL TRAVEL** *London HAW 2160*	6	3 wks
31 Oct 59	● **SPECIALLY FOR YOU** *London HAW 2191*	6	8 wks
19 Mar 60	● **THE TWANG'S THE THANG** *London HA 2236*	2	25 wks
26 Nov 60	**SONGS OF OUR HERITAGE** *London HAW 2285*	13	5 wks
1 Apr 61	● **A MILLION DOLLARS' WORTH OF TWANG** *London HAW 2325*	5	19 wks
9 Jun 62	**A MILLION DOLLARS WORTH OF TWANG VOL.2** *London HAW 2435*	18	1 wk
21 Jul 62	● **TWISTIN' & TWANGIN'** *RCA RD 27264*	8	12 wks
8 Dec 62	**TWANGY GUITAR - SILKY STRINGS** *RCA RD 7510*	13	11 wks
16 Mar 63	**DANCE WITH THE GUITAR MAN** *RCA RD 7545*	14	4 wks

Dave EDMUNDS

UK, male vocalist/multi-instrumentalist

Date	Title *Label Number*	Position	
23 Jun 79	**REPEAT WHEN NECESSARY** *Swansong SSK 59409*	39	12 wks
18 Apr 81	**TWANGIN'** *Swansong SSK 59411*	37	4 wks
3 Apr 82	**DE7** *Arista SPART 1184*	60	3 wks

EEK-A-MOUSE

Jamaica, male vocalist

Date	Title *Label Number*	Position	
14 Aug 82	**SKIDIP** *Greensleeves GREL 41*	61	3 wks

801

UK, male vocal/instrumental group

Date	Title *Label Number*	Position	
20 Nov 76	**801 LIVE** *Island ILPS 9444*	52	2 wks

Date	Title *Label Number*	Position	Date	Title *Label Number*	Position

ELECTRIC LIGHT ORCHESTRA

UK, male vocal/instrumental group

Date	Title *Label Number*	Position	Wks
12 Aug 72	**QUEEN OF THE HOURS** *Harvest SHVL 797*	32	4 wks
31 Mar 73	**ELO 2** *Harvest SHVL 806*	35	1 wk
11 Dec 76	● **A NEW WORLD RECORD** *United Artists UAG 30017*	6	100 wks
12 Nov 77	● **OUT OF THE BLUE** *United Artists UAR 100*	4	108 wks
6 Jan 79	**THREE LIGHT YEARS** *Jet JET BX 1*	38	9 wks
16 Jun 79	☆ **DISCOVERY** *Jet JET LX 500*	1	46 wks
1 Dec 79	● **ELO'S GREATEST HITS** *Jet JET LX 525*	7	18 wks
8 Aug 81	☆ **TIME** *Jet LP 236*	1	32 wks

Out Of The Blue *changed label number to JET DP 400 and* A New World Record *changed to JET LP 200 during their chart runs.*

Duke ELLINGTON

US, orchestra

Date	Title *Label Number*	Position	Wks
8 Apr 61	**NUT CRACKER SUITE** *Philips BBL 7418*	11	2 wks

EMERSON, LAKE and PALMER

US, male instrumental group

Date	Title *Label Number*	Position	Wks
5 Dec 70	● **EMERSON, LAKE AND PALMER** *Island ILPS 9132*	4	28 wks
19 Jun 71	☆ **TARKUS** *Island ILPS 9155*	1	17 wks
4 Dec 71	● **PICTURES AT AN EXHIBITION** *Island HELP 1*	3	5 wks
8 Jul 72	● **TRILOGY** *Island ILPS 9186*	2	29 wks
22 Dec 73	● **BRAIN SALAD SURGERY** *Manticore K 53501*	2	17 wks
24 Aug 74	● **WELCOME BACK MY FRIENDS TO THE SHOW THAT NEVER ENDS - LADIES AND GENTLEMEN: EMERSON, LAKE AND PALMER** *Manticore K 63500*	5	5 wks
9 Apr 77	● **WORKS** *Atlantic K 80009*	9	25 wks
10 Dec 77	**WORKS VOL.2** *Atlantic K 50422*	20	5 wks
9 Dec 78	**LOVE BEACH** *Atlantic K 50552*	48	4 wks

See also Greg Lake. Pictures At An Exhibition' was a budget album and after spending 5 weeks on the chart, budget albums were separated from the main chart so the album disappeared instantly.

ENGLAND FOOTBALL WORLD CUP SQUAD 1970

UK, football team

Date	Title *Label Number*	Position	Wks
16 May 70	● **THE WORLD BEATERS SING THE WORLD BEATERS** *Pye NSPL 18337*	4	8 wks

ENGLAND FOOTBALL WORLD CUP SQUAD 1982

UK, football team

Date	Title *Label Number*	Position	Wks
15 May 82	**THIS TIME** *K-Tel NE 1169*	37	10 wks

ENIGMA

UK, male vocal/instrumental group

Date	Title *Label Number*	Position	Wks
5 Sep 81	**AIN'T NO STOPPIN'** *Creole CRX 1*	80	3 wks

Brian ENO

UK, male instrumentalist - keyboards

Date	Title *Label Number*	Position	Wks
9 Mar 74	**HERE COME THE WARM JETS** *Island ILPS 9268*	26	2 wks
21 Oct 78	**MUSIC FOR FILMS** *Polydor 2310 623*	55	1 wk

See also Brian Eno and David Byrne.

Brian ENO and David BYRNE

UK, male instrumentalist and US, male vocalist/instrumentalist - guitar

Date	Title *Label Number*	Position	Wks
21 Feb 81	**MY LIFE IN THE BUSH OF GHOSTS** *Polydor EGLP 48*	29	8 wks

See also Brian Eno.

EQUALS

UK, male vocal/instrumental group

Date	Title *Label Number*	Position	Wks
18 Nov 67	● **UNEQUALLED EQUALS** *President PTL 1006*	10	9 wks
9 Mar 68	**EQUALS EXPLOSION** *President PTLS 1015*	32	1 wk

David ESSEX

UK, male vocalist

Date	Title *Label Number*	Position	Wks
24 Nov 73	● **ROCK ON** *CBS 65823*	7	22 wks
19 Oct 74	● **DAVID ESSEX** *CBS 69088*	2	24 wks
27 Sep 75	● **ALL THE FUN OF THE FAIR** *CBS 69160*	3	20 wks
5 Jun 76	**ON TOUR** *CBS 95000*	51	1 wk
30 Oct 76	**OUT ON THE STREET** *CBS 86017*	31	9 wks
8 Oct 77	**GOLD AND IVORY** *CBS 86038*	29	4 wks
6 Jan 79	**DAVID ESSEX ALBUM** *CBS 10011*	29	7 wks
31 Mar 79	**IMPERIAL WIZARD** *Mercury 9109 616*	12	9 wks
12 Jun 80	**HOT LOVE** *Mercury 6359 017*	75	1 wk
19 Jun 82	**STAGE-STRUCK** *Mercury/Phonogram MERS 4*	31	15 wks
27 Nov 82	**THE VERY BEST OF DAVID ESSEX** *TV Records TVA 4*	38†	5 wks

DUANE EDDY Twanged successfully from 1960-1963.

THE EVERLY BROTHERS Don and Phil 1961.

57

Don ESTELLE and Windsor DAVIES

UK, male vocal duo

| 10 Jan 76 | ● **SING LOFTY** *EMI EMC 3102* | 10 | 8 wks |

EVERLY BROTHERS

US, male vocal duo

2 Jul 60	● **IT'S EVERLY TIME** *Warner Bros. WM 4006*	2	23 wks
15 Oct 60	● **FABULOUS STYLE OF THE EVERLY BROTHERS** *London HAA 2266*	4	11 wks
4 Mar 61	● **A DATE WITH THE EVERLY BROTHERS** *Warner Bros. WM 4028*	3	14 wks
21 Jul 62	**INSTANT PARTY** *Warner Bros. WM 4061*	20	1 wk
12 Sep 70	● **ORIGINAL GREATEST HITS** *CBS 66255*	7	16 wks
8 Jun 74	**THE VERY BEST OF THE EVERLY BROTHERS** *Warner Bros. K 46008*	43	1 wk
29 Nov 75	**WALK RIGHT BACK WITH THE EVERLYS** *Warner Bros. K56118*	56	1 wk
9 Apr 77	**LIVING LEGENDS** *Warwick WW 5027*	12	10 wks
18 Dec 82	**LOVE HURTS** *K-Tel NE 1197*	46†	2 wks

EXPLOITED

UK, male vocal/instrumental group

16 May 81	**PUNK'S NOT DEAD** *Secret SEC 1*	20	11 wks
14 Nov 81	**EXPLOITED LIVE** *Superville EXPLP 2001*	52	3 wks
19 Jun 82	**TROOPS OF TOMORROW** *Secret SEC 8*	17	12 wks

FACES

UK, male vocal/instrumental group

4 Apr 70	**FIRST STEP** *Warner Bros. WS 3000*	45	1 wk
8 May 71	**LONG PLAYER** *Warner Bros. W 3011*	31	7 wks
25 Dec 71	● **A NOD'S AS GOOD AS A WINK....TO A BLIND HORSE** *Warner Bros. K 56006*	2	22 wks
21 Apr 73	★ **OOH-LA-LA** *Warner Bros. K 56011*	1	13 wks
21 May 77	**THE BEST OF THE FACES** *Riva RVLP 3*	24	6 wks

Donald FAGEN

US, male vocalist

| 30 Oct 82 | **THE NIGHTFLY** *Warner Bros. 923696* | 44† | 9 wks |

FAIRPORT CONVENTION

UK, male/female vocal instrumental group

2 Aug 69	**UNHALFBRICKING** *Island ILPS 9102*	12	8 wks
17 Jan 70	**LIEGE AND LIEF** *Island ILPS 9115*	17	15 wks
18 Jul 70	**FULL HOUSE** *Island ILPS 9130*	13	11 wks
3 Jul 71	● **ANGEL DELIGHT** *Island ILPS 9162*	8	5 wks
12 Jul 75	**RISING FOR THE MOON** *ILPS 9313*	52	1 wk

Adam FAITH

UK, male vocalist

19 Nov 60	● **ADAM** *Parlophone PMC 1128*	6	36 wks
11 Feb 61	**BEAT GIRL** *Columbia 33SX 1225*	11	3 wks
24 Mar 62	**ADAM FAITH** *Parlophone PMC 1162*	20	1 wk
25 Sep 65	**FAITH ALIVE** *Parlophone PMC 1249*	19	1 wk
19 Dec 81	**20 GOLDEN GREATS** *Warwick WW 5113*	61	3 wks

Marianne FAITHFULL

UK, female vocalist

5 Jun 65	**COME MY WAY** *Decca LK 4688*	12	7 wks
5 Jun 65	**MARIANNE FAITHFULL** *Decca LK 4689*	15	2 wks
24 Nov 79	**BROKEN ENGLISH** *Island M1*	57	3 wks
17 Oct 81	**DANGEROUS ACQUAINTANCES** *Island ILPS 9648*	45	4 wks

Date	Title Label Number	Position		Date	Title Label Number	Position	

FALL
UK, male vocal/instrumental group

20 Mar 82	HEX ENDUCTION HOUR *Kamera KAM 005*	71	3 wks

Georgie FAME
UK, male vocalist

17 Oct 64	FAME AT LAST *Columbia 33SX 1638*	15	8 wks
14 May 66	● SWEET THINGS *Columbia SX 6043*	6	22 wks
15 Oct 66	● SOUND VENTURE *Columbia SX 6076*	9	9 wks
11 Mar 67	HALL OF FAME *Columbia SX 6120*	12	18 wks
1 Jul 67	TWO FACES OF FAME *CBS SBPG 63018*	22	15 wks

FAMILY
UK, male vocal/instrumental group

10 Aug 68	MUSIC IN THE DOLLS HOUSE *Reprise RLP 6312*	35	3 wks
22 Mar 69	● FAMILY ENTERTAINMENT *Reprise RSLP 6340*	6	3 wks
7 Feb 70	● A SONG FOR ME *Reprise RSLP 9001*	4	13 wks
28 Nov 70	● ANYWAY *Reprise RSX 9005*	7	7 wks
20 Nov 71	FEARLESS *Reprise K 54003*	14	2 wks
30 Sep 72	BANDSTAND *Reprise K 54006*	15	10 wks
29 Sep 73	IT'S ONLY A MOVIE *Raft RA 58501*	30	3 wks

FAMILY STONE — See *SLY and the FAMILY STONE*

Chris FARLOWE
UK, male vocalist

2 Apr 66	14 THINGS TO THINK ABOUT *Immediate IMLP 005*	19	1 wk
10 Dec 66	THE ART OF CHRIS FARLOWE *Immediate IMLP 006*	37	2 wks

FASHION
UK, male vocal/instrumental group

3 Jul 82	● FABRIQUE *Arista SPART 1185*	10	16 wks

FAT LARRY'S BAND
US, male vocal/instrumental group

9 Oct 82	BREAKIN' OUT *Virgin V 2229*	58	4 wks

FATBACK BAND
US, male vocal/instrumental group

6 Mar 76	RAISING HELL *Polydor 2391 203*	19	6 wks

Jose FELICIANO
US, male vocalist/instrumentalist - guitar

2 Nov 68	● FELICIANO *RCA Victor SF 7946*	6	36 wks
29 Nov 69	JOSE FELICIANO *RCA Victor SF 8044*	29	2 wks
14 Feb 70	10 TO 23 *RCA SF 7946*	38	1 wk
22 Aug 70	FIREWORKS *RCA SF 8124*	65	1 wk

Julie FELIX
US, female vocalist

11 Sep 66	CHANGES *Fontana TL 5368*	27	4 wks

Bryan FERRY
UK, male vocalist

3 Nov 73	● THESE FOOLISH THINGS *Island ILPS 9249*	5	42 wks
20 Jul 74	● ANOTHER TIME, ANOTHER PLACE *Island ILPS 9284*	4	25 wks
2 Oct 76	LET'S STICK TOGETHER *Island ILPSX 1*	19	5 wks
5 Mar 77	● IN YOUR MIND *Polydor 2302 055*	5	17 wks
30 Sep 78	THE BRIDE STRIPPED BARE *Polydor POLD 5003*	13	5 wks

Gracie FIELDS
UK, female vocalist

20 Dec 75	THE GOLDEN YEARS *Warwick WW 5007*	48	3 wks

FISCHER-Z
UK, male vocal/instrumental group

23 Jun 79	WORD SALAD *United Artists UAG 30232*	66	1 wk

Ella FITZGERALD
US, female vocalist

11 Jun 60	ELLA SINGS GERSHWIN *Brunswick LA 8648*	13	3 wks
18 Jun 60	ELLA AT THE OPERA HOUSE *Columbia 33SX 10126*	16	1 wk
23 Jul 60	ELLA SINGS GERSHWIN VOL.5 *HMV CLP 1353*	18	2 wks
10 May 80	THE INCOMPARABLE ELLA *Polydor POLTV 9*	40	7 wks

Date	Title *Label Number*	Position

FIVE PENNY PIECE

UK, male/female vocal/instrumental group

| 24 Mar 73 | **MAKING TRACKS** *Columbia SCX 6536* | 37 | 1 wk |
| 3 Jul 76 | ● **KING COTTON** *EMI EMC 3129* | 9 | 5 wks |

FIXX

UK, male vocal/instrumental group

| 22 May 82 | **SHUTTERED ROOM** *MCA FX 1001* | 54 | 6 wks |

Roberta FLACK

US, female vocalist

| 15 Jul 72 | **FIRST TAKE** *Atlantic K 40040* | 47 | 2 wks |
| 13 Oct 73 | **KILLING ME SOFTLY** *Atlantic K 50021* | 40 | 2 wks |

See also Roberta Flack and Donny Hathaway.

Roberta FLACK and Donny HATHAWAY

US, female/male vocal duo

| 7 Jun 80 | **ROBERTA FLACK AND DONNY HATHAWAY** *Atlantic K 50696* | 31 | 7 wks |

See also Roberta Flack.

Grandmaster FLASH and the FURIOUS FIVE

US, male vocal group

| 23 Oct 82 | **THE MESSAGE** *Sugarhill SHLP 1007* | 77 | 3 wks |

FLEETWOOD MAC

UK/US, male/female vocal instrumental group

2 Mar 68	● **FLEETWOOD MAC** *Blue Horizon BPG 7-63200*	4	37 wks
7 Sep 68	● **MR. WONDERFUL** *Blue Horizon 7–63205*	10	11 wks
30 Aug 69	**PIOUS BIRD OF GOOD OMEN** *Blue Horizon 7–63205*	18	4 wks
4 Oct 69	● **THEN PLAY ON** *Reprise RSLP 9000*	6	11 wks
10 Oct 70	**KILN HOUSE** *Reprise RSLP 9004*	39	2 wks
19 Feb 72	**GREATEST HITS** *Reprise K 44162*	36	5 wks
7 Jul 73	**GREATEST HITS** *CBS 69011*	37	6 wks
6 Nov 76	**FLEETWOOD MAC** *Reprise K 54043*	23	19 wks
26 Feb 77	☆ **RUMOURS** *Warner Bros. K 56344*	1	271 wks
27 Oct 79	☆ **TUSK** *Warner Bros. K 66088*	1	23 wks
13 Dec 80	**FLEETWOOD MAC LIVE** *Warner Bros. K 66097*	31	9 wks
10 Jul 82	● **MIRAGE** *Warner Bros K 56592*	5	23 wks

Berni FLINT

UK, male vocalist

| 2 Jul 77 | **I DON'T WANT TO PUT A HOLD ON YOU** *EMI EMC 3184* | 37 | 6 wks |

FLOATERS

US, male vocal/instrumental group

| 20 Aug 77 | **FLOATERS** *ABC ABCL 5229* | 17 | 8 wks |

FLOCK

UK, male vocal/instrumental group

| 2 May 70 | **FLOCK** *CBS 63733* | 59 | 2 wks |

FLOCK OF SEAGULLS

UK, male vocal/instrumental group

| 17 Apr 82 | **A FLOCK OF SEAGULLS** *Jive HOP 201* | 32† | 29 wks |

Eddie FLOYD

US, male vocalist

| 29 Apr 67 | **KNOCK ON WOOD** *Stax 589-006* | 36 | 5 wks |

FLYING LIZARDS

UK, male/female vocal instrumental group

| 16 Feb 80 | **FLYING LIZARDS** *Virgin V 2150* | 60 | 3 wks |

FOCUS

Holland, male instrumental group

11 Nov 72	● **MOVING WAVES** *Polydor 2931 002*	2	34 wks
2 Dec 72	● **FOCUS 3** *Polydor 2383 016*	6	15 wks
20 Oct 73	**FOCUS AT THE RAINBOW** *Polydor 2442 118*	23	5 wks
25 May 74	**HAMBURGER CONCERTO** *Polydor 2442 124*	20	5 wks
9 Aug 75	**FOCUS** *Polydor 2384 070*	23	6 wks

Dan FOGELBERG

US, male vocalist

| 29 Mar 80 | **PHOENIX** *Epic EPC 83317* | 42 | 3 wks |

Date	Title Label Number	Position		Date	Title Label Number	Position	

Ellen FOLEY

US, female vocalist

| 17 Nov 79 | **NIGHT OUT** *Epic EPC 83718* | 68 | 1 wk |
| 4 Apr 81 | **SPIRIT OF ST.LOUIS** *Epic EPC 84809* | 57 | 2 wks |

Wayne FONTANA and the MINDBENDERS

UK, male vocalist and male vocal/instrumental group

| 20 Feb 65 | **WAYNE FONTANA AND THE MINDBENDERS** *Fontana TL 5230* | 18 | 1 wk |

See also The Mindbenders.

Steve FORBERT

US, male vocalist

| 9 Jun 79 | **ALIVE ON ARRIVAL** *Epic EPC 83308* | 56 | 1 wk |
| 24 Nov 79 | **JACK RABBIT SLIM** *Epic EPC 83879* | 54 | 2 wks |

Clinton FORD

UK, male vocalist

| 26 May 62 | **CLINTON FORD** *Oriole PS 40021* | 16 | 4 wks |

FOREIGNER

UK/US, male vocal/instrumental group

26 Aug 78	**DOUBLE VISION** *Atlantic K 50476*	32	5 wks
25 Jul 81	● **4** *Atlantic K 50796*	5	62 wks
18 Dec 82	**RECORDS** *Atlantic A 0999*	62†	2 wks

FOTHERINGAY

UK, male/female vocal/instrumental group

| 11 Jul 70 | **FOTHERINGAY** *Island ILPS 9125* | 18 | 6 wks |

FOUR PENNIES

UK, male vocal/instrumental group

| 7 Nov 64 | **TWO SIDES OF FOUR PENNIES** *Philips BL 7642* | 13 | 5 wks |

FOUR SEASONS

US, male vocal group

6 Jul 63	**SHERRY** *Stateside SL 10033*	20	1 wk
10 Apr 71	**EDIZIONE D'ORO** *Philips 6640-002*	11	7 wks
20 Nov 71	**THE BIG ONES** *Philips 6336-208*	37	1 wk
6 Mar 76	**THE FOUR SEASONS STORY** *Private Stock DAPS 1001*	20	8 wks
6 Mar 76	**WHO LOVES YOU** *Warner Bros. K 56179*	12	17 wks
20 Nov 76	● **GREATEST HITS OF** *K-Tel NE 942*	4	6 wks

Greatest Hits album credited to Frankie Valli and the Four Seasons. It contains some solo Valli items.

4-SKINS

UK, male vocal/instrumental group

| 17 Apr 82 | **THE GOOD, THE BAD AND THE 4-SKINS** *Secret SEC 4* | 80 | 4 wks |

FOUR TOPS

US, male vocal group

19 Nov 66	● **FOUR TOPS ON TOP** *Tamla Motown TML 11037*	9	23 wks
11 Feb 67	● **FOUR TOPS LIVE!** *Tamla Motown STML 11041*	4	72 wks
25 Nov 67	● **REACH OUT** *Tamla Motown STML 11056*	4	34 wks
20 Jan 68	☆ **GREATEST HITS** *Tamla Motown STML 11061*	1	67 wks
8 Feb 69	**YESTERDAY'S DREAMS** *Tamla Motown STML 11087*	37	1 wk
27 Jun 70	**STILL WATERS RUN DEEP** *Tamla Motown STML 11149*	29	8 wks
27 Nov 71	**FOUR TOPS' GREATEST HITS VOL.2** *Tamla Motown STML 11195*	25	10 wks
10 Nov 73	**THE FOUR TOPS STORY 1964-72** *Tamla Motown TMSP 11241/2*	35	5 wks
13 Feb 82	**THE BEST OF THE FOUR TOPS** *K-Tel NE 1160*	13	13 wks

See also Supremes and Four Tops.

FOX

UK, male/female vocal instrumental group

| 17 May 75 | ● **FOX** *GTO GTLP 001* | 7 | 8 wks |

John FOXX

UK, male vocalist

| 2 Feb 80 | **METAMATIX** *Metalbeat V 2146* | 18 | 7 wks |
| 3 Oct 81 | **THE GARDEN** *Virgin V 2194* | 24 | 6 wks |

BRYAN FERRY The Newcastle Ferry who led Roxy Music in uncharted territory until July 1972.

FOCUS Clearly a picture of Focus.

BILLY FURY One of the Rock & Roll greats, whose 'Sound of Fury' featuring Joe Brown on lead guitar was Britain's only really original home-grown self-penned rockabilly album.

FOUR TOPS Levi & The Tops in Parliament Square.

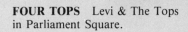

63

Date	Title Label Number	Position	Date	Title Label Number	Position

Peter FRAMPTON

UK, male vocalist

22 May 76	● FRAMPTON COMES ALIVE	6	39 wks
	A & M AMLM 63703		
18 Jun 77	I'M IN YOU A & M AMLK 64039	19	10 wks

Connie FRANCIS

US, female vocalist

26 Mar 60	ROCK 'N' ROLL MILLION SELLERS	12	1 wk
	MGM C 804		
11 Feb 61	CONNIE'S GREATEST HITS MGM C 831	16	3 wks
18 Jun 77	★ 20 ALL TIME GREATS Polydor 2391 290	1	22 wks

Aretha FRANKLIN

US, female vocalist

12 Aug 67	I NEVER LOVED A MAN Atlantic 587-006	36	2 wks
13 Apr 68	LADY SOUL Atlantic 588-099	25	18 wks
14 Sep 68	● ARETHA NOW Atlantic 588-114	6	11 wks

Rodney FRANKLIN

US, male instrumentalist - piano

24 May 80	YOU'LL NEVER KNOW CBS 83812	64	2 wks

FREDDIE and the DREAMERS

UK, male vocal/instrumental group

9 Nov 63	● FREDDIE AND THE DREAMERS	5	26 wks
	Columbia 33SX 1577		

FREDERICK — See *NINA and FREDERICK*

FREE

UK, male vocal/instrumental group

11 Jul 70	● FIRE AND WATER Island ILPS 9120	2	18 wks
23 Jan 71	HIGHWAY Island ILPS 9138	41	10 wks
26 Jun 71	● FREE LIVE! Island ILPS 9160	4	12 wks
17 Jun 72	● FREE AT LAST Island ILPS 9192	9	9 wks
3 Feb 73	● HEARTBREAKER Island ILPS 9217	9	7 wks
16 Mar 74	● THE FREE STORY Island ISLD 4	2	6 wks

FREEEZ

UK, male instrumental group

7 Feb 81	SOUTHERN FREEEZ Beggars Banquet BEGA 22	17	15 wks

FRIDA

Sweden, female vocalist

18 Sep 82	SOMETHING'S GOING ON Epic EPC 85966	18	7 wks

Dean FRIEDMAN

US, male vocalist

21 Oct 78	WELL, WELL, SAID THE ROCKING CHAIR	21	14 wks
	Lifesong LSLP 6019		

Robert FRIPP

UK, male vocalist/instrumentalist - guitar

12 May 79	EXPOSURE Polydor EGLP 101	71	1 wk

FUNBOY THREE

UK, male vocal/instrumental group

20 Mar 82	● FUNBOY THREE Chrysalis CHR 1383	7	20 wks

FUNKADELIC

US, male vocal/instrumental group

23 Dec 78	ONE NATION UNDER A GROOVE	56	5 wks
	Warner Bros. K 56539		

FUREYS AND DAVEY ARTHUR

Ireland, male vocal/instrumental group

8 May 82	WHEN YOU WERE SWEET SIXTEEN	99	1 wk
	Ritz RITZLP 0004		

Date	Title *Label Number*	Position		Date	Title *Label Number*	Position

Billy FURY

UK, male vocalist

Date	Title *Label Number*	Position	
4 Jun 60	THE SOUND OF FURY *Decca LF 1329*	18	2 wks
23 Sep 61	● HALFWAY TO PARADISE *Ace Of Clubs ACL 1083*	5	9 wks
11 May 63	● BILLY *Decca LK 4533*	6	21 wks
26 Oct 63	WE WANT BILLY *Decca LK 4548*	14	2 wks

Peter GABRIEL

UK, male vocalist

Date	Title *Label Number*	Position	
12 Mar 77	● PETER GABRIEL *Charisma CDS 4006*	7	19 wks
17 Jun 78	● PETER GABRIEL *Charisma CDS 4013*	10	8 wks
7 Jun 80	★ PETER GABRIEL *Charisma CDS 4019*	1	18 wks
18 Sep 82	● PETER GABRIEL *Charisma PG 4*	6†	15 wks

All four albums are different.

GALLAGHER and LYLE

UK, male vocal/instrumental duo

Date	Title *Label Number*	Position	
28 Feb 76	● BREAKAWAY *A & M AMLH 68348*	6	35 wks
29 Jan 77	LOVE ON THE AIRWAYS *A & M AMLH 64620*	19	9 wks

Rory GALLAGHER

UK, male vocalist/instrumentalist - guitar

Date	Title *Label Number*	Position	
29 May 71	RORY GALLAGHER *Polydor 2383-044*	32	2 wks
4 Dec 71	DEUCE *Polydor 2383-076*	39	1 wk
20 May 72	● LIVE IN EUROPE *Polydor 2383 112*	9	15 wks
24 Feb 73	BLUE PRINT *Polydor 2383 189*	12	7 wks
17 Nov 73	TATTOO *Polydor 2383 230*	32	3 wks
27 Jul 74	IRISH TOUR '74 *Polydor 2659 031*	36	2 wks
30 Oct 76	CALLING CARD *Chrysalis CHR 1124*	32	1 wk
22 Sep 79	TOP PRIORITY *Chrysalis CHR 1235*	56	4 wks
8 Nov 80	STAGE STRUCK *Chrysalis CHR 1280*	40	3 wks
8 May 82	JINX *Chrysalis CHR 1359*	68	5 wks

James GALWAY

Ireland, male vocalist/instrumentalist - flute

Date	Title *Label Number*	Position	
27 May 78	THE MAGIC FLUTE OF JAMES GALWAY *RCA Red Seal LRL1 5131*	43	6 wks
1 Jul 78	THE MAN WITH THE GOLDEN FLUTE *RCA Red Seal LRL1 5127*	52	3 wks
9 Sep 78	● JAMES GALWAY PLAYS SONGS FOR ANNIE *RCA Red Seal RL 25163*	7	40 wks
15 Dec 79	SONGS OF THE SEASHORE *Solar RL 25253*	39	6 wks
18 Dec 82	THE JAMES GALWAY COLLECTION *Telstar STAR 2224*	41†	2 wks

GANG — See *KOOL and the GANG*

GANG OF FOUR

UK, male vocal/instrumental group

Date	Title *Label Number*	Position	
13 Oct 79	ENTERTAINMENT *EMI EMC 3313*	45	3 wks
21 Mar 81	SOLID GOLD *EMI EMC 3364*	52	2 wks
29 May 82	SONGS OF THE FREE *EMI EMC 3412*	61	4 wks

Art GARFUNKEL

US, male vocalist

Date	Title *Label Number*	Position	
13 Oct 73	ANGEL CLARE *CBS 69021*	14	7 wks
1 Nov 75	● BREAKAWAY *CBS 86002*	7	10 wks
18 Mar 78	WATER MARK *CBS 86054*	25	5 wks
21 Apr 79	● FATE FOR BREAKFAST *CBS 86082*	2	20 wks
19 Sep 81	SCISSORS CUT *CBS 85259*	51	3 wks

See also Simon and Garfunkel.

Judy GARLAND

US, female vocalist

Date	Title *Label Number*	Position	
3 Mar 62	JUDY AT CARNEGIE HALL *Capitol W 1569*	13	3 wks

Errol GARNER

US, male instrumentalist - piano

Date	Title *Label Number*	Position	
14 Jul 62	CLOSE UP IN SWING *Philips BBL 7579*	20	1 wk

David GATES

US, male vocalist

Date	Title *Label Number*	Position	
31 May 75	NEVER LET HER GO *Elektra K 52012*	32	1 wk
29 Jul 78	GOODBYE GIRL *Elektra K 52091*	28	3 wks

Marvin GAYE

US, male vocalist

Date	Title *Label Number*	Position	
16 Mar 68	**GREATEST HITS** *Tamla Motown STML 11065*	40	1 wk
10 Nov 73	**LET'S GET IT ON** *Tamla Motown STMA 8013*	39	1 wk
15 May 76	**I WANT YOU** *Tamla Motown STML 12025*	22	5 wks
30 Oct 76	**THE BEST OF MARVIN GAYE** *Tamla Motown STML 12042*	56	1 wk
28 Feb 81	**IN OUR LIFETIME** *Motown STML 12149*	48	4 wks
20 Nov 82	● **MIDNIGHT LOVE** *CBS 85977*	10†	6 wks

See also Marvin Gaye and Tammi Terrell, Diana Ross and Marvin Gaye

Marvin GAYE and Tammi TERRELL

US male/female vocal duo

Date	Title *Label Number*	Position	
22 Aug 70	**GREATEST HITS** *Tamla Motown STML 11153*	60	4 wks

See also Marvin Gaye, Diana Ross and Marvin Gaye

Crystal GAYLE

US, female vocalist

Date	Title *Label Number*	Position	
21 Jan 78	**WE MUST BELIEVE IN MAGIC** *United Artists UAG 30108*	15	7 wks
23 Sep 78	**WHEN I DREAM** *United Artists UAG 30169*	25	8 wks
22 Mar 80	● **THE CRYSTAL GAYLE SINGLES ALBUM** *United Artists UAG 30287*	7	10 wks

Gloria GAYNOR

US, female vocalist

Date	Title *Label Number*	Position	
8 Mar 75	**NEVER CAN SAY GOODBYE** *MGM 2315 321*	32	8 wks
24 Mar 79	**LOVE TRACKS** *Polydor 2391 385*	31	7 wks

J. GEILS BAND

US, male vocal/instrumental group

Date	Title *Label Number*	Position	
27 Feb 82	**FREEZE FRAME** *EMI America AML 3020*	12	15 wks

GENERATION X

UK, male vocal/instrumental group

Date	Title *Label Number*	Position	
8 Apr 78	**GENERATION X** *Chrysalis CHR 1169*	29	4 wks
17 Feb 79	**VALLEY OF THE DOLLS** *Chrysalis CHS 1193*	51	5 wks

GENESIS

UK, male vocal/instrumental group

Date	Title *Label Number*	Position	
14 Oct 72	**FOXTROT** *Charisma CAS 1058*	12	7 wks
11 Aug 73	● **GENESIS LIVE** *Charisma CLASS 1*	9	10 wks
20 Oct 73	● **SELLING ENGLAND BY THE POUND** *Charisma CAS 1074*	3	21 wks
11 May 74	**NURSERY CRYME** *Charisma CAS 1052*	39	1 wk
7 Dec 74	● **THE LAMB LIES DOWN ON BROADWAY** *Charisma CGS 101*	10	6 wks
28 Feb 76	● **A TRICK OF THE TRAIL** *Charisma CDS 4001*	3	39 wks
15 Jan 77	● **WIND AND WUTHERING** *Charisma CDS 4005*	7	22 wks
29 Oct 77	● **SECONDS OUT** *Charisma GE 2001*	4	17 wks
15 Apr 78	● **AND THEN THERE WERE THREE** *Charisma CDS 4010*	3	32 wks
5 Apr 80	★ **DUKE** *Charisma CBR 101*	1	30 wks
26 Sep 81	★ **ABACAB** *Charisma CBR 102*	1	27 wks
12 Jun 82	● **3 SIDES LIVE** *Charisma/Phonogram GE 2002*	2	19 wks

Bobbie GENTRY

US, female vocalist

Date	Title *Label Number*	Position	
25 Oct 69	**TOUCH 'EM WITH LOVE** *Capitol EST 155*	21	1 wk

See also Bobbie Gentry and Glen Campbell.

Bobbie GENTRY and Glen CAMPBELL

US, female/male vocal duo

Date	Title *Label Number*	Position	
28 Feb 70	**BOBBIE GENTRY AND GLEN CAMPBELL** *Capitol ST 2928*	50	1 wk

See also Bobbie Gentry, Glen Campbell.

Lowell GEORGE

US, male vocalist

Date	Title *Label Number*	Position	
21 Apr 79	**THANKS BUT I'LL EAT IT HERE** *Warner Bros. K 56487*	71	1 wk

GERRY and the PACEMAKERS

UK, male vocal/instrumental group

Date	Title *Label Number*	Position	
26 Oct 63	● **HOW DO YOU LIKE IT?** *Columbia 33SX 1546*	2	28 wks
6 Feb 65	**FERRY CROSS THE MERSEY** *Columbia 33SX 1676*	19	1 wk

Stan GETZ and Charlie BYRD

US, male instrumental duo, saxophone and guitar

Date	Title *Label Number*	Position	
23 Feb 63	**JAZZ SAMBA** *Verve SULP 9013*	15	7 wks

Date	Title *Label Number*	Position		Date	Title *Label Number*	Position	

Andy GIBB

UK, male vocalist

19 Aug 78	**SHADOW DANCING** *RSO RSS 0001*	15	9 wks

Steve GIBBONS BAND

UK, male vocal/instrumental group

22 Oct 77	**CAUGHT IN THE ACT** *Polydor 2478 112*	22	3 wks

Don GIBSON

US, male vocalist

22 Mar 80	**COUNTRY NUMBER ONE** *Warwick WW 5079*	13	10 wks

GIBSON BROTHERS

Martinique, male vocal/instrumental group

30 Aug 80	**ON THE RIVIERA** *Island ILPS 9620*	50	3 wks

GILLAN

UK, male vocal/instrumental group

17 Jul 76	**CHILD IN TIME** *Polydor 2490 136*	55	1 wk
20 Oct 79	**MR. UNIVERSE** *Acrobat ACRO 3*	11	6 wks
16 Aug 80	● **GLORY ROAD** *Virgin V 2171*	3	12 wks
25 Apr 81	● **FUTURE SHOCK** *Virgin VK 2196*	2	13 wks
7 Nov 81	**DOUBLE TROUBLE** *Virgin VGD 3506*	12	15 wks
2 Oct 82	**MAGIC** *Virgin V 2238*	17	6 wks

Child In Time *credited to Ian Gillan Band.*

David GILMOUR

UK, male instrumentalist - guitar

10 Jun 78	**DAVID GILMOUR** *Harvest SHVL 817*	17	9 wks

Gordon GILTRAP

UK, male instrumentalist - guitar

18 Feb 78	**PERILOUS JOURNEY** *Electric TRIX 4*	29	7 wks

GIRL

UK, male vocal/instrumental group

9 Feb 80	**SHEER GREED** *Jet JETLP 224*	33	5 wks
23 Jan 82	**WASTED YOUTH** *Jet JETLP 238*	92	1 wk

GIRLS AT OUR BEST

UK, male/female vocal/instrumental group

7 Nov 81	**PLEASURE** *Happy Birthday RVLP 1*	60	3 wks

GIRLSCHOOL

UK, female vocal/instrumental group

5 Jul 80	**DEMOLITION** *Bronze BRON 525*	28	10 wks
25 Apr 81	● **HIT 'N' RUN** *Bronze BRON 534*	5	6 wks
12 Jun 82	**SCREAMING BLUE MURDER** *Bronze BRON 541*	27	6 wks

Gary GLITTER

UK, male vocalist

21 Oct 72	● **GLITTER** *Bell BELLS 216*	8	40 wks
16 Jun 73	● **TOUCH ME** *Bell BELLS 222*	2	33 wks
29 Jun 74	● **REMEMBER ME THIS WAY** *Bell BELLS 237*	5	14 wks
27 Mar 76	**GARY GLITTER'S GREATEST HITS** *Bell BELLS 262*	33	5 wks

GLITTER BAND

UK, male vocal/instrumental group

14 Sep 74	**HEY** *Bell BELLS 241*	13	12 wks
3 May 75	**ROCK 'N' ROLL DUDES** *Bell BELLS 253*	17	4 wks
19 Jun 76	**GREATEST HITS** *Bell BELLS 264*	52	1 wk

GODLEY and CREME

UK, male audiovisual duo

19 Nov 77	**CONSEQUENCES** *Mercury CONS 017*	52	1 wk
9 Sep 78	**L** *Mercury 9109 611*	47	2 wks
17 Oct 81	**ISMISM** *Polydor POLD 5043*	29	13 wks

Consequences *credited to Kevin Godley and Lol Creme.*

GO-GO'S

US, female vocal/instrumental group

21 Aug 82	**VACATION** *IRS/A&M SP 70031*	75	3 wks

Top **GILLAN** The ex-Deep Purple frontman lurks second from the left.

Above **GERRY & THE PACEMAKERS** Their hit album was a blend of their first two singles 'How Do You Do It' and 'I Like It'.

Date	Title Label Number	Position		Date	Title Label Number	Position	

Andrew GOLD

US, male vocalist/instrumentalist - piano

15 Apr 78	ALL THIS AND HEAVEN TOO *Asylum K 53072*	31	7 wks

GOLDEN EARRING

Holland, male vocal/instrumental group

2 Feb 74	MOONTAN *Track 2406 112*	24	4 wks

GOODIES

UK, male vocal group

8 Nov 75	THE NEW GOODIES LP *Bradley's BRADL 1010*	25	11 wks

Benny GOODMAN

US, male instrumentalist - clarinet

3 Apr 71	BENNY GOODMAN TODAY *Decca DDS 3*	49	1 wk

Ron GOODWIN

UK, orchestra

2 May 70	LEGEND OF THE GLASS MOUNTAIN *Studio two TWO 220*	49	1 wk

GOOMBAY DANCE BAND

Germany, male/female vocal group

10 Apr 82	SEVEN TEARS *Epic EPC 85702*	16	9 wks

GOONS

UK, male vocal group

28 Nov 59	● BEST OF THE GOON SHOWS *Parlophone PMC 1108*	8	14 wks
17 Dec 60	BEST OF THE GOON SHOWS VOL.2 *Parlophone PMC 1129*	12	6 wks
4 Nov 72	● LAST GOON SHOW OF ALL *BBC Radio Enterprises REB 142*	8	11 wks

GORDON — See *PETER and GORDON*

Eddy GRANT

Guyana, male vocalist/multi-instrumentalist

30 May 81	CAN'T GET ENOUGH *Ice ICEL 21*	39	6 wks
27 Nov 82	KILLER ON THE RAMPAGE *Ice ICELP 3023*	34†	5 wks

GRATEFUL DEAD

US, male vocal/instrumental group

19 Sep 70	WORKINGMAN'S DEAD *Warner Bros. WS 1869*	69	2 wks
3 Aug 74	GRATEFUL DEAD FROM THE MARS HOTEL *Atlantic K 59302*	47	1 wk
1 Nov 75	BLUES FOR ALLAH *United Artists UAS 29895*	45	1 wk
4 Sep 76	STEAL YOUR FACE *United Artists UAS 60131/2*	42	1 wk
20 Aug 77	TERRAPIN STATION *Arista SPARTY 1016*	30	1 wk

David GRAY and Tommy TYCHO

UK, male arrangers

16 Oct 76	ARMCHAIR MELODIES *K-Tel NE 927*	21	6 wks

Al GREEN

US, male vocalist

26 Apr 75	AL GREEN'S GREATEST HITS *London SHU 8481*	18	16 wks

Peter GREEN

UK, male vocalist/instrumentalist - guitar

9 Jun 79	IN THE SKIES *Creole PULS 101*	32	13 wks
24 May 80	LITTLE DREAMER *PUK PULS 102*	34	4 wks

GREENSLADE

UK, male vocal/instrumental group

14 Sep 74	SPYGLASS GUEST *Warner Bros. K 56055*	34	3 wks

Christina GREGG

UK, female vocalist - exercise record

27 May 78	MUSIC 'N' MOTION *Warwick WW 5041*	51	1 wk

Date	Title *Label Number*	Position

GROUNDHOGS

UK, male vocal/instrumental group

6 Jun 70	● THANK CHRIST FOR THE BOMB	9	13 wks
	Liberty LBS 83295		
3 Apr 71	● SPLIT *Liberty LBG 83401*	5	27 wks
18 Mar 72	● WHO WILL SAVE THE WORLD	8	9 wks
	United Artists UAG 29237		
13 Jul 74	SOLID *WWA WWA 004*	31	1 wk

GUILDFORD CATHEDRAL CHOIR

UK, choir

10 Dec 66	CHRISTMAS CAROLS FROM GUILDFORD	24	4 wks
	CATHEDRAL *MFP 1104*		

Record credits Barry Rose as conductor.

David GUNSON

US, male vocalist

25 Dec 82	WHAT GOES UP MIGHT COME DOWN	92†	1 wk
	Big Ben BB0012		

G.U.S. (FOOTWEAR) BAND and the MORRISTOWN ORPHEUS CHOIR

UK, male instrumental group and male/female vocal group

3 Oct 70	LAND OF HOPE AND GLORY	54	1 wk
	Columbia SCX 6406		

Arlo GUTHRIE

US, male vocalist

7 Mar 70	ALICE'S RESTAURANT *Reprise RSLP 6267*	44	1 wk

GUYS 'N' DOLLS

UK, male/female vocal group

31 May 75	GUYS 'N' DOLLS *Magnet MAG 5005*	43	1 wk

H

Steve HACKETT

UK, male vocalist/instrumentalist - guitar

1 Nov 75	VOYAGE OF THE ACOLYTE	26	4 wks
	Charisma CAS 1111		
6 May 78	PLEASE DON'T TOUCH *Charisma CDS 4012*	38	5 wks
26 May 79	SPECTRAL MORNINGS *Charisma CDS 4017*	22	11 wks
21 Jun 80	● DEFECTOR *Charisma CDS 4018*	9	7 wks
29 Aug 81	CURED *Charisma CDS 4021*	15	5 wks

Sammy HAGAR

US, male vocalist/instrumentalist - guitar

29 Sep 79	STREET MACHINE *Capitol EST 11983*	38	4 wks
22 Mar 80	LOUD AND CLEAR *Capitol EST 25330*	12	8 wks
7 Jun 80	DANGER ZONE *Capitol EST 12069*	25	3 wks
13 Feb 82	STANDING HAMPTON *Geffen GEF 85456*	84	2 wks

HAIRCUT 100

UK, male vocal/instrumental group

6 Mar 82	● PELICAN WEST *Arista HCC 100*	2	34 wks

Bill HALEY and his COMETS

US, male vocalist/guitarist, male vocal instrumental backing group

18 May 68	ROCK AROUND THE CLOCK	34	5 wks
	Ace Of Hearts AH 13		

Daryl HALL and John OATES

US, male vocal/instrumental duo

3 Jul 76	HALL AND OATES *RCA Victor APL1 1144*	56	1 wk
18 Sep 76	BIGGER THAN BOTH OF US	25	7 wks
	RCA Victor APL1 1467		
15 Oct 77	BEAUTY ON A BACK STREET *RCA PL 12300*	40	2 wks
6 Feb 82	● PRIVATE EYES *RCA RCALP 6001*	8	21 wks

TONY HANCOCK Anthony Aloysius St John Hancock of Railway Cuttings, East Cheam spent 14448 Hancock's Half Hours on the chart.

THE GOONS Major Bloodnok, Eccles and Bluebottle hit the chart courtesy of Messrs Secombe, Milligan and Sellers.

71

ARLO GUTHRIE 'You can get anything you
want at Alice's Restaurant—exceptin' Alice!'

Right **HAIRCUT ONE HUNDRED** Only a one line entry in
this book but an impressive 34 weeks on chart.

Below **GRATEFUL DEAD** Kings of the late 60s San Francisco
scene who were born out of 1963 group Mother McCree's
Uptown Jug Champions, part of whom became the Warlocks in
1965 before expanding both in mind and music into Acid Rock
band, the Grateful Dead.

Date	Title Label Number	Position		Date	Title Label Number	Position	

HAMBURG STUDENTS' CHOIR

Germany, male vocal group

17 Dec 60	HARK THE HERALD ANGELS SING *Pye GGL 0023*	11	6 wks

George HAMILTON IV

US, male vocalist

10 Apr 71	CANADIAN PACIFIC *RCA SF 8062*	45	1 wk
10 Feb 79	REFLECTIONS *Lotus WH 5008*	25	9 wks
13 Nov 82	SONGS FOR A WINTER'S NIGHT *Ronco RTL 2082*	94	1 wk

Herbie HANCOCK

US, male vocalist/instrumentalist - keyboards

9 Sep 78	SUNLIGHT *CBS 82240*	27	6 wks
24 Feb 79	FEETS DON'T FAIL ME NOW *CBS 83491*	28	8 wks

Tony HANCOCK

UK, male comedian

9 Apr 60	● THIS IS HANCOCK *Pye NPL 10845*	2	22 wks
12 Nov 60	PIECES OF HANCOCK *Pye NPL 18054*	17	2 wks
3 Mar 62	HANCOCK *Pye NPL 18068*	12	14 wks
14 Sep 63	THIS IS HANCOCK (re-issue) *Pye Golden Guinea GGL 0206*	16	4 wks

Bo HANNSON

Sweden, multi-instrumentalist

18 Nov 72	LORD OF THE RINGS *Charisma CAS 1059*	34	2 wks

John HANSON

UK, male vocalist

23 Apr 60	THE STUDENT PRINCE *Pye NPL 18046*	17	1 wk
2 Sep 61	● THE STUDENT PRINCE/VAGABOND KING *Pye GGL 0086*	9	7 wks
10 Dec 77	JOHN HANSON SINGS 20 SHOWTIME GREATS *K-Tel NE 1002*	16	4 wks

Mike HARDING

UK, male comedian

30 Aug 75	MRS 'ARDIN'S KID *Rubber RUB 011*	24	6 wks
10 Jul 76	ONE MAN SHOW *Philips 6625 022*	19	10 wks
11 Jun 77	OLD FOUR EYES IS BACK *Philips 6308 290*	31	6 wks
24 Jun 78	CAPTAIN PARALYTIC AND THE BROWN ALE COWBOY *Philips 6641 798*	60	2 wks

HARDY — See *LAUREL and HARDY*

Steve HARLEY and COCKNEY REBEL

UK, male vocalist and male vocal instrumental group

22 Jun 74	● THE PSYCHOMODO *EMI EMC 3033*	8	20 wks
22 Mar 75	● THE BEST YEARS OF OUR LIVES *EMI EMC 3068*	4	19 wks
14 Feb 76	TIMELESS FLIGHT *EMI EMA 775*	18	6 wks
27 Nov 76	LOVE'S A PRIMMA DONNA *EMI EMC 3156*	28	3 wks
30 Jul 77	FACE TO FACE - A LIVE RECORDING *EMI EMSP 320*	40	4 wks

First album credited to Cockney Rebel.

Roy HARPER

UK, male vocalist/instrumentalist - guitar

9 Mar 74	VALENTINE *Harvest SHSP 4027*	27	1 wk
21 Jun 75	H.Q. *Harvest SHSP 4046*	31	2 wks
12 Mar 77	BULLINAMINGVASE *Harvest SHSP 4060*	25	2 wks

Anita HARRIS

UK, female vocalist

27 Jan 68	JUST LOVING YOU *CBS SBPG 63182*	29	5 wks

Emmylou HARRIS

US, female vocalist

14 Feb 76	ELITE HOTEL *Reprise K 54060*	17	11 wks
29 Jan 77	LUXURY LINER *Warner Bros. K 56344*	17	6 wks
4 Feb 78	QUARTER MOON IN A TEN CENT TOWN *Warner Bros. K 56443*	40	5 wks
29 Mar 80	HER BEST SONGS *K-Tel NE 1058*	36	3 wks
14 Feb 81	EVANGELINE *Warner Bros. K 56880*	53	4 wks

GEORGE HARRISON
The first Beatle to make an album without the other three (Wonderwall) bites his thumbnail in anticipation as his triple album 'All Things Must Pass' passes most other things in the chart.

DEBBIE HARRY Despite a valiant effort, Miss Harry soloist could not match the success she achieved as singer with the Anglo-American Blondie.

EMMYLOU HARRIS The popular country singer's first UK hit checked in at number 17 and the next cruised to the same spot almost a year later. Since then even her best songs have failed to make the top twenty.

George HARRISON

UK, male vocalist/instrumentalist - guitar

Date	Title *Label Number*	Position	
26 Dec 70	● ALL THINGS MUST PASS *Apple STCH 639*	4	24 wks
7 Jul 73	● LIVING IN THE MATERIAL WORLD *Apple PAS 10006*	2	12 wks
18 Oct 75	EXTRA TEXTURE (READ ALL ABOUT IT) *Apple PAS 10009*	16	4 wks
18 Dec 76	THIRTY THREE AND A THIRD *Dark Horse K 56319*	35	4 wks
17 Mar 79	GEORGE HARRISON *Dark Horse K 56562*	39	5 wks
13 Jun 81	SOMEWHERE IN ENGLAND *Dark Horse K 56870*	13	4 wks

Debbie HARRY

US, female vocalist

Date	Title *Label Number*	Position	
8 Aug 81	● KOO KOO *Chrysalis CHR 1347*	6	7 wks

Keef HARTLEY BAND

UK, male vocal/instrumental group

Date	Title *Label Number*	Position	
5 Sep 70	THE TIME IS NEAR *Deram SML 1071*	41	3 wks

Sensational Alex HARVEY BAND

UK, male vocal/instrumental group

Date	Title *Label Number*	Position	
26 Oct 74	THE IMPOSSIBLE DREAM *Vertigo 6360 112*	16	4 wks
10 May 75	● TOMORROW BELONGS TO ME *Vertigo 9102 003*	9	10 wks
23 Aug 75	NEXT *Vertigo 6360 103*	37	5 wks
27 Sep 75	SENSATIONAL ALEX HARVEY BAND LIVE *Vertigo 6360 122*	14	7 wks
10 Apr 76	PENTHOUSE TAPES *Vertigo 9102 007*	14	7 wks
31 Jul 76	SAHB STORIES *Mountain TOPS 112*	11	9 wks

HATFIELD and The NORTH

UK, male/female vocal/instrumental group

Date	Title *Label Number*	Position	
29 Mar 75	ROTTERS CLUB *Virgin V 2030*	43	1 wk

Donny HATHAWAY — See *Roberta FLACK and Donny HATHAWAY*

HAWKWIND

UK, male vocal/instrumental group

Date	Title *Label Number*	Position	
6 Nov 71	IN SEARCH OF SPACE *United Artists UAS 29202*	18	19 wks
23 Dec 72	DOREMI FASOL LATIDO *United Artists UAS 29364*	14	5 wks
2 Jun 73	● SPACE RITUAL ALIVE *United Artists UAD 60037/8*	9	5 wks
21 Sep 74	HALL OF THE MOUNTAIN GRILL *United Artists UAG 29672*	16	5 wks
31 May 75	WARRIOR ON THE EDGE OF TIME *United Artists UAG 29766*	13	7 wks
24 Apr 76	ROAD HAWKS *United Artists UAK 29919*	34	4 wks
18 Sep 76	ASTONISHING SOUNDS, AMAZING MUSIC *Charisma CDS 4004*	33	5 wks
9 Jul 77	QUARK STRANGENESS AND CHARM *Charisma CDS 4008*	30	6 wks
21 Oct 78	25 YEARS ON *Charisma CD 4014*	48	3 wks
30 Jun 79	PXR 5 *Charisma CDS 4016*	59	5 wks
9 Aug 80	LIVE 1979 *Bronze Bron 527*	15	7 wks
8 Nov 80	LEVITATION *Bronze Bron 530*	21	4 wks
24 Oct 81	SONIC ATTACK *RCA RCALP 5004*	19	5 wks
22 May 82	CHURCH OF HAWKWIND *RCA RCALP 9004*	26	6 wks
23 Oct 82	CHOOSE YOUR MASQUES *RCA RCALP 6055*	29	5 wks

25 Years On *credited to Hawklords which was just a pseudonym for Hawkwind.*

Isaac HAYES

US, male vocalist/multi-instrumentalist

Date	Title *Label Number*	Position	
18 Dec 71	SHAFT *Polydor 2659 007*	17	13 wks
12 Feb 72	BLACK MOSES *Stax 2628 004*	38	1 wk

Justin HAYWARD

UK, male vocalist

Date	Title *Label Number*	Position	
5 Mar 77	SONGWRITER *Deram SDL 15*	28	5 wks
19 Jul 80	NIGHT FLIGHT *Decca TXS 138*	41	4 wks

See also Justin Hayward and John Lodge.

Justin HAYWARD and John LODGE

UK, male vocal/instrumental duo

Date	Title *Label Number*	Position	
29 Mar 75	● BLUE JAYS *Threshold THS 12*	4	18 wks

See also Justin Hayward.

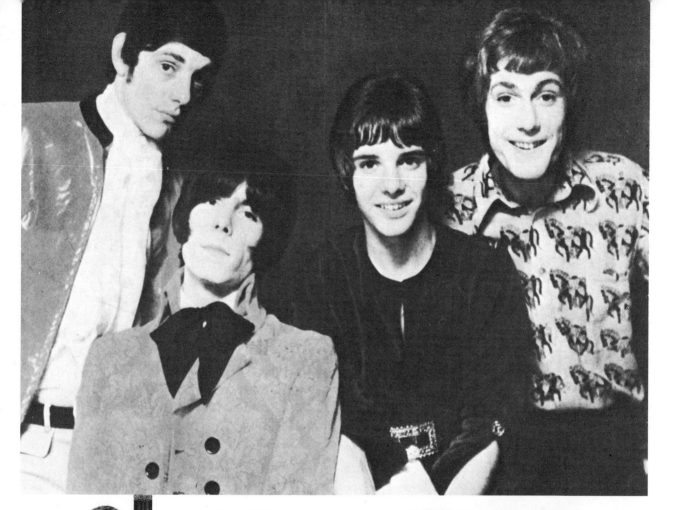

Above **THE HERD** They made a mockery of the Victorian adage by proving that young lads could be both seen and Herd.

Left **HERMAN'S HERMITS** Originally the Heartbeats, the Hermits were (l—r) Keith Hopwood, Derek Leckenby, Peter Noone, Karl Green, and Barry Whitwam.

HOT CHOCOLATE Slade's naughty Dave Hill attempts to slide an unwanted forkful of curry onto the clean plate of Hot Chocolate's Errol Brown.

Date	Title Label Number	Position		Date	Title Label Number	Position	

HEART

Canada, male/female vocal instrumental group

Date	Title Label Number	Position	
22 Jan 77	**DREAMBOAT ANNIE** *Arista ARTY 139*	36	8 wks
23 Jul 77	**LITTLE QUEEN** *Portrait PRT 82075*	34	4 wks
19 Jun 82	**PRIVATE AUDITION** *Epic EPC 85792*	77	2 wks

HEARTBREAKERS

US, male vocal/instrumental group

Date	Title Label Number	Position	
5 Nov 77	**L.A.M.F.** *Track 2409 218*	55	1 wk

Ted HEATH AND HIS MUSIC

UK, conductor and orchestra

Date	Title Label Number	Position	
21 Apr 62	**BIG BAND PERCUSSION** *Decca PFM 24004*	17	5 wks

HEATWAVE

UK/US, male vocal/instrumental group

Date	Title Label Number	Position	
11 Jun 77	**TOO HOT TO HANDLE** *GTO GTLP 013*	46	2 wks
6 May 78	**CENTRAL HEATING** *GTO GLP 027*	26	15 wks
14 Feb 81	**CANDLES** *GTO GTLP 047*	29	9 wks

HEAVEN 17

UK, male vocal/instrumental group

Date	Title Label Number	Position	
26 Sep 81	**PENTHOUSE AND PAVEMENT** *Virgin V 2208*	14	47 wks

Jimi HENDRIX

US, male vocalist/instrumentalist - guitar

Date	Title Label Number	Position	
27 May 67	● **ARE YOU EXPERIENCED** *Track 612-001*	2	33 wks
16 Dec 67	● **AXIS: BOLD AS LOVE** *Track 613-003*	5	16 wks
27 Apr 68	● **SMASH HITS** *Track 613-004*	4	25 wks
16 Nov 68	● **ELECTRIC LADY LAND** *Track 613-008/9*	6	12 wks
4 Jul 70	● **BAND OF GYPSIES** *Track 2406-001*	6	30 wks
3 Apr 71	● **CRY OF LOVE** *Track 2408-101*	2	14 wks
28 Aug 71	● **EXPERIENCE** *Ember NR 5057*	9	6 wks
20 Nov 71	**JIMI HENDRIX AT THE ISLE OF WIGHT** *Track 2302 016*	17	2 wks
4 Dec 71	**RAINBOW BRIDGE** *Reprise K 44159*	16	8 wks
5 Feb 72	● **HENDRIX IN THE WEST** *Polydor 2302 018*	7	14 wks
11 Dec 72	**WAR HEROES** *Polydor 2302 020*	23	3 wks

Date	Title Label Number	Position	
21 Jul 73	**SOUNDTRACK RECORDINGS FROM THE FILM 'JIMI HENDRIX'** *Warner Bros. K 64017*	37	1 wk
29 Mar 75	**JIMI HENDRIX** *Polydor 2343 080*	35	4 wks
30 Aug 75	**CRASH LANDING** *Polydor 2310 398*	35	3 wks
29 Nov 75	**MIDNIGHT LIGHTNING** *Polydor 2310 415*	46	1 wk
14 Aug 82	**THE JIMI HENDRIX CONCERTS** *CBS 88592*	16	11 wks

See also Jimi Hendrix and Curtis Knight. Act billed as Jimi Hendrix Experience for first four hits.

Jimi HENDRIX and Curtis KNIGHT

US, male vocal/instrumental duo

Date	Title Label Number	Position	
18 May 68	**GET THAT FEELING** *London HA 8349*	39	2 wks

See also Jimi Hendrix.

HER MAJESTY'S GUARDS DIVISION, BAND AND CHORUS OF

UK, military band

Date	Title Label Number	Position	
22 Nov 75	**30 SMASH HITS OF THE WAR YEARS** *Warwick WW 5006*	38	4 wks

HERD

UK, male vocal/instrumental group

Date	Title Label Number	Position	
24 Feb 68	**PARADISE LOST** *STL 5458*	38	1 wk

HERMAN'S HERMITS

UK, male vocal/instrumental group

Date	Title Label Number	Position	
18 Sep 65	**HERMAN'S HERMITS** *Columbia 33SX 1727*	16	2 wks
25 Sep 71	**THE MOST OF HERMAN'S HERMITS** *MFP 5216*	14	5 wks
8 Oct 77	**GREATEST HITS** *K-Tel NE 1001*	37	4 wks

HERMITS — See *HERMAN'S HERMITS*

HI TENSION

UK, male vocal/instrumental group

Date	Title Label Number	Position	
6 Jan 79	**HI TENSION** *Island ILPS 9564*	74	4 wks

Benny HILL

UK, male vocalist

Date	Title Label Number	Position	
11 Dec 71	● **WORDS AND MUSIC** *Columbia SCX 6479*	9	8 wks

Below **ENGELBERT HUMPERDINCK** Engelbert, sits nervously on the trainer's bench with the other substitutes urging the 1st XI to victory.

BUDDY HOLLY Buddy Holly (centre) outside the house of Crickets drummer Jerry Allison (right) just after a heavy fall of snow—a rare sight in Lubbock.

JOHNNY AND THE HURRICANES The first Rock & Roll instrumental group to hit the chart.

Date	Title Label Number	Position		Date	Title Label Number	Position	

Vince HILL

UK, male vocalist

20 May 67	**EDELWEISS** *Columbia SCX 6141*	23	9 wks
29 Apr 78	**THAT LOVING FEELING** *K-Tel NE 1017*	51	1 wk

Steve HILLAGE

UK, male vocalist/instrumentalist - guitar

3 May 75	**FISH RISING** *Virgin V 2031*	33	3 wks
16 Oct 76	● **L** *Virgin V 2066*	10	12 wks
22 Oct 77	**MOTIVATION RADIO** *Virgin V 2777*	28	5 wks
29 Apr 78	**GREEN** *V 2098*	30	8 wks
17 Feb 79	**LIVE HERALD** *Virgin VGD 3502*	54	5 wks
5 May 79	**RAINBOW DOME MUSIC** *Virgin VR 1*	52	5 wks
27 Oct 79	**OPEN** *Virgin V 2135*	71	1 wk

Gerrard HOFFNUNG

UK, male comedian

3 Sep 60	● **AT THE OXFORD UNION** *Decca LF 1330*	4	19 wks

HOLLIES

UK, male vocal/instrumental group

15 Feb 64	● **STAY WITH THE HOLLIES** *Parlophone PMC 1220*	2	25 wks
2 Oct 65	● **HOLLIES** *Parlophone PMC 1261*	8	14 wks
16 Jul 66	**WOULD YOU BELIEVE** *Parlophone PMC 7008*	16	8 wks
17 Dec 66	**FOR CERTAIN BECAUSE** *Parlophone PCS 17011*	23	7 wks
17 Jun 67	**EVOLUTION** *Parlophone PCS 7022*	13	10 wks
17 Aug 68	★ **GREATEST HITS** *Parlophone PCS 7057*	1	27 wks
17 May 69	● **HOLLIES SING DYLAN** *Parlophone PCS 7078*	3	7 wks
28 Nov 70	**CONFESSIONS OF THE MIND** *Parlophone PCS 7117*	30	5 wks
16 Mar 74	**HOLLIES** *Polydor 2383 262*	38	3 wks
19 Mar 77	● **HOLLIES LIVE HITS** *Polydor 2383 428*	4	12 wks
22 Jul 78	● **20 GOLDEN GREATS** *EMI EMTV 11*	2	15 wks

Buddy HOLLY and the CRICKETS

US, male vocalist/male vocal/instrumental group

2 May 59	● **BUDDY HOLLY STORY** *Coral No. LVA 9105*	2	156 wks
15 Oct 60	● **BUDDY HOLLY STORY VOL.2** *Coral LVA 9127*	7	14 wks
21 Oct 61	● **THAT'LL BE THE DAY** *Ace Of Hearts AH 3*	5	14 wks
6 Apr 63	● **REMINISCING** *Coral LVA 9212*	2	31 wks
13 Jun 64	● **BUDDY HOLLY SHOWCASE** *Coral LVA 9222*	3	16 wks
26 Jun 65	**HOLLY IN THE HILLS** *Coral LVA 9227*	13	6 wks
15 Jul 67	● **BUDDY HOLLY'S GREATEST HITS** *Ace Of Hearts AH 148*	9	40 wks
12 Apr 69	**GIANT** *MCA MUPS 371*	13	1 wk

21 Aug 71	**BUDDY HOLLY'S GREATEST HITS** *Coral CP 8*	32	6 wks
12 Jul 75	**BUDDY HOLLY'S GREATEST HITS** *MCA/Coral CDLM 8007*	42	3 wks
11 Mar 78	★ **20 GOLDEN GREATS** *MCA EMTV 8*	1	20 wks

See also The Crickets, Bobby Vee and the Crickets. Most albums feature the Crickets on at least some tracks.

John HOLT

Jamaica, male vocalist

1 Feb 75	**A THOUSAND VOLTS OF HOLT** *Trojan TRLS 75*	42	2 wks

HOME

UK, male vocal/instrumental group

11 Nov 72	**DREAMER** *CBS 67522*	41	1 wk

John Lee HOOKER

US, male vocalist

4 Feb 67	**HOUSE OF THE BLUES** *Marble Arch MAL 663*	34	2 wks

Mary HOPKINS

UK, female vocalist

1 Mar 69	● **POSTCARD** *Apple SAPCOR 5*	3	9 wks

HORSLIPS

Ireland, male vocal/instrumental group

30 Apr 77	**THE BOOK OF INVASIONS - A CELTIC SYMPHONY** *DJM DJF 20498*	39	3 wks

HOT CHOCOLATE

UK, male vocal/instrumental group

15 Nov 75	**HOT CHOCOLATE** *RAK SRAK 516*	34	7 wks
7 Aug 76	**MAN TO MAN** *RAK SRAK 522*	32	7 wks
20 Nov 76	● **GREATEST HITS** *RAK SRAK 524*	6	35 wks
8 Apr 78	**EVERY 1'S A WINNER** *RAK SRAK 531*	30	8 wks
15 Dec 79	● **20 HOTTEST HITS** *RAK EMTV 22*	3	19 wks
25 Sep 82	**MYSTERY** *RAK SRAK 549*	24	7 wks

Date	Title Label Number	Position		Date	Title Label Number	Position	

Steve HOWE

UK, male vocalist/instrumentalist - guitar

| 15 Nov 75 | **BEGINNINGS** *Atlantic K 50151* | 22 | 4 wks |
| 24 Nov 79 | **STEVE HOWE ALBUM** *Atlantic K 50621* | 68 | 2 wks |

Alan HULL

UK, male vocalist

| 28 Jul 73 | **PIPEDREAM** *Charisma CAS 1069* | 29 | 3 wks |

HUMAN LEAGUE

UK, male/female vocal/instrumental group

31 May 80	**TRAVELOGUE** *Virgin V 2160*	16	42 wks
22 Aug 81	**REPRODUCTION** *Virgin V 2133*	49	23 wks
24 Oct 81 ★	**DARE** *Virgin V 2192*	1†	62 wks

HUMBLE PIE

UK, male vocal/instrumental group

6 Sep 69	**AS SAFE AS YESTERDAY IS** *Immediate IMSP 025*	32	1 wk
22 Jan 72	**ROCKING AT THE FILLMORE** *A & M AMLH 63506*	32	2 wks
15 Apr 72	**SMOKIN'** *A & M AMLS 64342*	28	5 wks
7 Apr 73	**EAT IT** *A & M AMLS 6004*	34	2 wks

Engelbert HUMPERDINCK

UK, male vocalist

20 May 67	● **RELEASE ME** *Decca SKL 4868*	6	58 wks
25 Nov 67	● **THE LAST WALTZ** *Decca SKL 4901*	3	33 wks
3 Aug 68	● **A MAN WITHOUT LOVE** *Decca SKL 4939*	3	45 wks
1 Mar 69	● **ENGELBERT** *Decca SKL 4985*	3	8 wks
6 Dec 69	● **ENGELBERT HUMPERDINCK** *Decca SKL 5030*	5	23 wks
11 Jul 70	**WE MADE IT HAPPEN** *Decca SKL 5054*	17	11 wks
18 Sep 71	**ANOTHER TIME, ANOTHER PLACE** *Decca SKL 5097*	48	1 wk
26 Feb 72	**LIVE AT THE RIVIERA LAS VEGAS** *Decca TXS 105*	45	1 wk
21 Dec 74 ★	**ENGELBERT HUMPERDINCK - HIS GREATEST HITS** *Decca SKL 5198*	1	34 wks

Ian HUNTER

UK, male vocalist

12 Apr 75	**IAN HUNTER** *CBS 80710*	21	15 wks
29 May 76	**ALL AMERICAN ALIEN BOY** *CBS 81310*	29	4 wks
5 May 79	**YOU'RE NEVER ALONE WITH A SCHIZOPHRENIC** *Chrysalis CHR 1214*	49	3 wks
26 Apr 80	**WELCOME TO THE CLUB** *Chrysalis CJT 6*	61	2 wks
29 Aug 81	**SHORT BACK AND SIDES** *Chrysalis CHR 1326*	79	2 wks

HURRICANES — See *JOHNNY and the HURRICANES*

I

Frank IFIELD

UK, male vocalist

16 Feb 63	● **I'LL REMEMBER YOU** *Columbia 33SX 1467*	3	36 wks
21 Sep 63	● **BORN FREE** *Columbia 33SX 1462*	3	32 wks
28 Mar 64	● **BLUE SKIES** *Columbia 33SX 1588*	10	12 wks
19 Dec 64	● **GREATEST HITS** *Columbia 33SX 1633*	9	3 wks

Julio IGLESIAS

Spain, male vocalist

7 Nov 81	**DE NINA A MUJER** *CBS 85063*	43	5 wks
28 Nov 81	● **BEGIN THE BEGUINE** *CBS 85462*	5	28 wks
16 Oct 82	**AMOR** *CBS 25103*	14†	11 wks

IMAGINATION

UK, male vocal group

| 24 Oct 81 | **BODY TALK** *R & B RBLP 1001* | 22 | 11 wks |
| 11 Sep 82 | ● **IN THE HEAT OF THE NIGHT** *R&B RBLP 1002* | 7† | 16 wks |

INCANTATION

UK, male instrumental group

| 11 Dec 82 | **CACHARPAYA (PANPIPES OF THE ANDES)** *Beggars Banquet BEGA 39* | 31† | 3 wks |

INCOGNITO

France, male instrumental group

18 Apr 81	**JAZZ FUNK** *Ensign ENVY 504*	28	8 wks

INCREDIBLE STRING BAND

UK, male/female vocal instrumental group

21 Oct 67	**5,000 SPIRITS OR THE LAYERS OF THE ONION** *Elektra EUKS 257*	26	4 wks
6 Apr 68	● **HANGMAN'S BEAUTIFUL DAUGHTER** *Elektra EVKS7 258*	5	21 wks
20 Jul 68	**INCREDIBLE STRING BAND** *Elektra EKL 254*	34	3 wks
24 Jan 70	**CHANGING HORSES** *Elektra EKS 74057*	30	1 wk
9 May 70	**I LOOKED UP** *Elektra 2469-002*	30	4 wks
31 Oct 70	**U** *Elektra 2665-001*	34	2 wks
30 Oct 71	**LIQUID ACROBAT AS REGARDS THE AIR** *Island ILPS 9172*	46	1 wk

INFA RIOT

UK, male vocal/instrumental group

7 Aug 82	**STILL OUT OF ORDER** *Secret SEC 7*	42	4 wks

INVISIBLE GIRLS — See *Pauline MURRAY and the INVISIBLE GIRLS*

IRON MAIDEN

UK, male vocal/instrumental group

26 Apr 80	● **IRON MAIDEN** *EMI EMC 3330*	4	15 wks
28 Feb 81	**KILLERS** *EMI EMC 3357*	12	8 wks
10 Apr 82	★ **THE NUMBER OF THE BEAST** *EMI EMC 3400*	1	28 wks

Gregory ISAACS

Jamaica, male vocalist

12 Sep 81	**MORE GREGORY** *Charisma PREX 9*	93	1 wk
4 Sep 82	**NIGHT NURSE** *Island ILPS 9721*	32	5 wks

ISLEY BROTHERS

US, male vocal/instrumental group

14 Dec 68	**THIS OLD HEART OF MINE** *Tamla Motown STML 11034*	23	6 wks
14 Aug 76	**HARVEST FOR THE WORLD** *Epic EPC 81268*	50	5 wks
14 May 77	**GO FOR YOUR GUNS** *Epic EPC 86027*	46	2 wks
24 Jun 78	**SHOWDOWN** *Epic EPC 86039*	50	1 wk

IT'S A BEAUTIFUL DAY

US, male vocal/instrumental group

23 May 70	**IT'S A BEAUTIFUL DAY** *CBS 63722*	58	1 wk
18 Jul 70	**MARRYING MAIDEN** *CBS 66236*	45	2 wks

J

Jermaine JACKSON

US, male vocalist

31 May 80	**LET'S GET SERIOUS** *Motown STML 12127*	22	6 wks

Joe JACKSON

US, male vocalist

17 Mar 79	**LOOK SHARP** *A & M AMLH 64743*	40	11 wks
13 Oct 79	**I'M THE MAN** *A & M AMLH 64794*	12	16 wks
18 Oct 80	**BEAT CRAZY** *A & M AMLH 64837*	42	3 wks
4 Jul 81	**JUMPIN' JIVE** *A & M AMLH 68530*	14	14 wks
3 Jul 82	**NIGHT AND DAY** *A&M AMLH 64906*	44	11 wks

Jumpin' Jive *credited to Joe Jackson's Jumpin' Jive.*

Michael JACKSON

US, male vocalist

3 Jun 72	**GOT TO BE THERE** *Tamla Motown STML 11205*	37	5 wks
13 Jan 73	**BEN** *Tamla Motown STML 11220*	17	7 wks
29 Sep 79	● **OFF THE WALL** *Epic EPC 83468*	5	78 wks
20 Jun 81	**BEST OF** *Motown STMI 9009*	11	18 wks
18 Jul 81	**ONE DAY IN YOUR LIFE** *Motown STML 12158*	29	8 wks
11 Dec 82	**THRILLER** *Epic EPC 85930*	15†	3 wks

JACKSON FIVE

US, male vocal group

21 Mar 70	**DIANA ROSS PRESENTS THE JACKSON FIVE** *Tamla Motown STML 11142*	16	4 wks
15 Aug 70	**ABC** *Tamla Motown STML 11153*	22	6 wks
7 Oct 72	**GREATEST HITS** *Tamla Motown STML 11212*	26	14 wks
18 Nov 72	**LOOKIN' THROUGH THE WINDOWS** *Tamla Motown STML 11214*	16	8 wks

See also Jacksons.

JAPAN Maybe the lack of polaroids speaks for itself!

Centre Left **JEAN-MICHEL JARRE** Just think-if you looked like this *you* could be gazing at Charlotte Rampling over your Sugar Puffs.

Above **JACKSONS** Originally presented by Diana Ross.

Left **JAM** Their debut album 'In The City' stayed on the charts for over 4 months for the group who were all mod and no con.

83

Date	Title Label Number	Position		Date	Title Label Number	Position	

JACKSONS

US, male vocal group

16 Jul 77	**THE JACKSONS** *Epic EPC 86009*	54	1 wk
3 Dec 77	**GOIN' PLACES** *Epic EPC 86035*	45	1 wk
5 May 79	**DESTINY** *Epic EPC 83200*	33	7 wks
11 Oct 80	**TRIUMPH** *Epic EPC 86112*	13	16 wks
12 Dec 81	**THE JACKSONS** *Epic EPC 88562*	53	9 wks

See also Jackson Five.

JAM

UK, male vocal/instrumental group

28 May 77	**IN THE CITY** *Polydor 2383 447*	20	18 wks
26 Nov 77	**THIS IS THE MODERN WORLD** *Polydor 2383 475*	22	5 wks
11 Nov 78	● **ALL MOD CONS** *Polydor POLD 5008*	6	16 wks
24 Nov 79	● **SETTING SONS** *Polydor POLD 5028*	4	19 wks
6 Dec 80	● **SOUND AFFECTS** *Polydor POLD 5035*	2	19 wks
20 Mar 82	★ **THE GIFT** *Polydor POLD 5055*	1	24 wks
18 Dec 82	● **DIG THE NEW BREED** *Polydor POLD 5075*	2†	2 wks

Rick JAMES

US, male vocalist

24 Jul 82	**THROWIN' DOWN** *Motown STML 12167*	93	2 wks

JAN and DEAN

US, male vocal duo

12 Jul 80	**THE JAN AND DEAN STORY** *K-Tel NE 1084*	67	2 wks

JAPAN

UK, male vocal/instrumental group

9 Feb 80	**QUIET LIFE** *Ariola Hansa AHAL 8011*	53	8 wks
15 Nov 80	**GENTLEMEN TAKE POLAROIDS** *Virgin V 2180*	45	10 wks
26 Sep 81	**ASSEMBLAGE** *Hansa HANLP 1*	26	40 wks
28 Nov 81	**TIN DRUM** *Virgin V 2209*	12	46 wks

Jeff JARRATT and Don REEDMAN

UK, male producers

22 Nov 80	**MASTERWORKS** *K-Tel ONE 1093*	39	8 wks

Jean-Michel JARRE

France, male instrumentalist/producer

20 Aug 77	● **OXYGENE** *Polydor 2310 555*	2	23 wks
16 Dec 78	**EQUINOXE** *Polydor POLD 5007*	11	26 wks
6 Jun 81	● **MAGNETIC FIELDS** *Polydor POLS 1033*	6	17 wks
15 May 82	● **THE CONCERTS IN CHINA** *Polydor PODV 3*	6	17 wks

Al JARREAU

US, male vocalist

5 Sep 81	**BREAKING AWAY** *Warner Bros. K 56917*	60	8 wks

JEFFERSON AIRPLANE

US, female/male vocal/instrumental group

28 Jun 69	**BLESS ITS POINTED LITTLE HEAD** *RCA SF 8019*	38	1 wk
7 Mar 70	**VOLUNTEERS** *RCA SF 8076*	34	7 wks
2 Oct 71	**BARK** *Grunt FTR 1001*	42	1 wk
2 Sep 72	**LONG JOHN SILVER** *Grunt FTR 1007*	30	1 wk

JEFFERSON STARSHIP

US, male vocal/instrumental group

31 Jul 76	**SPITFIRE** *Grunt RFL 1557*	30	2 wks
9 Feb 80	**FREEDOM AT POINT ZERO** *Grunt FL 13452*	22	11 wks

JETHRO TULL

UK, male vocal/instrumental group

2 Nov 68	● **THIS WAS** *Island ILPS 9085*	10	22 wks
9 Aug 69	★ **STAND UP** *Island ILPS 9103*	1	29 wks
9 May 70	● **BENEFIT** *Island ILPS 9123*	3	13 wks
3 Apr 71	● **AQUALUNG** *Island ILPS 9145*	4	21 wks
18 Mar 72	● **THICK AS A BRICK** *Chrysalis CHR 1003*	5	14 wks
15 Jul 72	● **LIVING IN THE PAST** *Chrysalis CJT 1*	8	11 wks
28 Jul 73	**A PASSION PLAY** *Chrysalis CHR 1040*	13	8 wks
2 Nov 74	**WAR CHILD** *Chrysalis CHR 1067*	14	4 wks
27 Sep 75	**MINSTREL IN THE GALLERY** *Chrysalis CHR 1082*	20	6 wks
31 Jan 76	**M.U. THE BEST OF JETHRO TULL** *Chrysalis CHR 1078*	44	5 wks
15 May 76	**TOO OLD TO ROCK 'N' ROLL TOO YOUNG TO DIE** *Chrysalis CHR 1111*	25	10 wks
19 Feb 77	**SONGS FROM THE WOOD** *Chrysalis CHR 1132*	13	12 wks
29 Apr 78	**HEAVY HORSES** *Chrysalis CHR 1175*	20	10 wks
14 Oct 78	**LIVE BURSTING OUT** *Chrysalis CJT 4*	17	8 wks

Date	Title Label Number	Position		Date	Title Label Number	Position	
6 Oct 79	**STORM WATCH** Chrysalis CDL 1238	27	4 wks	30 May 81	**THE FOX** Rocket TRAIN 16	12	12 wks
6 Sep 80	**A** Chrysalis CDL 1301	25	5 wks	17 Apr 82	**JUMP UP** Rocket HISPD 127	13	12 wks
17 Apr 82	**BROADSWORD AND THE BEAST** Chrysalis CDL 1380	27	19 wks	6 Nov 82	**LOVE SONGS** TV Records TVA 3	39†	8 wks

JETS

UK, male vocal/instrumental group

10 Apr 82	**100 PERCENT COTTON** EMI EMC 3399	30	6 wks

Joan JETT and the BLACKHEARTS

US, female/male vocal/instrumental group.

8 May 82	**I LOVE ROCK 'N' ROLL** Epic EPC 85686	25	7 wks

Billy JOEL

US, male vocalist

25 Mar 78	**THE STRANGER** CBS 82311	25	34 wks
25 Nov 78	● **52ND STREET** CBS 83181	10	41 wks
22 Mar 80	● **GLASS HOUSES** CBS 86108	9	23 wks
10 Oct 81	**SONGS IN THE ATTIC** CBS 85273	57	3 wks
2 Oct 82	**NYLON CURTAIN** CBS 85959	27	5 wks

Elton JOHN

UK, male vocalist/instrumentalist - piano

23 May 70	**ELTON JOHN** DJM DJLPS 406	11	14 wks
16 Jan 71	● **TUMBLEWEED CONNECTION** DJM DJLPS 410	6	20 wks
1 May 71	**THE ELTON JOHN LIVE ALBUM 17-11-70** DJM DJLPS 414	20	2 wks
20 May 72	**MADMAN ACROSS THE WATER** DJM DJLPH 420	41	2 wks
3 Jun 72	● **HONKY CHATEAU** DJM DJLPH 423	2	23 wks
10 Feb 73	★ **DON'T SHOOT ME I'M ONLY THE PIANO PLAYER** DJM DJLPH 427	1	42 wks
3 Nov 73	★ **GOODBYE YELLOW BRICK ROAD** DJM DJLPO 1001	1	84 wks
13 Jul 74	★ **CARIBOU** DJM DJLPH 439	1	18 wks
23 Nov 74	★ **ELTON JOHN'S GREATEST HITS** DJM DJLPH 442	1	84 wks
7 Jun 75	● **CAPTAIN FANTASTIC AND THE BROWN DIRT COWBOY** DJM DJLPX 1	2	24 wks
8 Nov 75	● **ROCK OF WESTIES** DJM DJLPH 464	5	12 wks
15 May 76	● **HERE AND THERE** DJM DJLPH 473	6	9 wks
6 Nov 76	● **BLUE MOVES** Rocket ROSP 1	3	15 wks
15 Oct 77	● **GREATEST HITS VOL. 2** DJM DJH 20520	6	24 wks
4 Nov 78	● **A SINGLE MAN** Rocket TRAIN 1	8	26 wks
20 Oct 79	**VICTIM OF LOVE** Rocket HISPD 125	41	3 wks
8 Mar 80	**LADY SAMANTHA** DJM 22085	56	2 wks
31 May 80	**21 AT 33** Rocket HISPD 126	12	13 wks
25 Oct 80	**THE VERY BEST OF ELTON JOHN** K-Tel NE 1094	24	13 wks

JOHNNY and The HURRICANES

US, male instrumental group

3 Dec 60	**STORMSVILLE** London HAI 2269	18	1 wk
1 Apr 61	**BIG SOUND OF JOHNNY AND THE HURRICANES** London HAK 2322	14	4 wks

Linton Kwesi JOHNSON

Jamaica, male poet

30 Jun 79	**FORCE OF VICTORY** Island ILPS 9566	66	1 wk
31 Oct 80	**BASS CULTURE** Island ILPS 9605	46	5 wks

Al JOLSON

US, male vocalist

14 Mar 81	**20 GOLDEN GREATS** MCA MCTV 4	18	7 wks

JON and VANGELIS

UK, male vocalist and Greece, male instrumentalist - keyboards

26 Jan 80	● **SHORT STORIES** Polydor POLD 5030	4	11 wks
11 Jul 81	● **THE FRIENDS OF MR. CAIRO** Polydor POLD 5039	6	23 wks

See also Jon Anderson, Vangelis.

Grace JONES

US, female vocalist

30 Aug 80	**WARM LEATHERETTE** Island ILPS 9592	45	2 wks
23 May 81	**NIGHTCLUBBING** Island ILPS 9624	35	16 wks
20 Nov 82	**LIVING MY LIFE** Island ILPS 9722	15	6 wks

Jack JONES

US, male vocalist

29 Apr 72	● **A SONG FOR YOU** RCA Victor SF 8228	9	6 wks
3 Jun 72	● **BREAD WINNERS** RCA Victor SF 8280	7	36 wks
7 Apr 73	● **TOGETHER** RCA Victor SF 8342	8	10 wks
23 Feb 74	● **HARBOUR** RCA Victor APL1 0408	10	5 wks
19 Feb 77	**THE FULL LIFE** RCA Victor PL 12067	41	5 wks
21 May 77	**ALL TO YOURSELF** RCA TVL 2	13	8 wks

TOM JONES The most successful Welshman ever in the album chart topped Otis Redding by 14 weeks to become Album Champion of 1968 (135 wks).

JETHRO TULL Originally from Blackpool the John Evan Band evolved into Jethro Tull in 1968 at the suggestion of flautist and vocalist—Ian Anderson

Above **ELTON JOHN** Elton Hercules John, 1975 Album Champion.

JEFFERSON AIRPLANE Although an integral part of the San Franciscan scene, their classic albums 'After Bathing at Baxters' and 'Surrealistic Pillow' failed to chart in Britain.

Left **KINKS** The Village Green Preservation Society hold their annual meeting to discuss why their album of the same name didn't make the chart.

Left **GLADYS KNIGHT AND THE PIPS** Originally formed in 1952 when Gladys was 8, they first toured four years later with Jackie Wilson & Sam Cooke.

Date	Title *Label Number*	Position		Date	Title *Label Number*	Position	

Quincy JONES

US, male arranger/instrumentalist - keyboards

| 18 Apr 81 | THE DUDE *A & M AMLK 63721* | 19 | 25 wks |
| 20 Mar 82 | THE BEST *A&M AMLH 68542* | 41 | 4 wks |

Rickie Lee JONES

US, female vocalist

| 16 Jun 79 | RICKIE LEE JONES *Warner Bros. K 56628* | 18 | 19 wks |
| 8 Aug 81 | PIRATES *Warner Bros. K 56816* | 37 | 11 wks |

Tammy JONES

UK, female vocalist

| 12 Jul 75 | LET ME TRY AGAIN *Epic EPC 80853* | 38 | 5 wks |

Tom JONES

UK, male vocalist

5 Jun 65	ALONG CAME JONES *Decca LK 6693*	11	5 wks
8 Oct 66	FROM THE HEART *Decca LK 4814*	23	8 wks
8 Apr 67	● GREEN GREEN GRASS OF HOME *Decca SKL 4855*	3	49 wks
24 Jun 67	● LIVE AT THE TALK OF THE TOWN *Decca SKL 4874*	6	90 wks
30 Dec 67	● 13 SMASH HITS *Decca SKL 4909*	5	49 wks
27 Jul 68	★ DELILAH *Decca SKL 4946*	1	29 wks
21 Dec 68	● HELP YOURSELF *Decca SKL 4982*	4	9 wks
28 Jun 69	● THIS IS TOM JONES *Decca SKL 5007*	2	20 wks
15 Nov 69	● TOM JONES LIVE IN LAS VEGAS *Decca SKL 5032*	3	45 wks
25 Apr 70	● TOM *Decca SKL 5045*	4	18 wks
14 Nov 70	● I WHO HAVE NOTHING *Decca SKL 5072*	10	10 wks
29 May 71	● SHE'S A LADY *Decca SKL 5089*	9	7 wks
27 Nov 71	LIVE AT CAESAR'S PALACE *Decca 1/1-1/2*	27	5 wks
24 Jun 72	CLOSE UP *Decca SKL 5132*	17	4 wks
23 Jun 73	THE BODY AND SOUL OF TOM JONES *Decca SKL 5162*	31	1 wk
5 Jan 74	GREATEST HITS *Decca SKL 5162*	15	13 wks
22 Mar 75	★ 20 GREATEST HITS *Decca TJD 1/11/2*	1	21 wks
7 Oct 78	I'M COMING HOME *Lotus WH 5001*	12	9 wks

Janis JOPLIN

US, female vocalist

| 17 Apr 71 | PEARL *CBS 64188* | 50 | 1 wk |
| 22 Jul 72 | JANIS JOPLIN IN CONCERT *CBS 67241* | 30 | 6 wks |

JOURNEY

US, male vocal/instrumental group

| 20 Mar 82 | ESCAPE *CBS 85138* | 32 | 16 wks |

JOY DIVISION

UK, male vocal/instrumental group

26 Jul 80	● CLOSER *Factory FACT 25*	6	8 wks
30 Aug 80	UNKNOWN PLEASURES *Factory FACT 10*	71	1 wk
17 Oct 81	● STILL *Factory FACT 40*	5	12 wks

JUDAS PRIEST

UK, male vocal/instrumental group

14 May 77	SIN AFTER SIN *CBS 82008*	23	6 wks
25 Feb 78	STAINED GLASS *CBS 82430*	27	5 wks
11 Nov 78	KILLING MACHINE *CBS 83135*	32	9 wks
6 Oct 79	● UNLEASHED IN THE EAST *CBS 83852*	10	8 wks
19 Apr 80	● BRITISH STEEL *CBS 84160*	4	17 wks
7 Mar 81	POINT OF ENTRY *CBS 84834*	14	5 wks
17 Jul 82	SCREAMING FOR VENGEANCE *CBS 85941*	11	9 wks

JUDGE DREAD

UK, male vocalist

| 6 Dec 75 | BEDTIME STORIES *Cactus CTLP 113* | 26 | 12 wks |
| 7 Mar 81 | 40 BIG ONES *Creole BIG 1* | 51 | 2 wks |

JUICY LUCY

UK, male vocal/instrumental group

| 18 Apr 70 | JUICY LUCY *Vertigo VO 2* | 41 | 4 wks |
| 21 Nov 70 | LIE BACK AND ENJOY IT *Vertigo 6360 014* | 53 | 1 wk |

JUNIOR

UK, male vocalist

| 5 Jun 82 | JI *Mercury/Phonogram MERS 3* | 28 | 14 wks |

Date	Title Label Number	Position		Date	Title Label Number	Position	

Bert KAEMPFERT

Germany, orchestra

5 Mar 66	● BYE BYE BLUES *Polydor BM 84086*	4	22 wks
16 Apr 66	BEST OF BERT KAEMPFERT *Polydor 84-012*	27	1 wk
28 May 66	SWINGING SAFARI *Polydor LPHM 46-384*	20	15 wks
30 Jul 66	STRANGERS IN THE NIGHT *Polydor LPHM 84-053*	13	26 wks
4 Feb 67	RELAXING SOUND OF BERT KAEMPFERT *Polydor 583-501*	33	3 wks
18 Feb 67	BERT KAEMPFERT - BEST SELLER *Polydor 583-551*	25	18 wks
29 Apr 67	HOLD ME *Polydor 184-072*	36	5 wks
26 Aug 67	KAEMPFERT SPECIAL *Polydor 236-207*	24	5 wks
19 Jun 71	ORANGE COLOURED SKY *Polydor 2310-091*	49	1 wk
5 Jul 80	SOUNDS SENSATIONAL *Polydor POLTB 10*	17	8 wks

Mick KARN

UK, male vocalist/instrumentalist - bass

| 20 Nov 82 | TITLES *Virgin V 2249* | 74 | 3 wks |

K.C. and The SUNSHINE BAND

US, male vocal/instrumental group

| 30 Aug 75 | K.C. AND THE SUNSHINE BAND *Jayboy JSL 9* | 26 | 7 wks |
| 1 Mar 80 | ● GREATEST HITS *TK TKR 83385* | 10 | 6 wks |

Felicity KENDALL

UK, female vocalist - exercise record

| 19 Jun 82 | SHAPE UP AND DANCE WITH FELICITY KENDALL (VOL 1) *Lifestyle LEG 1* | 53 | 14 wks |

KENNY

UK, male vocal/instrumental group

| 17 Jan 76 | THE SOUND OF SUPER K *RAK SRAK 518* | 56 | 1 wk |

Gerard KENNY

US, male vocalist

| 21 Jul 79 | MADE IT THROUGH THE RAIN *RCA Victor PL 25218* | 19 | 4 wks |

Aram KHATCHATURIAN/VIENNA PHILHARMONIC ORCHESTRA

Russia, male conductor, Austria orchestra

| 22 Jan 72 | SPARTACUS *Decca SXL 6000* | 16 | 15 wks |

KIDS FROM FAME

US, male/female vocal/instrumental group

| 24 Jul 82 | ★ KIDS FROM FAME *BBC REP 447* | 1† | 23 wks |
| 16 Oct 82 | ● KIDS FROM FAME AGAIN *RCA RCALP 6057* | 2† | 11 wks |

KILLING JOKE

UK, male vocal/instrumental group

25 Oct 80	KILLING JOKE *Polydor EGMD 545*	39	4 wks
20 Jun 81	WHAT'S THIS FOR *Malicious Damage EG MD 550*	42	4 wks
8 May 82	REVELATIONS *Malicious Damage/Polydor EGMD 3*	12	6 wks
27 Nov 82	'HA'-KILLING JOKE LIVE *EG(Polydor) EGMDT 4*	66	2 wks

B.B. KING

US, male vocalist/instrumentalist - guitar

| 25 Aug 79 | TAKE IT HOME *MCA MCF 3010* | 60 | 5 wks |

Ben E. KING

UK, male vocalist

| 1 Jul 67 | SPANISH HARLEM *Atlantic 590-001* | 30 | 3 wks |

Carole KING

US, female vocalist

24 Jul 71	● TAPESTRY *A & M AMLS 2025*	4	90 wks
15 Jan 72	MUSIC *A & M AMLH 67013*	18	10 wks
2 Dec 72	RHYMES AND REASONS *Ode 77016*	40	2 wks

Date	Title Label Number	Position	

Evelyn KING

US, female vocalist

Date	Title Label Number	Position	
11 Sep 82	**GET LOOSE** RCA RCALP 3093	35	9 wks

Solomon KING

US, male vocalist

22 Jun 68	**SHE WEARS MY RING** Columbia SCX 6250	40	1 wk

KING CRIMSON

UK, male vocal/instrumental group

1 Nov 69	● **IN THE COURT OF THE CRIMSON KING**	5	18 wks
	Island ILPS 9111		
30 May 70	● **IN THE WAKE OF POSEIDON** Island ILPS 9127	4	13 wks
16 Jan 71	**LIZARD** Island ILPS 9141	30	1 wk
8 Jan 72	**ISLANDS** Island ILPS 9175	30	1 wk
7 Apr 73	**LARKS' TONGUES IN ASPIC** Island ILPS 9230	20	4 wks
13 Apr 74	**STARLESS AND BIBLE BLACK**	28	2 wks
	Island ILPS 9275		
26 Oct 74	**RED** Island ILPS 9308	45	1 wk
10 Oct 81	**DISCIPLINE** EG/Polydor EGLP 49	41	4 wks
26 Jun 82	**BEAT** EG/Polydor EGLP 51	39	5 wks

The Choir Of KING'S COLLEGE, CAMBRIDGE

UK, choir

11 Dec 71	**THE WORLD OF CHRISTMAS** Argo SPAA 104	38	3 wks

KINGS OF SWING ORCHESTRA

Australia, orchestra

29 May 82	**SWITCHED ON SWING** K-Tel ONE 1166	28	11 wks

KINKS

UK, male vocal/instrumental group

17 Oct 64	● **KINKS** Pye NPL 18096	3	25 wks
13 Mar 65	● **KINDA KINKS** Pye NPL 18112	3	15 wks
4 Dec 65	● **KINKS KONTROVERSY** Pye NPL 18131	9	12 wks
11 Sep 66	● **WELL RESPECTED KINKS**	5	31 wks
	Marble Arch MAL 612		
5 Nov 66	**FACE TO FACE** Pye NPL 18149	12	11 wks
14 Oct 67	**SOMETHING ELSE** Pye NSPL 18193	35	2 wks

2 Dec 67	● **SUNNY AFTERNOON** Marble Arch MAL 716	9	11 wks
23 Oct 71	**GOLDEN HOUR OF THE KINKS**	21	4 wks
	Golden Hour GH 501		
14 Oct 78	**20 GOLDEN GREATS** Ronco RPL 2031	19	6 wks

Kathy KIRBY

UK, female vocalist

4 Jan 64	**16 HITS FROM STARS AND GARTERS**	11	8 wks
	Decca LK 4575		

KISS

US, male vocal/instrumental group

29 May 76	**DESTROYER** Casablanca CBSP 4008	22	5 wks
25 Jun 76	**ALIVE!** Casablanca CBSP 401	49	2 wks
17 Dec 77	**ALIVE** Casablanca CALD 5004	60	1 wk
7 Jul 79	**DYNASTY** Casablanca CALH 2051	50	6 wks
28 Jun 80	**UNMASKED** Mercury 6302 032	48	3 wks
5 Dec 81	**THE ELDER** Casablanca 6302 163	51	3 wks
26 Jun 82	**KILLERS** Casablanca/Phonogram CANL 1	42	6 wks
6 Nov 82	**CREATURES OF THE NIGHT**	22	4 wks
	Casablanca/Phonogram CANL 4		

Eartha KITT

US, female vocalist

11 Feb 61	**REVISITED** London HA 2296	17	1 wk

KNACK

US, male vocal/instrumental group

4 Aug 79	**GET THE KNACK** Capitol EST 11948	65	2 wks

Gladys KNIGHT and The PIPS

US, female vocalist/male vocal backing group

31 May 75	**I FEEL A SONG** Buddah BDLP 4030	20	15 wks
28 Feb 76	● **THE BEST OF GLADYS KNIGHT & THE PIPS**	6	43 wks
	Buddah BDLH 5013		
16 Jul 77	**STILL TOGETHER** Buddah BDLH 5014	42	3 wks
12 Nov 77	● **30 GREATEST** K-Tel NE 1004	3	22 wks
4 Oct 80	**A TOUCH OF LOVE** K-Tel NE 1090	16	6 wks

KNIGHTSBRIDGE STRINGS

UK, male orchestra

25 Jun 60	**STRING SWAY** Top Rank BUY 017	20	1 wk

Date	Title *Label Number*	Position		Date	Title *Label Number*	Position	

John KONGOS

South Africa, male vocalist/multi-instrumentalist

15 Jan 72	**KONGOS** *Fly HIFLY 7*	29	2 wks

KOOL AND THE GANG

US, male vocal/instrumental group

21 Nov 81	● **SOMETHING SPECIAL** *De-Lite DCR 001*	10	20 wks
2 Oct 82	**AS ONE** *De-Lite/Phonogram DSR 3*	49	9 wks

KORGIS

UK, male vocal/instrumental duo

26 Jul 80	**DUMB WAITERS** *Rialto TENOR 104*	40	4 wks

KRAFTWERK

Germany, male vocal/instrumental group

17 May 75	● **AUTOBAHN** *Vertigo 6360 620*	4	18 wks
20 May 78	● **THE MAN-MACHINE** *Capitol EST 11728*	9	13 wks
23 May 81	**COMPUTER WORLD** *EMI EMC 3370*	15	22 wks
6 Feb 82	**TRANS-EUROPE EXPRESS** *Capitol EST 11603*	56	7 wks

Billy J. KRAMER and The DAKOTAS

UK, male vocalist/male instrumental backing group

16 Nov 63	**LISTEN TO BILLY J. KRAMER** *Parlophone PMC 1209*	11	17 wks

Kris KRISTOFFERSON and Rita COOLIDGE

US, male/female vocal duo

6 May 78	**NATURAL ACT** *A & M AMLH 64690*	35	4 wks

See also Rita Coolidge.

KROKUS

Switzerland/Malta, male vocal/instrumental group

21 Feb 81	**HARDWARE** *Ariola ARL 5064*	44	4 wks
20 Feb 82	**ONE VICE AT A TIME** *Arista SPART 1189*	28	5 wks

Charlie KUNZ

US, male instrumentalist - piano

14 Jun 69	● **THE WORLD OF CHARLIE KUNZ** *Decca SPA 15*	9	11 wks

L

Cleo LAINE

UK, female vocalist

2 Dec 78	**CLEO** *Arcade ADEP 37*	68	1 wk

See also Cleo Laine and John Williams, Cleo Laine and James Galway.

Cleo LAINE and James GALWAY

UK, female vocalist and Ireland, male instrumentalist - flute

31 May 80	**SOMETIMES WHEN WE TOUCH** *RCA PL 25296*	15	14 wks

See also Cleo Laine, James Galway, Cleo Laine and John Williams.

Cleo LAINE and John WILLIAMS

UK, female vocalist/male instrumentalist - guitar

7 Jan 78	**BEST OF FRIENDS** *RCA RS 1094*	18	22 wks

See also Cleo Laine, John Williams, Cleo Laine and James Galway.

Frankie LAINE

US, male vocalist

24 Jun 61	● **HELL BENT FOR LEATHER** *Philips BBL 7468*	7	23 wks
24 Sep 77	● **THE VERY BEST OF FRANKIE LAINE** *Warwick PR 5032*	7	6 wks

Greg LAKE

UK, male vocalist

17 Oct 81	**GREG LAKE** *Chrysalis CHR 1357*	62	3 wks

See also Emerson, Lake and Palmer.

Left **BRENDA LEE** "Little Miss Dynamite".

Below **JERRY LEE LEWIS** "The Killer".

Above **JAMES LAST** He that is Last shall be first-if it hadn't been for Elvis and Frank.

Date	Title Label Number	Position

LAMBRETTAS

UK, male vocal/instrumental group

5 Jul 80	**BEAT BOYS IN THE JET AGE** *Rocket TRAIN 10*	28	8 wks

LANDSCAPE

UK, male vocal/instrumental group

21 Mar 81	**FROM THE TEAROOMS** *RCA RCALP 5003*	16	12 wks

Ronnie LANE and the BAND SLIM CHANCE

UK, male vocal/instrumental group

17 Aug 74	**ANYMORE FOR ANYMORE** *GM GML 1013*	48	1 wk

See also Pete Townshend and Ronnie Lane.

Mario LANZA

US, male vocalist

6 Dec 58	● **THE STUDENT PRINCE/THE GREAT CARUSO** *RCA RB 16113*	4	21 wks
23 Jul 60	● **THE GREAT CARUSO** *RCA RB 16112*	3	15 wks
9 Jan 71	**HIS GREATEST HITS VOL.1** *RCA LSB 4000*	39	1 wk
5 Sep 81	**THE LEGEND OF MARIO LANZA** *K-Tel NE 1110*	29	11 wks

The Great Caruso side of the first album is a film soundtrack.

James LAST

UK, orchestra

15 Apr 67	● **THIS IS JAMES LAST** *Polydor 104-678*	6	48 wks
22 Jul 67	**HAMMOND A-GO-GO** *Polydor 249-043*	27	10 wks
26 Aug 67	**NON-STOP DANCING** *Polydor 236-203*	35	1 wk
26 Aug 67	**LOVE THIS IS MY SONG** *Polydor 583-553*	32	2 wks
22 Jun 68	**JAMES LAST GOES POP** *Polydor 249-160*	32	3 wks
8 Feb 69	**DANCING '68 VOL. 1** *Polydor 249-216*	40	1 wk
31 May 69	**TRUMPET A-GO-GO** *Polydor 249-239*	13	1 wk
9 Aug 69	**NON-STOP DANCING '69** *Polydor 249-294*	26	1 wk
24 Jan 70	**NON-STOP DANCING '69/2** *Polydor 249-354*	27	3 wks
23 May 70	**NON-STOP EVERGREENS** *Polydor 249-370*	26	1 wk
11 Jul 70	**CLASSICS UP TO DATE** *Polydor 249-371*	44	1 wk
11 Jul 70	**NON-STOP DANCING '70** *Polydor 2371-04*	67	1 wk
24 Oct 70	**VERY BEST OF JAMES LAST** *Polydor 2371-054*	45	4 wks
8 May 71	**NON-STOP DANCING '71** *Polydor 2371-111*	21	4 wks
26 Jun 71	**SUMMER HAPPENING** *Polydor 2371-133*	38	1 wk
18 Sep 71	**BEACH PARTY 2** *Polydor 2371-211*	47	1 wk
2 Oct 71	**YESTERDAY'S MEMORIES** *Contour 2870-117*	17	14 wks
16 Oct 71	**NON-STOP DANCING 12** *Polydor 2371-141*	30	3 wks
19 Feb 72	**NON-STOP DANCING 13** *Polydor 2371-189*	32	2 wks

Date	Title Label Number	Position
4 Mar 72	**POLKA PARTY** *Polydor 2371-190*	22	3 wks
29 Apr 72	**JAMES LAST IN CONCERT** *Polydor 2371-191*	13	6 wks
24 Jun 72	**VOODOO PARTY** *Polydor 2371-235*	45	1 wk
16 Sep 72	**CLASSICS UP TO DATE VOL.2** *Polydor 184-061*	49	1 wk
30 Sep 72	**LOVE MUST BE THE REASON** *Polydor 2371-281*	32	2 wks
27 Jan 73	**THE MUSIC OF JAMES LAST** *Polydor 2683 010*	19	12 wks
24 Feb 73	**JAMES LAST IN RUSSIA** *Polydor 2371 293*	12	9 wks
24 Feb 73	**NON STOP DANCING VOL 14** *Polydor 2371-319*	27	3 wks
28 Jul 73	**OLE** *Polydor 2371 384*	24	5 wks
1 Sep 73	**NON-STOP DANCING VOL. 15** *Polydor 2371-376*	34	2 wks
20 Apr 74	**NON-STOP DANCING VOL. 16** *Polydor 2371-444*	43	2 wks
29 Jun 74	**IN CONCERT VOL. 2** *Polydor 2371-320*	49	1 wk
23 Nov 74	**GOLDEN MEMORIES** *Polydor 2371-472*	39	2 wks
26 Jul 75	● **TEN YEARS NON-STOP JUBILEE** *Polydor 2660-111*	5	16 wks
2 Aug 75	**VIOLINS IN LOVE** *K-tel*	60	1 wk
22 Nov 75	● **MAKE THE PARTY LAST** *Polydor 2371-612*	3	19 wks
8 May 76	**CLASSICS UP TO DATE VOL.3** *Polydor*	54	1 wk
6 May 78	**EAST TO WEST** *Polydor 2630-092*	49	4 wks
14 Apr 79	● **LAST THE WHOLE NIGHT LONG** *Polydor PTD 5008*	2	45 wks
23 Aug 80	**THE BEST FROM 150 GOLD** *Polydor 2681 211*	56	3 wks
1 Nov 80	**CLASSICS FOR DREAMING** *Polydor POLTV 11*	12	18 wks
14 Feb 81	**ROSES FROM THE SOUTH** *Polydor 2372 051*	41	5 wks
21 Nov 81	**HANSIMANIA** *Polydor POLTV 14*	18	13 wks
28 Nov 81	**LAST FOREVER** *Polydor 2630 135*	88	2 wks

LAUREL and HARDY

US, male comic duo

6 Dec 75	**THE GOLDEN AGE OF HOLLYWOOD COMEDY** *United Artists UAG 29676*	55	4 wks

Syd LAWRENCE

UK, male orchestra

8 Aug 70	**MORE MILLER AND OTHER BIG BAND MAGIC** *Philips 6642 001*	14	4 wks
25 Dec 71	**SYD LAWRENCE WITH THE GLENN MILLER SOUND** *Fontana SFL 13178*	31	2 wks
25 Dec 71	**MUSIC OF GLENN MILLER IN SUPER STEREO** *Philips 6641-017*	43	2 wks
26 Feb 72	**SOMETHING OLD, SOMETHING NEW** *Philips 6308 090*	34	1 wk

Ronnie LAWS

US, male vocalist/instrumentalist - saxophone

17 Oct 81	**SOLID GROUND** *Liberty/EMI LBG 30336*	100	1 wk

LEAGUE UNLIMITED ORCHESTRA

UK, male instrumental group

17 Jul 82	● LOVE AND DANCING *Virgin OVED 6*	3†	24 wks

This album is an instrumental version of previously recorded Human League songs re-mixed by UK producer Martin Rushent.

LED ZEPPELIN

UK, male vocal/instrumental group

12 Apr 69	● LED ZEPPELIN *Atlantic 588-171*	6	79 wks
8 Nov 69	★ LED ZEPPELIN 2 *Atlantic 588-198*	1	138 wks
7 Nov 70	★ LED ZEPPELIN 3 *Atlantic 2401-002*	1	40 wks
27 Nov 71	★ FOUR SYMBOLS *Atlantic 2401-012*	1	61 wks
14 Apr 73	★ HOUSES OF THE HOLY *Atlantic K 50014*	1	13 wks
15 Mar 75	★ PHYSICAL GRAFFITI *Swan Song SSK 89400*	1	27 wks
24 Apr 76	★ PRESENCE *Swan Song SSK 59402*	1	14 wks
6 Nov 76	★ THE SONG REMAINS THE SAME *Swan Song SSK 89402*	1	15 wks
8 Sep 79	★ IN THROUGH THE OUT DOOR *Swan Song SSK 59410*	1	16 wks
4 Dec 82	● CODA *Swansong A 0051*	4†	4 wks

Led Zeppelin 2 *changed label/number to Atlantic K 40037,* Four Symbols *changed to Atlantic K 50008 during their runs. The fourth Led Zeppelin album appeared in the chart under various guises;* The Fourth Led Zeppelin Album, Runes, The New Led Zeppelin Album, Led Zeppelin 4 *and* Four Symbols. *We call it* Four Symbols.

LEE — See *PETERS and LEE*

Brenda LEE

US, female vocalist

24 Nov 62	ALL THE WAY *Brunswick LAT 8383*	20	2 wks
16 Feb 63	BRENDA - THAT'S ALL *Brunswick LAT 8516*	13	9 wks
13 Apr 63	● ALL ALONE AM I *Brunswick LAT 8530*	8	20 wks
16 Jul 66	BYE BYE BLUES *Brunswick LAT 8649*	21	2 wks
1 Nov 80	LITTLE MISS DYNAMITE *Warwick WW 5083*	15	11 wks

Peggy LEE

US, female vocalist

4 Jun 60	● LATIN A LA LEE *Capitol T 1290*	8	15 wks
20 May 61	BEST OF PEGGY LEE VOL. 2 *Brunswick LAT 8355*	18	1 wk
21 Oct 61	BLACK COFFEE *Ace of Hearts AH 5*	20	1 wk

See also Peggy Lee and George Shearing.

Peggy LEE and George SHEARING

US, female vocalist and male band leader

11 Jun 60	BEAUTY AND THE BEAT *Capitol T 1219*	16	6 wks

See also Peggy Lee, and Nat "King" Cole and the George Shearing Quintet.

Raymond LEFEVRE

France, orchestra

7 Oct 67	● RAYMOND LEFEVRE *Major Minor MMLP 4*	10	7 wks
17 Feb 68	RAYMOND LEFEVRE VOL.2 *Major Minor SMLP 13*	37	2 wks

Tom LEHRER

US, male comic vocalist

8 Nov 58	● SONGS BY TOM LEHRER *Decca LF 1311*	7	19 wks
25 Jun 60	● AN EVENING WASTED WITH TOM LEHRER *Decca LK 4332*	7	7 wks

John LENNON

UK, male vocalist

16 Jan 71	JOHN LENNON AND THE PLASTIC ONO BAND *Apple PCS 7124*	11	11 wks
30 Oct 71	★ IMAGINE *Apple PAS 10004*	1	101 wks
14 Oct 72	SOMETIME IN NEW YORK CITY *Apple PCSP 716*	11	6 wks
8 Dec 73	MIND GAMES *Apple PCS 7165*	13	12 wks
19 Oct 74	● WALLS AND BRIDGES *Apple PCTC 253*	6	10 wks
8 Mar 75	ROCK 'N' ROLL *Apple PCS 7169*	6	28 wks
8 Nov 75	● SHAVED FISH *Apple PCS 7173*	8	29 wks
22 Nov 80	★ DOUBLE FANTASY *Geffen K 99131*	1	36 wks
20 Nov 82	★ THE JOHN LENNON COLLECTION *Parlophone EMTV 37*	1	6 wks

Imagine *changed its label credit to Parlophone PAS 10004 between its initial chart run and later runs.* John Lennon and the Plastic Ono Band *is credited to John Lennon and the Plastic Ono Band.* Imagine *is credited to John Lennon and the Plastic Ono Band with the Flux Fiddlers.* Sometime In New York City *is credited to John and Yoko Lennon with the Plastic Ono Band and Elephant's Memory.* Double Fantasy *is credited to John Lennon and Yoko Ono.* Shaved Fish *and* The John Lennon Collection *are compilations and so have various credits. See also Yoko Ono.*

Deke LEONARD

UK, male vocalist/instrumentalist - guitar

13 Apr 74	KAMIKAZE *United Artists UAG 29544*	50	1 wk

Right **JOHN LENNON** Technically Lennon's first non-Beatle album was the avant-garde 'Unfinished Music No. 1—Two Virgins' in 1968 but the 'John Lennon/Plastic Ono Band' is accepted as his first real long playing solo effort.

Below Right **LOVE** Fronted by dual vocalists Arthur Lee & Bryan Maclean their 'Forever Changes' included the classic singles 'Alone Again Or' and 'Andmoreagain', neither of which were hits in Britain.

Below **ANDREW LLOYD WEBBER** One Variation.

95

Date	Title Label Number	Position		Date	Title Label Number	Position	

LEVEL 42

UK, male vocal/instrumental group

29 Aug 81	**LEVEL 42** *Polydor POLS 1036*	20	18 wks
10 Apr 82	**THE EARLY TAPES JULY-AUGUST 1980** *Polydor POLS 1064*	46	6 wks
18 Sep 82	**THE PURSUIT OF ACCIDENTS** *Polydor POLD 5067*	17	8 wks

Jerry Lee LEWIS

US, male vocalist/instrumentalist - piano

| 2 Jun 62 | **JERRY LEE LEWIS VOL.2** *London HA 2440* | 14 | 6 wks |

Linda LEWIS

UK, female vocalist

| 9 Aug 75 | **NOT A LITTLE GIRL ANYMORE** *Arista ARTY 109* | 40 | 4 wks |

Ramsey LEWIS TRIO

US, male vocal instrumental trio

| 21 May 66 | **HANG ON RAMSEY** *Chess CRL 4520* | 20 | 4 wks |

LIGHT OF THE WORLD

UK, male vocal/instrumental group

| 24 Jan 81 | **ROUND TRIP** *Ensign ENVY 14* | 73 | 1 wk |

Gordon LIGHTFOOT

Canada, male vocalist

| 20 May 72 | **DON QUIXOTE** *Reprise K 44166* | 44 | 1 wk |
| 17 Aug 74 | **SUNDOWN** *Reprise K 54020* | 45 | 1 wk |

LINDISFARNE

UK, male vocal/instrumental group

30 Oct 71	⭐ **FOG ON THE TYNE** *Charisma CAS 1050*	1	56 wks
5 Jan 72	● **NICELY OUT OF TUNE** *Charisma CAS 1025*	8	30 wks
30 Sep 72	● **DINGLY DELL** *Charisma CAS 1057*	5	10 wks
11 Aug 73	**LINDISFARNE LIVE** *Charisma Class 2*	25	6 wks
18 Oct 75	**FINEST HOUR** *Charisma CAS 1108*	55	1 wk
24 Jun 78	**BACK AND FOURTH** *Mercury 9109 609*	22	11 wks
9 Dec 78	**MAGIC IN THE AIR** *Mercury 6641 877*	71	1 wk
23 Oct 82	**SLEEPLESS NIGHT** *LMP GET 1*	59	4 wks

LINX

UK, male vocal/instrumental group

| 28 Mar 81 | ● **INTUITION** *Chrysalis CHR 1332* | 8 | 19 wks |
| 31 Oct 81 | **GO AHEAD** *Chrysalis CHR 1358* | 35 | 4 wks |

LIQUID GOLD

UK, male/female vocal instrumental group

| 16 Aug 80 | **LIQUID GOLD** *Polo POLP 101* | 34 | 3 wks |

LITTLE FEAT

US, male vocal/instrumental group

6 Dec 75	**THE LAST RECORD ALBUM** *Warner Bros. K 56156*	36	3 wks
21 May 77	● **TIME LOVES A HERO** *Warner Bros. K 56349*	8	11 wks
11 Mar 78	**WAITING FOR COLUMBUS** *Warner Bros. K 66075*	43	1 wk
1 Dec 79	**DOWN ON THE FARM** *Warner Bros. K 56667*	46	3 wks
8 Aug 81	**HOY HOY** *Warner Bros. K 666100*	76	1 wk

Andrew LLOYD WEBBER

UK, male composer/producer

| 11 Feb 78 | ● **VARIATIONS** *MCA MCF 2824* | 2 | 19 wks |

This album features the cello playing of Julian Lloyd Webber.

Josef LOCKE

Ireland, male vocalist

| 28 Jun 69 | **THE WORLD OF JOSEF LOCKE TODAY** *Decca SPA 21* | 29 | 1 wk |

John LODGE

UK, male vocalist/instrumentalist - guitar

| 19 Feb 77 | **NATURAL AVENUE** *Decca TXS 120* | 38 | 2 wks |

See also Justin Hayward and John Lodge.

Nils LOFGREN

US, male vocalist

17 Apr 76	● CRY TOUGH *A & M AMLH 64573*	8	11 wks
26 Mar 77	I CAME TO DANCE *A & M AMLH 64628*	30	4 wks
5 Nov 77	NIGHT AFTER NIGHT *A & M AMLH AMLM*	38	2 wks
26 Sep 81	NIGHT FADES AWAY *Backstreet MCF 3121*	50	3 wks
1 May 82	A RHYTHM ROMANCE *A&M AMLH 68543*	100	1 wk

LONDON PHILHARMONIC CHOIR/John ALLDIS/NATIONAL PHILHARMONIC ORCHESTRA

UK, choir/male conductor/orchestra

13 Nov 76	● SOUND OF GLORY *Arcade ADEP 25*	10	10 wks

See also London Philharmonic Choir.

LONDON PHILHARMONIC CHOIR

UK, choir

3 Dec 60	● THE MESSIAH *Pye Golden Guinea GGL 0062*	10	7 wks

Full label credits: with the London Orchestra conducted by Walter Susskind. See also London Philharmonic Choir/John Alldis/National Philharmonic Orchestra.

LONDON PHILHARMONIC ORCHESTRA

UK, orchestra

23 Apr 60	RAVEL'S BOLERO *London HAV 2189*	15	4 wks
8 Apr 61	VICTORY AT SEA *PYE GGL 0073*	12	1 wk

LONDON SYMPHONY ORCHESTRA

UK, orchestra

18 Mar 72	TOP TV THEMES *Studio Two STWO 372*	13	7 wks
5 Jul 75	MUSIC FROM 'EDWARD VII' *Polydor 2659 041*	52	1 wk
21 Jan 78	STAR WARS (SOUNDTRACK) *20th Centuary BTD 541*	21	12 wks
8 Jul 78	● CLASSIC ROCK - ROCK CLASSICS *K-Tel ONE 1009*	3	39 wks
10 Feb 79	CLASSIC ROCK - THE SECOND MOVEMENT *K-Tel NE 1039*	26	8 wks
5 Jan 80	SYMPHONY IN BLACK *K-Tel ONE 1063*	34	5 wks
1 Aug 81	● CLASSIC ROCK-ROCK CLASSICS *K-Tel ONE 1123*	5	23 wks

Music from Edward VII was conducted by Cyril Ornandel. See also Cyril Ornandel and London Symphony Orchestra.

LONDON WELSH MALE VOICE CHOIR

UK, male choir

5 Sep 81	SONGS OF THE VALLEYS *K-Tel NE 1117*	61	10 wks

LONE STAR

UK, male vocal/instrumental group

2 Oct 76	LONE STAR *Epic EPC 81545*	47	1 wk
17 Sep 77	FIRING ON ALL SIX *CBS 82213*	36	6 wks

Trini LOPEZ

US, male vocalist

26 Oct 63	● TRINI LOPEZ AT P.J.'S *Reprise R 6093*	7	25 wks
25 Mar 67	● TRINI LOPEZ IN LONDON *Reprise RSLP 6238*	6	17 wks

Sophia LOREN — See *Peter SELLERS and Sophia LOREN*

Joe LOSS

UK, orchestra

30 Oct 71	ALL-TIME PARTY HITS *MFP 5227*	24	10 wks

LOVE

US, male vocal/instrumental group

24 Feb 68	FOREVER CHANGES *Elektra EKS7 4013*	24	6 wks
16 May 70	OUT HERE *Transatlantic TRA 205*	29	2 wks

Geoff LOVE

UK, orchestra

7 Aug 71	BIG WAR MOVIE THEMES *MFP 5171*	11	20 wks
21 Aug 71	BIG WESTERN MOVIE THEMES *MFP 5204*	38	3 wks
30 Oct 71	BIG LOVE MOVIE THEMES *MFP 5171*	28	5 wks

Lene LOVICH

US, female vocalist

17 Mar 79	STATELESS *Stiff SEEZ 7*	35	11 wks
2 Feb 80	FLEX *Stiff SEEZ 19*	19	6 wks

Above
MADNESS They charted with 'The Prince' in 1979, and met a real one in 1982.

Top Right **JOHN MARTYN** 'Fool Glorious Fool'.

Right **BOB MARLEY** Waiting for the bus to Babylon in 1979.

Left **MAMAS & PAPAS** Papas: Denny Doherty & John Phillips and Mamas: Michelle Phillips & Cass Elliot.

Date	Title *Label Number*	Position		Date	Title *Label Number*	Position	

LOVIN' SPOONFUL

US/Canada, male vocal/instrumental group

7 May 66	● **DAYDREAM** *Pye NPL 28078*	8	11 wks

Nick LOWE

UK, male vocalist

11 Mar 78	**THE JESUS OF COOL** *Radar RAD 1*	22	9 wks
23 Jun 79	**LABOUR OF LUST** *Radar RAD 21*	43	6 wks
20 Feb 82	**NICK THE KNIFE** *F.Beat XXLP 14*	99	2 wks

LULU

UK, female vocalist

25 Sep 71	**THE MOST OF LULU** *MFP 5215*	15	6 wks

Bob LUMAN

US, male vocalist

14 Jan 61	**LET'S THINK ABOUT LIVING** *Warner Bros. WM 4025*	18	1 wk

LURKERS

UK, male vocal/instrumental group

1 Jul 78	**FULHAM FALLOUT** *Beggars Banquet BEGA 2*	57	1 wk

LYLE — See *GALLAGHER and LYLE*

Vera LYNN

UK, female vocalist

21 Nov 81	**20 FAMILY FAVOURITES** *EMI EMTV 28*	25	8 wks

Philip LYNOTT

Ireland, male vocalist

26 Apr 80	**SOLO IN SOHO** *Vertigo 9102 038*	28	6 wks

LYNYRD SKYNYRD

US, male vocal/instrumental group

3 May 75	**NUTHIN' FANCY** *MCA MCF 2700*	43	1 wk
28 Feb 76	**GIMME BACK MY BULLETS** *MCA MCF 2744*	34	5 wks
6 Nov 76	**ONE MORE FOR THE ROAD** *MCA MCPS 279*	17	4 wks
12 Nov 77	**STREET SURVIVORS** *MCA MCG 3525*	13	4 wks
4 Nov 78	**SKYNYRD'S FIRST AND LAST** *MCA MCG 3529*	50	1 wk
9 Feb 80	**GOLD AND PLATINUM** *MCA MCSP 308*	49	4 wks

M

Frankie McBRIDE

Ireland, male vocalist

17 Feb 68	**FRANKIE MCBRIDE** *Emerald SLD 28*	29	3 wks

Paul McCARTNEY

UK, male vocalist

2 May 70	● **McCARTNEY** *Apple PCS 7102*	2	32 wks
5 Jun 71	★ **RAM** *Apple PAS 10003*	1	24 wks
31 May 80	**McCARTNEY II** *Parlophone PCTC 258*	1	18 wks
7 Mar 81	**McCARTNEY INTERVIEW** *EMI CHAT 1*	34	4 wks
8 May 82	★ **TUG OF WAR** *Parlophone PCTC 259*	1	27 wks

Ram credited to Paul and Linda McCartney. See also Wings.

Van McCOY and The SOUL CITY SYMPHONY

US, orchestra

5 Jul 75	**DISCO BABY** *Avco 9109 004*	32	11 wks

George McCRAE

US, male vocalist

3 Aug 74	**ROCK YOUR BABY** *Jayboy JSL 3*	13	28 wks
13 Sep 75	**GEORGE MCCRAE** *Jayboy JSL 10*	54	1 wk

Kate and Anna McGARRIGLE

Canada, female vocal duo

26 Feb 77	**DANCER WITH BRUISED KNEES**	35	4 wks
	Warner Bros. K 56356		

Mary MacGREGOR

US, female vocalist

23 Apr 77	**TORN BETWEEN TWO LOVERS**	59	1 wk
	Ariola America AAS 1504		

McGUINNESS FLINT

UK, male vocal/instrumental group

23 Jan 71	● **McGUINNESS FLINT** *Capitol EA-ST 22625*	9	10 wks

Kenneth McKELLAR

UK, male vocalist

28 Jun 69	**THE WORLD OF KENNETH MCKELLAR**	27	7 wks
	Decca SPA 11		
31 Jan 70	**ECCO DI NAPOLI** *Decca SKL 5018*	45	3 wks

Don McLEAN

US, male vocalist

11 Mar 72	● **AMERICAN PIE** *United Artists UAS 29285*	3	54 wks
17 Jun 72	**TAPESTRY** *United Artists UAS 29350*	16	12 wks
24 Nov 73	**PLAYIN' FAVORITES** *United Artists UAG 29528*	42	2 wks
14 Jun 80	**CHAIN LIGHTNING** *EMI International INS 3025*	19	9 wks
27 Sep 80	● **THE VERY BEST OF DON MCLEAN**	4	12 wks
	United Artists UAG 30314		

Ralph McTELL

UK, male vocalist

18 Nov 72	**NOT TILL TOMORROW** *Reprise K 44210*	36	1 wk
2 Mar 74	**EASY** *Reprise K 54013*	31	4 wks
15 Feb 75	**STREETS** *Warner Bros. K 56105*	13	12 wks

David McWILLIAMS

UK, male vocalist

10 Jun 67	**DAVID MCWILLIAMS SINGS**	38	2 wks
	Major Minor MMLP 2		
4 Nov 67	**DAVID MCWILLIAMS VOL.2**	23	6 wks
	Major Minor MMLP 10		
9 Mar 68	**DAVID MCWILLIAMS VOL.3**	39	1 wk
	Major Minor MMLP 11		

MADNESS

UK, male vocal/instrumental group

3 Nov 79	● **ONE STEP BEYOND** *Stiff SEEZ 17*	2	78 wks
4 Oct 80	● **ABSOLUTELY** *Stiff SEEZ 29*	2	46 wks
10 Oct 81	● **MADNESS 7** *Stiff SEEZ 39*	5	29 wks
1 May 82	★ **COMPLETE MADNESS** *Stiff HIT-TV 1*	1	35 wks
13 Nov 82	● **THE RISE AND FALL** *Stiff SEEZ 46*	10†	7 wks

MAGAZINE

UK, male vocal/instrumental group

24 Jun 78	**REAL LIFE** *Virgin V 2100*	29	8 wks
14 Apr 79	**SECONDHAND DAYLIGHT** *Virgin V 2121*	38	8 wks
10 May 80	**CORRECT USE OF SOAP** *Virgin V 2156*	28	4 wks
13 Dec 80	**PLAY** *Virgin V 2184*	69	1 wk
27 Jun 81	**MAGIC, MURDER AND THE WEATHER**	39	3 wks
	Virgin V 2200		

MAGIC BAND — See *Captain BEEFHEART and his MAGIC BAND*

MAGNA CARTA

UK, male vocal/instrumental group

8 Aug 70	**SEASONS** *Vertigo 6360 003*	55	2 wks

MAGNUM

UK, male vocal/instrumental group

16 Sep 78	**KINGDOM OF MADNESS** *Jet JETLP 210*	58	1 wk
19 Apr 80	**MARAUDER** *Jet JETLP 230*	34	5 wks
6 Mar 82	**CHASE THE DRAGON** *Jet JETLP 235*	17	7 wks

MAHAVISHNU ORCHESTRA

UK/US, male vocal/instrumental group

31 Mar 73	**BIRDS OF FIRE** *CBS 65321*	20	5 wks
See also Carlos Santana and Mahavishnu John McLaughlin.			

Right **JOHN MAYALL'S BLUEBREAKERS** John McVie, Hughie Flint, Peter Green, John Mayall.

Far Left **DEAN MARTIN** Dino Crocetti: steel worker, gas station attendant, prize-fighter and singer. *Left* **JOHNNY MATHIS** The George Washington High School athlete who graduated to show business millionaire.

MANFRED MANN'S EARTH BAND 'The Roaring Silence' sounded the start of their chart success.

Tommy MAKEM — See *CLANCY BROTHERS and Tommy MAKEM*

MAMAS and The PAPAS

US, male/female vocal group

25 Jun 66	● THE MAMAS AND THE PAPAS	3	18 wks
	RCA Victor RD 7803		
28 Jan 67	CASS, JOHN, MICHELLE, DENNY	24	6 wks
	RCA Victor SF 7639		
24 Jun 67	● MAMAS AND THE PAPAS DELIVER	4	22 wks
	RCA Victor SF 7880		
26 Apr 69	● HITS OF GOLD *Stateside S 5007*	7	2 wks
18 Jun 77	● THE BEST OF THE MAMAS AND THE PAPAS	6	13 wks
	Arcade ADEP 30		

MAN

UK, male vocal/instrumental group

20 Oct 73	BACK INTO THE FUTURE	23	3 wks
	United Artists UAD 60053/4		
25 May 74	RHINOS WINOS AND LUNATICS	24	4 wks
	United Artists UAG 29631		
11 Oct 75	MAXIMUM DARKNESS	25	2 wks
	United Artists UAG 29872		
17 Apr 76	WELSH CONNECTION *MCA MCF 2753*	40	2 wks

Henry MANCINI

US, orchestra/chorus

| 16 Oct 76 | HENRY MANCINI *Arcade ADEP 24* | 26 | 8 wks |

MANFRED MANN

UK, male vocal/instrumental group

19 Sep 64	● FIVE FACES OF MANFRED MANN	3	24 wks
	HMV CLP 1731		
23 Oct 65	● MANN MADE *HMV CLP 1911*	7	11 wks
17 Sep 66	MANN MADE HITS *HMV CLP 3559*	11	18 wks
29 Oct 66	AS IS *Fontana TL 5377*	22	4 wks
21 Jan 67	SOUL OF MANN *HMV CSD 3594*	40	1 wk
15 Sep 79	● SEMI-DETACHED SUBURBAN *EMI EMTV 19*	9	14 wks

MANHATTAN TRANSFER

US, male/female vocal group

12 Mar 77	COMING OUT *Atlantic K 50291*	12	20 wks
19 Mar 77	MANHATTAN TRANSFER *Atlantic K 50138*	49	7 wks
25 Feb 78	● PASTICHE *Atlantic K 50444*	10	34 wks
11 Nov 78	● LIVE *Atlantic K 50540*	4	17 wks
17 Nov 79	EXTENSIONS *Atlantic K 50674*	63	3 wks

MANHATTANS

US, male vocal group

| 14 Aug 76 | MANHATTANS *CBS 81513* | 37 | 3 wks |

Barry MANILOW

US, male vocalist

23 Sep 78	EVEN NOW *Arista SPART 1047*	12	28 wks
3 Mar 79	● MANILOW MAGIC *Arista ARTV 2*	3	151 wks
20 Oct 79	ONE VOICE *Arista SPART 1106*	18	7 wks
29 Nov 80	● BARRY *Arista DLART 2*	5	34 wks
25 Apr 81	GIFT SET *Arista BOX 1*	62	1 wk
3 Oct 81	● IF I SHOULD LOVE AGAIN *Arista BMAN 1*	5	26 wks
1 May 82	★ BARRY LIVE IN BRITAIN *Arista ARTV 4*	1	23 wks
27 Nov 82	● I WANNA DO IT WITH YOU *Arista BMAN 2*	7†	5 wks

Roberto MANN

UK, male orchestra leader

| 9 Dec 67 | GREAT WALTZES *Deram SML 1010* | 19 | 9 wks |

Shelley MANNE

US, male instrumentalist - drums

| 18 Jun 60 | MY FAIR LADY *Vogue LAC 12100* | 20 | 1 wk |

Manfred MANN'S EARTH BAND

UK, male vocal/instrumental group

18 Sep 76	● THE ROARING SILENCE *Bronze ILPS 9357*	10	9 wks
17 Jun 78	WATCH *Bronze BRON 507*	33	6 wks
24 Mar 79	ANGEL STATION *Bronze BRON 516*	30	8 wks

MANTOVANI

UK, orchestra

21 Feb 59	● CONTINENTAL ENCORES *Decca LK 4298*	4	12 wks
18 Feb 61	CONCERT SPECTACULAR *Decca LK 4377*	16	2 wks
16 Apr 66	● MANTOVANI MAGIC *Decca LK 7949*	3	15 wks
15 Oct 66	MR MUSIC - MANTOVANI *Decca LK 4809*	24	3 wks
14 Jan 67	● MANTOVANI'S GOLDEN HITS *Decca SKL 4818*	10	43 wks
30 Sep 67	HOLLYWOOD *Decca SKL 4887*	37	1 wk
14 Jun 69	● THE WORLD OF MANTOVANI *Decca SPA 1*	6	31 wks
4 Oct 69	● THE WORLD OF MANTOVANI VOL 2	4	19 wks
	Decca SPA 36		
16 May 70	MANTOVANI TODAY *Decca SKL 5003*	16	8 wks
26 Feb 72	TO LOVERS EVERYWHERE *Decca SKL 5112*	44	1 wk
3 Nov 79	● 20 GOLDEN GREATS *Warwick WW 5067*	9	13 wks

MANUEL and his MUSIC OF THE MOUNTAINS

UK, orchestra, leader Geoff Love

Date	Title *Label Number*	Position	
10 Sep 60	**MUSIC OF THE MOUNTAINS** *Columbia 33SX 1212*	17	1 wk
7 Aug 71	**THIS IS MANUEL** *Studio Two STWO 5*	18	19 wks
31 Jan 76	● **CARNIVAL** *Studio Two TWO 337*	3	18 wks

Phil MANZANERA

UK, male vocalist/instrumentalist - guitar

Date	Title *Label Number*	Position	
24 May 75	**DIAMOND HEAD** *Island ILPS 9315*	40	1 wk

MARC and the MAMBAS

UK, male/female vocal instrumental group

Date	Title *Label Number*	Position	
16 Oct 82	**UNTITLED** *Some Bizarre/Phonogram BZA 13*	42	4 wks

Yannis MARKOPOULOS

Greece, orchestra

Date	Title *Label Number*	Position	
26 Aug 78	**WHO PAYS THE FERRYMAN** *BBC REB 315*	22	8 wks

Bob MARLEY and The WAILERS

Jamaica, male vocal/instrumental group

Date	Title *Label Number*	Position	
4 Oct 75	**NATTY DREAD** *Island ILPS 9281*	43	5 wks
20 Dec 75	**LIVE** *Island ILPS 9376*	38	5 wks
8 May 76	**RASTAMAN VIBRATION** *Island ILPS 9383*	15	13 wks
11 Jun 77	● **EXODUS** *Island ILPS 9498*	8	56 wks
1 Apr 78	● **KAYA** *Island ILPS 9517*	4	24 wks
16 Dec 78	**BABYLON BY BUS** *Island ISLD 11*	40	11 wks
13 Oct 79	**SURVIVAL** *Island ILPS 9542*	20	6 wks
28 Jun 80	● **UPRISING** *Island ILPS 9596*	6	17 wks
25 Jul 81	**LIVE AT THE LYCEUM** *Island ILPS 9376*	68	6 wks

Bernie MARSDEN

UK, male vocalist/instrumentalist - guitar

Date	Title *Label Number*	Position	
5 Sep 81	**LOOK AT ME NOW** *Parlophone PCF 7217*	71	2 wks

Lena MARTELL

UK, female vocalist

Date	Title *Label Number*	Position	
25 May 74	**THAT WONDERFUL SOUND OF LENA MARTELL** *Pye SPL 18427*	35	2 wks
8 Jan 77	**THE BEST OF LENA MARTELL** *Pye NSPL 18506*	13	16 wks
27 May 78	**THE LENA MARTELL COLLECTION** *Ronco RTL 2028*	12	19 wks
20 Oct 79	● **LENA'S MUSIC ALBUM** *Pye N 123*	5	18 wks
19 Apr 80	● **BY REQUEST** *Ronco RTL 2046*	9	9 wks
29 Nov 80	**BEAUTIFUL SUNDAY** *Ronco RTL 2052*	23	7 wks

MARTHA and The MUFFINS

Canada, male/female vocal instrumental group

Date	Title *Label Number*	Position	
15 Mar 80	**METRO MUSIC** *DinDisc DID 1*	34	6 wks

Dean MARTIN

US, male vocalist

Date	Title *Label Number*	Position	
13 May 61	**THIS TIME I'M SWINGING** *Capitol T 1442*	18	1 wk
25 Feb 67	**AT EASE WITH DEAN** *Reprise RSLP 6322*	35	1 wk
4 Nov 67	**WELCOME TO MY WORLD** *Philips DBL 001*	39	1 wk
12 Oct 68	**GREATEST HITS VOL.1** *Reprise RSLP 6301*	40	1 wk
22 Feb 69	● **BEST OF DEAN MARTIN** *Capitol ST 21194*	9	1 wk
22 Feb 69	● **GENTLE ON MY MIND** *Reprise RSLP 6330*	9	8 wks
13 Nov 76	● **20 ORIGINAL DEAN MARTIN HITS** *Reprise K 54066*	7	11 wks

John MARTYN

UK, male vocalist/instrumentalist - guitar

Date	Title *Label Number*	Position	
4 Feb 78	**ONE WORLD** *Island ILPS 9492*	54	1 wk
1 Nov 80	**GRACE AND DANGER** *Island ILPS 9560*	54	2 wks
26 Sep 81	**GLORIOUS FOOL** *Geffen K 99178*	25	7 wks
4 Sep 82	**WELL KEPT SECRET** *WEA K 99255*	20	7 wks

Hank MARVIN

UK, male vocalist/instrumentalist - guitar

Date	Title *Label Number*	Position	
22 Nov 69	**HANK MARVIN** *Columbia SCX 6352*	14	2 wks
20 Mar 82	**WORDS AND MUSIC** *Polydor POLD 5054*	66	3 wks

See also Marvin, Welch and Farrar.

MARVIN, WELCH and FARRAR

UK, male instrumental group

3 Apr 71	**MARVIN, WELCH AND FARRAR** *Regal Zonophone SRZA 8502*	30	4 wks

See also Hank Marvin.

MARY — See *PETER, PAUL and MARY*

MASSED WELSH CHOIRS

UK, male voice choir

9 Aug 69	● **CYMANSA GANN** *BBC REC 53 M*	5	7 wks

MATCHBOX

UK, male vocal/instrumental group

2 Feb 80	**MATCHBOX** *Magnet MAG 5031*	44	5 wks
11 Oct 80	**MIDNITE DYNAMOS** *Magnet MAG 5036*	23	9 wks

Mireille MATHIEU

France, female vocalist

2 Mar 68	**MIREILLE MATHIEU** *Columbia SCX 6210*	39	1 wk

Johnny MATHIS

US, male vocalist

8 Nov 58	● **WARM** *Fontana TBA TFL 5015*	6	2 wks
24 Jan 59	● **SWING SOFTLY** *Fontana TBA TFL 5039*	10	1 wk
13 Feb 60	● **RIDE ON A RAINBOW** *Fontana TFL 5061*	10	2 wks
10 Dec 60	● **RHYTHMS AND BALLADS OF BROADWAY** *Fontana SET 101*	6	10 wks
17 Jun 61	**I'LL BUY YOU A STAR** *Fontana TFL 5143*	18	1 wk
16 May 70	**RAINDROPS KEEP FALLING ON MY HEAD** *CBS 63587*	23	10 wks
3 Apr 71	**LOVE STORY** *CBS 64334*	27	5 wks
9 Sep 72	**FIRST TIME EVER I SAW YOUR FACE** *CBS 64930*	40	3 wks
16 Dec 72	**MAKE IT EASY ON YOURSELF** *CBS 65161*	49	1 wk
8 Mar 75	**I'M COMING HOME** *CBS 65690*	18	11 wks
5 Apr 75	**THE HEART OF A WOMAN** *CBS 80533*	39	2 wks
26 Jul 75	**WHEN WILL I SEE YOU AGAIN** *CBS 80738*	13	10 wks
3 Jul 76	**I ONLY HAVE EYES FOR YOU** *CBS 81329*	14	12 wks
19 Feb 77	**GREATEST HITS VOL. IV** *CBS 86022*	31	5 wks
18 Jun 77	★ **THE JOHNNY MATHIS COLLECTION** *CBS 10003*	1	40 wks
17 Dec 77	**SWEET SURRENDER** *CBS 86036*	55	1 wk
29 Apr 78	● **YOU LIGHT UP MY LIFE** *CBS 86055*	3	19 wks
7 Apr 79	**THE BEST DAYS OF MY LIFE** *CBS 86080*	38	5 wks
3 Nov 79	**MATHIS MAGIC** *CBS 86103*	59	4 wks
8 Mar 80	★ **TEARS AND LAUGHTER** *CBS 10019*	1	15 wks
12 Jul 80	**ALL FOR YOU** *CBS 86115*	20	8 wks
19 Sep 81	● **CELEBRATION** *CBS 10028*	9	16 wks
15 May 82	**FRIENDS IN LOVE** *CBS 85652*	34	7 wks

See also Johnny Mathis and Deniece Williams.

Johnny MATHIS and Deniece WILLIAMS

US, male/female vocal duo

26 Aug 78	**THAT'S WHAT FRIENDS ARE FOR** *CBS 86068*	16	11 wks

See also Johnny Mathis, Deniece Williams.

MATTHEWS' SOUTHERN COMFORT

UK, male vocal/instrumental group

25 Jul 70	**SECOND SPRING** *Uni UNLS 112*	52	4 wks

John MAYALL

US, male vocalist

4 Mar 67	● **A HARD ROAD** *Decca SKL 4853*	10	19 wks
23 Sep 67	● **CRUSADE** *Decca SKL 4890*	8	14 wks
25 Nov 67	**BLUES ALONE** *Ace Of Clubs SCL 1243*	24	5 wks
16 Mar 68	**DIARY OF A BAND VOL.1** *Decca SKL 4918*	27	9 wks
16 Mar 68	**DIARY OF A BAND VOL.2** *Decca SKL 4919*	28	5 wks
20 Jul 68	● **BARE WIRES** *Decca SKL 4945*	3	17 wks
18 Jan 69	**BLUES FROM LAUREL CANYON** *Decca SKL 4972*	33	3 wks
23 Aug 69	**LOOKING BACK** *Decca SKL 5010*	14	7 wks
15 Nov 69	**TURNING POINT** *Polydor 583-571*	11	7 wks
11 Apr 70	● **EMPTY ROOMS** *Polydor 583-580*	9	8 wks
12 Dec 70	**U.S.A. UNION** *Polydor 2425-020*	50	1 wk
26 Jun 71	**BACK TO THE ROOTS** *Polydor 2657-005*	31	2 wks

A Hard Road *Credited to John Mayall and the Bluesbreakers.* Crusade *to John Mayall and his Bluesbreakers,* Diary Of A Band Vols 1 & 2 *to John Mayall's Bluesbreakers,* Bare Wire *to John Mayall Bluesbreakers.*

John MAYALL and Eric CLAPTON

UK, male instrumental duo

30 Jul 66	● **BLUES BREAKERS** *Decca LK 4804*	6	17 wks

See also John Mayall, Eric Clapton.

Curtis MAYFIELD

US, male vocalist

31 Mar 73	**SUPER FLY** *Buddah 2318 065*	26	2 wks

STEVE MILLER This is a "fun" caption-it-yourself picture.

Left **MANTOVANI** Annunzio Paolo Mantovani, famous for his cascading strings.

Spike MILLIGAN

UK, male comedian

25 Nov 61	**MILLIGAN PRESERVED** *Parlophone PMC 1152*	11	4 wks
18 Dec 76	**THE SNOW GOOSE** *RCA RS 1088*	49	1 wk

Second album featured credit - with the London Symphony Orchestra. See also Harry Secombe, Peter Sellers and Spike Milligan.

Mrs. MILLS

UK, female instrumentalist - piano

10 Dec 66	**COME TO MY PARTY** *Parlophone PMC 7010*	17	7 wks
28 Dec 68	**MRS. MILLS' PARTY PIECES** *Parlophone PCS 7066*	32	3 wks
13 Dec 69	**LET'S HAVE ANOTHER PARTY** *Parlophone PCS 7035*	23	2 wks
6 Nov 71	**I'M MIGHTY GLAD** *MFP 5225*	49	1 wk

MINDBENDERS

UK, male vocal/instrumental group

25 Jun 66	**THE MINDBENDERS** *Fontana TL 5324*	28	4 wks

See also Wayne Fontana and the Mindbenders.

Liza MINELLI

US, female vocalist

7 Apr 73	● **LIZA WITH A 'Z'** *CBS 65212*	9	15 wks
16 Jun 73	**THE SINGER** *CBS 65555*	45	1 wk

Joni MITCHELL

Canada, female vocalist

6 Jun 70	● **LADIES OF THE CANYON** *Reprise RSLP 6376*	8	25 wks
24 Jul 71	● **BLUE** *Reprise K 44128*	3	18 wks
16 Mar 74	**COURT AND SPARK** *Asylum SYLA 8756*	14	11 wks
1 Feb 75	**MILES OF AISLES** *Asylum SYSP 902*	34	4 wks
27 Dec 75	**THE HISSING OF SUMMER LAWNS** *Asylum SYLA 8763*	14	10 wks
11 Dec 76	**HEJIRA** *Asylum K 53063*	11	5 wks
21 Jan 78	**DON JUAN'S RECKLESS DAUGHTER** *Asylum K 63003*	20	7 wks
14 Jul 79	**MINGUS** *Asylum K 53091*	24	7 wks
4 Oct 80	**SHADOWS AND LIGHT** *Elektra K 62030*	63	3 wks
4 Dec 82	**WILD THINGS RUN FAST** *Geffen GEF 25102*	32†	4 wks

George MITCHELL MINSTRELS

UK, male/female vocal group

26 Nov 60	★ **THE BLACK AND WHITE MINSTREL SHOW** *HMV CLP 1399*	1	90 wks
21 Oct 61	★ **ANOTHER BLACK AND WHITE MINSTREL SHOW** *HMV CLP 1460*	1	64 wks
20 Oct 62	★ **ON STAGE WITH THE GEORGE MITCHELL MINSTRELS** *HMV CLP 1599*	1	26 wks
2 Nov 63	● **ON TOUR WITH THE GEORGE MITCHELL MINSTRELS** *HMV CLP 1667*	6	18 wks
12 Dec 64	● **SPOTLIGHT ON THE GEORGE MITCHELL MINSTRELS** *HMV CLP 1803*	6	7 wks
4 Dec 65	● **MAGIC OF THE MINSTRELS** *HMV CLP 1917*	9	7 wks
26 Nov 66	**HERE COME THE MINSTRELS** *HMV CLP 3579*	11	11 wks
16 Dec 67	**SHOWTIME** *HMV CSD 3642*	26	2 wks
14 Dec 68	**SING THE IRVING BERLIN SONGBOOK** *Columbia SCX 6267*	33	1 wk
19 Dec 70	**THE MAGIC OF CHRISTMAS** *Columbia SCX 6431*	32	4 wks

MODERN EON

UK, male vocal/instrumental group

13 Jun 81	**FICTION TALES** *Dindisc DID 11*	65	1 wk

MODERN LOVERS — See *Jonathan RICHMAN and the MODERN LOVERS*

Zoot MONEY and the BIG ROLL BAND

UK, male vocalist and male instrumental backing group

15 Oct 66	**ZOOT** *Columbia SX 6075*	23	3 wks

MONKEES

US/UK, male vocal/instrumental group

28 Jan 67	★ **THE MONKEES** *RCA Victor SF 7844*	1	36 wks
15 Apr 67	★ **MORE OF THE MONKEES** *RCA Victor SF 7868*	1	25 wks
8 Jul 67	● **HEADQUARTERS** *RCA Victor SF 7886*	2	19 wks
13 Jan 68	● **PISCES, AQUARIUS, CAPRICORN & JONES LTD.** *RCA Victor SF 7912*	5	11 wks
28 Nov 81	**THE MONKEES** *Arista DARTY 12*	99	1 wk

MONOCHROME SET

UK, male vocal/instrumental group

3 May 80	**STRANGE BOUTIQUE** *DinDisc DID 4*	62	4 wks

Date	Title Label Number	Position		Date	Title Label Number	Position	

Tony MONOPOLY

Australia, male vocalist

12 Jun 76	**TONY MONOPOLY** *BUK BULP 2000*	25	4 wks

Matt MONRO

UK, male vocalist

7 Aug 65	**I HAVE DREAMED** *Parlophone PMC 1250*	20	1 wk
17 Sep 66	**THIS IS THE LIFE** *Capitol T 2540*	25	2 wks
26 Aug 67	**INVITATION TO THE MOVIES** *Capitol ST 2730*	30	1 wk
15 Mar 80	●**HEARTBREAKERS** *EMI EMTV 23*	5	11 wks

MONTROSE

US, male vocal/instrumental group

15 Jun 74	**MONTROSE** *Warner Bros. K 46276*	43	1 wk

MONTY PYTHON'S FLYING CIRCUS

UK, male comedy group

30 Oct 71	**ANOTHER MONTY PYTHON RECORD** *Charisma CAS 1049*	26	3 wks
27 Jan 73	**MONTY PYTHON'S PREVIOUS ALBUM** *Charisma CAS 1063*	39	3 wks
23 Feb 74	**MATCHING TIE AND HANDKERCHIEF** *Charisma CAS 1080*	49	2 wks
27 Jul 74	**LIVE AT DRURY LANE** *Charisma CLASS 4*	19	8 wks
9 Aug 75	**MONTY PYTHON** *Charisma CAS 1003*	45	4 wks
24 Nov 79	**THE LIFE OF BRIAN** *Warner Bros. K 56751*	63	3 wks
18 Oct 80	**CONTRACTUAL OBLIGATION ALBUM** *Charisma CAS 1152*	13	8 wks

MOODY BLUES

UK, male vocal/instrumental group

27 Jan 68	**DAYS OF FUTURE PASSED** *Deram SML 707*	27	16 wks
3 Aug 68	●**IN SEARCH OF THE LOST CHORD** *Deram SML 711*	5	32 wks
3 May 69	★**ON THE THRESHOLD OF A DREAM** *Deram SML 1035*	1	73 wks
6 Dec 69	●**TO OUR CHILDREN'S CHILDREN'S CHILDREN** *Threshold THS 1*	2	44 wks
15 Aug 70	★**A QUESTION OF BALANCE** *Threshold THS 3*	1	19 wks
7 Aug 71	★**EVERY GOOD BOY DESERVES FAVOUR** *Threshold THS 5*	1	21 wks
2 Dec 72	●**SEVENTH SOJOURN** *Threshold THS 7*	5	18 wks
16 Nov 74	**THIS IS THE MOODY BLUES** *Threshold MB 1/2*	14	18 wks

24 Jun 78	●**OCTAVE** *Decca TXS 129*	6	18 wks
10 Nov 79	**OUT OF THIS WORLD** *K-Tel NE 1051*	15	10 wks
23 May 81	●**LONG DISTANCE VOYAGER** *Threshold TXS 139*	7	19 wks

Dudley MOORE

UK, male vocalist/instrumentalist - piano

4 Dec 65	**THE OTHER SIDE OF DUDLEY MOORE** *Decca LK 4732*	11	9 wks
11 Jun 66	**GENUINE DUD** *Decca LK 4788*	13	10 wks

Second album credited to the Dudley Moore Trio. See also Peter Cook and Dudley Moore.

Gary MOORE

UK, male instrumentalist - guitar

3 Feb 79	**BACK ON THE STREETS** *MCA MCE 2853*	70	1 wk
16 Oct 82	**CORRIDORS OF POWER** *Virgin V 2245*	30	6 wks

Patrick MORAZ

Switzerland, male instrumentalist - keyboards

10 Apr 76	**PATRICK MORAZ** *Charisma CDS 4002*	28	7 wks
23 Jul 77	**OUT IN THE SUN** *Charisma CDS 4007*	44	1 wk

Ennio MORRICONE

Italy, orchestra

2 May 81	**THIS IS...** *EMI THIS 33*	23	5 wks
9 May 81	**CHI MAI** *BBC REH 414*	29	6 wks

Van MORRISON

UK, male vocalist

18 Apr 70	**MOON DANCE** *Warner Bros. WS 1835*	32	2 wks
11 Aug 73	**HARD NOSE THE HIGHWAY** *Warner Bros. K 46242*	22	3 wks
16 Nov 74	**VEEDON FLEECE** *Warner Bros. K 56068*	41	1 wk
7 May 77	**A PERIOD OF TRANSITION** *Warner Bros. K 56322*	23	5 wks
21 Oct 78	**WAVELENGTH** *Warner Bros. K 56526*	27	6 wks
8 Sep 79	**INTO THE MYSTIC** *Vertigo 9120 852*	21	9 wks
20 Sep 80	**THE COMMON ONE** *Mercury 6302 021*	53	3 wks
27 Feb 82	**BEAUTIFUL VISION** *Mercury/Phonogram 6302 122*	31	14 wks

Above **MOTT THE HOOPLE** Originally a Herefordshire group Silence, they added vocalist Ian Hunter and re-named themselves after a Willard Mans novel.

Top Right **MARVIN WELCH & FARRAR** Having been enlisted by Hank & Bruce, John Farrar correctly anticipated the blistering British summers.

Right **VAN MORRISON** From Them to just him.

THE MONKEES Jones, Aquarius, Pisces and Capricorn.

MOODY BLUES On The Threshold of Past Days.

111

MORRISSEY MULLEN

UK, male vocal/instrumental duo

18 Jul 81	**BADNESS** *Beggars Banquet BEGA 27*	43	5 wks
3 Apr 82	**LIFE ON THE WIRE** *Beggars Banquet BEGA 33*	47	5 wks

MOTHERS OF INVENTION

US, male vocal/instrumental group

29 Jun 68	**WE'RE ONLY IN IT FOR THE MONEY** *Verve SVLP 9199*	32	5 wks
28 Mar 70	**BURNT WEENY SANDWICH** *Reprise RSLP 6370*	17	3 wks
3 Oct 70	**WEASELS RIPPED MY FLESH** *Reprise RSLP 2028*	28	4 wks

See also Frank Zappa.

MOTORHEAD

UK, male vocal/instrumental group

24 Sep 77	**MOTORHEAD** *Chiswick WIK 2*	43	5 wks
24 Mar 79	**OVERKILL** *Bronze BRON 515*	24	11 wks
8 Dec 79	**ON PARADE** *United Artists LBR 1004*	65	2 wks
8 Nov 80	● **ACE OF SPADES** *Bronze BRON 531*	4	16 wks
27 Jun 81	☆ **NO SLEEP TILL HAMMERSMITH** *Bronze BRON 535*	1	21 wks
17 Apr 82	● **IRONFIST** *Bronze BRNA 539*	6	9 wks

MOTORS

UK, male vocal/instrumental group

15 Oct 77	**THE MOTORS** *Virgin V 2089*	46	5 wks
3 Jun 78	**APPROVED BY THE MOTORS** *Virgin V 2101*	60	1 wk

MOTT THE HOOPLE

UK, male vocal/instrumental group

2 May 70	**MOTT THE HOOPLE** *Island ILPS 9108*	66	1 wk
17 Oct 70	**MAD SHADOWS** *Island ILPS 9119*	48	2 wks
17 Apr 71	**WILD LIFE** *Island ILPS 9144*	44	2 wks
23 Sep 72	**ALL THE YOUNG DUDES** *CBS 65184*	21	4 wks
11 Aug 73	● **MOTT** *CBS 69038*	7	15 wks
13 Apr 74	**THE HOOPLE** *CBS 69062*	11	5 wks
23 Nov 74	**LIVE** *CBS 69093*	32	2 wks
4 Oct 75	**DRIVE ON** *CBS 69154*	45	1 wk

MOUNTAIN

US/Canada, male vocal/instrumental group

5 Jun 71	**NANTUCKET SLEIGHRIDE** *Island ILPS 9148*	43	1 wk
8 Jul 72	**THE ROAD GOES ON** *Island ILPS 9199*	21	3 wks

Nana MOUSKOURI

Greece, female vocalist

7 Jun 69	● **OVER AND OVER** *Fontana S 5511*	10	105 wks
4 Apr 70	● **THE EXQUISITE NANA MOUSKOURI** *Fontana STL 5536*	10	25 wks
10 Oct 70	**RECITAL '70** *Fontana 6312 003*	68	1 wk
3 Apr 71	**TURN ON THE SUN** *Fontana 6312 008*	16	15 wks
29 Jul 72	**BRITISH CONCERT** *Fontana 6651 003*	29	11 wks
28 Apr 73	**SONGS FROM HER TV SERIES** *Fontana 6312 036*	29	11 wks
28 Sep 74	**SPOTLIGHT ON NANA MOUSKOURI** *Fontana 6641 197*	38	6 wks
10 Jul 76	● **PASSPORT** *Philips 9101 061*	3	16 wks

MOVE

UK, male vocal/instrumental group

13 Apr 68	**MOVE** *Regal Zonophone SLPZ 1002*	15	9 wks

MUD

UK, male vocal/instrumental group

28 Sep 74	● **MUD ROCK** *RAK SRAK 508*	8	35 wks
26 Jul 75	● **MUD ROCK VOL 2** *RAK SRAK 513*	6	12 wks
1 Nov 75	**MUD'S GREATEST HITS** *RAK SRAK 6755*	25	6 wks
27 Dec 75	**USE YOUR IMAGINATION** *Private Stock PVLP 1003*	33	5 wks

MUFFINS — See *MARTHA and the MUFFINS*

Gerry MULLIGAN and Ben WEBSTER

US, male instrumental duo - baritone and tenor sax

24 Sep 60	**GERRY MULLIGAN MEETS BEN WEBSTER** *HMV CLP 1373*	15	1 wk

MUNGO JERRY

UK, male vocal/instrumental group

8 Aug 70	**MUNGO JERRY** *Dawn DNLS 3008*	13	6 wks
10 Apr 71	**ELECTRONICALLY TESTED** *Dawn DNLS 3020*	14	8 wks

Date	Title Label Number	Position		Date	Title Label Number	Position

MUPPETS

US, puppets

| 11 Jun 77 | ★ THE MUPPET SHOW *Pye NSPH 19* | 1 | 35 wks |
| 25 Feb 78 | THE MUPPET SHOW VOL.2 *Pye NSPH 21* | 16 | 10 wks |

Anne MURRAY

Canada, female vocalist

| 3 Oct 81 | VERY BEST OF *Capitol EMTV 31* | 14 | 10 wks |

Pauline MURRAY and the INVISIBLE GIRLS

UK, female vocalist with male (sic) vocal/instrumental group

| 11 Oct 80 | PAULINE MURRAY AND THE INVISIBLE GIRLS *Elusive 2394 227* | 25 | 4 wks |

MUSIC OF THE MOUNTAINS — See *MANUEL and his MUSIC OF THE MOUNTAINS*

MUSICAL YOUTH

UK, male vocal/instrumental group

| 4 Dec 82 | THE YOUTH OF TODAY *MCA YOULP 1* | 24† | 4 wks |

N

Graham NASH

UK, male vocalist

| 26 Jun 71 | SONGS FOR BEGINNERS *Atlantic 2401-011* | 13 | 8 wks |

See also Crosby, Stills and Nash, and Crosby, Stills, Nash and Young, and Graham Nash and David Crosby.

Graham NASH and David CROSBY

UK/US, male vocal duo

| 13 May 72 | GRAHAM NASH AND DAVID CROSBY *Atlantic K 50011* | 13 | 5 wks |

See also Dave Crosby, and Crosby, Stills and Nash, and Crosby, Stills, Nash and Young, and Graham Nash.

Johnny NASH

US, male vocalist

| 5 Aug 72 | I CAN SEE CLEARLY NOW *CBS 64860* | 39 | 6 wks |
| 10 Dec 77 | JOHNNY NASH COLLECTION *Epic EPC 10008* | 18 | 11 wks |

NASH THE SLASH

Canada, male vocalist/multi-instrumentalist

| 21 Feb 81 | CHILDREN OF THE NIGHT *DinDisc DID 9* | 61 | 1 wk |

NATASHA

UK, female vocalist

| 9 Oct 82 | CAPTURED *Towerbell TOWLP 2* | 53 | 3 wks |

NATIONAL BRASS BAND

UK, orchestra

| 10 May 80 | GOLDEN MEMORIES *K-Tel ONE 1075* | 15 | 10 wks |

NAZARETH

UK, male vocal/instrumental group

26 May 73	RAZAMANAZ *Mooncrest CREST 1*	11	25 wks
24 Nov 73	● LOUD 'N' PROUD *Mooncrest CREST 4*	10	7 wks
18 May 74	RAMPANT *Mooncrest CREST 15*	13	3 wks
13 Dec 75	GREATEST HITS *Mountain TOPS 108*	54	1 wk
3 Feb 79	NO MEAN CITY *Mountain TOPS 123*	34	9 wks
28 Feb 81	THE FOOL CIRCLE *NEMS NEL 6019*	60	3 wks
3 Oct 81	NAZARETH LIVE *NEMS NELD 102*	78	3 wks

MOTORHEAD Hammersm
boarding house landlady's fro
doorstep view of Motorhead.

Above **THE NICE**   "Here comes the nice looking
so good"—Small Faces 1967. Keith Emerson,
Blinky Davison, Lee Jackson & David O'List.

JOHNY NASH
N.A.S.H.
at T.O.T.P.

114

Above **PINK FLOYD** The original line-up for their debut album 'Piper At The Gates Of Dawn' named by leader Syd Barrett (2nd left) after one of the chapters of 'Wind In The Willows''. Barrett left in April 1968 and was replaced by Dave Gilmour.

Right **ROY ORBISON** 3 hit albums in the 1st year on the charts for the Big O.

Left **MIKE OLDFIELD** He made his debut album in 1968 with his sister Sally as folk duo Sally-Angie but had to wait until 1973 for his first success.

Bill NELSON

UK, male vocalist/multi-instrumentalist

Date	Title *Label Number*	Position	
23 May 81	● **QUIT DREAMING AND GET ON THE BEAM** *Mercury 6359 055*	7	6 wks
3 Jul 82	**THE LOVE THAT WHIRLS (DIARY OF A THINKING HEART)** *Mercury/Phonogram WHIRL 3*	28	4 wks

See also Bill Nelson's Red Noise.

Bill NELSON'S RED NOISE

UK, male vocal/instrumental group

24 Feb 79	**SOUND ON SOUND** *Harvest SHSP 4095*	33	5 wks

See also Bill Nelson.

NEW MUSIK

UK, male vocal/instrumental group

17 May 80	**FROM A TO B** *GTO GTLP 041*	35	9 wks
14 Mar 81	**ANYWHERE** *GTO GTLP 044*	68	2 wks

NEW ORDER

UK, male vocal/instrumental group

28 Nov 81	**MOVEMENT** *Factory FACT 50*	30	10 wks

NEW SEEKERS

UK, male/female vocal instrumental group

5 Feb 72	**NEW COLOURS** *Polydor 2383 066*	40	4 wks
1 Apr 72	● **WE'D LIKE TO TEACH THE WORLD TO SING** *Polydor 2883 103*	2	25 wks
12 Aug 72	**NEVER ENDING SONG OF LOVE** *Polydor 2383 126*	35	4 wks
14 Oct 72	**CIRCLES** *Polydor 2442 102*	23	5 wks
21 Apr 73	**NOW** *Polydor 2383 195*	47	2 wks
30 Mar 74	**TOGETHER** *Polydor 2383 264*	12	9 wks

NEW WORLD THEATRE ORCHESTRA

UK, orchestra

24 Dec 60	**LET'S DANCE TO THE HITS OF THE 30'S AND 40'S** *Pye Golden Guinea GGL 0026*	20	1 wk

Bob NEWHART

US, male comedian

1 Oct 60	● **BUTTON-DOWN MIND OF BOB NEWHART** *Warner Bros. WM 4010*	2	37 wks

Anthony NEWLEY

UK, male vocalist

14 May 60	**LOVE IS A NOW AND THEN THING** *Decca LK 4343*	19	2 wks
8 Jul 61	● **TONY** *Decca LK 4406*	5	12 wks

Anthony NEWLEY, Peter SELLERS, Joan COLLINS

UK, male/female stage cast

28 Sep 63	● **FOOL BRITANNIA** *Ember CEL 902*	10	10 wks

Although this was a stage production featuring various artists, the above three were most prominently associated with it.

Olivia NEWTON-JOHN

UK, female vocalist

2 Mar 74	**MUSIC MAKES MY DAY** *Pye NSPL 28186*	37	3 wks
29 Jun 74	**LONG LIVE LOVE** *EMI EMC 3028*	40	2 wks
26 Apr 75	**HAVE YOU NEVER BEEN MELLOW** *EMI EMC 3069*	37	2 wks
29 May 76	**COME ON OVER** *EMI EMC 3124*	49	4 wks
27 Aug 77	**MAKING A GOOD THING BETTER** *EMI EMC 3192*	60	1 wk
6 Jan 79	**TOTALLY HOT** *EMI EMA 789*	30	14 wks
21 Jan 78	**GREATEST HITS** *EMI EMA 785*	19	9 wks
31 Oct 81	**PHYSICAL** *EMI EMC 3386*	11	22 wks
23 Oct 82	● **GREATEST HITS** *EMI EMTV 36*	9†	10 wks

NICE

UK, male instrumental group

13 Sep 69	● **NICE** *Immediate IMSP 026*	3	6 wks
27 Jun 70	● **FIVE BRIDGES** *Charisma CAS 1014*	2	21 wks
17 Apr 71	● **ELEGY** *Charisma CAS 1030*	5	11 wks

Stevie NICKS

US, female vocalist

8 Aug 81	**BELLA DONNA** *WEA K 99169*	11	15 wks

Date	Title *Label Number*	Position		Date	Title *Label Number*	Position	

NICOLE

Germany, female vocalist

2 Oct 82	**A LITTLE PEACE** *CBS 85011*	85	2 wks

NILSSON

US, male vocalist

29 Jan 72	**THE POINT** *RCA Victor SF 8166*	46	1 wk
5 Feb 72	● **NILSSON SCHMILSSON** *RCA Victor SF 8242*	4	22 wks
19 Aug 72	**SON OF SCHMILSSON** *RCA Victor SF 8297*	41	1 wk
28 Jul 73	**A LITTLE TOUCH OF SCHMILSSON IN THE NIGHT** *RCA Victor SF 8371*	20	19 wks

NINA and FREDERICK

Denmark, male/female vocal duo

13 Feb 60	● **NINA AND FREDERICK** *Pye NPT 19023*	9	2 wks
29 Apr 61	**NINA AND FREDERICK** *Columbia COL 1314*	11	4 wks

These two albums, although identically named, are different.

9 BELOW ZERO

UK, male vocal/instrumental group

14 Mar 81	**DON'T POINT YOUR FINGER** *A & M AMLH 68521*	56	6 wks
20 Mar 82	**THIRD DEGREE** *A&M AMLH 68537*	38	6 wks

999

UK, male vocal/instrumental group

25 Mar 78	**999** *United Artists UAG 30199*	53	1 wk

NOLANS

Ireland, female vocal group

20 Jul 78	● **20 GIANT HITS** *Target TGS 502*	3	12 wks
19 Jan 80	**NOLANS** *Epic EPC 83892*	15	13 wks
25 Oct 80	**MAKING WAVES** *Epic EPC 10023*	11	33 wks
27 Mar 82	● **PORTRAIT** *Epic EPC 10033*	7	10 wks
20 Nov 82	**ALTOGETHER** *Epic EPC 10037*	52	5 wks

First album credited to Nolan Sisters.

NORTH — See *HATFIELD and the NORTH*

NOT THE 9 O'CLOCK NEWS CAST

UK, male/female TV cast

8 Nov 80	● **NOT THE 9 O'CLOCK NEWS** *BBC REB 400*	5	23 wks
17 Oct 81	● **HEDGEHOG SANDWICH** *BBC REB 421*	5	24 wks
23 Oct 82	**THE MEMORY KINDA LINGERS** *BBC REF 453*	63	4 wks

NUCLEUS

UK, male instrumental group

11 Jul 70	**ELASTIC ROCK** *Vertigo 6360 006*	46	1 wk

Ted NUGENT

US, male vocal/instrumental group

4 Sep 76	**TED NUGENT** *Epic EPC 81268*	56	1 wk
30 Oct 76	**FREE FOR ALL** *Epic EPC 81397*	33	2 wks
2 Jul 77	**CAT SCRATCH FEVER** *Epic EPC 82010*	28	5 wks
11 Mar 78	**DOUBLE LIVE GONZO** *Epic EPC 88282*	47	2 wks
14 Jun 80	**SCREAM DREAM** *Epic EPC 86111*	37	3 wks
25 Apr 81	**IN 10 CITIES** *Epic EPC 84917*	75	1 wk

Gary NUMAN

UK, male vocalist

22 Sep 79	☆ **THE PLEASURE PRINCIPLE** *Beggars Banquet BEGA 10*	1	21 wks
13 Sep 80	☆ **TELEKON** *Beggars Banquet BEGA 19*	1	11 wks
2 May 81	● **LIVING ORNAMENTS 1979-1980** *Beggars Banquet BOX 1*	2	4 wks
2 May 81	**LIVING ORNAMENTS 1979** *Beggars Banquet BEGA 24*	47	3 wks
2 May 81	**LIVING ORNAMENTS 1980** *Beggars Banquet BEGA 25*	39	3 wks
12 Sep 81	● **DANCE** *Beggars Banquet BEGA 28*	3	8 wks
18 Sep 82	● **I, ASSASSIN** *Beggars Banquet BEGA 40*	8	6 wks
27 Nov 82	**NEW MAN NUMAN - THE BEST OF GARY NUMAN** *TV Records TVA 7*	45†	5 wks

Living Ornaments 1979-1980 *is a boxed set of* Living Ornaments 1979 *and* Living Ornaments 1980. *See also* Tubeway Army.

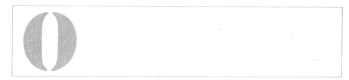

OATES — See *Daryl HALL and John OATES*

Date	Title *Label Number*	Position	

Des O'CONNOR

UK, male vocalist

Date	Title *Label Number*	Position	
7 Dec 68	● I PRETEND *Columbia SCX 6295*	8	10 wks
5 Dec 70	WITH LOVE *Columbia SCX 6417*	40	4 wks
2 Dec 72	SING A FAVOURITE SONG *Pye NSPL 18390*	25	6 wks
2 Feb 80	JUST FOR YOU *Warwick WW 5071*	17	7 wks

Hazel O'CONNOR

UK, female vocalist

9 Aug 80	● BREAKING GLASS (film soundtrack) *A & M AMLH 64820*	5	37 wks
12 Sep 81	COVER PLUS *Albion ALB 108*	32	7 wks

ODYSSEY

US, male/female vocal group

16 Aug 80	HANG TOGETHER *RCA PL 13526*	38	3 wks
4 Jul 81	I'VE GOT THE MELODY *RCA RCALP 5028*	29	7 wks
3 Jul 82	HAPPY TOGETHER *RCA RCALP 6036*	21	9 wks
20 Nov 82	THE MAGIC TOUCH OF ODYSSEY *Telstar STAR 2223*	69	5 wks

Esther and Abi OFARIM

Israel, male/female vocal duo

24 Feb 68	● 2 IN 3 *Philips SBL 7825*	6	20 wks
12 Jul 69	OFARIM CONCERT - LIVE '69 *Philips XL 4*	29	4 wks

Mary O'HARA

UK, female vocalist/instrumentalist - harp

8 Apr 78	MARY O'HARA AT THE ROYAL FESTIVAL HALL *Chrysalis CHR 1159*	37	3 wks
1 Dec 79	TRANQUILLITY *Warwick WW 5072*	12	9 wks

Mike OLDFIELD

UK, male multi-instrumentalist/vocalist

14 Jul 73	★ TUBULAR BELLS *Virgin V 2001*	1	247 wks
14 Sep 74	★ HERGEST RIDGE *Virgin V 2013*	1	17 wks
8 Feb 75	THE ORCHESTRAL TUBULAR BELLS (WITH THE ROYAL PHILHARMONIC ORCHESTRA) *Virgin V 2026*	17	7 wks
15 Nov 75	● OMMADAWN *Virgin V 2043*	4	23 wks
20 Nov 76	BOXED *Virgin V BOX 1*	22	13 wks
9 Dec 78	INCANTATIONS *Virgin VDT 101*	14	17 wks
11 Aug 79	EXPOSED *Virgin VD 2511*	16	9 wks

8 Dec 79	PLATINUM *Virgin V 2141*	24	9 wks
8 Nov 80	QE 2 *Virgin V 2181*	27	8 wks
27 Mar 82	● FIVE MILES OUT *Virgin V 2222*	7	27 wks

101 STRINGS

Germany, orchestra

26 Sep 59	● GYPSY CAMPFIRES *Pye GGL 0009*	9	7 wks
26 Mar 60	SOUL OF SPAIN *Pye GGL 0017*	17	1 wk
16 Apr 60	● GRAND CANYON SUITE *Pye GGL 0048*	10	1 wk
27 Aug 60	★ DOWN DRURY LANE TO MEMORY LANE *Pye GGL 0061*	1	21 wks

ONLY ONES

UK, male vocal/instrumental group

3 Jun 78	THE ONLY ONES *CBS 82830*	56	1 wk
31 Mar 79	EVEN SERPENTS SHINE *CBS 83451*	42	2 wks
3 May 80	BABY'S GOT A GUN *CBS 84089*	37	5 wks

Yoko ONO

Japan, female vocalist

20 Jun 81	SEASON OF GLASS *Geffen K 99164*	47	2 wks

See also John Lennon.

ORANGE JUICE

UK, male vocal/instrumental group

6 Mar 82	YOU CAN'T HIDE YOUR LOVE FOREVER *Polydor POLS 1057*	21	6 wks
20 Nov 82	RIP IT UP *Holden Caulfield Universal/Polydor POLS 1076*	39	2 wks

Roy ORBISON

US, male vocalist

8 Jun 63	LONELY AND BLUE *London HAU 2342*	15	8 wks
29 Jun 63	CRYING *London HAU 2437*	17	3 wks
30 Nov 63	● IN DREAMS *London HAU 8108*	6	57 wks
25 Jul 64	EXCITING SOUNDS OF ROY ORBISON *Ember NR 5013*	17	2 wks
5 Dec 64	● OH PRETTY WOMAN *London HAU 8207*	4	16 wks
25 Sep 65	● THERE IS ONLY ONE ROY ORBISON *London HAU 8252*	10	12 wks
26 Feb 66	THE ORBISON WAY *London HAU 8279*	11	10 wks
24 Sep 66	THE CLASSIC ROY ORBISON *London HAU 8297*	12	8 wks
22 Jul 67	ORBISONGS *Monument SMO 5004*	40	1 wk
30 Sep 67	ROY ORBISON'S GREATEST HITS *Monument SMO 5007*	40	1 wk

Date	Title *Label Number*	Position		
27 Jan 73	**ALL-TIME GREATEST HITS** *Monument MNT 67290*	39	3 wks
29 Nov 75	★ **THE BEST OF ROY ORBISON** *Arcade ADEP 19*	1	20 wks
18 Jul 81	**GOLDEN DAYS** *CBS 10026*	63	1 wk

ORCHESTRAL MANOEUVRES IN THE DARK

UK, male vocal/instrumental duo

1 Mar 80	**ORCHESTRAL MANOEUVRES IN THE DARK** *DinDisc DIND 2*	27	29 wks
1 Nov 80	● **ORGANISATION** *DinDisc DID 6*	6	25 wks
14 Nov 81	● **ARCHITECTURE AND MORALITY** *DinDisc DID 12*	3	39 wks

Cyril ORNANDEL/LONDON SYMPHONY ORCHESTRA

UK, conductor and orchestra

16 Dec 72	● **THE STRAUSS FAMILY** *Polydor 2659 014*	2	21 wks

See also London Symphony Orchestra.

Ozzy OSBOURNE

UK, male vocalist

7 Nov 81	**DIARY OF A MADMAN** *Jet JETLP 237*	14	12 wks
27 Nov 82	**TALK OF THE DEVIL** *Jet JETDP 401*	21†	5 wks

See also Ozzy Osbourne's Blizzard Of Oz.

Ozzy OSBOURNE'S BLIZZARD OF OZ

UK/US, male vocal/instrumental group

20 Sep 80	● **OZZY OSBOURNE'S BLIZZARD OF OZ** *Jet JETLP 234*	7	8 wks

See also Ozzy Osbourne.

OSIBISA

Ghana/Nigeria, male vocal/instrumental group

22 May 71	**OSIBISA** *MCA MDKS 8001*	11	10 wks
5 Feb 72	**WOYAYA** *MCA MDKS 8005*	11	7 wks

Donny OSMOND

US, male vocalist

23 Sep 72	● **PORTRAIT OF DONNY** *MGM 2315 108*	5	43 wks
16 Dec 72	● **TOO YOUNG** *MGM 2315 113*	7	24 wks
26 May 73	● **ALONE TOGETHER** *MGM 2315 210*	6	19 wks
15 Dec 73	● **A TIME FOR US** *MGM 2315 273*	4	13 wks
8 Feb 75	**DONNY** *MGM 2315 314*	16	4 wks
2 Oct 76	**DISCOTRAIN** *Polydor 2391 226*	59	1 wk

See also Osmonds, Donny and Marie Osmond.

Donny and Marie OSMOND

US, male/female duo

2 Nov 74	**I'M LEAVING IT ALL UP TO YOU** *MGM 2315 307*	13	15 wks
26 Jul 75	**MAKE THE WORLD GO AWAY** *MGM 2315 343*	30	3 wks
5 Jun 76	**DEEP PURPLE** *Polydor 2391 220*	48	1 wk

See also Osmonds, Donny Osmond, Marie Osmond.

Little Jimmy OSMOND

US, male vocalist

17 Feb 73	**KILLER JOE** *MGM 2315 157*	20	12 wks

See also Osmonds.

Marie OSMOND

UK, female vocalist

9 Feb 74	**PAPER ROSES** *MGM 2315 262*	46	1 wk

See also Donny and Marie Osmond.

OSMONDS

US, male vocal/instrumental group

18 Nov 72	**OSMONDS LIVE** *MGM 2315 117*	13	22 wks
16 Dec 72	● **CRAZY HORSES** *MGM 2315 123*	9	19 wks
25 Aug 73	● **THE PLAN** *MGM 2315 251*	6	25 wks
17 Aug 74	● **OUR BEST TO YOU** *MGM 2315 300*	5	20 wks
7 Dec 74	**LOVE ME FOR A REASON** *MGM 2315 312*	13	9 wks
14 Jun 75	**I'M STILL GONNA NEED YOU** *MGM 2315 342*	19	7 wks
10 Jan 76	**AROUND THE WORLD - LIVE IN CONCERT** *MGM 2659 044*	41	1 wk

See also Donny Osmond, Little Jimmy Osmond, Donny and Marie Osmond.

Gilbert O'SULLIVAN

UK, male vocalist

25 Sep 71	**HIMSELF** *MAM 501*	15	82 wks
18 Nov 72	★**BACK TO FRONT** *MAM 502*	1	64 wks
6 Oct 73	●**I'M A WRITER NOT A FIGHTER** *MAMS 505*	2	25 wks
26 Oct 74	●**STRANGER IN MY OWN BACK YARD** *MAM MAMS 506*	9	8 wks
18 Dec 76	**GREATEST HITS** *MAM MAMA 2003*	13	11 wks
12 Sep 81	**20 GOLDEN GREATS** *K-Tel NE 1133*	98	1 wk

John OTWAY and Wild Willy BARRETT

UK, male vocal/instrumental duo

1 Jul 78	**DEEP AND MEANINGLESS** *Polydor 2383 501*	44	1 wk

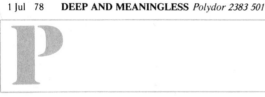

PACEMAKERS — See *GERRY and the PACEMAKERS*

Jimmy PAGE

UK, male vocalist/instrumentalist - guitar

27 Feb 82	**DEATHWISH II** *Swansong SSK 59415*	40	4 wks

Elaine PAIGE

UK, female vocalist

1 May 82	**ELAINE PAIGE** *WEA K 58385*	56	6 wks

Robert PALMER

UK, male vocalist

6 Nov 76	**SOME PEOPLE CAN DO WHAT THEY LIKE** *Island ILPS 9420*	46	1 wk
14 Jul 79	**SECRETS** *Island ILPS 9544*	54	4 wks
6 Sep 80	**CLUES** *Island ILPS 9595*	31	8 wks
3 Apr 82	**MAYBE IT'S LIVE** *Island ILPS 9665*	32	6 wks

See also Emerson, Lake and Palmer.

PAPAS — See *MAMAS and the PAPAS*

Graham PARKER and the RUMOUR

UK, male vocal/instrumental group

27 Nov 76	**HEAT TREATMENT** *Vertigo 6360 137*	52	2 wks
12 Nov 77	**STICK TO ME** *Vertigo 9102 017*	19	4 wks
27 May 78	**PARKERILLA** *Vertigo 6641 797*	14	5 wks
7 Apr 79	**SQUEEZING OUT SPARKS** *Vertigo 9102 030*	18	8 wks
7 Jun 80	**THE UP ESCALATOR** *Stiff SEEZ 23*	11	10 wks
27 Mar 82	**ANOTHER GREY AREA** *RCA RCALP 6029*	40	6 wks

Another Grey Area credited to Graham Parker.

Alan PARSONS PROJECT

UK, male vocal/instrumental group

28 Aug 76	**TALES OF MYSTERY AND IMAGINATION** *Charisma CDS 4003*	56	1 wk
13 Aug 77	**I ROBOT** *Arista SPARTY 1016*	30	1 wk
10 Jun 78	**PYRAMID** *Arista SPART 1054*	49	4 wks
29 Sep 79	**EVE** *Arista SPARTY 1100*	74	1 wk
15 Nov 80	**THE TURN OF A FRIENDLY CARD** *Arista DLART 1*	38	4 wks
29 May 82	**EYE IN THE SKY** *Arista 204 6666*	28	11 wks

Dolly PARTON

US, female vocalist

25 Nov 78	**DOLLY PARTON** *Lotus WH 5006*	24	6 wks
6 Jan 79	**BOTH SIDES** *Lotus WH 5006*	45	6 wks

PARTRIDGE FAMILY

US, male/female vocal group

8 Jan 72	**UP TO DATE** *Bell SBLL 143*	46	2 wks
22 Apr 72	**THE PARTRIDGE FAMILY SOUND MAGAZINE** *Bell BELLS 206*	14	7 wks
30 Sep 72	**SHOPPING BAG** *Bell BELLS 212*	28	3 wks
9 Dec 72	**CHRISTMAS CARD** *Bell BELLS 214*	45	1 wk

PASSIONS

UK, male/female vocal instrumental group

3 Oct 81	**THIRTY THOUSAND FEET OVER CHINA** *Polydor POLS 1041*	92	1 wk

PAUL — See *PETER, PAUL and MARY*

Luciano PAVAROTTI

Italy, male vocalist

15 May 82	**PAVAROTTI'S GREATEST HITS** *Decca D 2362*	95	1 wk

Tom PAXTON

US, male vocalist

13 Jun 70	**NO.6** *Elektra 2469-003*	23	5 wks
3 Apr 71	**THE COMPLEAT TOM PAXTON** *Elektra EKD 2003*	18	4 wks
1 Jul 72	**PEACE WILL COME** *Reprise K 44182*	47	1 wk

PEDDLERS

UK, male vocal/instrumental group

16 Mar 68	**FREE WHEELERS** *CBS SBPG 63183*	27	13 wks
7 Feb 70	**BIRTHDAY** *CBS 63682*	16	3 wks

Kevin PEEK

UK, male instrumentalist - guitar

21 Mar 81	**AWAKENING** *Ariola ARL 5065*	52	2 wks

PENETRATION

UK, male/female vocal instrumental group

28 Oct 78	**MOVING TARGETS** *Virgin V 2109*	22	4 wks
6 Oct 79	**COMING UP FOR AIR** *Virgin V 2131*	36	4 wks

PENTANGLE

UK, male/female vocal instrumental group

15 Jun 68	**THE PENTANGLE** *Transatlantic TRA 162*	21	9 wks
1 Nov 69	● **BASKET OF LIGHT** *Transatlantic TRA 205*	5	28 wks
12 Dec 70	**CRUEL SISTER** *Transatlantic TRA 228*	51	2 wks

Carl PERKINS

US, male vocalist

15 Apr 78	**OL' BLUE SUEDES IS BACK** *Jet UATV 30146*	38	3 wks

PESTALOZZI CHILDREN'S CHOIR

UK, male/female vocal group

26 Dec 81	**SONGS OF JOY** *K-Tel NE 1140*	65	2 wks

PETER and GORDON

UK, male vocal duo

20 Jun 64	**PETER AND GORDON** *Columbia 33SX 1630*	18	1 wk

PETER, PAUL and MARY

US, male/female vocal/instrumental group

4 Jan 64	**PETER PAUL & MARY** *Warner Bros. WM 4064*	18	1 wk
21 Mar 64	**IN THE WIND** *Warner Bros. WM 8142*	11	19 wks
13 Feb 65	**IN CONCERT VOL.1** *Warner Bros. WM 8158*	20	2 wks
5 Sep 70	**TEN YEARS TOGETHER** *Warner Bros. WS 2552*	60	4 wks

PETERS and LEE

UK, male/female vocal duo

30 Jun 73	★ **WE CAN MAKE IT** *Philips 6308 165*	1	55 wks
22 Dec 73	● **BY YOUR SIDE** *Philips 6308 192*	9	48 wks
21 Sep 74	● **RAINBOW** *Philips 6308 208*	6	27 wks
4 Oct 75	● **FAVOURITES** *Philips 9109 205*	2	32 wks
18 Dec 76	**INVITATION** *Philips 9101 027*	44	4 wks

Tom PETTY and the HEARTBREAKERS

US, male vocal/instrumental group

4 Jun 77	**TOM PETTY AND THE HEARTBREAKERS** *Shelter ISA 5014*	24	12 wks
1 Jul 78	**YOU'RE GONNA GET IT** *Island ISA 5017*	34	5 wks
17 Nov 79	**DAMN THE TORPEDOES** *MCA MCF 3044*	57	4 wks
23 May 81	**HARD PROMISES** *MCA/Backstreet MCF 3098*	32	5 wks
20 Nov 82	**LONG AFTER DARK** *MCA MCF 3155*	45	4 wks

PhD

UK, male vocal/instrumental group

1 May 82	**PHD** *WEA K 99150*	33	8 wks

Arlene PHILIPS

UK, female vocalist - exercise record

28 Aug 82	**KEEP IN SHAPE SYSTEM** *Ferroway SUP 01*	41	10 wks

Above **PROCOL HAREM** Their 'Salty Dog' album was a parody of the Players cigarette packet. *Top Left* **ELVIS PRESLEY** Elvis in 'King Creole'.

Left **PRETENDERS** This their first album simply titled Pretenders made No. 1 and registered 35 weeks on the chart.

Below **PRETTY THINGS** Formed in 1963 at Sidcup Art College (left to right); Dick Taylor (original bass player with the Rolling Stones) John Stax, Phil May, Skip Alan (who replaced Viv Prince late in 1965) and Brian Pendleton.

Above **POLICE** "Ello Ello Ello off to Reggatta de Henley then are we?"

Left **GARY PUCKETT AND THE UNION GAP** Originally The Outcasts from San Diego they kept together as the Union Gap until 1971.

PHOTOS

UK, male/female vocal/instrumental group

21 Jun 80	● THE PHOTOS *CBS PHOTO 5*	4	9 wks

PIGBAG

UK, male instrumental group

13 Mar 82	DR HECKLE AND MR JIVE *Y Y 17*	18	14 wks

PILOT

UK, male vocal/instrumental group

31 May 75	SECOND FLIGHT *EMI EMC 3075*	48	1 wk

PINK FAIRIES

UK, male vocal/instrumental group

29 Jul 72	WHAT A BUNCH OF SWEETIES *Polydor 2383 132*	48	1 wk

PINK FLOYD

UK, male vocal/instrumental group

19 Aug 67	● PIPER AT THE GATES OF DAWN *Columbia SCX 6157*	6	14 wks
13 Jul 68	● SAUCERFUL OF SECRETS *Columbia SCX 6258*	9	11 wks
28 Jun 69	● MORE (FILM SOUNDTRACK) *Columbia SCX 6346*	9	5 wks
15 Nov 69	● UMMAGUMMA *Harvest SHDW 1/2*	5	21 wks
24 Oct 70	★ ATOM HEART MOTHER *Harvest SHVL 781*	1	23 wks
7 Aug 71	RELICS *Starline SRS 5071*	32	6 wks
20 Nov 71	● MEDDLE *Harvest SHVL 795*	3	82 wks
17 Jun 72	● OBSCURED BY CLOUDS (FILM SOUNDTRACK) *Harvest SHSP 4020*	6	14 wks
31 Mar 73	● DARK SIDE OF THE MOON *Harvest SHVL 804*	2	292 wks
19 Jan 74	A NICE PAIR (DOUBLE RE-ISSUE) *Harvest SHDW 403*	21	20 wks
27 Sep 75	★ WISH YOU WERE HERE *Harvest SHVL 814*	1	83 wks
19 Feb 77	● ANIMALS *Harvest SHVL 815*	2	33 wks
8 Dec 79	● THE WALL *Harvest SHDW 411*	3	46 wks
5 Dec 81	A COLLECTION OF GREAT DANCE SONGS *Harvest SHVL 822*	37	10 wks

A Nice Pair *is a double re-issue of the first two albums.*

PIPS — See *Gladys KNIGHT and the PIPS*

PIRANHAS

UK, male vocal/instrumental group

20 Sep 80	PIRANHAS *Sire SRK 6098*	69	3 wks

PIRATES

UK, male vocal/instrumental group

19 Nov 77	OUT OF THEIR SKULLS *Warner Bros. K 56411*	57	3 wks

Gene PITNEY

US, male vocalist

11 Apr 64	● BLUE GENE *United Artists ULP 1061*	7	11 wks
6 Feb 65	GENE PITNEY'S BIG 16 *Stateside SL 10118*	12	6 wks
20 Mar 65	I'M GONNA BE STRONG *Stateside SL 10120*	15	2 wks
20 Nov 65	LOOKIN' THRU THE EYES OF LOVE *Stateside SL 10148*	15	5 wks
17 Sep 66	NOBODY NEEDS YOUR LOVE *Stateside SL 10183*	13	17 wks
4 Mar 67	YOUNG WARM AND WONDERFUL *Stateside SSL 10194*	39	1 wk
22 Apr 67	GENE PITNEY'S BIG SIXTEEN *Stateside SSL 10199*	40	1 wk
20 Sep 69	● BEST OF GENE PITNEY *Stateside SSL 10286*	8	9 wks
2 Oct 76	● HIS 20 GREATEST HITS *Arcade ADEP 22*	6	14 wks

Robert PLANT

UK, male vocalist

10 Jul 82	● PICTURES AT ELEVEN *Swansong SSK 59418*	2	15 wks

PLASMATICS

UK, female/male vocal/instrumental group

11 Oct 80	NEW HOPE FOR THE WRETCHED *Stiff SEEZ 24*	55	3 wks

PLATTERS

US, male/female vocal group

8 Apr 78	● 20 CLASSIC HITS *Mercury 9100 049*	8	13 wks

PLAYERS ASSOCIATION

US, male/female vocal instrumental group

17 Mar 79	TURN THE MUSIC UP *Vanguard VSD 79421*	54	4 wks

Date	Title Label Number	Position		Date	Title Label Number	Position	

POINTER SISTERS

US, female vocal group

| 29 Aug 81 | **BLACK AND WHITE** *Planet K 52300* | 21 | 13 wks |

POLECATS

UK, male vocal/instrumental group

| 4 Jul 81 | **POLECATS** *Vertigo 6359 057* | 28 | 2 wks |

POLICE

UK, male vocal/instrumental group

21 Apr 79	● **OUTLANDOS D'AMOUR** *A & M AMLH 68502*	6	96 wks
13 Oct 79	★ **REGGATTA DE BLANC** *A & M AMLH 64792*	1	74 wks
11 Oct 80	★ **ZENYATTA MONDATTA** *A & M AMLH 64831*	1	31 wks
10 Oct 81	★ **GHOST IN THE MACHINE** *A & M AMLK 63730*	1	27 wks

Iggy POP

UK, male vocalist

9 Apr 77	**THE IDIOT** *RCA Victor PL 12275*	30	3 wks
4 Jun 77	**RAW POWER** *Embassy 31464*	44	2 wks
1 Oct 77	**LUST FOR LIFE** *RCA PL 12488*	28	5 wks
19 May 79	**NEW VALUES** *Arista SPART 1092*	60	4 wks
16 Feb 80	**SOLDIER** *Arista SPART 1117*	62	2 wks

Raw Power *credited to Iggy and the Stooges*

Sandy POSEY

US, female vocalist

| 11 Mar 67 | **BORN A WOMAN** *MGM MGMCS 8035* | 39 | 1 wk |

Frank POURCEL

France, male vocalist

| 20 Nov 71 | ● **THIS IS POURCEL** *Studio Two STWO 7* | 8 | 7 wks |

Cozy POWELL

UK, male instrumentalist - drums

| 26 Jan 80 | ● **OVER THE TOP** *Ariola ARL 5038* | 4 | 11 wks |
| 19 Sep 81 | **TILT** *Polydor POLD 5047* | 58 | 4 wks |

PRAYING MANTIS

UK, male vocal/instrumental group

| 11 Apr 81 | **TIME TELLS NO LIES** *Arista SPART 1153* | 60 | 2 wks |

Elvis PRESLEY

US, male vocalist

8 Nov 58	● **ELVIS' GOLDEN RECORDS** *RCA RB 16069*	3	44 wks
8 Nov 58	● **KING CREOLE (FILM SOUNDTRACK)** *RCA RD 27086*	4	14 wks
4 Apr 59	● **ELVIS (ROCK 'N' ROLL NO.1)** *HMV CLP 1093*	4	9 wks
8 Aug 59	● **A DATE WITH ELVIS** *RCA RD 27128*	4	15 wks
18 Jun 60	★ **ELVIS IS BACK** *RCA RD 27171*	1	27 wks
18 Jun 60	● **ELVIS' GOLDEN RECORDS VOL.2** *RCA RD 27159*	4	20 wks
10 Dec 60	★ **G-I BLUES (FILM SOUNDTRACK)** *RCA RD 27192*	1	55 wks
20 May 61	● **HIS HAND IN MINE** *RCA RD 27211*	3	25 wks
4 Nov 61	● **SOMETHING FOR EVERYBODY** *RCA RD 27224*	2	18 wks
9 Dec 61	★ **BLUE HAWAII (FILM SOUNDTRACK)** *RCA RD 27238*	1	65 wks
7 Jul 62	★ **POT LUCK** *RCA RD 27265*	1	25 wks
8 Dec 62	● **ROCK 'N' ROLL NO.2** *RCA RD 7528*	3	17 wks
26 Jan 63	● **GIRLS! GIRLS! GIRLS! (FILM SOUNDTRACK)** *RCA RD 7534*	2	21 wks
11 May 63	● **IT HAPPENDED AT THE WORLD'S FAIR (FILM SOUNDTRACK)** *RCA RD 7565*	4	21 wks
28 Dec 63	● **FUN IN ACAPULCO (FILM SOUNDTRACK)** *RCA RD 7609*	9	14 wks
11 Apr 64	● **ELVIS' GOLDEN RECORDS VOL.3** *RCA RD 7630*	6	13 wks
4 Jul 64	● **KISSIN' COUSINS (FILM SOUNDTRACK)** *RCA RD 7645*	5	17 wks
9 Jan 65	**ROUSTABOUT (FILM SOUNDTRACK)** *RCA RD 7678*	12	4 wks
1 May 65	● **GIRL HAPPY** *RCA RD 7714*	8	18 wks
25 Sep 65	**FLAMING STAR AND SUMMER KISSES** *RCA RD 7723*	11	4 wks
4 Dec 65	● **ELVIS FOR EVERYBODY** *RCA RD 7782*	8	8 wks
15 Jan 66	**HAREM HOLIDAY** *RCA RD 7767*	11	5 wks
30 Apr 66	**FRANKIE AND JOHNNY (FILM SOUNDTRACK)** *RCA RD 7793*	11	5 wks
6 Aug 66	● **PARADISE HAWAIIAN STYLE (FILM SOUNDTRACK)** *RCA Victor RD 7810*	7	9 wks
26 Nov 66	**CALIFORNIA HOLIDAY** *RCA Victor RD 7820*	17	6 wks
8 Apr 67	**HOW GREAT THOU ART** *RCA Victor SF 7867*	11	14 wks
2 Sep 67	**DOUBLE TROUBLE (FILM SOUNDTRACK)** *RCA Victor SF 7892*	34	1 wk
20 Apr 68	**CLAMBAKE (FILM SOUNDTRACK)** *RCA Victor SD 7917*	39	1 wk
3 May 69	● **ELVIS - NBC TV SPECIAL** *RCA RD 8011*	2	26 wks
5 Jul 69	● **FLAMING STAR** *RCA International INTS 1012*	2	14 wks
23 Aug 69	★ **FROM ELVIS IN MEMPHIS** *RCA SF 8029*	1	13 wks
28 Feb 70	**PORTRAIT IN MUSIC (IMPORT)** *RCA 558*	36	1 wk
14 Mar 70	● **FROM MEMPHIS TO VEGAS - FROM VEGAS TO MEMPHIS** *RCA SF 8080/1*	3	16 wks

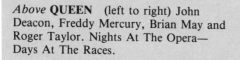

Above **QUEEN** (left to right) John Deacon, Freddy Mercury, Brian May and Roger Taylor. Nights At The Opera—Days At The Races.

Right **SUZI QUATRO** Holding on to her "Rear of the Year" award—and not an "all bum" in sight.

Date	Title Label Number	Position	
5 Dec 70	ELVIS' GOLDEN RECORDS VOL.1 (re-issue) RCA SF 8129	21	11 wks
5 Dec 70	ELVIS' GOLDEN RECORDS VOL.1 (re-issue) RCA SF 8129	21	11 wks
12 Dec 70	WORLDWIDE 50 GOLD AWARD HITS VOL 1 RCA LPM 6401	49	2 wks
30 Jan 71	THAT'S THE WAY IT IS RCA SF 8162	12	41 wks
10 Apr 71	● ELVIS COUNTRY RCA SF 8172	6	9 wks
24 Jul 71	● LOVE LETTERS FROM ELVIS RCA SF 8202	7	5 wks
7 Aug 71	● C'MON EVERYBODY RCA International INTS 1286	5	21 wks
7 Aug 71	YOU'LL NEVER WALK ALONE RCA Camden CDM 1088	20	4 wks
25 Sep 71	ALMOST IN LOVE RCA International INTS 1206	38	2 wks
4 Dec 71	● ELVIS' CHRISTMAS ALBUM RCA International INTS 1126	7	5 wks
18 Dec 71	I GOT LUCKY RCA International INTS 1322	26	3 wks
27 May 72	ELVIS NOW RCA Victor SF 8266	12	8 wks
3 Jun 72	ROCK AND ROLL (re-issue of rock 'n' roll no.1) RCA Victor SF 8233	34	4 wks
3 Jun 72	ELVIS FOR EVERYONE RCA Victor SF 8232	48	1 wk
15 Jul 72	● ELVIS AT MADISON SQUARE GARDEN RCA Victor SF 8296	3	20 wks
12 Aug 72	HE TOUCHED ME RCA Victor SF 8275	38	3 wks
24 Feb 73	ALOHA FROM HAWAII VIA SATELLITE RCA Victor DPS 2040	11	10 wks
15 Sep 73	ELVIS RCA Victor SF 8378	16	4 wks
2 Mar 74	A LEGENDARY PERFORMER VOL.1 RCA Victor CPL1 0341	20	3 wks
25 May 74	GOOD TIMES RCA Victor APL1 0475	42	1 wk
7 Sep 74	ELVIS PRESLEY LIVE ON STAGE IN MEMPHIS RCA Victor APL1 0606	44	1 wk
22 Feb 75	PROMISED LAND RCA Victor APL1 0873	21	4 wks
14 Jun 75	TODAY RCA Victor RS 1011	48	3 wks
5 Jul 75	★ 40 GREATEST HITS Arcade ADEP 12	1	38 wks
6 Sep 75	THE ELVIS PRESLEY COLLECTION RCA Starcall HY 1001	16	13 wks
19 Jun 76	FROM ELVIS PRESLEY BOULEVARD, MEMPHIS, TENNESSEE RCA Victor RS 1060	29	5 wks
19 Feb 77	ELVIS IN DEMAND RCA Victor PL 42003	12	11 wks
27 Aug 77	● MOODY BLUE RCA PL 12428	3	15 wks
3 Sep 77	● WELCOME TO MY WORLD RCA PL 12274	7	9 wks
3 Sep 77	G-I BLUES (re-issue) RCA SF5078	14	10 wks
10 Sep 77	ELVIS GOLDEN RECORDS VOL.2 (re-issue) RCA SF 8151	27	4 wks
10 Sep 77	HITS OF THE 70'S RCA LPL1 7527	30	4 wks
10 Sep 77	BLUE HAWAII (re-issue) RCA SF 8145	26	6 wks
10 Sep 77	ELVIS' GOLDEN RECORDS VOL 3 (re-issue) RCA SF 7630	49	2 wks
10 Sep 77	PICTURES OF ELVIS RCA Starcall HY 1023	52	1 wk
8 Oct 77	THE SUN YEARS Charly Sun 1001	31	2 wks
15 Oct 77	LOVING YOU RCA PL 42358	24	3 wks
19 Nov 77	ELVIS IN CONCERT RCA PL 02578	13	11 wks
22 Apr 78	HE WALKS BESIDE ME RCA PL 12772	37	1 wk
3 Jun 78	THE '56 SESSIONS VOL 1 RCA PL 42101	47	4 wks
2 Sep 78	TV SPECIAL RCA PL 42370	50	2 wks
11 Nov 78	40 GREATEST RCA PL 42691	40	14 wks
3 Feb 79	A LEGENDARY PERFORMER VOL 3 RCA PL 13082	43	3 wks
5 May 79	OUR MEMORIES OF ELVIS RCA PL 13279	72	1 wk
24 Nov 79	● LOVE SONGS K-Tel NE 1062	4	13 wks

Date	Title Label Number	Position	
21 Jun 80	ELVIS PRESLEY SINGS LIEBER AND STOLLER RCA International INTS 5031	32	5 wks
23 Aug 80	ELVIS ARON PRESLEY RCA ELVIS 25	21	4 wks
23 Aug 80	PARADISE HAWAIIAN STYLE (re-issue) RCA International INTS 5037	53	2 wks
29 Nov 80	● INSPIRATION K-Tel NE 1101	6	8 wks
14 Mar 81	GUITAR MAN RCA RCALP 5010	33	5 wks
9 May 81	THIS IS ELVIS PRESLEY RCA RCALP 5029	47	4 wks
28 Nov 81	THE ULTIMATE PERFORMANCE K-Tel NE 1141	45	6 wks
13 Feb 82	THE SOUND OF YOUR CRY RCA RCALP 3060	31	12 wks
6 Mar 82	ELVIS PRESLEY EP PACK RCA EP1	97	1 wk
21 Aug 82	ROMANTIC ELVIS/ROCKIN' ELVIS RCA RCALP 1000/1	62	5 wks
18 Dec 82	IT WON'T SEEM LIKE CHRISTMAS WITHOUT YOU RCA INTS 5235	80	1 wk

PRETENDERS

UK/US, male/female vocal/instrumental group

Date	Title Label Number	Position	
19 Jan 80	★ PRETENDERS Real RAL 3	1	35 wks
15 Aug 81	● PRETENDERS II Real SRK 3572	7	27 wks

PRETTY THINGS

UK, male vocal/instrumental group

Date	Title Label Number	Position	
27 Mar 65	● PRETTY THINGS Fontana TL 5239	6	10 wks
27 Jun 70	PARACHUTE Harvest SHVL 774	43	3 wks

Alan PRICE

UK, male vocalist/instrumentalist - keyboards

Date	Title Label Number	Position	
8 Jun 74	● BETWEEN TODAY AND YESTERDAY Warner Bros. K 56032	9	10 wks

Charley PRIDE

US, male vocalist

Date	Title Label Number	Position	
10 Apr 71	CHARLEY PRIDE SPECIAL RCA SF 8171	29	1 wk
28 May 77	SHE'S JUST AN OLD LOVE TURNED MEMORY RCA Victor PL 12261	34	2 wks
3 Jun 78	SOMEONE LOVES YOU HONEY RCA PL 12478	48	2 wks
26 Jan 80	● GOLDEN COLLECTION K-Tel NE 1056	6	12 wks

P.J. PROBY

US, male vocalist

Date	Title Label Number	Position	
27 Feb 65	I'M P.J. PROBY Liberty LBY 1235	16	3 wks

PROCOL HARUM

UK, male vocal/instrumental group

19 Jul 69	**A SALTY DOG** *Regal Zonophone SLRZ 1009*	27	2 wks
27 Jun 70	**HOME** *Regal Zonophone SLRZ 1014*	49	1 wk
3 Jul 71	**BROKEN BARRICADES** *Island ILPS 9158*	42	1 wk
6 May 72	**A WHITER SHADE OF PALE/A SALTY DOG** (DOUBLE RE-ISSUE) *Fly Double Back TOOFA 7/8*	26	4 wks
6 May 72	**PROCOL HARUM IN CONCERT WITH THE EDMONTON SYMPHONY ORCHESTRA** *Chrysalis CHR 1004*	48	1 wk
30 Aug 75	**PROCOL'S NINTH** *Chrysalis CHR 1080*	41	2 wks

A Whiter Shade Of Pale/A Salty Dog *is a double re-issue although* A Whiter Shade Of Pale *was not previously a hit. The Edmonton Symphony Orchestra is a US orchestra.*

Dorothy PROVINE

US, female vocalist

| 2 Dec 61 | ● **THE ROARING TWENTIES SONGS FROM THE TV SERIES** *Warner Bros. WM 4035* | 3 | 42 wks |
| 10 Feb 62 | ● **VAMP OF THE ROARING TWENTIES** *Warner Bros. WM 4053* | 9 | 7 wks |

PSYCHEDELIC FURS

UK, male vocal/instrumental group

15 Mar 80	**PSYCHEDELIC FURS** *CBS 84084*	18	6 wks
23 May 81	**TALK TALK TALK** *CBS 84892*	30	9 wks
2 Oct 82	**FOREVER NOW** *CBS 85909*	20	6 wks

PUBLIC IMAGE LTD.

UK, male vocal/instrumental group

23 Dec 78	**PUBLIC IMAGE** *Virgin V 2114*	22	11 wks
8 Dec 79	**METAL BOX** *Virgin METAL 1*	18	8 wks
8 Mar 80	**SECOND EDITION OF PIL** *Virgin VD 2512*	46	2 wks
22 Nov 80	**PARIS IN THE SPRING** *Virgin V 2183*	61	2 wks
18 Apr 81	**FLOWERS OF ROMANCE** *Virgin V 2189*	11	5 wks

Gary PUCKETT and the UNION GAP

US, male vocalist, male vocal/instrumental backing group

| 29 Jun 68 | **UNION GAP** *CBS 63342* | 24 | 4 wks |

Q-TIPS

UK, male vocal/instrumental group

| 30 Aug 80 | **Q-TIPS** *Chrysalis* | 50 | 1 wk |

Suzi QUATRO

US, female vocalist/instrumentalist - guitar

| 13 Oct 73 | **SUZI QUATRO** *RAK SRAK 505* | 32 | 4 wks |
| 26 Apr 80 | ● **SUZI QUATRO'S GREATEST HITS** *RAK EMTV 24* | 4 | 9 wks |

QUEDO BRASS — See *CHAQUITO and QUEDO BRASS*

QUEEN

UK, male vocal/instrumental group

23 Mar 74	● **QUEEN 2** *EMI EMA 767*	5	29 wks
30 Mar 74	**QUEEN** *EMI EMC 3006*	24	18 wks
23 Nov 74	● **SHEER HEART ATTACK** *EMI EMC 3061*	2	42 wks
13 Dec 75	☆ **A NIGHT AT THE OPERA** *EMI EMTC 103*	1	48 wks
25 Dec 76	☆ **A DAY AT THE RACES** *EMI EMTC 104*	1	24 wks
12 Nov 77	● **NEWS OF THE WORLD** *EMI EMA 784*	4	20 wks
25 Nov 78	● **JAZZ** *EMI EMA 788*	2	27 wks
7 Jul 79	● **LIVE KILLERS** *EMI EMSP 330*	3	27 wks
12 Jul 80	☆ **THE GAME** *EMI EMA 795*	1	18 wks
20 Dec 80	**FLASH GORDON (FILM SOUNDTRACK)** *EMI EMC 3351*	17	15 wks
7 Nov 81	☆ **GREATEST HITS** *EMI EMTV 30*	1†	58 wks
15 May 82	● **HOT SPACE** *EMI EMA 797*	4	19 wks

QUINTESSENCE

UK/Australia, male vocal/instrumental group

27 Jun 70	**QUINTESSENCE** *Island ILPS 9128*	22	4 wks
3 Apr 71	**DIVE DEEP** *Island ILPS 9143*	43	1 wk
27 May 72	**SELF** *RCA Victor SF 8273*	50	1 wk

Date	Title Label Number	Position		Date	Title Label Number	Position

RACING CARS

UK, male vocal/instrumental group

19 Feb 77	**DOWNTOWN TONIGHT** *Chrysalis CHR 1099*	39	6 wks

Gerry RAFFERTY

UK, male vocalist

25 Feb 78	● **CITY TO CITY** *United Artists UAS 30104*	6	37 wks
2 Jun 79	● **NIGHT OWL** *United Artists UAK 30238*	9	24 wks
26 Apr 80	**SNAKES AND LADDERS** *United Artists UAK 30298*	15	9 wks
25 Sep 82	**SLEEPWALKING** *Liberty LBG 30352*	39	4 wks

RAINBOW

UK, male vocal/instrumental group

13 Sep 75	**RITCHIE BLACKMORE'S RAINBOW** *Oyster OYA 2001*	11	6 wks
5 Jun 76	**RAINBOW RISING** *Polydor 2490 137*	11	33 wks
30 Jul 77	● **ON STAGE** *Polydor 2657 016*	7	10 wks
6 May 78	● **LONG LIVE ROCK 'N' ROLL** *Polydor POLD 5002*	7	12 wks
18 Aug 79	● **DOWN TO EARTH** *Polydor POLD 5023*	6	37 wks
21 Feb 81	● **DIFFICULT TO CURE** *Polydor POLD 5036*	3	22 wks
8 Aug 81	**RITCHIE BLACKMORE'S RAINBOW** (re-issue) *Polydor 2490 141*	91	2 wks
21 Nov 81	**BEST OF RAINBOW** *Polydor POLDV 2*	14	17 wks
24 Apr 82	● **STRAIGHT BETWEEN THE EYES** *Polydor POLD 5056*	5	14 wks

First two albums and re-issue of first album credited to Ritchie Blackmore's Rainbow.

RAMONES

US, male vocal/instrumental group

23 Apr 77	**LEAVE HOME** *Philips 9103 254*	45	1 wk
24 Dec 77	**ROCKET TO RUSSIA** *Sire 9103 255*	60	2 wks
7 Oct 78	**ROAD TO RUIN** *Sire SRK 6063*	32	2 wks
16 Jun 79	**IT'S ALIVE** *Sire SRK 26074*	27	8 wks
19 Jan 80	**END OF THE CENTURY** *Sire SRK 6077*	14	8 wks

RAVEN

UK, male vocal/instrumental group

17 Oct 81	**ROCK UNTIL YOU DROP** *Neat NEAT 1001*	63	3 wks

Chris REA

UK, male vocalist

28 Apr 79	**DELTICS** *Magnet MAG 5028*	54	3 wks
12 Apr 80	**TENNIS** *Magnet MAG 5032*	60	1 wk
3 Apr 82	**CHRIS REA** *Magnet MAGL 5040*	52	4 wks

REAL THING

UK, male vocal/instrumental group

6 Nov 76	**REAL THING** *Pye NSPL 18507*	34	3 wks
7 Apr 79	**CAN YOU FEEL THE FORCE** *Pye NSPH 18601*	73	1 wk
10 May 80	**20 GREATEST HITS** *K-Tel NE 1073*	56	2 wks

REBEL ROUSERS — See *Cliff BENNETT and the REBEL ROUSERS*

RED NOISE — See *Bill NELSON'S RED NOISE*

Sharon REDD

US, female vocalist

23 Oct 82	**REDD HOTT** *Prelude PRL 25056*	59	5 wks

Otis REDDING

US, male vocalist

19 Feb 66	● **OTIS BLUE** *Atlantic ATL 5041*	6	21 wks
23 Apr 66	**SOUL BALLADS** *Atlantic ATL 5029*	30	1 wk
23 Jul 66	**SOUL ALBUM** *Atlantic 587-011*	22	9 wks
21 Jan 67	**OTIS REDDING'S DICTIONARY OF SOUL** *Atlantic 588-050*	23	16 wks
21 Jan 67	● **OTIS BLUE** (re-issue) *Atlantic 587-036*	7	54 wks
29 Apr 67	**PAIN IN MY HEART** *Atlantic 587-042*	28	9 wks
10 Feb 68	● **HISTORY OF OTIS REDDING** *Volt S 418*	2	43 wks
30 Mar 68	**OTIS REDDING IN EUROPE** *Stax 589-016*	14	16 wks
1 Jun 68	★ **DOCK OF THE BAY** *Stax 231-001*	1	15 wks
12 Oct 68	**IMMORTAL OTIS REDDING** *Atlantic 588-113*	19	8 wks

See also Otis Redding and Carla Thomas.

Otis REDDING and Carla THOMAS

US, male/female vocal duo

1 Jul 67	**KING AND QUEEN** *Atlantic 589-007*	18	17 wks

See also Otis Redding.

Far Left **OTIS REDDING** Onstage at the Paris Olympia.

Left **JIM REEVES** Despite charting 26 albums he only just pipped ''The Sound of Music'' by seven weeks.

Below **CLIFF RICHARD** Cliff and Sue Barker watching a video of the highly seeded Beatles at Abbey Road. (No. 2 court).

Date	Title Label Number	Position		Date	Title Label Number	Position	

Helen REDDY

Australia, female vocalist

Date	Title Label Number	Position	
8 Feb 75	**FREE AND EASY** Capitol E-ST 11348	17	9 wks
14 Feb 76	● **THE BEST OF HELEN REDDY** Capitol E-ST 11467	5	18 wks

Lou REED

US, male vocalist

Date	Title Label Number	Position	
21 Apr 73	**TRANSFORMER** RCA Victor LSP 4807	13	25 wks
20 Oct 73	● **BERLIN** RCA Victor RCA Victor	7	5 wks
16 Mar 74	**ROCK 'N' ROLL ANIMAL** RCA Victor APLI 0472	26	1 wk
14 Feb 76	**CONEY ISLAND BABY** RCA Victor RS 1035	52	1 wk
3 Jul 82	**TRANSFORMER** (re-issue) RCA INTS 5061	91	2 wks

Don REEDMAN — See *Jeff JARRATT and Don REEDMAN*

Jim REEVES

US, male vocalist

Date	Title Label Number	Position	
28 Mar 64	● **GOOD 'N' COUNTRY** RCA Camden CDN 5114	10	35 wks
9 May 64	● **GENTLEMAN JIM** RCA RD 7541	3	23 wks
15 Aug 64	● **A TOUCH OF VELVET** RCA RD 7521	8	9 wks
15 Aug 64	**INTERNATIONAL JIM REEVES** RCA RD 7577	11	15 wks
22 Aug 64	**HE'LL HAVE TO GO** RCA RD 27176	16	4 wks
29 Aug 64	**THE INTIMATE JIM REEVES** RCA RD 27193	12	4 wks
29 Aug 64	● **GOD BE WITH YOU** RCA RD 7636	10	10 wks
5 Sep 64	● **MOONLIGHT AND ROSES** RCA RD 7639	2	52 wks
19 Sep 64	**COUNTRY SIDE OF JIM REEVES** RCA Camden CDN 5100	12	5 wks
26 Sep 64	**WE THANK THEE** RCA RD 7637	17	3 wks
28 Nov 64	● **TWELVE SONGS OF CHRISTMAS** RCA RD 7663	3	17 wks
30 Jan 65	● **BEST OF JIM REEVES** RCA RD 7666	3	47 wks
10 Apr 65	**HAVE I TOLD YOU LATELY THAT I LOVE YOU** RCA Camden CDN 5122	12	5 wks
22 May 65	**THE JIM REEVES WAY** RCA RD 7694	16	4 wks
5 Nov 66	● **DISTANT DRUMS** RCA Victor RD 7814	2	34 wks
18 Jan 69	**A TOUCH OF SADNESS** RCA SF 7978	15	5 wks
5 Jul 69	★ **ACCORDING TO MY HEART** RCA International INTS 1013	1	14 wks
23 Aug 69	**JIM REEVES AND SOME FRIENDS** RCA SF 8022	24	4 wks
29 Nov 69	**ON STAGE** RCA SF 8047	13	4 wks
26 Dec 70	**MY CATHEDRAL** RCA SF 8146	48	2 wks
3 Jul 71	**JIM REEVES WRITES YOU A RECORD** RCA SF 8176	47	2 wks
7 Aug 71	● **JIM REEVES' GOLDEN RECORDS** RCA International INTS 1070	9	21 wks
14 Aug 71	● **THE INTIMATE JIM REEVES** (re-issue) RCA International INTS 1256	8	15 wks
21 Aug 71	**GIRLS I HAVE KNOWN** RCA International INTS 1140	35	5 wks
27 Nov 71	● **TWELVE SONGS OF CHRISTMAS** (re-issue) RCA International INTS 1188	3	6 wks
27 Nov 71	**A TOUCH OF VELVET** (re-issue) RCA International INTS 1089	49	2 wks
15 Apr 72	**MY FRIEND** RCA SF 8258	32	5 wks
20 Sep 75	★ **40 GOLDEN GREATS** Arcade ADEP 16	1	25 wks
6 Sep 80	**COUNTRY GENTLEMAN** K-Tel NE 1088	53	4 wks

Neil REID

UK, male vocalist

Date	Title Label Number	Position	
5 Feb 72	★ **NEIL REID** Decca SKL 5122	1	16 wks
2 Sep 72	**SMILE** Decca SKL 5136	47	2 wks

RENAISSANCE

UK, male/female vocal instrumental group

Date	Title Label Number	Position	
21 Feb 70	**RENAISSANCE** Island ILPS 9114	60	1 wk
19 Aug 78	**A SONG FOR ALL SEASONS** Warner Bros. K 56460	35	8 wks
2 Jun 79	**AZUR D'OR** Warner Bros. K 56633	73	1 wk

RENATO

Italy, male vocalist

Date	Title Label Number	Position	
25 Dec 82	**SAVE YOUR LOVE** Lifestyle LEG 9	91†	1 wk

REO SPEEDWAGON

US, male vocal/instrumental group

Date	Title Label Number	Position	
25 Apr 81	● **HI INFIDELITY** Epic EPC 84700	6	29 wks
17 Jul 82	**GOOD TROUBLE** Epic EPC 85789	29	7 wks

REZILLOS

UK, male/female vocal instrumental group

Date	Title Label Number	Position	
5 Aug 78	**CAN'T STAND THE REZILLOS** Sire WEA K 56530	16	10 wks
28 Apr 79	**MISSION ACCOMPLISHED BUT THE BEAT GOES ON** Sire SRK 6069	30	5 wks

Charlie RICH

US, male vocalist

Date	Title Label Number	Position	
23 Mar 74	● **BEHIND CLOSED DOORS** Epic 65716	4	26 wks
13 Jul 74	**VERY SPECIAL LOVE SONGS** Epic 80031	34	2 wks

Date	Title *Label Number*	Position		Date	Title *Label Number*	Position	

RICH KIDS

UK, male vocal/instrumental group

Date	Title *Label Number*	Position	
7 Oct 78	**GHOST OF PRINCES IN TOWERS** *EMI EMC 3263*	51	1 wk

Cliff RICHARD

UK, male vocalist

Date	Title *Label Number*	Position	
18 Apr 59	● **CLIFF** *Columbia 33SX 1147*	4	31 wks
14 Nov 59	● **CLIFF SINGS** *Columbia 33SX 1192*	2	36 wks
15 Oct 60	● **ME AND MY SHADOWS** *Columbia 33SX 1261*	2	33 wks
22 Apr 61	● **LISTEN TO CLIFF** *Columbia 33SX 1320*	2	28 wks
21 Oct 61	★ **I'M 21 TODAY** *Columbia 33SX 1368*	1	16 wks
23 Dec 61	★ **THE YOUNG ONES (FILM SOUNDTRACK)** *Columbia 33SX 1384*	1	42 wks
29 Sep 62	● **32 MINUTES AND 17 SECONDS** *Columbia 33SX 1431*	3	21 wks
26 Jan 63	★ **SUMMER HOLIDAY (FILM SOUNDRACK)** *Columbia 33SX 1472*	1	36 wks
13 Jul 63	● **CLIFF'S HIT ALBUM** *Columbia 33SX 1512*	2	19 wks
28 Sep 63	● **WHEN IN SPAIN** *Columbia 33SX 1541*	8	10 wks
11 Jul 64	● **WONDERFUL LIFE** *Columbia 33SX 1628*	2	23 wks
9 Jan 65	**ALADDIN** *Columbia 33SX 1676*	13	5 wks
17 Apr 65	● **CLIFF RICHARD** *Columbia 33SX 1709*	9	5 wks
14 Aug 65	**MORE HITS BY CLIFF** *Columbia 33SX 1737*	20	1 wk
8 Jan 66	**LOVE IS FOREVER** *Columbia 33SX 1769*	19	1 wk
21 May 66	● **KINDA LATIN** *Columbia SX 6039*	9	12 wks
17 Dec 66	● **FINDERS KEEPERS** *Columbia SX 6079*	6	18 wks
7 Jan 67	**CINDERELLA (PANTOMIME)** *Columbia 33SCX 6103*	30	6 wks
15 Apr 67	**DON'T STOP ME NOW...** *Columbia SCX 6133*	23	9 wks
11 Nov 67	**GOOD NEWS** *Columbia SCX 6167*	37	1 wk
1 Jun 68	**CLIFF IN JAPAN** *Columbia SCX 6244*	29	2 wks
16 Nov 68	**ESTABLISHED 1958** *Columbia SCX 6282*	30	4 wks
12 Jul 69	● **BEST OF CLIFF** *Columbia SCX 6343*	5	11 wks
27 Sep 69	**SINCERELY** *Columbia SCX 6357*	24	3 wks
31 Jan 70	**BEST OF CLIFF RICHARD** *Columbia SCX 6342*	43	6 wks
12 Dec 70	**TRACKS 'N' GROOVES** *Columbia SCX 6435*	37	2 wks
23 Dec 72	**BEST OF CLIFF VOL.2** *Columbia SCX 6519*	49	2 wks
19 Jan 74	**TAKE ME HIGH** *EMI EMC 3016*	41	4 wks
29 May 76	● **I'M NEARLY FAMOUS** *EMI EMC 3122*	5	21 wks
26 Mar 77	● **EVERY FACE TELLS A STORY** *EMI EMC 3172*	8	10 wks
22 Oct 77	★ **40 GOLDEN GREATS** *EMI EMTV 6*	1	19 wks
4 Mar 78	**SMALL CORNERS** *EMI EMC 3219*	33	5 wks
21 Oct 78	**GREEN LIGHT** *EMI EMC 3231*	25	3 wks
17 Feb 79	● **THANK YOU VERY MUCH - REUNION CONCERT AT THE LONDON PALLADIUM** *EMI EMTV 15*	5	12 wks
15 Sep 79	● **ROCK 'N' ROLL JUVENILE** *EMI EMC 3307*	3	22 wks
13 Sep 80	● **I'M NO HERO** *EMI EMA 796*	4	11 wks
4 Jul 81	★ **LOVE SONGS** *EMI EMTV 27*	1	43 wks
26 Sep 81	● **WIRED FOR SOUND** *EMI EMC 3377*	4	25 wks
4 Sep 82	● **NOW YOU SEE ME, NOW YOU DON'T** *EMI EMC 3415*	4†	12 wks

Cliff *credited to Cliff Richard and the Drifters. The Shadows featured on all or some tracks of the following albums;* Cliff Sings, Me And My Shadows, Listen To Cliff, I'm 21 Today, 32 Minutes And 17 Seconds, Summer Holiday, Cliffs Hits, When In Spain, Wonderful Life, Aladdin, More Hits, Love Is Forever, Finders Keepers, Cinderella, Est 1958, Best Of Cliff *and most of the later compilations and the* Reunion *album. See also the Shadows.*

Lionel RICHIE

US, male vocalist

Date	Title *Label Number*	Position	
27 Nov 82	**LIONEL RICHIE** *Motown STMA 8037*	18†	5 wks

Jonathan RICHMAN and the MODERN LOVERS

US, male vocal/instrumental group

Date	Title *Label Number*	Position	
27 Aug 77	**ROCK 'N' ROLL WITH THE MODERN LOVERS** *Beserkeley BSERK 9*	50	3 wks

RICHMOND STRINGS/MIKE SAMMES SINGERS

UK, orchestra/male/female vocal group

Date	Title *Label Number*	Position	
19 Jan 76	**MUSIC OF AMERICA** *Ronco TRD 2016*	18	7 wks

RIP RIG and PANIC

UK, male/female vocal/instrumental group

Date	Title *Label Number*	Position	
26 Jun 82	**I AM GOLD** *Virgin V 2228*	67	3 wks

Minnie RIPERTON

US, female vocalist

Date	Title *Label Number*	Position	
17 May 75	**PERFECT ANGEL** *Epic EPC 80426*	33	3 wks

Marty ROBBINS

US, male vocalist

Date	Title *Label Number*	Position	
13 Aug 60	**GUNFIGHTER BALLADS** *Fontana TFL 5063*	20	1 wk
10 Feb 79	● **MARTY ROBBINS COLLECTION** *Lotus WH 5009*	5	14 wks

Paddy ROBERTS

South Africa, male vocalist

26 Sep 59	● STRICTLY FOR GROWN-UPS *Decca LF 1322*	8	5 wks
17 Sep 60	PADDY ROBERTS TRIES AGAIN *Decca LK 4358*	16	1 wk

B.A. ROBERTSON

UK, male vocalist

29 Mar 80	INITIAL SUCCESS *Asylum K 52216*	32	8 wks
4 Apr 81	BULLY FOR YOU *Asylum K 52275*	61	2 wks

Smokey ROBINSON

US, male vocalist

20 Jun 81	BEING WITH YOU *Motown STML 12151*	17	10 wks

Tom ROBINSON BAND

UK, male vocal/instrumental group

3 Jun 78	● POWER IN THE DARKNESS *EMI EMC 3226*	4	12 wks
24 Mar 79	TRB2 *EMI EMC 3296*	18	6 wks

ROCKIN' BERRIES

UK, male vocal/instrumental group

19 Jun 65	IN TOWN *Pye NPL 38013*	15	1 wk

ROCKPILE

UK, male vocal/instrumental group

18 Oct 80	SECONDS OF PLEASURE *F-Beat XXLP 7*	34	5 wks

Clodagh RODGERS

Ireland, female vocalist

13 Sep 69	CLODAGH RODGERS *RCA SF 8033*	27	1 wk

RODS

US, male vocal/instrumental group

24 Jul 82	WILD DOGS *Arista SPART 1196*	75	4 wks

Kenny ROGERS

US, male vocalist

18 Jun 77	KENNY ROGERS *United Artists UAS 30046*	14	7 wks
6 Oct 79	THE KENNY ROGERS SINGLES ALBUM *United Artists UAK 30263*	12	22 wks
9 Feb 80	● KENNY *United Artists UAG 30273*	7	10 wks
31 Jan 81	LADY *Liberty LBG 30334*	40	5 wks

ROLLING STONES

UK, male vocal/instrumental group

25 Apr 64	★ ROLLING STONES *Decca LK 4805*	1	51 wks
23 Jan 65	★ ROLLING STONES NO.2 *Decca LK 4661*	1	37 wks
2 Oct 65	● OUT OF OUR HEADS *Decca LK 4733*	2	24 wks
23 Apr 66	★ AFTERMATH *Decca LK 4786*	1	28 wks
12 Nov 66	● BIG HITS (HIGH TIDE AND GREEN GRASS) *Decca TXS 101*	4	43 wks
28 Jan 67	● BETWEEN THE BUTTONS *Decca SKL 4852*	3	22 wks
23 Dec 67	● THEIR SATANIC MAJESTIES REQUEST *Decca TXS 103*	3	13 wks
21 Dec 68	● BEGGARS BANQUET *Decca SKL 4955*	3	12 wks
27 Sep 69	● THROUGH THE PAST DARKLY (BIG HITS VOL.2) *Decca SKL 5019*	2	37 wks
20 Dec 69	★ LET IT BLEED *Decca SKL 5025*	1	29 wks
19 Sep 70	★ GET YOUR YA-YAS OUT *Decca SKL 5065*	1	15 wks
3 Apr 71	● STONE AGE *Decca SKL 5084*	4	7 wks
8 May 71	★ STICKY FINGERS *Rolling Stones COC 59100*	1	25 wks
18 Sep 71	GIMME SHELTER *Decca SKL 5101*	19	5 wks
11 Mar 72	MILESTONES *Decca SKL 5098*	14	8 wks
10 Jun 72	★ EXILE ON MAIN STREET *Rolling Stones COC 69100*	1	16 wks
11 Nov 72	ROCK 'N' ROLLING STONES *Decca SKL 5149*	41	1 wk
22 Sep 73	★ GOAT'S HEAD SOUP *Rolling Stones COC 59101*	1	14 wks
2 Nov 74	● IT'S ONLY ROCK 'N' ROLL *Rolling Stones COC 59103*	2	9 wks
28 Jun 75	MADE IN THE SHADE *Rolling Stones COC 59104*	14	12 wks
28 Jun 75	METAMORPHIS *Decca SKL 5212*	45	1 wk
29 Nov 75	● ROLLED GOLD - THE VERY BEST OF THE ROLLING STONES *Decca ROST 1/2*	7	50 wks
8 May 76	● BLACK & BLUE *Rolling Stones COC 59106*	2	14 wks
8 Oct 77	● LOVE YOU LIVE *Rolling Stones COC 89101*	3	8 wks
5 Nov 77	GET STONED *Arcade ADEP 32*	13	15 wks
24 Jun 78	● SOME GIRLS *Rolling Stones CUN 39108*	2	25 wks
5 Jul 80	★ EMOTIONAL RESCUE *Rolling Stones CUN 39111*	1	18 wks
12 Sep 81	● TATTOO YOU *Rolling Stones CUNS 39114*	2	29 wks
12 Jun 82	● STILL LIFE (AMERICAN CONCERTS 1981) *Rolling Stones CUN 39115*	4	18 wks
31 Jul 82	IN CONCERT (IMPORT) *Decca (Holland) 6640 037*	94	3 wks
11 Dec 82	STORY OF THE STONES *K-Tel NE 1200*	24†	3 wks

Mick RONSON

UK, male vocalist/instrumentalist - guitar

Date	Title Label Number	Pos	Wks
16 Mar 74	● SLAUGHTER ON TENTH AVENUE *RCA Victor APLI 0353*	9	7 wks
8 Mar 75	PLAY DON'T WORRY *RCA Victor APL1 0681*	29	3 wks

Linda RONSTADT

US, female vocalist

Date	Title Label Number	Pos	Wks
4 Sep 76	HASTEN DOWN THE WIND *Asylum K 53045*	32	8 wks
25 Dec 76	GREATEST HITS *Asylum K 53055*	37	9 wks
1 Oct 77	SIMPLE DREAMS *Asylum K 53065*	15	5 wks
14 Oct 78	LIVING IN THE USA *Asylum K 53085*	39	2 wks
8 Mar 80	MAD LOVE *Asylum K 52210*	65	1 wk

ROSE ROYCE

US, male/female vocal instrumental group

Date	Title Label Number	Pos	Wks
22 Oct 77	IN FULL BLOOM *Warner Bros. K 56394*	18	13 wks
30 Sep 78	● STRIKES AGAIN *Whitfield K 56257*	7	11 wks
22 Sep 79	RAINBOW CONNECTION IV *Atlantic K 56714*	72	2 wks
1 Mar 80	★ GREATEST HITS *Whitfield K RRTV 1*	1	34 wks

ROSE TATTOO

Austrialia, male vocal/instrumental group

Date	Title Label Number	Pos	Wks
26 Sep 81	ASSAULT AND BATTERY *Carrere CAL 127*	40	4 wks

Diana ROSS

US, female vocalist

Date	Title Label Number	Pos	Wks
24 Oct 70	DIANA ROSS *Tamla Motown STML 11159*	14	5 wks
19 Jun 71	EVERYTHING IS EVERYTHING *Tamla Motown STML 11178*	31	3 wks
9 Oct 71	● I'M STILL WAITING *Tamla Motown STML 11193*	10	11 wks
9 Oct 71	DIANA *Tamla Motown STMA 8001*	43	1 wk
11 Nov 72	GREATEST HITS *Tamla Motown STMA 8006*	34	10 wks
1 Sep 73	● TOUCH ME IN THE MORNING *Tamla Motown STML 11239*	7	35 wks
27 Oct 73	LADY SINGS THE BLUES *Tamla Motown TMSP 1131*	50	1 wk
2 Mar 74	LAST TIME I SAW HIM *Tamla Motown STML 11255*	41	1 wk
8 Jun 74	LIVE *Tamla Motown STML 11248*	21	8 wks
27 Mar 76	● DIANA ROSS *Tamla Motown STML 12022*	4	26 wks
7 Aug 76	● GREATEST HITS 2 *Tamla Motown STML 12036*	2	29 wks
19 Mar 77	AN EVENING WITH DIANA ROSS *Motown TMSP 6005*	52	1 wk
4 Aug 79	THE BOSS *Motown STML 12118*	52	2 wks
17 Nov 79	● 20 GOLDEN GREATS *Motown EMTV 21*	2	29 wks
21 Jun 80	DIANA *Motown STMA 8033*	12	32 wks
28 Mar 81	TO LOVE AGAIN *Motown STML 12152*	26	10 wks
7 Nov 81	WHY DO FOOLS FALL IN LOVE *Capitol EST 26733*	17	24 wks
21 Nov 81	ALL THE GREATEST HITS *Motown STMA 8036*	21	31 wks
13 Feb 82	DIANA ROSS *Motown STML 12163*	43	6 wks
23 Oct 82	SILK ELECTRIC *Capitol EAST 27313*	33†	10 wks
4 Dec 82	● LOVE SONGS *K-Tel NE 1200*	5†	4 wks

See also Diana Ross and Marvin Gaye, and Diana Ross and the Supremes with the Temptations.

Diana ROSS and Marvin GAYE

US, female/male vocal duo

Date	Title Label Number	Pos	Wks
19 Jan 74	● DIANA AND MARVIN *Tamla Motown STMA 8015*	6	43 wks
29 Aug 81	DIANA AND MARVIN (re-issue) *Motown STMS 5001*	78	2 wks

See also Marvin Gaye, and Marvin Gaye and Tammi Terrell, and Diana Ross and the Supremes with the Temptations.

Diana ROSS and the SUPREMES with the TEMPTATIONS

US, male/female vocal instrumental group

Date	Title Label Number	Pos	Wks
25 Jan 69	★ DIANA ROSS AND THE SUPREMES JOIN THE TEMPTATIONS *Tamla Motown STML 11096*	1	15 wks
28 Jun 69	TCB *Tamla Motown STML 11110*	11	12 wks
14 Feb 70	TOGETHER *Tamla Motown STML 11122*	28	4 wks

See also Diana Ross, and Diana Ross and Marvin Gaye, and Supremes, and Supremes and the Four Tops, and Temptations.

ROSTAL and SCHAEFER

UK, male instrumental duo

Date	Title Label Number	Pos	Wks
14 Jul 79	BEATLES CONCERTO *Parlophone PAS 10014*	61	2 wks

Thomas ROUND — See *June BRONHILL and Thomas ROUND*

Demis ROUSSOS

Greece, male vocalist

Date	Title Label Number	Pos	Wks
22 Jun 74	● FOREVER AND EVER *Philips 6325 021*	2	68 wks
19 Apr 75	SOUVENIRS *Philips 6325 201*	25	18 wks
24 Apr 76	● HAPPY TO BE *Philips 9101 027*	4	34 wks
3 Jul 76	MY ONLY FASCINATION *Philips 6325 094*	39	6 wks
16 Apr 77	THE MAGIC OF DEMIS ROUSSOS *Philips 9101 131*	29	6 wks
28 Oct 78	LIFE AND LOVE *Philips 9199 873*	36	11 wks

ROXY MUSIC

UK, male vocal/instrumental group

29 Jul 72	● **ROXY MUSIC** *Island ILPS 9200*	10	16 wks
7 Apr 73	● **FOR YOUR PLEASURE** *Island ILPS 9232*	4	27 wks
1 Dec 73	★ **STRANDED** *Island ILPS 9252*	1	17 wks
30 Nov 74	● **COUNTRY LIFE** *Island ILPS 9303*	3	10 wks
8 Nov 75	● **SIREN** *Island ILPS 9344*	4	17 wks
31 Jul 76	● **VIVA ROXY MUSIC** *Island ILPS 9400*	6	12 wks
19 Nov 77	**GREATEST HITS** *Polydor 2302 073*	20	11 wks
24 Mar 79	● **MANIFESTO** *Polydor POLH 001*	7	34 wks
31 May 80	★ **FLESH AND BLOOD** *Polydor POLH 002*	1	60 wks
5 Jun 82	★ **AVALON** *EG/Polydor EGHP 50*	1	30 wks

ROYAL CHORAL SOCIETY — See *LONDON SYMPHONY ORCHESTRA*

ROYAL PHILHARMONIC ORCHESTRA

UK, orchestra

23 Dec 78	**CLASSIC GOLD VOL.2** *Ronco RTD 42032*	31	4 wks
13 Jan 79	**CLASSICAL GOLD** *Ronco RTV 42020*	65	1 wk

See also Louis Clark/Royal Philharmonic Orchestra.

RUBETTES

UK, male vocal/instrumental group

10 May 75	**WE CAN DO IT** *State ETAT 001*	41	1 wk

Jimmy RUFFIN

US, male vocalist

13 May 67	**JIMMY RUFFIN WAY** *Tamla Motown STML 11048*	32	6 wks
1 Jun 74	**GREATEST HITS** *Tamla Motown STML 11259*	41	4 wks

RUFUS

US, male/female vocal instrumental group

12 Apr 75	**RUFUSIZED** *ABC ABCL 5063*	48	2 wks

RUMOUR — See *Graham PARKER and the RUMOUR*

Todd RUNDGREN

US, male vocalist

29 Jan 77	**RA** *Bearsville K 55514*	27	6 wks
6 May 78	**HERMIT OF MINK HOLLOW** *Bearsville K 55521*	42	3 wks

RUSH

Canada, male vocal/instrumental group

8 Oct 77	**FAREWELL TO KINGS** *Mercury 9100 042*	22	4 wks
25 Nov 78	**HEMISPHERES** *Mercury 9100 059*	14	6 wks
26 Jan 80	● **PERMANENT WAVES** *Mercury 9100 071*	3	16 wks
21 Feb 81	● **MOVING PICTURES** *Mercury 6337 160*	3	11 wks
7 Nov 81	● **EXIT STAGE LEFT** *Mercury 6619 053*	6	14 wks
18 Sep 82	● **SIGNALS** *Mercury/Phonogram 6337 243*	3	8 wks

Patrice RUSHEN

US, female vocalist

1 May 82	**STRAIGHT FROM THE HEART** *Elektra K 52532*	24	14 wks

Leon RUSSELL

US, male vocalist

3 Jul 71	**LEON RUSSELL AND THE SHELTER PEOPLE** *A & M AMLS 65003*	29	1 wk

Mike RUTHERFORD

UK, male vocalist/instrumentalist - guitar

23 Feb 80	**SMALL CREEPS DAY** *Charisma CAS 1149*	13	7 wks
18 Sep 82	**ACTING VERY STRANGE** *WEA K 99249*	23	4 wks

RUTLES

UK, male vocal group

15 Apr 78	**THE RUTLES** *Warner Bros. K 56459*	12	11 wks

RUTS

UK, male vocal/instrumental group

13 Oct 79	**THE CRACK** *Virgin V 2132*	16	6 wks

See also Ruts D.C.

RUTS D.C.

UK, male vocal/instrumental group

18 Oct 80	**GRIN AND BEAR IT** *Virgin V 2188*	28	4 wks

See also Ruts.

Left **ROLLING STONES**   4th Most Top Ten Albums (23), 4th Most Hit Albums (31), 5th Most Weeks In Chart (592). *Below Right* **ROXY MUSIC**   The 'Flesh + Blood' album cover encloses their most successful release to date, spending over a year on the chart.

Top Left **SMALL FACES**   Steve, Plonk, Ian & Kenny beaming out of the corner of their eponymous Decca 12″ mono L.P. record sleeve. *Left* **DIANA ROSS & THE SUPREMES**   Diana Ross et les Supremes avec le chanteur Cliff Richard à la Maison de la Radio en Paris, with a couple of French chappies.

Date	Title Label Number	Position

S

SAD CAFE

UK, male vocal/instrumental group

Date	Title Label Number	Position	
1 Oct 77	**FANX TA RA** *RCA PL 25101*	56	1 wk
29 Apr 78	**MISPLACED IDEALS** *RCA PL 25133*	50	1 wk
29 Sep 79	● **FACADES** *RCA PL 25249*	8	23 wks
25 Oct 80	**SAD CAFE** *RCA SADLP 4*	46	5 wks
21 Mar 81	**LIVE** *RCA SAD LP 5*	37	4 wks
24 Oct 81	**OLE** *Polydor POLD 5045*	72	2 wks

SAILOR

UK, male vocal/instrumental group

Date	Title Label Number	Position	
7 Feb 76	**TROUBLE** *Epic*	45	8 wks

ST. PAUL'S BOYS' CHOIR

UK, choir

Date	Title Label Number	Position	
29 Nov 80	**REJOICE** *K-Tel NE 1064*	36	8 wks

SALVATION ARMY

UK, Salvation Army Band

Date	Title Label Number	Position	
24 Dec 77	**BY REQUEST** *Warwick WW 5038*	16	5 wks

SAM and DAVE

US, male vocal duo

Date	Title Label Number	Position	
21 Jan 67	**HOLD ON I'M A COMIN'** *Atlantic 588-045*	35	7 wks
22 Apr 67	**DOUBLE DYNAMITE** *Stax 589-003*	28	5 wks
23 Mar 68	**SOUL MAN** *Stax 589-015*	32	8 wks

Mike SAMMES SINGERS — See *RICHMOND STRINGS/Mike SAMMES SINGERS*

SAMSON

UK, male vocal/instrumental group

Date	Title Label Number	Position	
26 Jul 80	**HEAD ON** *Gem GEMLP 108*	34	6 wks

SANTANA

US, male vocal/instrumental group

Date	Title Label Number	Position	
2 May 70	**SANTANA** *CBS 63815*	26	11 wks
28 Nov 70	● **ABRAXAS** *CBS 64807*	7	52 wks
13 Nov 71	● **SANTANA 3** *CBS 69015*	6	14 wks
29 Nov 72	● **CARAVANSERAI** *CBS 65299*	6	11 wks
8 Dec 73	● **WELCOME** *CBS 69040*	8	6 wks
21 Sep 74	**GREATEST HITS** *CBS 69081*	14	15 wks
30 Nov 74	**BARBOLETTA** *CBS 69084*	18	5 wks
10 Apr 76	**AMIGOS** *CBS 86005*	21	9 wks
8 Jan 77	**FESTIVAL** *CBS 86020*	27	3 wks
5 Nov 77	● **MOONFLOWER** *CBS 88272*	7	27 wks
11 Nov 78	**INNER SECRETS** *CBS 86075*	17	16 wks
27 Oct 79	**MARATHON** *CBS 86098*	28	5 wks
18 Apr 81	**ZE BOP** *CBS 84946*	33	4 wks
14 Aug 82	**SHANGO** *CBS 85914*	35	7 wks

See also *Carlos Santana, and Carlos Santana and Alice Coltrane, and Carlos Santana and Mahavishnu John McLaughlin, and Carlos Santana and Buddy Miles.*

Carlos SANTANA

US, male instrumentalist-guitar

Date	Title Label Number	Position	
24 Mar 79	**ONENESS - SILVER DREAMS GOLDEN REALITY** *CBS 86037*	55	4 wks
20 Sep 80	**THE SWING OF DELIGHT** *CBS 22075*	74	2 wks

See also *Santana, and Carlos Santana and Alice Coltrane and Carlos Santana and Mahavishnu John McLaughlin, and Carlos Santana and Buddy Miles.*

Carlos SANTANA and Alice COLTRANE

US, male instrumental duo

Date	Title Label Number	Position	
2 Nov 74	**ILLUMINATIONS** *CBS 69063*	40	1 wk

See also *Santana, and Carlos Santana, and Carlos Santana and Mahavishnu John McLaughlin, and Carlos Santana and Buddy Miles.*

Carlos SANTANA and Mahavishnu John McLAUGHLIN

US, male instrumental duo

Date	Title Label Number	Position	
28 Jul 73	● **LOVE DEVOTION SURRENDER** *CBS 69037*	7	9 wks

See also *Mahavishnu Orchestra, and Santana, and Carlos Santana, and Carlos Santana and Alice Coltrane, and Carlos Santana and Buddy Miles.*

Carlos SANTANA and Buddy MILES

US, male instrumental duo

26 Aug 72	**CARLOS SANTANA AND BUDDY MILES LIVE** *CBS 65142*	29	4 wks

See also Santana, and Carlos Santana, and Carlos Santana and Alice Coltrane, and Carlos Santana and Mahavishnu John McLaughlin.

Peter SARSTEDT

UK, male vocalist

15 Mar 69	● **PETER SARSTEDT** *United Artists SULP 1219*	8	4 wks

Telly SAVALAS

US, male vocalist

22 Mar 75	**TELLY** *MCA MCF 2699*	12	10 wks

SAVOY BROWN

UK, male vocal/instrumental group

28 Nov 70	**LOOKIN' IN** *Decca SKL 5066*	50	1 wk

SAXON

UK, male vocal/instrumental group

12 Apr 80	● **WHEELS OF STEEL** *Carrere CAL 115*	5	29 wks
15 Nov 80	**STRONG ARM OF THE LAW** *Carrere CAL 120*	11	11 wks
3 Oct 81	● **DENIM AND LEATHER** *Carrere CAL 128*	9	11 wks

Leo SAYER

UK, male vocalist

5 Jan 74	● **SILVER BIRD** *Chrysalis CHR 1050*	2	22 wks
26 Oct 74	● **JUST A BOY** *Chrysalis CHR 1068*	4	14 wks
20 Sep 75	● **ANOTHER YEAR** *Chrysalis CHR 1087*	8	9 wks
27 Nov 76	● **ENDLESS FLIGHT** *Chrysalis CHR 1125*	4	66 wks
22 Oct 77	● **THUNDER IN MY HEART** *Chrysalis CDL 1154*	8	16 wks
2 Sep 78	**LEO SAYER** *Chrysalis CDL 1198*	15	25 wks
31 Mar 79	★ **THE VERY BEST OF LEO SAYER** *Chrysalis CDL 1222*	1	37 wks
13 Oct 79	**HERE** *Chrysalis CDL 1240*	44	4 wks
23 Aug 80	**LIVING IN A FANTASY** *Chrysalis CDL 1297*	15	9 wks
8 May 82	**WORLD RADIO** *Chrysalis CDL 1345*	30	12 wks

Boz SCAGGS

US, male vocalist

12 Mar 77	**SILK DEGREES** *CBS 81193*	37	24 wks
17 Dec 77	**DOWN TWO, THEN LEFT** *CBS 86036*	55	1 wk
3 May 80	**MIDDLE MAN** *CBS 86094*	52	4 wks

SCARS

UK, male vocal/instrumental group

18 Apr 81	**AUTHOR AUTHOR** *Pre PREX 5*	67	3 wks

SCHAEFER — See *ROSTAL and SCHAEFER*

Michael SCHENKER GROUP

Germany/UK, male vocal/instrumental group

6 Sep 80	● **MICHAEL SCHENKER GROUP** *Chrysalis CHR 1302*	8	8 wks
19 Sep 81	**MICHAEL SCHENKER GROUP** (re-issue) *Chrysalis CHR 1336*	14	8 wks
13 Mar 82	● **ONE NIGHT AT BUDOKAN** *Chrysalis CTY 1375*	5	11 wks
23 Oct 82	**ASSAULT ATTACK** *Chrysalis CHR 1393*	19	5 wks

SCORPIONS

Germany, male vocal/instrumental group

21 Apr 79	**LOVE DRIVE** *Harvest SHSP 4097*	36	11 wks
3 May 80	**ANIMAL MAGNETISM** *Harvest SHSP 4113*	23	6 wks
10 Apr 82	**BLACKOUT** *Harvest SHVL 823*	11	11 wks

SCOTLAND FOOTBALL WORLD CUP SQUAD 1974

UK, male football team vocalists

25 May 74	● **EASY EASY** *Polydor 2383 282*	3	9 wks

Band Of The SCOTS GUARDS

UK, military band

28 Jun 69	**BAND OF THE SCOTS GUARDS** *Fontana SFXL 54*	25	2 wks

Date	Title Label Number	Position		Date	Title Label Number	Position

Jack SCOTT

Canada, male vocalist

7 May 60	● I REMEMBER HANK WILLIAMS	7	11 wks
	Top Rank BUY 034		
3 Sep 60	WHAT IN THE WORLD'S COME OVER YOU	11	1 wk
	Top Rank 25/024		

SCRITTI POLITTI

UK, male vocal/instrumental group

| 11 Sep 82 | SONGS TO REMEMBER | 12 | 7 wks |
| | *Rough Trade ROUGH 20* | | |

SEARCHERS

UK, male vocal/instrumental group

10 Aug 63	● MEET THE SEARCHERS *Pye NPL 18086*	2	44 wks
16 Nov 63	● SUGAR AND SPICE *Pye NPL 18089*	5	21 wks
30 May 64	● IT'S THE SEARCHERS *Pye NPL 18092*	4	17 wks
27 Mar 65	● SOUNDS LIKE THE SEARCHERS	8	5 wks
	Pye NPL 18111		

Harry SECOMBE

UK, male vocalist

31 Mar 62	SACRED SONGS *Philips RBL 7501*	16	1 wk
22 Apr 67	● SECOMBE'S PERSONAL CHOICE	6	13 wks
	Philips BETS 707		
7 Aug 71	IF I RULED THE WORLD *Contour 6870 501*	17	20 wks
16 Dec 78	● 20 SONGS OF JOY *Warwick WW 5052*	8	12 wks

See also Harry Secombe and Moira Anderson, and Harry Secombe, Peter Sellers and Spike Milligan.

Harry SECOMBE and Moira ANDERSON

UK, male/female vocal duo

| 5 Dec 81 | GOLDEN MEMORIES *Warwick WW 5107* | 46 | 5 wks |

See also Harry Secombe, and Harry Secombe, Peter Sellers and Spike Milligan.

Harry SECOMBE, Peter SELLERS and Spike MILLIGAN

UK, male vocal group

| 18 Apr 64 | HOW TO WIN AN ELECTION *Philips AL 3464* | 20 | 1 wk |

See also Spike Milligan, and Harry Secombe, and Harry Secombe and Moira Anderson, and Peter Sellers, and Peter Sellers and Sophia Loren.

SECRET AFFAIR

UK, male vocal/instrumental group

1 Dec 79	GLORY BOYS *I-Spy 1*	41	8 wks
20 Sep 80	BEHIND CLOSED DOORS *I-Spy 2*	48	4 wks
13 Mar 82	BUSINESS AS USUAL *I-Spy 3*	84	3 wks

Neil SEDAKA

US, male vocalist

1 Sep 73	THE TRA-LA DAYS ARE OVER *MGM 2315 248*	13	10 wks
22 Jun 74	LAUGHTER IN THE RAIN *Polydor 2383 265*	17	10 wks
23 Nov 74	LIVE AT THE ROYAL FESTIVAL HALL	48	1 wk
	Polydor 2383 299		
1 Mar 75	OVERNIGHT SUCCESS *Polydor 2442 131*	31	6 wks
10 Jul 76	● LAUGHTER AND TEARS - THE BEST OF NEIL	2	25 wks
	SEDAKA TODAY *Polydor 2383 399*		

SEEKERS

Australia, male/female vocal group

3 Jul 65	● A WORLD OF OUR OWN *Columbia 33SX 1722*	5	36 wks
3 Jul 65	THE SEEKERS *Decca LK 4694*	16	1 wk
19 Nov 66	● COME THE DAY *Columbia SX 6093*	3	67 wks
25 Nov 67	SEEKERS - SEEN IN GREEN	15	10 wks
	Columbia SCX 6193		
14 Sep 68	● LIVE AT THE TALK OF THE TOWN	2	30 wks
	Columbia SCX 6278		
16 Nov 68	★ BEST OF THE SEEKERS *Columbia SCX 6268*	1	125 wks

Bob SEGER and the SILVER BULLET BAND

US, male vocal/instrumental group

3 Jun 78	STRANGER IN TOWN *Capitol EAST 11698*	31	6 wks
15 Mar 80	AGAINST THE WIND *Capitol EA-ST 12041*	26	6 wks
26 Sep 81	NINE TONIGHT *Capitol ESTSP 23*	24	10 wks

The SELECTER

UK, male/female vocal instrumental group

| 23 Feb 80 | ● TOO MUCH PRESSURE *Two Tone CDL TT 5002* | 5 | 13 wks |
| 7 Mar 81 | CELEBRATE THE BULLET *Chrysalis CHR 1306* | 41 | 4 wks |

Date	Title *Label Number*	Position	

Peter SELLERS

UK, male vocalist

Date	Title *Label Number*	Position	
14 Feb 59	● THE BEST OF SELLERS *Parlophone PMD 1069*	3	47 wks
12 Dec 59	● SONGS FOR SWINGING SELLERS *Parlophone PMC 1111*	3	37 wks

See also Harry Secombe, Peter Sellers and Spike Milligan, and Peter Sellers and Sophia Loren.

Peter SELLERS and Sophia LOREN

UK/Italy, male/female vocal duo

3 Dec 60	● PETER AND SOPHIA *Parlophone PMC 1131*	5	18 wks

See also Peter Sellers, and Harry Secombe, Peter Sellers and Spike Milligan.

Captain SENSIBLE

UK, male vocalist

11 Sep 82	WOMEN AND CAPTAIN FIRST *A&M AMLH 68548*	64	3 wks

SEX PISTOLS

UK, male vocal/instrumental group

12 Nov 77	★ NEVER MIND THE BOLLOCKS HERE'S THE SEX PISTOLS *Virgin V 2086*	1	48 wks
10 Mar 79	● THE GREAT ROCK 'N' ROLL SWINDLE *Virgin VD 2410*	7	33 wks
11 Aug 79	● SOME PRODUCT - CARRI ON SEX PISTOLS *Virgin VR 2*	6	10 wks
16 Feb 80	FLOGGING A DEAD HORSE *Virgin V 2142*	23	6 wks

SHADOWS

UK, male instrumental group

16 Sep 61	★ THE SHADOWS *Columbia 33SX 1374*	1	57 wks
13 Oct 62	★ OUT OF THE SHADOWS *Columbia 33SX 1458*	1	38 wks
22 Jun 63	● GREATEST HITS *Columbia 33SX 1522*	2	49 wks
9 May 64	● DANCE WITH THE SHADOWS *Columbia 33SX 1619*	2	27 wks
17 Jul 65	● SOUND OF THE SHADOWS *Columbia 33SX 1736*	4	17 wks
21 May 66	● SHADOW MUSIC *Columbia SX 6041*	5	17 wks
15 Jul 67	● JIGSAW *Columbia SCX 6148*	8	16 wks
24 Oct 70	SHADES OF ROCK *Columbia SCX 6420*	30	4 wks
13 Apr 74	ROCKIN' WITH CURLY LEADS *EMI EMA 762*	45	1 wk
11 May 74	GREATEST HITS (re-issue) *Columbia SCX 1522*	48	6 wks
29 Mar 75	SPECS APPEAL *EMI EMC 3066*	30	5 wks
12 Feb 77	★ 20 GOLDEN GREATS *EMI EMTV 3*	1	38 wks
15 Sep 79	★ STRING OF HITS *EMI EMC 3310*	1	41 wks
26 Jul 80	ANOTHER STRING OF HITS *EMI EMC 3339*	16	8 wks

13 Sep 80	CHANGE OF ADDRESS *Polydor 2442 179*	17	6 wks
19 Sep 81	HITS RIGHT UP YOUR STREET *Polydor POLD 5046*	15	16 wks
25 Sep 82	LIFE IN THE JUNGLE/LIVE AT ABBEY ROAD *Polydor SHADS 1*	24	6 wks

See also Cliff Richard.

SHAKATAK

UK, male/female vocal/instrumental group

30 Jan 82	DRIVIN' HARD *Polydor POLS 1030*	35	17 wks
15 May 82	● NIGHT BIRDS *Polydor POLS 1059*	4	28 wks
27 Nov 82	INVITATIONS *Polydor POLD 5068*	30†	5 wks

SHAKIN' PYRAMIDS

UK, male vocal/instrumental group

4 Apr 81	SKIN 'EM UP *Cuba/Libra V 2199*	48	4 wks

SHALAMAR

US, male/female vocal instrumental group

27 Mar 82	FRIENDS *Solar K 52345*	11†	40 wks
11 Sep 82	GREATEST HITS *Solar SOLA 3001*	71	5 wks

SHAM 69

UK, male vocal/instrumental group

11 Mar 78	TELL US THE TRUTH *Polydor 2383 491*	25	8 wks
2 Dec 78	THAT'S LIFE *Polydor POLD 5010*	27	11 wks
29 Sep 79	● THE ADVENTURES OF THE HERSHAM BOYS *Polydor POLD 5025*	8	8 wks

Del SHANNON

US, male vocalist

11 May 63	● HATS OFF TO DEL SHANNON *London HAX 8071*	9	17 wks
2 Nov 63	LITTLE TOWN FLIRT *London HAX 8091*	15	6 wks

Helen SHAPIRO

UK, female vocalist

10 Mar 62	● TOPS WITH ME *Columbia 33SX 1397*	2	25 wks

Date	Title Label Number	Position		Date	Title Label Number	Position	

Sandie SHAW

UK, female vocalist

6 Mar 65	● SANDIE *Pye NPL 18110*	3	13 wks

SHOWADDYWADDY

UK, male vocal/instrumental group

7 Dec 74	● SHOWADDYWADDY *Bell BELLS 248*	9	19 wks
12 Jul 75	● STEP TWO *Bell BELLS 256*	7	17 wks
29 May 76	TROCADERO *Bell SYBEL 8003*	41	3 wks
25 Dec 76	● GREATEST HITS *Arista ARTY 145*	4	26 wks
3 Dec 77	RED STAR *Arista SPARTY 1023*	20	10 wks
9 Dec 78	★ GREATEST HITS *Arista ARTV 1*	1	17 wks
10 Nov 79	● CREPES AND DRAPES *Arista ARTV 3*	8	14 wks
20 Dec 80	BRIGHT LIGHTS *Arista SPART 1142*	54	8 wks
7 Nov 81	THE VERY BEST OF *Arista SPART 1178*	33	11 wks

Labi SIFFRE

UK, male vocalist

24 Jul 71	SINGER AND THE SONG *Pye NSPL 28147*	47	1 wk
14 Oct 72	CRYING, LAUGHING, LOVING, LYING *Pye NSPL 28163*	46	1 wk

SILVER BULLET BAND — See *Bob SEGER and the SILVER BULLET BAND*

SILVER CONVENTION

Germany/US, female vocal duo

25 Jun 77	SILVER CONVENTION: GREATEST HITS *Magnet*	34	3 wks

SIMON and GARFUNKEL

US, male vocal duo

16 Apr 66	SOUNDS OF SILENCE *CBS 62690*	13	104 wks
3 Aug 68	★ BOOKENDS *CBS 63101*	1	77 wks
31 Aug 68	PARSLEY, SAGE, ROSEMARY & THYME *CBS 62860*	13	66 wks
26 Oct 68	● THE GRADUATE (FILM SOUNDTRACK) *CBS 70042*	3	71 wks
9 Nov 68	WEDNESDAY MORNING 3 A.M. *CBS 63370*	24	6 wks
21 Feb 70	★ BRIDGE OVER TROUBLED WATER *CBS 63699*	1	303 wks
22 Jul 72	● GREATEST HITS *CBS 69003*	2	281 wks
4 Apr 81	SOUNDS OF SILENCE (re-issue) *CBS 32020*	68	1 wk
21 Nov 81	● SIMON AND GARFUNKEL COLLECTION *CBS 10029*	4	35 wks
20 Mar 82	● THE CONCERT IN CENTRAL PARK *Geffen 96008*	6	33 wks

See also Paul Simon, Art Garfunkel.

Carly SIMON

US, female vocalist

20 Jan 73	● NO SECRETS *Elektra K 42127*	3	26 wks
16 Mar 74	HOT CAKES *Elektra K 52005*	19	9 wks

Paul SIMON

US, male vocalist

26 Feb 72	★ PAUL SIMON *CBS 69007*	1	26 wks
2 Jun 73	● THERE GOES RHYMIN' SIMON *CBS 69035*	4	22 wks
1 Nov 75	STILL CRAZY AFTER ALL THESE YEARS *CBS 86001*	11	31 wks
3 Dec 77	● GREATEST HITS, ETC. *CBS 10007*	6	15 wks
30 Aug 80	ONE-TRICK PONY *Warner Bros. K 56846*	17	12 wks

See also Simon and Garfunkel.

Nina SIMONE

US, female vocalist/instrumentalist - piano

24 Jul 65	I PUT A SPELL ON YOU *Philips BL 7671*	18	3 wks
15 Feb 69	'NUFF SAID *RCA SF 7979*	11	1 wk

SIMPLE MINDS

UK, male vocal/instrumental group

5 May 79	A LIFE IN THE DAY *Zoom ZULP 1*	30	6 wks
27 Sep 80	EMPIRES AND DANCE *Arista SPART 1140*	41	3 wks
12 Sep 81	SONS AND FASCINATIONS/SISTERS FEELINGS CALL *Virgin 2207*	11	7 wks
27 Feb 82	CELEBRATION *Arista SPART 1183*	45	7 wks
25 Sep 82	● NEW GOLD DREAM (81,82,83,84) *Virgin V 2230*	3†	14 wks

Frank SINATRA

US, male vocalist

8 Nov 58	● COME FLY WITH ME *Capitol LCT 6154*	2	18 wks
15 Nov 58	● SONGS FOR SWINGING LOVERS *Capitol LCT 6106*	8	8 wks
29 Nov 58	● FRANK SINATRA STORY *Fontana TFL 5030*	8	1 wk
13 Dec 58	● FRANK SINATRA SINGS FOR ONLY THE LONELY *Capitol LCT 6168*	5	13 wks
16 May 59	● COME DANCE WITH ME *Capitol LCT 6179*	2	30 wks
22 Aug 59	● LOOK TO YOUR HEART *Capitol LCT 6181*	5	8 wks

Date	Title Label Number	Position	
11 Jun 60	● COME BACK TO SORRENTO *Fontana TFL 5082*	6	9 wks
29 Oct 60	● SWING EASY *Capitol W 587*	5	17 wks
21 Jan 61	● NICE 'N EASY *Capitol W 1417*	4	27 wks
15 Jul 61	SINATRA SOUVENIR *Fontana TFL 5138*	18	1 wk
19 Aug 61	● WHEN YOUR LOVER HAS GONE *Encore ENC 101*	6	10 wks
23 Sep 61	● SINATRA'S SWINGING SESSION *Capitol W 1491*	6	8 wks
28 Oct 61	● SINATRA SWINGS *Reprise R 1002*	8	8 wks
25 Nov 61	● SINATRA PLUS *Fontana SET 303*	7	9 wks
16 Dec 61	● RING-A-DING-DING *Reprise R 1001*	8	9 wks
17 Feb 62	COME SWING WITH ME *Capitol W 1594*	13	4 wks
7 Apr 62	● I REMEMBER TOMMY *Reprise R 1003*	10	12 wks
9 Jun 62	● SINATRA AND STRINGS *Reprise R 1004*	6	20 wks
27 Oct 62	GREAT SONGS FROM GREAT BRITAIN *Reprise R 1006*	12	9 wks
29 Dec 62	SINATRA WITH SWINGING BRASS *Reprise R 1005*	14	11 wks
27 Jul 63	● CONCERT SINATRA *Reprise R 1009*	8	18 wks
5 Oct 63	● SINATRA'S SINATRA *Reprise R 1010*	9	24 wks
19 Sep 64	IT MIGHT AS WELL BE SWING *Reprise R 1012*	17	4 wks
20 Mar 65	SOFTLY AS I LEAVE YOU *Reprise R 1013*	20	1 wk
22 Jan 66	● A MAN AND HIS MUSIC *Reprise R 1016*	9	19 wks
21 May 66	MOONLIGHT SINATRA *Reprise R 1018*	18	8 wks
2 Jul 66	● STRANGERS IN THE NIGHT *Reprise R 1017*	4	18 wks
1 Oct 66	● SINATRA AT THE SANDS *Reprise RLP 1019*	7	18 wks
3 Dec 66	FRANK SINATRA SINGS SONGS FOR PLEASURE *MFP 1120*	26	2 wks
25 Feb 67	THAT'S LIFE *Reprise RSLP 1020*	22	12 wks
7 Oct 67	FRANK SINATRA *Reprise RSLP 1022*	28	5 wks
19 Oct 68	● GREATEST HITS *Reprise RSLP 1025*	8	38 wks
7 Dec 68	BEST OF FRANK SINATRA *Capitol ST 21140*	17	10 wks
7 Jun 69	● MY WAY *Reprise RSLP 1029*	2	59 wks
4 Oct 69	A MAN ALONE *Reprise RSLP 1030*	18	7 wks
9 May 70	WATERTOWN *Reprise RSLP 1031*	14	9 wks
12 Dec 70	● GREATEST HITS VOL.2 *Reprise RSLP 1032*	6	40 wks
5 Jun 71	● SINATRA AND COMPANY *Reprise RSLP 1033*	9	9 wks
27 Nov 71	FRANK SINATRA SINGS RODGERS AND HART *Starline SRS 5083*	35	1 wk
8 Jan 72	MY WAY (re-issue) *Reprise K 44015*	35	1 wk
8 Jan 72	GREATEST HITS VOL.2 *Reprise K 44018*	29	3 wks
1 Dec 73	OL' BLUE EYES IS BACK *Warner Bros. K 44249*	12	13 wks
17 Aug 74	SOME NICE THINGS WE MISSED *Reprise K 54020*	35	3 wks
15 Feb 75	THE MAIN EVENT (TV SOUNDTRACK) *Reprise K 54031*	30	2 wks
14 Jun 75	THE BEST OF OL' BLUE EYES *Reprise K 54042*	30	3 wks
19 Mar 77	★ PORTRAIT OF SINATRA *Reprise K 64039*	1	18 wks
13 May 78	● 20 GOLDEN GREATS *Capitol EMTV 10*	4	11 wks

See also Frank Sinatra and Count Basie.

Frank SINATRA and Count BASIE

US, male vocalist and male orchestra leader/instrumentalist - piano

Date	Title Label Number	Position	
23 Feb 63	● SINATRA - BASIE *Reprise R 1008*	2	23 wks

See also Frank Sinatra, Count Basie.

Nancy SINATRA

US, female vocalist

Date	Title Label Number	Position	
16 Apr 66	BOOTS *Reprise R 6202*	12	9 wks
18 Jun 66	HOW DOES THAT GRAB YOU *Reprise R 6207*	12	3 wks
10 Oct 70	NANCY'S GREATEST HITS *Reprise RSLP 6409*	39	3 wks

See also Nancy Sinatra and Lee Hazlewood.

Nancy SINATRA and Lee HAZLEWOOD

US, female/male vocal duo

Date	Title Label Number	Position	
29 Jun 68	NANCY AND LEE *Reprise RSLP 6273*	17	12 wks
25 Sep 71	NANCY AND LEE *Reprise K 44126*	42	1 wk
29 Jan 72	DID YOU EVER *RCA Victor SF 8240*	31	4 wks

See also Nancy Sinatra.

SIOUXSIE and the BANSHEES

UK, male/female vocal instrumental group

Date	Title Label Number	Position	
2 Dec 78	THE SCREAM *Polydor POLD 5009*	12	11 wks
22 Sep 79	JOIN HANDS *Polydor POLD 5024*	13	5 wks
16 Aug 80	● KALEIDOSCOPE *Polydor 2442 177*	5	6 wks
27 Jun 81	● JU JU *Polydor POLS 1034*	7	17 wks
12 Dec 81	ONCE UPON A TIME *Polydor POLS 1056*	21	26 wks
13 Nov 82	A KISS IN THE DREAMHOUSE *Polydor POLD 5064*	11†	7 wks

SISTER SLEDGE

US, female vocal duo

Date	Title Label Number	Position	
12 May 79	WE ARE FAMILY *Atlantic K 50587*	15	23 wks

Peter SKELLERN

UK, male vocalist

Date	Title Label Number	Position	
9 Sep 78	SKELLERN *Mercury 9109 701*	48	3 wks
8 Dec 79	ASTAIRE *Mercury 9102 702*	23	20 wks
4 Dec 82	A STRING OF PEARLS *Mercury/Phonogram MERC 10*	67†	4 wks

SKID ROW

UK, male vocal/instrumental group

Date	Title Label Number	Position	
17 Oct 70	SKID *CBS 63965*	30	3 wks

Above **LEO SAYER** Six top ten albums spread over 214 weeks of the year (Leo is the one on the right).

Right **SQUEEZE** 'Five cool cats'.

Right **RINGO STARR** His debut album was loaded with evergreen songs and became a hit—the follow up ''Beaucoups Of Blues'' was loaded with evergreen musicians (Charlie Daniels, Jerry Reed, The Jordanaires, Charlie McCoy) and didn't.

Above **SIMON AND GARFUNKEL** Although 2nd to the Beatles in the Most Weeks On Chart List, adding their solo efforts gives Paul Simon 1,083 weeks and Art Garfunkel 1,022. Here (foreground) giving a radio interview.

JIMMY SMITH The legendary jazz organist had to wait until he was forty to have his first long playing success in Britain.

Left **SOFT MACHINE** Mike Ratledge, Robert Wyatt, Kevin Ayers and Australian David Allen took their name from a William Burroughs novel for which he gave them permission.

Date	Title *Label Number*	Position	

SKIDS

UK, male vocal/instrumental group

Date	Title *Label Number*	Position	
17 Mar 79	**SCARED TO DANCE** *Virgin V 2116*	19	10 wks
27 Oct 79	**DAYS IN EUROPE** *Virgin V 2138*	32	5 wks
27 Sep 80	● **THE ABSOLUTE GAME** *Virgin V 2174*	9	5 wks

SKY

UK/Australia, male instrumental group

Date	Title *Label Number*	Position	
2 Jun 79	● **SKY** *Ariola ARLH 5022*	9	56 wks
26 Apr 80	★ **SKY 2** *Ariola ADSKY 2*	1	53 wks
28 Mar 81	● **SKY 3** *Ariola ASKY 3*	3	23 wks
3 Apr 82	● **SKY 4-FORTHCOMING** *Ariola ASKY 4*	7	22 wks

SLADE

UK, male vocal/instrumental group

Date	Title *Label Number*	Position	
8 Apr 72	● **SLADE ALIVE** *Polydor 2383 101*	2	58 wks
9 Dec 72	★ **SLAYED?** *Polydor 2383 163*	1	34 wks
6 Oct 73	★ **SLADEST** *Polydor 2442 119*	1	24 wks
23 Feb 74	★ **OLD NEW BORROWED AND BLUE** *Polydor 2383 261*	1	16 wks
14 Dec 74	● **SLADE IN FLAME** *Polydor 2442 126*	6	18 wks
27 Mar 76	**NOBODY'S FOOL** *Polydor 2383 377*	14	4 wks
22 Nov 80	**SLADE SMASHES** *Polydor POLTV 13*	25	53 wks
21 Mar 81	**WE'LL BRING THE HOUSE DOWN** *Cheapskate SKATE 1*	25	4 wks
28 Nov 81	**TILL DEAF US DO PART** *RCA RCALP 6021*	68	2 wks
18 Dec 82	**SLADE ON STAGE** *RCA RCALP 3107*	58†	2 wks

Grace SLICK

US, female vocalist

Date	Title *Label Number*	Position	
31 May 80	**DREAMS** *RCA PL 13544*	28	6 wks

SLIK

UK, male vocal/instrumental group

Date	Title *Label Number*	Position	
12 Jun 76	**SLIK** *Bell SYBEL 8004*	58	1 wk

SLITS

UK, female vocal/instrumental group

Date	Title *Label Number*	Position	
22 Sep 79	**CUT** *Island ILPS 9573*	30	5 wks

SLY and the FAMILY STONE

US, male/female vocal/instrumental group

Date	Title *Label Number*	Position	
5 Feb 72	**THERE'S A RIOT GOIN' ON** *Epic EPC 64613*	31	2 wks

SMALL FACES

UK, male vocal/instrumental group

Date	Title *Label Number*	Position	
14 May 66	● **SMALL FACES** *Decca LK 4790*	3	25 wks
17 Jun 67	**FROM THE BEGINNING** *Decca LK 4879*	17	5 wks
1 Jul 67	**SMALL FACES** *Immediate IMSP 008*	12	17 wks
15 Jun 68	★ **OGDEN'S NUT GONE FLAKE** *Immediate IMLP 012*	1	19 wks

Brian SMITH and his HAPPY PIANO

UK, male instrumentalist - piano

Date	Title *Label Number*	Position	
19 Sep 81	**PLAY IT AGAIN** *Deram DS 047*	97	1 wk

Jimmy SMITH

US, male instrumentalist - organ

Date	Title *Label Number*	Position	
18 Jun 66	**GOT MY MOJO WORKING** *Verve VLP 912*	19	3 wks

Keely SMITH

US, female vocalist

Date	Title *Label Number*	Position	
16 Jan 65	**LENNON-MCCARTNEY SONGBOOK** *Reprise R 6142*	12	9 wks

O.C. SMITH

US, male vocalist

Date	Title *Label Number*	Position	
17 Aug 68	**HICKORY HOLLER REVISITED** *CBS 63362*	40	1 wk

Steven SMITH and FATHER

UK, male instrumental duo

Date	Title *Label Number*	Position	
13 May 72	**STEVEN SMITH AND FATHER AND 16 GREAT SONGS** *Decca SKL 5128*	17	3 wks

Date	Title *Label Number*	Position		Date	Title *Label Number*	Position

Patti SMITH GROUP

US, female vocalist and male instrumental backing group

| 1 Apr 78 | **EASTER** *Arista SPARI 1043* | **16** | 14 wks |
| 19 May 79 | **WAVE** *Arista SPART 1086* | **41** | 6 wks |

SMOKIE

UK, male vocal/instrumental group

1 Nov 75	**SMOKIE/CHANGING ALL THE TIME** *RAK SRAK 517*	**18**	5 wks
30 Apr 77	● **GREATEST HITS** *RAK SRAK 526*	**6**	22 wks
4 Nov 78	**THE MONTREUX ALBUM** *RAK SRAK 6757*	**52**	2 wks
11 Oct 80	**SMOKIE'S HITS** *RAK SRAK 540*	**23**	13 wks

SOFT CELL

UK, male vocal/instrumental duo

| 12 Dec 81 | ● **NON-STOP EROTIC CABARET** *Some Bizzare BZLP 2* | **5** | 45 wks |
| 26 Jun 82 | ● **NON-STOP ECSTATIC DANCING** *Some Bizarre BZX 1012* | **6** | 18 wks |

SOFT MACHINE

UK, male vocal/instrumental group

| 4 Jul 70 | **THIRD** *CBS 66246* | **18** | 6 wks |
| 3 Apr 71 | **FOURTH** *CBS 64280* | **32** | 2 wks |

SOLID SENDERS

UK, male vocal/instrumental group

| 23 Sep 78 | **SOLID SENDERS** *Virgin V 2105* | **42** | 3 wks |

Diane SOLOMON

UK, female vocalist

| 9 Aug 75 | **TAKE TWO** *Philips 6308 236* | **26** | 6 wks |

SONNY and CHER

US, male/female vocal duo

| 16 Oct 65 | ● **LOOK AT US** *Atlantic ATL 5036* | **7** | 13 wks |
| 14 May 66 | **THE WONDROUS WORLD OF SONNY & CHER** *Atlantic 587-006* | **15** | 7 wks |

See also Cher.

David SOUL

US, male vocalist

| 27 Nov 76 | ● **DAVID SOUL** *Private Stock PVLP 1012* | **2** | 28 wks |
| 17 Sep 77 | ● **PLAYING TO AN AUDIENCE OF ONE** *Private Stock PVLP 1026* | **8** | 23 wks |

SOUL CITY SYMPHONY — See *Van McCOY and the SOUL CITY SYMPHONY*

SOUNDS ORCHESTRAL

UK, orchestra

| 12 Jun 65 | **CAST YOUR FATE TO THE WIND** *Piccadilly NPL 38041* | **17** | 1 wk |

SOUNDTRACKS (films, tv etc) — See *VARIOUS ARTISTS*

SOUTH BANK ORCHESTRA conducted by Joseph MOROVITZ and Laurie HOLLOWAY

UK, orchestra and conductors

| 2 Dec 78 | **LILLIE** *Sounds MOR 516* | **47** | 6 wks |

SPACE

France, male instrumental group

| 17 Sep 77 | **MAGIC FLY** *Pye NSPL 28232* | **11** | 9 wks |

SPANDAU BALLET

UK, male vocal/instrumental group

| 14 Mar 81 | ● **JOURNEY TO GLORY** *Reformation/Chrysalis CHR 1331* | **5** | 29 wks |
| 20 Mar 82 | **DIAMOND** *Reformation CDL 1353* | **15** | 18 wks |

SPARKS

US/UK, male vocal/instrumental group

1 Jun 74	● **KIMONO MY HOUSE** *Island ILPS 9272*	**4**	24 wks
23 Nov 74	● **PROPAGANDA** *Island ILPS 9312*	**9**	13 wks
18 Oct 75	**INDISCREET** *Island ILPS 9345*	**18**	4 wks
8 Sep 79	**NUMBER ONE IN HEAVEN** *Virgin V 2115*	**73**	1 wk

Billie Jo SPEARS

US, female vocalist

11 Sep 76	**WHAT I'VE GOT IN MIND** *United Artists UAS 29955*	47	2 wks
19 May 79	● **THE BILLIE JO SPEARS SINGLES ALBUM** *United Artists UAK 30231*	7	17 wks
21 Nov 81	**COUNTRY GIRL** *Warwick WW 5109*	17	9 wks

SPECIALS

UK, male vocal/instrumental group

3 Nov 79	● **SPECIALS** *Two-Tone CDL TT 5001*	4	45 wks
4 Oct 80	● **MORE SPECIALS** *Two-Tone CHR TT 5003*	5	19 wks

SPIDER

UK, male vocal/instrumental group

23 Oct 82	**ROCK 'N' ROLL GYPSIES** *RCA RCALP 3101*	75	1 wk

SPINNERS

UK, male/female vocal group

5 Sep 70	**THE SPINNERS ARE IN TOWN** *Fontana 6309 014*	40	5 wks
7 Aug 71	**SPINNERS LIVE PERFORMANCE** *Contour 6870 502*	14	12 wks
13 Nov 71	**THE SWINGING CITY** *Philips 6382 002*	20	3 wks
8 Apr 72	**LOVE IS TEASING** *Columbia SCX 6493*	33	4 wks

SPIRIT

US, male vocal/instrumental duo

18 Apr 81	**POTATO LAND** *Beggars Banquet BEGA 23*	40	2 wks

SPLIT ENZ

New Zealand/UK, male vocal/instrumental group

30 Aug 80	**TRUE COLOURS** *A & M AMLH 64822*	42	8 wks
8 May 82	**TIME AND TIDE** *A&M AMLH 64894*	71	1 wk

SPOTNICKS

Sweden, male instrumental group

9 Feb 63	**OUT-A-SPACE** *Oriole PS 40036*	20	1 wk

Dusty SPRINGFIELD

UK, female vocalist

25 Apr 64	● **A GIRL CALLED DUSTY** *Philips BL 7594*	6	23 wks
23 Oct 65	● **EVERYTHING COMES UP DUSTY** *Philips RBL 1002*	6	12 wks
22 Oct 66	● **GOLDEN HITS** *Philips BL 7737*	2	36 wks
11 Nov 67	**WHERE AM I GOING** *Philips SBL 7820*	40	1 wk
21 Dec 68	**DUSTY...DEFINITELY** *Philips SBL 7864*	30	6 wks
2 May 70	**FOR YOU - LOVE DUSTY** *Philips SBL 7927*	35	2 wks
4 Mar 78	**IT BEGINS AGAIN** *Mercury 9109 607*	41	2 wks

Bruce SPRINGSTEEN

US, male vocalist

1 Nov 75	**BORN TO RUN** *CBS 69170*	36	20 wks
17 Jun 78	**DARKNESS ON THE EDGE OF TOWN** *CBS 86061*	16	12 wks
25 Oct 80	● **THE RIVER** *CBS 88510*	2	52 wks
2 Oct 82	● **NEBRASKA** *CBS 25100*	3	10 wks

SPYRO GYRA

US, male instrumental group

14 Jul 79	**MORNING DANCE** *Infinity INS 2003*	11	16 wks
23 Feb 80	**CATCHING THE SUN** *MCA MCG 4009*	31	6 wks

SQUEEZE

UK, male vocal/instrumental group

28 Apr 79	**COOL FOR CATS** *A & M AMLH 68503*	45	11 wks
16 Feb 80	**ARGY BARGY** *A & M AMLH 64802*	32	15 wks
23 May 81	**EAST SIDE STORY** *A & M AMLH 64854*	19	26 wks
15 May 82	**SWEETS FROM A STRANGER** *A&M AMLH 64899*	37	10 wks
6 Nov 82	● **SINGLES-45'S AND UNDER** *A&M AMLH 68522*	3†	8 wks

Chris SQUIRE

UK, male vocalist/instrumentalist - bass

6 Dec 75	**FISH OUT OF WATER** *Atlantic K 50203*	25	7 wks

STAGE CAST RECORDINGS — See *VARIOUS ARTISTS*

Date	Title Label Number	Position

Alvin STARDUST

UK, male vocalist

Date	Title Label Number	Position	
16 Mar 74	● THE UNTOUCHABLE *Magnet MAG 5001*	4	12 wks
21 Dec 74	ALVIN STARDUST *Magnet MAG 5004*	37	3 wks
4 Oct 75	ROCK WITH ALVIN *Magnet MAG 5007*	52	2 wks

Kay STARR

US, female vocalist

26 Mar 60	MOVIN' *Capitol T 1254*	16	1 wk

Ringo STARR

UK, male vocalist

18 Apr 70	● SENTIMENTAL JOURNEY *Apple PCS 7101*	7	6 wks
8 Dec 73	● RINGO *Apple PCTC 252*	7	20 wks
7 Dec 74	GOODNIGHT VIENNA *Apple PMC 7168*	30	2 wks

STARSOUND

Holland, disco aggregation

16 May 81	★ STARS ON 45 *CBS 86132*	1	21 wks
19 Sep 81	STARS ON 45 VOL.2 *CBS 85181*	18	6 wks
3 Apr 82	STARS MEDLEY *CBS 85651*	94	1 wk

STARTRAX

UK, disco aggregation

1 Aug 81	STARTRAX CLUB DISCO *Picksy KSYA 1001*	26	7 wks

Candi STATON

US, female vocalist

24 Jul 76	YOUNG HEARTS RUN FREE *Warner Bros. K 56259*	34	3 wks

STATUS QUO

UK, male vocal/instrumental group

20 Jan 73	● PILEDRIVER *Vertigo 6360 082*	5	37 wks
9 Jun 73	THE BEST OF STATUS QUO *Pye NSPL 18402*	32	7 wks
6 Oct 73	★ HELLO *Vertigo 6360 098*	1	28 wks
18 May 74	● QUO *Vertigo 9102 001*	2	16 wks
1 Mar 75	★ ON THE LEVEL *Vertigo 9102 002*	1	27 wks
8 Nov 75	DOWN THE DUSTPIPE *Golden Hour CH 604*	20	6 wks
20 Mar 76	★ BLUE FOR YOU *Vertigo 9102 006*	1	30 wks
12 Mar 77	● LIVE *Vertigo 6641 580*	3	14 wks
26 Nov 77	● ROCKIN' ALL OVER THE WORLD *Vertigo 9102 014*	5	15 wks
11 Nov 78	● CAN'T STAND THE HEAT *Vertigo 9102 027*	3	14 wks
20 Oct 79	● WHATEVER YOU WANT *Vertigo 9102 037*	3	14 wks
22 Mar 80	● 12 GOLD BARS *Vertigo QUO TV1*	3	48 wks
25 Oct 80	● JUST SUPPOSIN' *Vertigo 6302 057*	4	18 wks
28 Mar 81	● NEVER TOO LATE *Vertigo 6302 104*	2	13 wks
10 Oct 81	FRESH QUOTA *PRT DOW 2*	74	1 wk
24 Apr 82	★ 1982 *Vertigo/Phonogram 6302 169*	1	20 wks
13 Nov 82	● FROM THE MAKERS OF... *Vertigo/Phonogram PROLP 1*	4†	7 wks

STEEL PULSE

UK, male vocal/instrumental group

5 Aug 78	● HANDSWORTH REVOLUTION *Island EMI ILPS 9502*	9	12 wks
14 Jul 79	TRIBUTE TO MARTYRS *Island ILPS 9568*	42	6 wks

STEELEYE SPAN

UK, male/female vocal instrumental group

10 Apr 71	PLEASE TO SEE THE KING *B & C CAS 1029*	45	2 wks
14 Oct 72	BELOW THE SALT *Chrysalis CHR 1008*	43	1 wk
28 Apr 73	PARCEL OF ROGUES *Chrysalis CHR 1046*	26	5 wks
23 Mar 74	NOW WE ARE SIX *Chrysalis CHR 1053*	13	13 wks
15 Feb 75	COMMONER'S CROWN *Chrysalis CHR 1071*	21	4 wks
25 Oct 75	● ALL AROUND MY HAT *Chrysalis CHR 1091*	7	20 wks
16 Oct 76	ROCKET COTTAGE *Chrysalis CHR 1123*	41	3 wks

STEELY DAN

US, male vocal/instrumental group

30 Mar 74	PRETZEL LOGIC *Probe SPBA 6282*	37	2 wks
3 May 75	KATY LIED *ABC*	13	6 wks
20 Sep 75	CAN'T BUY A THRILL *ABC ABCL 5024*	38	1 wk
22 May 76	ROYAL SCAM *ABC ABCL 5161*	11	13 wks
8 Oct 77	● AJA *ABC ABCL 5225*	5	10 wks
2 Dec 78	GREATEST HITS *ABC BLD 616*	41	18 wks
29 Nov 80	GAUCHO *MCA MCF 3090*	27	12 wks
3 Jul 82	GOLD *MCA MCF 3145*	44	6 wks

Woot STEINHOUS

Germany, male instrumentalist - organ

21 Nov 81	HAWAIIAN PARADISE/CHRISTMAS *Warwick WW 5106*	28	7 wks

BARBRA STREISAND Her "Love Songs" was the most successful album of 1982 and followed another No. 1 Album 'Guilty'.

STEPPENWOLF In common with Soft Machine and Mott the Hoople they took their name from a novel—in this case one from the pen of Herman Hesse.

Above **THE SEARCHERS** Waiting for the 3:43 to Lime Street.

150

Jim STEINMAN

US, male vocalist

9 May 81	● **BAD FOR GOOD** *Epic EPC 84361*	8	24 wks

STEPPENWOLF

US, male vocal/instrumental group

28 Feb 70	**MONSTER** *Stateside SSL 5021*	43	4 wks
25 Apr 70	**STEPPENWOLF** *Stateside SSL 5020*	59	2 wks
4 Jul 70	**STEPPENWOLF LIVE** *Stateside SSL 5029*	16	14 wks

Little STEVEN and the DISCIPLES

US, male vocal/instrumental group

6 Nov 82	**MEN WITHOUT WOMEN** *EMI America AML 3027*	73	2 wks

Cat STEVENS

UK, male vocalist

25 Mar 67	● **MATTHEW AND SON** *Deram SML 1004*	7	16 wks
11 Jul 70	**MONA BONE JAKON** *Island ILPS 9118*	63	4 wks
28 Nov 70	**TEA FOR THE TILLERMAN** *Island ILPS 9135*	20	39 wks
2 Oct 71	● **TEASER AND THE FIRECAT** *Island ILPS 9154*	3	93 wks
7 Oct 72	● **CATCH BULL AT FOUR** *Island ILPS 9206*	2	27 wks
21 Jul 73	● **FOREIGNER** *Island ILPS 9240*	3	10 wks
6 Apr 74	● **BUDDAH AND THE CHOCOLATE BOX** *Island ILPS 9274*	3	15 wks
19 Jul 75	● **GREATEST HITS** *Island ILPS 9310*	2	24 wks
14 May 77	**IZITSO** *Island ILPS 9451*	18	15 wks

Ray STEVENS

US, male vocalist

26 Sep 70	**EVERYTHING IS BEAUTIFUL** *CBS 64074*	62	1 wk
13 Sep 75	**MISTY** *Janus 9109 401*	23	7 wks

Shakin' STEVENS

UK, male vocalist

15 Mar 80	**TAKE ONE** *Epic EPC 83978*	62	2 wks
4 Apr 81	● **THIS OLE HOUSE** *Epic EPC 84985*	2	28 wks
8 Aug 81	**SHAKIN' STEVENS** *Hallmark/Pickwick SHM 3065*	34	5 wks
19 Sep 81	★ **SHAKY** *Epic EPC 10027*	1	28 wks
9 Oct 82	● **GIVE ME YOUR HEART TONIGHT** *Epic EPC 10035*	3†	12 wks

Al STEWART

UK, male vocalist

11 Apr 70	**ZERO SHE FLIES** *CBS 63848*	40	4 wks
5 Feb 77	**YEAR OF THE CAT** *RCA Victor RS 1082*	38	7 wks
21 Oct 78	**TIME PASSAGES** *RCA PL 25173*	39	1 wk
6 Sep 80	**24 CARAT** *RCA PL 25306*	55	6 wks

Andy STEWART

UK, male vocalist

3 Feb 82	**ANDY STEWART** *Top Rank 35-116*	13	2 wks

Rod STEWART

UK, male vocalist

3 Oct 70	**GASOLINE ALLEY** *Vertigo 6360 500*	62	1 wk
24 Jul 71	★ **EVERY PICTURE TELLS A STORY** *Mercury 6338 063*	1	81 wks
5 Aug 72	★ **NEVER A DULL MOMENT** *Philips 6499 153*	1	36 wks
25 Aug 73	★ **SING IT AGAIN ROD** *Mercury 6499 484*	1	30 wks
19 Oct 74	★ **SMILER** *Mercury 9104 011*	1	20 wks
30 Aug 75	★ **ATLANTIC CROSSING** *Warner Bros. K 56151*	1	88 wks
3 Jul 76	★ **A NIGHT ON THE TOWN** *Riva RVLP 1*	1	47 wks
16 Jul 77	**BEST OF ROD STEWART** *Mercury 6643 030*	18	22 wks
19 Nov 77	● **FOOT LOOSE AND FANCY FREE** *Riva RVLP 5*	3	26 wks
21 Jan 78	**ATLANTIC CROSSING** (re-issue) *Riva RVLP 4*	60	1 wk
9 Dec 78	● **BLONDES HAVE MORE FUN** *Riva RVLP 8*	3	31 wks
10 Nov 79	★ **GREATEST HITS** *Riva ROD TV 1*	1	26 wks
22 Nov 80	● **FOOLISH BEHAVIOUR** *Riva RVLP 11*	4	13 wks
14 Nov 81	● **TONIGHT I'M YOURS** *Riva RVLP 14*	8	21 wks
13 Nov 82	**ABSOLUTELY LIVE** *Riva RVLP 17*	35	5 wks

See also Rod Stewart and the Faces.

Rod STEWART and the FACES

UK, male vocal/instrumental group

26 Jan 74	● **OVERTURE AND BEGINNERS** *Mercury 9100 001*	3	7 wks

See also Rod Stewart, Faces.

STIFF LITTLE FINGERS

UK, male vocal/instrumental group

3 Mar 79	**INFLAMMABLE MATERIAL** *Rough Trade ROUGH 1*	14	19 wks
15 Mar 80	● **NOBODY'S HEROES** *Chrysalis CHR 1270*	8	10 wks
20 Sep 80	● **HANX** *Chrysalis CHR 1300*	9	5 wks
25 Apr 81	**GO FOR IT** *Chrysalis CHX 1339*	14	8 wks
2 Oct 82	**NOW THEN** *Chrysalis CHR 1400*	24	6 wks

Stephen STILLS

US, male vocalist

19 Dec 70	**STEPHEN STILLS** *Atlantic 2401 004*	30	1 wk
14 Aug 71	**STEPHEN STILLS 2** *Atlantic 2401 013*	22	3 wks
26 Jul 75	**STILLS** *CBS 69146*	31	1 wk
29 May 76	**ILLEGAL STILLS** *CBS 81330*	54	2 wks

See also Crosby, Stills and Nash, and Crosby, Stills, Nash and Young, and Stills-Young Band, and Stephen Stills' Manassas.

STILLS - YOUNG BAND

US/Canada, male vocal/instrumental group

9 Oct 76	**LONG MAY YOU RUN** *Reprise K 54081*	12	5 wks

See also Crosby, Stills and Nash, and Crosby, Stills, Nash and Young, and Stephen Stills, and Stephen Stills' Manassas, and Neil Young.

Stephen STILLS' MANASSAS

US, male vocal/instrumental group

20 May 72	**MANASSAS** *Atlantic K 60021*	30	5 wks
19 May 73	**DOWN THE ROAD** *Atlantic K 40440*	33	2 wks

See also Crosby, Stills and Nash, Crosby, Stills, Nash and Young, and Stephen Stills, and Stills-Young Band.

STONE THE CROWS

UK, female/male vocal/instrumental group

7 Oct 72	**ONTINUOUS PERFORMANCE** *Polydor 2391 043*	33	3 wks

STORYVILLE JAZZMEN — See *Bob WALLIS and his STORYVILLE JAZZMEN*

STRANGLERS

UK, male vocal/instrumental group

30 Apr 77	● **STRANGLERS IV (RATTUS NORVEGICUS)** *United Artists UAG 30045*	4	34 wks
8 Oct 77	● **NO MORE HEROES** *United Artists UAG 30200*	2	19 wks
3 Jun 78	● **BLACK AND WHITE** *United Artists UAK 30222*	2	18 wks
10 Mar 79	● **LIVE (X CERT)** *United Artists UAG 30224*	7	10 wks
6 Oct 79	● **THE RAVEN** *United Artists UAG 30262*	4	8 wks
21 Feb 81	● **THEMENINBLACK** *Liberty LBG 30313*	8	5 wks
21 Nov 81	**LA FOLIE** *Liberty LBG 30342*	11	18 wks
25 Sep 82	**THE COLLECTION 1977-1982** *Liberty LBS 30353*	12	9 wks

STRAWBS

UK, male vocal/instrumental group

21 Nov 70	**JUST A COLLECTION OF ANTIQUES AND CURIOS** *A & M AMLS 994*	27	2 wks
17 Jul 71	**FROM THE WITCHWOOD** *A & M AMLH 64304*	39	2 wks
26 Feb 72	**GRAVE NEW WORLD** *A & M AMLH 68078*	11	12 wks
24 Feb 73	● **BURSTING AT THE SEAMS** *A & M AMLH 68144*	2	12 wks
27 Apr 74	**HERO AND HEROINE** *A & M AMLH 63607*	35	3 wks

STRAY CATS

US, male vocal/instrumental group

28 Feb 81	● **STRAY CATS** *Arista STRAY 1*	6	22 wks
21 Nov 81	**GONNA BALL** *Arista STRAY 2*	48	4 wks

STREETWALKERS

UK, male vocal/instrumental group

12 Jun 76	**RED CARD** *Vertigo 9102 010*	16	6 wks

Barbra STREISAND

US, female vocalist

22 Jan 66	● **MY NAME IS BARBRA, TWO** *CBS BPG 62603*	6	22 wks
4 Apr 70	**GREATEST HITS** *CBS 63921*	44	2 wks
17 Apr 71	**STONEY END** *CBS 64269*	28	2 wks
15 Jun 74	**THE WAY WE WERE** *CBS 69057*	49	1 wk
23 Jul 77	**STREISAND SUPERMAN** *CBS 86030*	32	9 wks
15 Jul 78	**SONGBIRD** *CBS 86060*	50	1 wk
17 Mar 79	★ **BARBRA STREISAND HITS VOL.2** *CBS 10012*	1	30 wks
17 Nov 79	**WET** *CBS 86104*	25	13 wks
11 Oct 80	★ **GUILTY** *CBS 86122*	1	82 wks
16 Jan 82	★ **LOVE SONGS** *CBS 10031*	1†	50 wks

STRINGS FOR PLEASURE

UK, orchestra

4 Dec 71	**BEST OF BACHARACH** *MFP 1334*	49	1 wk

STYLISTICS

US, male vocal group

24 Aug 74	**ROCKIN' ROLL BABY** *Avco 6466 012*	42	3 wks
21 Sep 74	**LET'S PUT IT ALL TOGETHER** *Avoc 6466 013*	26	14 wks
1 Mar 75	**FROM THE MOUNTAIN** *Avco 9109 002*	36	1 wk
5 Apr 75	★ **THE BEST OF THE STYLISTICS** *Avco 9109 003*	1	63 wks
5 Jul 75	● **THANK YOU BABY** *Avco 9109 005*	5	23 wks

Date	Title Label Number	Position	
6 Dec 75	YOU ARE BEAUTIFUL *Avco 9109 006*	26	9 wks
12 Jun 76	FABULOUS *Avco 9109 008*	21	5 wks
18 Sep 76	★ BEST OF THE STYLISTICS VOL.2 *H & L 9109 010*	1	21 wks

STYX

US, male vocal/instrumental group

Date	Title Label Number	Position	
3 Nov 79	CORNERSTONE *A & M AMLK 63711*	36	8 wks
24 Jan 81	● PARADISE THEATER *A & M AMLH 63719*	8	8 wks

Donna SUMMER

US, female vocalist

Date	Title Label Number	Position	
31 Jan 76	LOVE TO LOVE YOU BABY *GTO GTLP 008*	16	9 wks
22 May 76	A LOVE TRILOGY *GTO GTLP 010*	41	10 wks
25 Jun 77	● I REMEMBER YESTERDAY *GTO GTLP 025*	3	23 wks
26 Nov 77	ONCE UPON A TIME *Casablanca CALD 5003*	24	13 wks
7 Jan 78	● GREATEST HITS *GTO GTLP 028*	4	18 wks
21 Oct 78	LIVE AND MORE *Casablanca CALD 5006*	16	16 wks
2 Jun 79	BAD GIRLS *Casablanca CALD 5007*	23	23 wks
10 Nov 79	ON THE RADIO - GREATEST HITS VOLS. 1 & 2 *Casablanca CALD 5008*	24	22 wks
1 Nov 80	THE WANDERER *Geffen K 99124*	55	2 wks
31 Jul 82	DONNA SUMMER *Warner Bros K 99193*	13†	15 wks

SUNSHINE BAND — See *KC and the SUNSHINE BAND*

SUPERTRAMP

UK/US, male vocal/instrumental group

Date	Title Label Number	Position	
23 Nov 74	● CRIME OF THE CENTURY *A & M AMLS 68258*	4	22 wks
6 Dec 75	CRISIS? WHAT CRISIS? *A & M AMLH 68347*	20	15 wks
23 Apr 77	EVEN IN THE QUIETEST MOMENTS *A & M AMLK 64634*	12	22 wks
31 Mar 79	● BREAKFAST IN AMERICA *A & M AMLK 63708*	3	52 wks
4 Oct 80	● PARIS *A & M AMLM 66702*	7	17 wks
6 Nov 82	● FAMOUS LAST WORDS *A&M AMLK 63732*	6†	8 wks

SUPREMES

US, female vocal group

Date	Title Label Number	Position	
5 Dec 64	● MEET THE SUPREMES *Stateside SL 10109*	8	6 wks
17 Dec 66	SUPREMES A GO-GO *Tamla Motown STML 11039*	15	21 wks
13 May 67	SUPREMES SING MOTOWN *Tamla Motown STML 11047*	15	16 wks
30 Sep 67	SUPREMES SING RODGERS AND HART *Tamla Motown STML 11054*	25	7 wks
20 Jan 68	GREATEST HITS *Tamla Motown STML 11063*	1	60 wks
30 Mar 68	LIVE AT THE TALK OF THE TOWN *Tamla Motown STML 11070*	6	18 wks

Date	Title Label Number	Position	
20 Jul 68	REFLECTIONS *Tamla Motown STML 11073*	30	2 wks
1 Feb 69	LOVE CHILD *Tamla Motown STML 11095*	8	6 wks
25 Sep 71	TOUCH *Tamla Motown STML 11189*	40	1 wk

See also Diana Ross and the Supremes with the Temptations, and the Supremes and the Four Tops.

SUPREMES and the FOUR TOPS

US, female and male vocal groups

Date	Title Label Number	Position	
29 May 71	● MAGNIFICENT SEVEN *Tamla Motown STML 11179*	6	11 wks

See also Diana Ross , and Diana Ross and the Supremes with the Temptations, and the Supremes.

SURVIVOR

US, male vocal/instrumental group

Date	Title Label Number	Position	
21 Aug 82	EYE OF THE TIGER *Scotti Bros SCT 85845*	12	10 wks

SUTHERLAND BROTHERS and QUIVER

UK, male vocal/instrumental group

Date	Title Label Number	Position	
15 May 76	REACH FOR THE SKY *CBS 69191*	26	8 wks
9 Oct 76	SLIPSTREAM *CBS 81593*	49	3 wks

SWEET

UK, male vocal/instrumental group

Date	Title Label Number	Position	
18 May 74	SWEET FANNY ADAMS *RCA LPI 5038*	27	2 wks

SWINGLE SINGERS

US/France, male/female vocal group

Date	Title Label Number	Position	
1 Feb 64	JAZZ SEBASTIAN BACH *Philips BL 7572*	13	18 wks

SYLVESTER

US, male vocalist

Date	Title Label Number	Position	
23 Jun 79	MIGHTY REAL *Fantasy FTA 3009*	62	3 wks

T. REX

UK, male vocal/instrumental group

Date	Title *Label Number*	Position	
13 Jul 68	**MY PEOPLE WERE FAIR AND HAD SKY IN THEIR HAIR BUT NOW THEY'RE CONTENT TO WEAR STARS ON THEIR BROW'S** *Regal Zonophone SLRZ 1003*	15	9 wks
7 Jun 69	**UNICORN** *Regal Zonophone S 1007*	12	3 wks
14 Mar 70	**A BEARD OF STARS** *Regal Zonophone SLRZ 1013*	21	6 wks
16 Jan 71	**T. REX** *Fly HIFLY 2*	13	24 wks
7 Aug 71	**THE BEST OF T. REX** *Flyback TON 2*	21	7 wks
9 Oct 71	★ **ELECTRIC WARRIOR** *Fly HIFLY 6*	1	44 wks
29 Mar 72	★ **PROPHETS, SEERS AND SAGES THE ANGELS OF THE AGES/MY PEOPLE WERE FAIR.....** *Fly Doubleback TOOFA 3/4*	1	12 wks
20 May 72	★ **BOLAN BOOGIE** *Fly HIFLY 8*	1	19 wks
5 Aug 72	● **THE SLIDER** *EMI BLN 5001*	4	18 wks
9 Dec 72	**BEARD OF STARS/UNICORN** *Cube TOOFA 9/10*	44	2 wks
31 Mar 73	● **TANX** *EMI BLN 5002*	4	12 wks
10 Nov 73	**GREAT HITS** *EMI BLN 5003*	32	3 wks
16 Mar 74	**ZINC ALLOY AND THE HIDDEN RIDERS OF TOMORROW** *EMI BLNA 7751*	12	3 wks
21 Feb 76	**FUTURISTIC DRAGON** *EMI BLN 5004*	50	1 wk
9 Apr 77	**DANDY IN THE UNDERWORLD** *EMI BLN 5005*	26	3 wks
30 Jun 79	**SOLID GOLD** *EMI NUT 5*	51	3 wks
12 Sep 81	**T. REX IN CONCERT** *Marc ABOLAN 1*	35	6 wks
7 Nov 81	**YOU SCARE ME TO DEATH** *Cherry Red ERED 20*	88	1 wk

Phrophets .../My People ... *is a double re-issue although* Phrophets *had not previously been a hit.* Beard Of Stars/Unicorn *is a double re-issue. The first three albums and the two double re-issues are credited to Tyrannosaurus Rex.* Zinc Alloy ... *is credited to Marc Bolan and T. Rex.* You Scare Me To Death *is credited to Marc Bolan.*

TALK TALK

UK, male vocal/instrumental group

Date	Title *Label Number*	Position	
24 Jul 82	**THE PARTY'S OVER** *EMI EMC 343*	21	22 wks

TALKING HEADS

UK, male vocal/instrumental group

Date	Title *Label Number*	Position	
25 Feb 78	**TALKING HEADS '77** *Sire 9103 328*	60	1 wk
29 Jul 78	**MORE SONGS ABOUT FOOD AND BUILDINGS** *Sire K 56531*	21	3 wks
15 Sep 79	**FEAR OF MUSIC** *Sire SRK 6076*	33	5 wks
1 Nov 80	**REMAIN IN LIGHT** *Sire SRK 6095*	21	17 wks
10 Apr 82	**THE NAME OF THIS BAND IS TALKING HEADS** *Sire SRK 23590*	22	5 wks

TANGERINE DREAM

Germany, male instrumental group

Date	Title *Label Number*	Position	
20 Apr 74	**PHAEDRA** *Virgin V 2010*	15	15 wks
5 Apr 75	**RUBYCON** *Virgin V 2025*	12	14 wks
20 Dec 75	**RICOCHET** *Virgin V 2044*	40	2 wks
13 Nov 76	**STRATOSFEAR** *Virgin V 2068*	39	4 wks
23 Jul 77	**SORCERER (FILM SOUNDTRACK)** *MCA MCF 2806*	25	7 wks
19 Nov 77	**ENCORE** *Virgin VD 2506*	55	1 wk
1 Apr 78	**CYCLONE** *Virgin V 2097*	37	4 wks
17 Feb 79	**FORCE MAJEURE** *Virgin V 2111*	26	5 wks
7 Jun 80	**TANGRAM** *Virgin V 2147*	36	5 wks
18 Apr 81	**THIEF** *Virgin V 2198*	43	3 wks
19 Sep 81	**EXIT** *Virgin V 2212*	43	5 wks
10 Apr 82	**WHITE EAGLE** *Virgin V 2226*	57	5 wks

TANK

UK, male vocal/instrumental group

Date	Title *Label Number*	Position	
13 Mar 82	**FILTH HOUNDS OF HADES** *Kamaflage KAMLP 1*	33	5 wks

TASTE

Ireland, male vocal/instrumental group

Date	Title *Label Number*	Position	
7 Feb 70	**ON THE BOARDS** *Polydor 583-083*	18	11 wks
9 Sep 72	**TASTE LIVE AT THE ISLE OF WIGHT** *Polydor 2383 120*	41	1 wk

TAVARES

US, male vocal group

Date	Title *Label Number*	Position	
21 Aug 76	**SKY HIGH** *Capitol EST 11533*	22	13 wks
1 Apr 78	**THE BEST OF TAVARES** *Capitol EST 11701*	39	2 wks

James TAYLOR

US, male vocalist

Date	Title *Label Number*	Position	
21 Nov 70	● **SWEET BABY JAMES** *Warner Bros. ES 1843*	7	53 wks
29 May 71	● **MUD SLIDE SLIM AND THE BLUE HORIZON** *Warner Bros. WS 2561*	4	41 wks
8 Jan 72	**SWEET BABY JAMES** (re-issue) *Warner Bros. K 46043*	34	6 wks
18 Mar 72	**MUD SLIDE SLIM & THE BLUE HORIZON** (re-issue) *Warner Bros. K 46085*	49	1 wk
9 Dec 72	**ONE MAN DOG** *Warner Bros. K 46185*	27	5 wks

Above **CAT STEVENS**   9 chart lives for Cat.

Above Left **TANGERINE DREAM**   Formed in 1967, the German trio have performed their experimental electronic music in such hallowed halls as York Minster and the cathedrals at Liverpool, Coventry and Rheims.

Below Left **THE SHADOWS**   A camel relaxing in the Shadows.

155

Roger TAYLOR

UK, male vocalist

18 Apr 81	**FUN IN SPACE** *EMI EMC 3369*	18	5 wks

The TEARDROP EXPLODES

UK, male vocal/instrumental group

18 Oct 80	**KILIMANJARO** *Mercury 6359 035*	24	35 wks
5 Dec 81	**WILDER** *Mercury 6359 056*	29	6 wks

TELEVISION

US, male vocal/instrumental group

26 Mar 77	**MARQUEE MOON** *Elektra K 52046*	28	13 wks
29 Apr 78	● **ADVENTURE** *Elektra K 52072*	7	4 wks

TEMPERANCE SEVEN

UK, male vocal/instrumental group

13 May 61	**TEMPERANCE SEVEN PLUS ONE** *Argo RG 11*	19	1 wk
25 Nov 61	**TEMPERANCE SEVEN 1961** *Parlophone PMC 1152*	11	4 wks
27 Jan 62	● **THE TEMPERANCE SEVEN** *Parlophone PMC 1152*	8	5 wks

TEMPLE CHURCH CHOIR

UK, male vocal/instrumental group

16 Dec 61	● **CHRISTMAS CAROLS** *HMV CLP 1309*	8	3 wks

TEMPTATIONS

US, male vocal group

24 Dec 66	**GETTING READY** *Tamla Motown STML 11035*	40	2 wks
11 Feb 67	**TEMPTATIONS GREATEST HITS** *Tamla Motown STML 11042*	26	40 wks
22 Jul 67	**TEMPTATIONS LIVE** *Tamla Motown STML 11053*	20	4 wks
18 Nov 67	**TEMPTATIONS WITH A LOT OF SOUL** *Tamla Motown STML 11057*	19	18 wks
20 Sep 69	**CLOUD NINE** *Tamla Motown STML 11109*	32	1 wk
14 Feb 70	**PUZZLE PEOPLE** *Tamla Motown STML 11133*	20	4 wks
11 Jul 70	**PSYCHEDELIC SHACK** *Tamla Motown STML 11147*	56	1 wk
26 Dec 70	**GREATEST HITS VOL.2** *Tamla Motown STML 11170*	35	12 wks
29 Apr 72	**SOLID ROCK** *Tamla Motown STML 11202*	34	2 wks
20 Jan 73	**ALL DIRECTIONS** *Tamla Motown STML 11218*	19	7 wks
7 Jul 73	**MASTERPIECE** *Tamla Motown STML 11229*	28	3 wks

See also Diana Ross and the Supremes with the Temptations.

10 C.C.

UK, male vocal/instrumental group

1 Sep 73	**10 C.C.** *UK UKAL 1005*	36	5 wks
15 Jun 74	● **SHEET MUSIC** *UK UKAL 1007*	9	24 wks
22 Mar 75	● **THE ORIGINAL SOUNDTRACK** *Mercury 9102 50Q*	4	40 wks
7 Jun 75	● **GREATEST HITS OF 10 C.C.** *Decca UKAL 1012*	9	18 wks
31 Jan 76	● **HOW DARE YOU?** *Mercury 9102 501*	5	31 wks
14 May 77	● **DECEPTIVE BENDS** *Mercury 9102 502*	3	21 wks
10 Dec 77	**LIVE AND LET LIVE** *Mercury 6641 698*	14	15 wks
23 Sep 78	● **BLOODY TOURISTS** *Mercury 9102 503*	3	15 wks
6 Oct 79	● **GREATEST HITS 1972-1978** *Mercury 9102 504*	5	21 wks
5 Apr 80	**LOOK HERE** *Mercury 9102 505*	35	5 wks

TEN POLE TUDOR

UK, male vocal/instrumental group

9 May 81	● **EDDIE, OLD BOB, DICK & GARRY** *Stiff SEEZ 31*	4	8 wks

TEN YEARS AFTER

UK, male vocal/instrumental group

21 Sep 68	**UNDEAD** *Deram SML 1023*	26	7 wks
22 Feb 69	● **STONEDHENGE** *Deram SML 1029*	6	5 wks
4 Oct 69	● **SSSSH** *Deram SML 1052*	4	18 wks
2 May 70	● **CRICKLEWOOD GREEN** *Deram SML 1065*	4	27 wks
9 Jan 71	● **WATT** *Deram SML 1078*	5	12 wks
13 Nov 71	**SPACE IN TIME** *Chrysalis CHR 1001*	36	1 wk
7 Oct 72	**ROCK AND ROLL** *Chrysalis CHR 1009*	27	1 wk
28 Jul 73	**RECORDED LIVE** *Chrysalis CHR 1049*	36	2 wks

TENNILLE — See *CAPTAIN and TENNILLE*

THEATRE OF HATE

UK, male vocal/instrumental group

13 Mar 82	**WESTWORLD** *Burning Rome ROME TOH 1*	17	6 wks

THIN LIZZY

Ireland, male vocal/instrumental group

27 Sep 75	**FIGHTING** *Vertigo 6360 121*	60	1 wk
10 Apr 76	● **JAILBREAK** *Vertigo 9102 008*	10	50 wks
6 Nov 76	**JOHNNY THE FOX** *Vertigo 9102 012*	11	24 wks

Date	Title Label Number	Position		Date	Title Label Number	Position	
1 Oct 77	● BAD REPUTATION *Vertigo 9102 016*	4	9 wks	3 Mar 79	● A COLLECTION OF THEIR 20 GREATEST HITS *Epic EPC 10013*	8	18 wks
17 Jun 78	● LIVE AND DANGEROUS *Vertigo 6641 807*	2	62 wks	15 Dec 79	3D *Ariola 3D1*	61	7 wks
5 May 79	● BLACK ROSE (A ROCK LEGEND) *Vertigo 9102 032*	2	21 wks	27 Sep 80	● GOLD *Ariola 3D 2*	9	15 wks
18 Oct 80	● CHINA TOWN *Vertigo 6359 030*	7	7 wks				
11 Apr 81	● ADVENTURES OF THIN LIZZY *Vertigo LIZTV 1*	6	13 wks				
5 Dec 81	RENEGADE *Vertigo 6359 083*	38	8 wks				

TICH — See *Dave DEE, DOZY, BEAKY, MICK and TICH*

THIRD EAR BAND

TIGHT FIT

UK, male instrumental group

UK, male/female vocal group

27 Jun 70	AIR, EARTH, FIRE, WATER *Harvest SHVL 773*	49	2 wks	26 Sep 81	BACK TO THE SIXTIES *Jive HIP 1*	38	4 wks
				4 Sep 82	TIGHT FIT *Jive HIP 2*	87	2 wks

THIRD WORLD

TOM TOM CLUB

Jamaica, male vocal/instrumental group

US, female/male vocal/instrumental group

21 Oct 78	JOURNEY TO ADDIS *Island ILPS 9554*	30	6 wks	24 Oct 81	TOM TOM CLUB *Island ILPS 9686*	78	1 wk
11 Jul 81	ROCKS THE WORLD *CBS 85027*	37	9 wks				
15 May 82	YOU'VE GOT THE POWER *CBS 85563*	87	3 wks				

Carla THOMAS — See *Otis REDDING and Carla THOMAS*

TOMITA

Japan, male instrumentalist - synthesiser

Ray THOMAS

7 Jun 75	SNOWFLAKES ARE DANCING *RCA Red Seal ARL 1 0488*	17	20 wks
16 Aug 75	PICTURES AT AN EXHIBITION *RCA Red Seal ARL 1 0838*	42	5 wks
7 May 77	HOLST: THE PLANETS *RCA Red Seal RL 11919*	41	6 wks
9 Feb 80	TOMITA'S GREATEST HITS *RCA Red Seal RL 43076*	66	2 wks

UK, male vocalist

26 Jul 75	FROM MIGHTY OAKS *Threshold THS 16*	23	3 wks

THOMPSON TWINS

UK, male/female vocal instrumental group

13 Mar 82	SET *Tee TELP 2*	48	3 wks

Bernie TORME

UK, male vocalist/instrumentalist - guitar

3 Jul 82	TURN OUT THE LIGHTS *Kamaflage KAMLP 2*	50	3 wks

George THOROGOOD and the DESTROYERS

US, male vocal/instrumental group

Peter TOSH

Jamaica, male vocalist

2 Dec 78	GEORGE THOROGOOD AND THE DESTROYERS *Sonet SNTF 781*	67	1 wk

25 Sep 76	LEGALIZE IT *Virgin V 2061*	54	1 wk

THREE DEGREES

TOTO

US, female vocal group

US, male vocal/instrumental group

31 Mar 79	TOTO *CBS 83148*	37	5 wks

10 Aug 74	THREE DEGREES *Philadelphia International 65858*	12	22 wks
17 May 75	● TAKE GOOD CARE OF YOURSELF *Philadelphia Int. PIR 69137*	6	16 wks
24 Feb 79	NEW DIMENSIONS *Ariola ARLH 5012*	34	13 wks

THE TREMELOES Originally formed as Brian Poole and the Tremeloes in 1959, they parted company with their singer in 1966, and are seen here a year later during the recording of their No. 1 single "Silence Is Golden".

Left **TEN YEARS AFTER** Seen here recording live at a Hampstead gig, they undertook no less than 28 American tours—more than any other British group in rock history.

Below Left **THE TEMPTATIONS** "Well, the agency said they'd send five temps" . . .

Below **TRAFFIC** They shed new light on the phrase "go and play in the traffic".

Right **TOYAH**   Her favourite album in this book is T.Rex's 1971 L.P. "Electric Warrior".

Below **U.F.O.**   Albumwise in the dark from 1970 until 'Lights Out'.

Right **ULTRAVOX**   Their first hit album was named after the birthplace of Mozart, Beethoven, Haydn, Brahms, Schubert and Mahler.

TOURISTS

UK, male/female vocal/instrumental group

14 Jul 79	**THE TOURISTS** *Logo GO 1018*	72	1 wk
3 Nov 79	**REALITY EFFECT** *Logo GO 1019*	23	16 wks
22 Nov 80	**LUMINOUS BASEMENT** *RCA RCALP 5001*	75	1 wk

Pete TOWNSHEND

UK, male vocalist/instrumentalist - guitar

21 Oct 72	**WHO CAME FIRST** *Track 2408 201*	30	2 wks
3 May 80	**EMPTY GLASS** *Atco K 50699*	11	14 wks
3 Jul 82	**ALL THE BEST COWBOYS HAVE CHINESE EYES** *Atco K 50889*	32	8 wks

See also Pete Townshend and Ronnie Lane.

Pete TOWNSHEND and Ronnie LANE

UK, male vocalists

| 15 Oct 77 | **ROUGH MIX** *Polydor 2442 147* | 44 | 3 wks |

See also Pete Townshend, Ronnie Lane and the Band Slim Chance.

TOYAH

UK, female vocalist

14 Jun 80	**THE BLUE MEANING** *Safari IEYA 666*	40	4 wks
17 Jan 81	**TOYAH TOYAH TOYAH** *Safari LIVE 2*	22	14 wks
30 May 81	● **ANTHEM** *Safari VOOR 1*	2	46 wks
19 Jun 82	● **THE CHANGELING** *Safari VOOR 9*	6	12 wks
13 Nov 82	**WARRIOR ROCK-TOYAH ON TOUR** *Safari TNT 1*	20	6 wks

TRAFFIC

UK, male vocal/instrumental group

30 Dec 67	● **MR. FANTASY** *Island ILP 9061*	8	16 wks
26 Oct 68	● **TRAFFIC** *Island ILPS 9081 T*	9	8 wks
8 Aug 70	**JOHN BARLEYCORN MUST DIE** *Island ILPS 9116*	11	9 wks
24 Nov 73	**ON THE ROAD** *Island ISLD 2*	40	3 wks
28 Sep 74	**WHEN THE EAGLE FLIES** *Island ILPS 9273*	31	1 wk

Pat TRAVERS

US, male instrumentalist - guitar

| 2 Apr 77 | **MAKIN' MAGIC** *Polydor 2383 436* | 40 | 3 wks |

John TRAVOLTA

US, male vocalist

| 23 Dec 78 | **SANDY** *Polydor POLD 5014* | 40 | 6 wks |

TREMELOES

UK, male vocal/instrumental group

| 3 Jun 67 | **HERE COME THE TREMELOES** *CBS SBPG 63017* | 15 | 7 wks |

TRIUMPH

Canada, male vocal/instrumental group

| 10 May 80 | **PROGRESSIONS OF POWER** *RCA PL 13524* | 61 | 5 wks |
| 3 Oct 81 | **ALLIED FORCES** *RCA RCALP 6002* | 64 | 3 wks |

TROGGS

UK, male vocal/instrumental group

30 Jul 66	● **FROM NOWHERE...THE TROGGS** *Fontana TL 5355*	6	16 wks
25 Feb 67	● **TROGGLODYNAMITE** *Page One POL 001*	10	11 wks
5 Aug 67	**BEST OF THE TROGGS** *Page One FOR 001*	24	5 wks

TROUBADOURS DU ROI BAUDOUIN

Zaire, male/female vocal group

| 22 May 76 | **MISSA! LUBA!** *Philips SBL 7952* | 59 | 1 wk |

Robin TROWER

UK, male instrumentalist - guitar

1 Mar 75	**FOR EARTH BELOW** *Chrysalis CHR 1073*	26	4 wks
13 Mar 76	**LIVE** *Chrysalis CHR 1089*	15	6 wks
30 Oct 76	**LONG MISTY DAYS** *Chrysalis CHR 1107*	31	1 wk
29 Oct 77	**IN CITY DREAMS** *Chrysalis CHR 1148*	58	1 wk
16 Feb 80	**VICTIMS OF THE FURY** *Chrysalis CHR 1215*	61	4 wks

TUBES

US, male vocal/instrumental group

| 4 Mar 78 | **WHAT DO YOU WANT FROM LIFE** *A & M AMS 68460* | 38 | 1 wk |
| 2 Jun 79 | **REMOTE CONTROL** *A & M AMLH 64751* | 40 | 5 wks |

Date	Title *Label Number*	Position		Date	Title *Label Number*	Position

TUBEWAY ARMY

UK, male vocal/instrumental group

9 Jun 79	★ **REPLICAS** *Beggars Banquet BEGA 7*	1	31 wks
25 Aug 79	**TUBEWAY ARMY** *Beggars Banquet BEGA 4*	14	10 wks

Ike and Tina TURNER

US, male instrumentalist - guitar and female vocalist

1 Oct 66	**RIVER DEEP - MOUNTAIN HIGH** *London HAU 8298*	27	1 wk

TURTLES

US, male vocal/instrumental group

22 Jul 67	**HAPPY TOGETHER** *London HAU 8330*	18	9 wks

TWIGGY

UK, female vocalist

21 Aug 76	**TWIGGY** *Mercury 9102 600*	33	8 wks
30 Apr 77	**PLEASE GET MY NAME RIGHT** *Mercury 9102 601*	35	3 wks

TWISTED SISTER

US, male vocal/instrumental group

25 Sep 82	**UNDER THE BLADE** *Secret SECX 9*	70	3 wks

TYGERS OF PAN TANG

UK, male vocal/instrumental group

30 Aug 80	**WILD CAT** *MCA MCF 3075*	18	5 wks
18 Apr 81	**SPELLBOUND** *MCA MCF 3104*	33	4 wks
21 Nov 81	**CRAZY NIGHTS** *MCA MCF 3123*	51	3 wks
28 Aug 82	**THE CAGE** *MCA MCF 3150*	13	8 wks

Judie TZUKE

UK, female vocalist

4 Aug 79	**WELCOME TO THE CRUISE** *Rocket TRAIN 7*	14	17 wks
10 May 80	● **SPORTS CAR** *Rocket TRAIN 9*	7	11 wks
16 May 81	**I AM PHOENIX** *Rocket TRAIN 15*	17	10 wks
17 Apr 82	**SHOOT THE MOON** *Chrysalis CDL 1382*	19	10 wks
30 Oct 82	**ROAD NOISE-THE OFFICIAL BOOTLEG** *Chrysalis CTY 1405*	39	4 wks

U

U 2

Ireland, male vocal/instrumental group

29 Aug 81	**BOY** *Island ILPS 9646*	52	9 wks
24 Oct 81	**OCTOBER** *Island ILPS 9680*	11	11 wks

UB 40

UK, male vocal/instrumental group

6 Sep 80	● **SIGNING OFF** *Graduate GRAD LP 2*	2	71 wks
6 Jun 81	● **PRESENT ARMS** *DEP International LP DEP 1*	2	38 wks
10 Oct 81	**PRESENT ARMS IN DUB** *DEP International LPS DEP 2*	38	7 wks
28 Aug 82	**THE SINGLES ALBUM** *Graduate GRADLSP 3*	17	8 wks
9 Oct 82	● **UB 44** *Dep International LP DEP 3*	4	8 wks

UFO

UK, male vocal/instrumental group

4 Jun 77	**LIGHTS OUT** *Chrysalis CHR 1127*	54	2 wks
15 Jul 78	**OBSESSION** *Chrysalis CDL 1182*	26	7 wks
10 Feb 79	● **STRANGERS IN THE NIGHT** *Chrysalis CJT 5*	8	11 wks
19 Jan 80	**NO PLACE TO RUN** *Chrysalis CDL 1239*	11	7 wks
24 Jan 81	**THE WILD THE WILLING AND THE INNOCENT** *Chrysalis CHR 1307*	19	5 wks
20 Feb 82	● **MECHANIX** *Chrysalis CHR 1360*	8	6 wks

U.K.

UK, male vocal/instrumental group

27 May 78	**U.K.** *Polydor 2302 080*	43	3 wks

U.K. SUBS

UK, male vocal/instrumental group

13 Oct 79	**ANOTHER KIND OF BLUES** *Gem GEMLP 100*	21	6 wks
19 Apr 80	**BRAND NEW AGE** *Gem GEMLP 106*	18	9 wks
27 Sep 80	● **CRASH COURSE** *Gem GEMLP 111*	8	6 wks
21 Feb 81	**DIMINISHED RESPONSIBILITY**	18	5 wks

VANILLA FUDGE Three years after the demise of the Fudge, the group's bass player and drummer Tim Bogart and Carmine Appice scored again in the chart as two-thirds of Beck, Bogart and Appice.

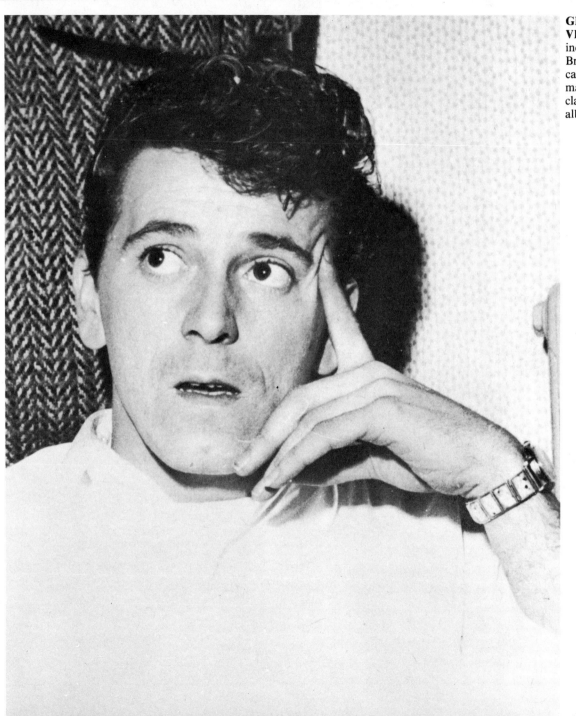

GENE VINCENT The inception of the British LP charts came too late for many of Gene's classic rock 'n' roll albums.

ULTRAVOX

UK, male vocal/instrumental group

19 Jul 80	● **VIENNA** *Chrysalis CHR 1296*	3	71 wks
19 Sep 81	● **RAGE IN EDEN** *Chrysalis CDL 1338*	4	23 wks
23 Oct 82	● **QUARTET** *Chrysalis CDL 1394*	6†	10 wks

UNDERTONES

UK, male vocal/instrumental group

19 May 79	**THE UNDERTONES** *Sire SRK 6071*	13	21 wks
26 Apr 80	● **HYPNOTISED** *Sire SRK 6088*	6	10 wks
16 May 81	**POSITIVE TOUCH** *Ardeck ARD 103*	17	6 wks

UNION GAP — See *Gary PUCKETT and the UNION GAP*

URIAH HEEP

UK, male vocal/instrumental group

13 Nov 71	**LOOK AT YOURSELF** *Island ILPS 9169*	39	1 wk
10 Jun 72	**DEMONS AND WIZARDS** *Bronze ILPS 9193*	20	11 wks
2 Dec 72	**THE MAGICIAN'S BIRTHDAY** *Bronze ILPS 9213*	28	3 wks
19 May 73	**LIVE** *Island ISLD 1*	23	8 wks
29 Sep 73	**SWEET FREEDOM** *Island ILPS 9245*	18	3 wks
29 Jun 74	**WONDERWORLD** *Bronze ILPS 9280*	23	3 wks
5 Jul 75	● **RETURN TO FANTASY** *Bronze ILPS 9335*	7	6 wks
12 Jun 76	**HIGH AND MIGHTY** *Island ILPS 9384*	55	1 wk
22 Mar 80	**CONQUEST** *Bronze BRON 524*	37	3 wks
17 Apr 82	**ABOMINOG** *Bronze BRON 538*	34	6 wks

UTOPIA

UK, male vocal/instrumental group

| 1 Oct 77 | **OOPS SORRY WRONG PLANET** *Bearsville K 53517* | 59 | 1 wk |
| 16 Feb 80 | **ADVENTURES IN UTOPIA** *Island ILPS 9602* | 57 | 2 wks |

VAN DE GRAAF GENERATOR

UK, male vocal/instrumental group

| 25 Apr 70 | **THE LEAST WE CAN DO IS WAVE TO EACH OTHER** *Charisma CAS 1007* | 47 | 2 wks |

VAN HALEN

US/Holland, male vocal/instrumental group

27 May 78	**VAN HALEN** *Warner Bros. K 56470*	34	11 wks
14 Apr 79	**VAN HALEN II** *Warner Bros. K 566116*	23	7 wks
5 Apr 80	**WOMEN AND CHILDREN FIRST** *Warner Bros. K 56793*	15	7 wks
23 May 81	**FAIR WARNING** *Warner Bros. K 56899*	49	4 wks
1 May 82	**DIVER DOWN** *Warner Bros. K 57003*	36	5 wks

VANGELIS

Greece, male instrumentalist - keyboards

10 Jan 76	**HEAVEN AND HELL** *RCA Victor RS 1025*	31	7 wks
9 Oct 76	**ALBEDO 0.39** *RCA Victor RS 1080*	18	6 wks
18 Apr 81	● **CHARIOTS OF FIRE** *Polydor POLS 1026*	5†	76 wks

See also *Jon and Vangelis.*

VANILLA FUDGE

US, male vocal/instrumental group

| 4 Nov 67 | **VANILLA FUDGE** *Atlantic 588-086* | 31 | 3 wks |

VAPORS

UK, male vocal/instrumental group

| 7 Jun 80 | **NEW CLEAR DAYS** *United Artists UAG 30300* | 44 | 6 wks |

VARDIS

UK, male vocal/instrumental group

| 1 Nov 80 | **100 MPH** *Logo MOGO 4012* | 52 | 1 wk |

Frankie VAUGHAN

UK, male vocalist

5 Sep 59	● **FRANKIE VAUGHAN AT THE LONDON PALLADIUM** *Philips BDL 7330*	6	2 wks
4 Nov 67	**FRANKIE VAUGHAN SONGBOOK** *Philips DBL 001*	40	1 wk
25 Nov 67	**THERE MUST BE A WAY** *Columbia SCX 6200*	22	8 wks
12 Nov 77	**100 GOLDEN GREATS** *Ronco RTDX 2021*	24	9 wks

Sarah VAUGHAN

US, female vocalist

| 26 Mar 60 | **NO COUNT - SARAH** *Mercury MMC 14021* | 19 | 1 wk |

Bobby VEE

US, male vocalist

Date	Title	Pos	Wks
24 Feb 62	● TAKE GOOD CARE OF MY BABY *London HAG 2428*	7	8 wks
31 Mar 62	HITS OF THE ROCKIN' 50'S *London HAG 2406*	20	1 wk
12 Jan 63	● A BOBBY VEE RECORDING SESSION *Liberty LBY 1084*	10	11 wks
20 Apr 63	● BOBBY VEE'S GOLDEN GREATS *Liberty LBY 1112*	10	14 wks
5 Oct 63	THE NIGHT HAS A THOUSAND EYES *Liberty LIB 1139*	15	2 wks
19 Apr 80	● THE BOBBY VEE SINGLES ALBUM *United Artists UAG 30253*	5	10 wks

See also Bobby Vee and the Crickets.

Bobby VEE and the CRICKETS

US, male vocalist and male vocal/instrumental group

Date	Title	Pos	Wks
27 Oct 62	● BOBBY VEE MEETS THE CRICKETS *Liberty LBY 1086*	2	27 wks

See also Bobby Vee, Crickets, Buddy Holly and the Crickets.

Anthony VENTURA ORCHESTRA

Swiss, orchestra

Date	Title	Pos	Wks
20 Jan 79	DREAM LOVER *Lotus WH 5007*	44	4 wks

VIBRATORS

UK, male vocal/instrumental group

Date	Title	Pos	Wks
25 Jun 77	THE VIBRATORS *Epic EPC 82907*	49	5 wks
29 Apr 78	V2 *Epic EPC 82495*	33	2 wks

VICE SQUAD

UK, male/female vocal instrumental group

Date	Title	Pos	Wks
24 Oct 81	NO CAUSE FOR CONCERN *Zonophone ZEM 103*	32	5 wks
22 May 82	STAND STRONG STAND PROUD *Zonophone ZEM 104*	47	5 wks

Sid VICIOUS

UK, male vocalist

Date	Title	Pos	Wks
15 Dec 79	SID SINGS *Virgin V 2144*	30	8 wks

VIENNA PHILHARMONIC ORCHESTRA — See *Aram KHATCHATURIAN/VIENNA PHILHARMONIC ORCHESTRA*

VILLAGE PEOPLE

US, male vocal/instrumental group

Date	Title	Pos	Wks
27 Jan 79	CRUISIN' *Mercury 9109 614*	24	9 wks
12 May 79	GO WEST *Mercury 9109 621*	14	19 wks

Gene VINCENT

US, male vocalist

Date	Title	Pos	Wks
16 Jul 60	CRAZY TIMES *Capitol T 1342*	12	2 wks

VIOLINSKI

UK, male instrumental group

Date	Title	Pos	Wks
26 May 79	NO CAUSE FOR ALARM *Jet JETLU 219*	49	1 wk

VISAGE

UK, male vocal/instrumental group

Date	Title	Pos	Wks
24 Jan 81	VISAGE *Polydor 2490 157*	13	20 wks
3 Apr 82	● THE ANVIL *Polydor POLD 5050*	6	16 wks

VOYAGE

UK/France, disco aggregation

Date	Title	Pos	Wks
9 Sep 78	VOYAGE *GTO GTLP 030*	59	1 wk

W

WAH!

UK, male vocal/instrumental group

Date	Title	Pos	Wks
18 Jul 81	NAH-POO THE ART OF BLUFF *Eternal CLASSIC 1*	33	5 wks

WAILERS — See *Bob MARLEY and the WAILERS*

Rick WAKEMAN

UK, male instrumentalist - keyboards

Date	Title	Pos	Wks
24 Feb 73	● THE SIX WIVES OF HENRY VIII *A & M AMLH 64361*	7	22 wks
18 May 74	★ JOURNEY TO THE CENTRE OF THE EARTH *A & M AMLH 63621*	1	30 wks
12 Apr 75	● THE MYTHS AND LEGENDS OF KING ARTHUR AND THE KNIGHTS OF THE ROUND TABLE *A & M AMLH 64515*	2	28 wks
24 Apr 76	● NO EARTHLY CONNECTION *A & M AMLK 64583*	9	9 wks
12 Feb 77	WHITE ROCK *A & M AMLH 64614*	14	9 wks
3 Dec 77	● CRIMINAL RECORD *A & M AMLK 64660*	25	5 wks
2 Jun 79	RHAPSODIES *A & M AMLX 68508*	25	10 wks
27 Jun 81	1984 *Charisma CDS 4022*	24	9 wks

Scott WALKER

US, male vocalist

Date	Title	Pos	Wks
16 Sep 67	● SCOTT *Philips SBL 7816*	3	17 wks
20 Apr 68	★ SCOTT 2 *Philips SBL 7840*	1	18 wks
5 Apr 69	● SCOTT 3 *Philips S 7882*	3	4 wks
5 Jul 69	● SONGS FROM HIS TV SERIES *Philips SBL 7900*	7	3 wks

WALKER BROTHERS

US, male vocal group

Date	Title	Pos	Wks
18 Dec 65	● TAKE IT EASY *Philips BL 7691*	3	36 wks
3 Sep 66	● PORTRAIT *Philips BL 7691*	3	23 wks
18 Mar 67	● IMAGES *Philips SBL 7770*	6	15 wks
16 Sep 67	● WALKER BROTHERS' STORY *Philips DBL 002*	9	19 wks
21 Feb 76	NO REGRETS *GTO GTLP 007*	49	3 wks

Bob WALLIS and his STORYVILLE JAZZMEN

UK, male vocal/instrumental group

Date	Title	Pos	Wks
11 Jun 60	EVERYBODY LOVES SATURDAY NIGHT *Top Rank BUY 023*	20	1 wk

Joe WALSH

US, male vocalist

Date	Title	Pos	Wks
17 Apr 76	YOU CAN'T ARGUE WITH A SICK MIND *Anchor ABCL 5156*	28	3 wks
10 Jun 78	BUT SERIOUSLY FOLKS *Asylum K 53081*	16	17 wks

WAR — See *Eric BURDEN and WAR*.

Clifford T. WARD

UK, male vocalist

Date	Title	Pos	Wks
21 Jul 73	HOME THOUGHTS *Charisma CAS 1066*	40	3 wks
16 Feb 74	MANTLE PIECES *Charisma CAS 1077*	42	2 wks

Michael WARD

UK, male vocalist

Date	Title	Pos	Wks
5 Jan 74	INTRODUCING MICHAEL WARD *Philips 6308 189*	26	3 wks

Dionne WARWICK

US, female vocalist

Date	Title	Pos	Wks
23 May 64	PRESENTING DIONNE WARWICK *Pye NPL 28037*	14	10 wks
7 May 66	● BEST OF DIONNE WARWICK *Pye NPL 28078*	8	11 wks
4 Feb 67	HERE WHERE THERE IS LOVE *Pye NPL 28096*	39	2 wks
18 May 68	● VALLEY OF THE DOLLS *Pye NSPL 28114*	10	13 wks
23 May 70	GREATEST HITS VOL.1 *Wand WNS 1*	31	26 wks
6 Jun 70	GREATEST HITS VOL.2 *Wand WNS 2*	28	14 wks
30 Oct 82	● HEARTBREAKER *Arista 204 974*	3†	9 wks

Geno WASHINGTON

UK, male vocalist

Date	Title	Pos	Wks
10 Dec 66	● HAND CLAPPIN' - FOOT STOMPIN' - FUNKY BUTT - LIVE! *Piccadilly NPL 38026*	5	38 wks
23 Sep 67	● HIPSTERS, FLIPSTERS, AND FINGER POPPIN' DADDIES *Piccadilly NSPL 38032*	8	13 wks

Grover WASHINGTON Jr

US, male instrumentalist - saxophone

Date	Title	Pos	Wks
9 May 81	WINELIGHT *Elektra K 52262*	34	9 wks
19 Dec 81	COME MORNING *Elektra K 52337*	98	1 wk

Jeff WAYNE

US/UK orchestra and cast

Date	Title	Pos	Wks
1 Jul 78	● WAR OF THE WORLDS *CBS 96000*	5	200 wks

This album featured various artists but is commonly credited to Jeff Wayne, it's 'creator' and producer.

KIM WILDE Just one good reason for supporting the 'Wilde Life'.

Right **WHITESNAKE** Cozy Powell, Colin 'Bomber' Hodgkinson, Jon Lord, David Coverdale, Micky Moody and Mel Galley.

Below **THE WHO** Moon the loon and the Ox with the bareheaded Roger and Pete.

WEATHER REPORT

US, male instrumental group

23 Apr 77	**HEAVY WEATHER** *CBS 81775*	43	6 wks
11 Nov 78	**MR. GONE** *CBS 82775*	47	3 wks
27 Feb 82	**WEATHER REPORT** *CBS 85326*	88	2 wks

Marti WEBB

UK, female vocalist

16 Feb 80	● **TELL ME ON A SUNDAY** *Polydor POLD 5031*	2	23 wks

Ben WEBSTER — See *Gerry MULLIGAN and Ben WEBSSTER*

Bert WEEDON

UK, male instrumentalist - guitar

16 Jul 60	**KING SIZE GUITAR** *Top Rank BUY 026*	18	1 wk
23 Oct 76	★ **22 GOLDEN GUITAR GREATS** *Warwick WW 5019*	1	25 wks

WHISPERS

US, male vocal group

14 Mar 81	**IMAGINATION** *Solar SOLA 7*	42	5 wks

Alan WHITE

UK, male instrumentalist - drums

13 Mar 76	**RAMSHACKLED** *Atlantic K 50217*	41	4 wks

Barry WHITE

US, male vocalist

9 Mar 74	**STONE GON'** *Pye NSPL 28186*	18	17 wks
6 Apr 74	**RHAPSODY IN WHITE** *Pye NSPL 28191*	50	1 wk
2 Nov 74	● **CAN'T GET ENOUGH** *20th Century BT 444*	4	34 wks
26 Apr 75	**JUST ANOTHER WAY TO SAY I LOVE YOU** *20th Century BT 466*	12	15 wks
22 Nov 75	**GREATEST HITS** *20th Century BTH 8000*	18	12 wks
21 Feb 76	**LET THE MUSIC PLAY** *20th Century BT 502*	22	14 wks
9 Apr 77	**BARRY WHITE'S GREATEST HITS VOL.2** *20th Century BTH 8001*	17	7 wks
10 Feb 79	**THE MAN** *20th Century BT 571*	46	4 wks

Tony Joe WHITE

US, male vocalist

26 Sep 70	**TONY JOE** *CBS 63800*	63	1 wk

WHITESNAKE

UK, male vocal/instrumental group

18 Nov 78	**TROUBLE** *EMI International INS 3022*	50	2 wks
13 Oct 79	**LOVE HUNTER** *United Artists UAG 30264*	29	7 wks
7 Jun 80	● **READY AND WILLING** *United Artists UAG 30302*	6	15 wks
8 Nov 80	● **LIVE IN THE HEART OF THE CITY** *United Artists SNAKE 1*	5	15 wks
18 Apr 81	● **COME AND GET IT** *Liberty LBG 30327*	2	23 wks
27 Nov 82	● **SAINTS 'N' SINNERS** *Liberty LBG 30354*	9†	5 wks

Slim WHITMAN

US, male vocalist

14 Dec 74	**HAPPY ANNIVERSARY** *United Artists UAS 29670*	44	2 wks
31 Jan 76	★ **THE VERY BEST OF SLIM WHITMAN** *United Artists UAS 29898*	1	17 wks
15 Jan 77	★ **RED RIVER VALLEY** *United Artists UAS 29993*	1	14 wks
15 Oct 77	● **HOME ON THE RANGE** *United Artists UATV 30102*	2	13 wks
13 Jan 79	**GHOST RIDERS IN THE SKY** *United Artists UATV 30202*	27	6 wks
22 Dec 79	**SLIM WHITMAN'S 20 GREATEST LOVE SONGS** *United Artists UAG 30270*	18	7 wks

Roger WHITTAKER

South Africa, male vocalist

27 Jun 70	**I DON'T BELIEVE IN IF ANYMORE** *Columbia SCX 6404*	23	1 wk
3 Apr 71	**NEW WORLD IN THE MORNING** *Columbia SCX 6456*	45	2 wks
6 Sep 75	● **THE VERY BEST OF ROGER WHITTAKER** *Columbia SCX 6560*	5	42 wks
15 May 76	**THE SECOND ALBUM OF THE VERY BEST OF ROGER WHITTAKER** *EMI EMC 3117*	27	7 wks
9 Dec 78	**ROGER WHITTAKER SINGS THE HITS** *Columbia SCX 6601*	52	5 wks
4 Aug 79	**20 ALL TIME GREATS** *Polydor POLTV 8*	24	9 wks
7 Feb 81	**THE ROGER WHITTAKER ALBUM** *K-Tel NE 1105*	18	14 wks

WHO

UK, male vocal/instrumental group

Date	Title *Label Number*	Position		
25 Dec 65	● MY GENERATION *Brunswick LAT 8616*	5	11 wks
17 Dec 66	● A QUICK ONE *Reaction 593-002*	4	17 wks
13 Jan 68	THE WHO SELL OUT *Track 613-002*	13	11 wks
7 Jun 69	● TOMMY *Track 613-013/4*	2	9 wks
6 Jun 70	● LIVE AT LEEDS *Track 2406-001*	3	21 wks
11 Sep 71	★ WHO'S NEXT *Track 2408-102*	1	13 wks
18 Dec 71	● MEATY, BEATY, BIG & BOUNCY *Track 2406-006*	9	8 wks
17 Nov 73	● QUADROPHENIA *Track 2657-013*	2	13 wks
26 Oct 74	● ODDS AND SODS *Track 2406-116*	10	4 wks
23 Aug 75	TOMMY (FILM SOUNDTRACK VERSION) *Track 2657-007*	30	2 wks
18 Oct 75	● THE WHO BY NUMBERS *Polydor 2490-129*	7	6 wks
9 Oct 76	● THE STORY OF THE WHO *Polydor 2683-069*	2	18 wks
9 Sep 78	● WHO ARE YOU *Polydor WHOD 5004*	6	9 wks
30 Jun 79	THE KIDS ARE ALRIGHT *Polydor 2675 174*	26	13 wks
25 Oct 80	MY GENERATION (re-issue) *Virgin V 2179*	20	7 wks
28 Mar 81	● FACE DANCES *Polydor WHOD 5037*	2	9 wks
11 Sep 82	IT'S HARD *Polydor WHOD 5066*	11	6 wks

WILD HORSES

UK, male vocal/instrumental group

| 26 Apr 80 | WILD HORSES *EMI EMC 3324* | 38 | 4 wks |

WILD WILLY BARRETT — See *John OTWAY and Wild Willy BARRETT*

Kim WILDE

UK, female vocalist

| 11 Jul 81 | ● KIM WILDE *RAK SRAK 544* | 3 | 14 wks |
| 22 May 82 | SELECT *RAK SRAK 548* | 19 | 11 wks |

Andy WILLIAMS

US, male vocalist

26 Jun 65	● ALMOST THERE *CBS BPG 62533*	4	46 wks
7 Aug 65	CAN'T GET USED TO LOSING YOU *CBS BPG 62146*	16	1 wk
19 Mar 66	MAY EACH DAY *CBS BPG 62658*	11	6 wks
30 Apr 66	GREAT SONGS FROM MY FAIR LADY *CBS BPG 62430*	30	1 wk
23 Jul 66	SHADOW OF YOUR SMILE *CBS 62633*	24	4 wks
29 Jul 67	BORN FREE *CBS SBPG 63027*	22	11 wks
11 May 68	★ LOVE ANDY *CBS 63167*	1	22 wks
6 Jul 68	● HONEY *CBS 63311*	4	17 wks
26 Jul 69	HAPPY HEART *CBS 63614*	22	9 wks
27 Dec 69	GET TOGETHER WITH ANDY WILLIAMS *CBS 63800*	13	12 wks

24 Jan 70	ANDY WILLIAMS' SOUND OF MUSIC *CBS 66214*	22	10 wks
11 Apr 70	★ GREATEST HITS *CBS 63920*	1	116 wks
20 Jun 70	● CAN'T HELP FALLING IN LOVE *CBS 64067*	7	48 wks
5 Dec 70	● ANDY WILLIAMS SHOW *CBS 64127*	10	6 wks
3 Apr 71	★ HOME LOVING MAN *CBS 64286*	1	25 wks
31 Jul 71	LOVE STORY *CBS 64467*	11	11 wks
29 Apr 72	THE IMPOSSIBLE DREAM *CBS 67236*	26	3 wks
29 Jul 72	LOVE THEME FROM "THE GODFATHER" *CBS 64869*	11	16 wks
16 Dec 72	GREATEST HITS VOL.2 *CBS 65151*	23	10 wks
22 Dec 73	● SOLITAIRE *CBS 65638*	3	26 wks
15 Jun 74	● THE WAY WE WERE *CBS 80152*	7	11 wks
11 Oct 75	THE OTHER SIDE OF ME *CBS 69152*	60	1 wk
28 Jan 78	● REFLECTIONS *CBS 10006*	2	17 wks

Deniece WILLIAMS

US, female vocalist

| 21 May 77 | THIS IS NIECEY *CBS 81869* | 31 | 12 wks |

See also Johnny Mathis and Deniece Williams.

Don WILLIAMS

US, male vocalist

10 Jul 76	GREATEST HITS VOL.1 *ABC ABCL 5147*	29	15 wks
19 Feb 77	VISIONS *ABC ABCL 5200*	13	20 wks
15 Oct 77	COUNTRY BOY *ABC ABCL 5233*	27	5 wks
5 Aug 78	● IMAGES *K-Tel NE 1033*	2	38 wks
5 Aug 78	YOU'RE MY BEST FRIEND *ABC ABCD 5127*	58	1 wk
4 Nov 78	EXPRESSIONS *ABC ABCL 5253*	28	8 wks
22 Sep 79	NEW HORIZONS *K-Tel NE 1048*	29	12 wks
15 Dec 79	PORTRAIT *MCA MCS 3045*	58	4 wks
6 Sep 80	I BELIEVE IN YOU *MCA MCF 3077*	36	5 wks
18 Jul 81	ESPECIALLY FOR YOU *MCA MCF 3114*	33	7 wks
17 Apr 82	LISTEN TO THE RADIO *MCA MCF 3135*	69	3 wks

Iris WILLIAMS

UK, female vocalist

| 22 Dec 79 | HE WAS BEAUTIFUL *Columbia SCX 6627* | 69 | 4 wks |

John WILLIAMS

UK, male instrumentalist - guitar

3 Oct 70	PLAYS SPANISH MUSIC *CBS 72860*	46	1 wk
17 Jun 78	TRAVELLING *Cube HIFLY 27*	23	5 wks
30 Jun 79	● BRIDGES *Lotus WH 5015*	5	22 wks
4 Aug 79	CAVATINA *Cube/Electric HIFLY 32*	64	3 wks

See also John Williams with the English Chamber Orchestra conducted by Daniel Barenboim.

Date	Title Label Number	Position		Date	Title Label Number	Position	

John WILLIAMS

US, male conductor

Date	Title	Pos	Wks
25 Dec 82	**ET-THE EXTRATERRESTRIAL** *MCA MCF 3160*	99†	1 wk

John WILLIAMS with the ENGLISH CHAMBER ORCHESTRA conducted by Daniel BARENBOIM

UK, male instrumentalist - guitar, UK orchestra and male conductor

28 Feb 76	**RODRIGO: CONCERTO DE ARANJUEZ** *CBS 76369*	20	9 wks

See also John Williams. (UK)

Sonny Boy WILLIAMSON

US, male vocalist/instrumentalist - guitar

20 Jun 64	**DOWN AND OUT BLUES** *Pye NPL 28036*	20	1 wk

WINGS

UK, male vocal/instrumental group

18 Dec 71	**WINGS WILDLIFE** *Apple PCS 7142*	11	9 wks
19 May 73	● **RED ROSE SPEEDWAY** *Apple PCTC 251*	5	16 wks
15 Dec 73	★ **BAND ON THE RUN** *Apple PAS 10007*	1	124 wks
21 Jun 75	★ **VENUS & MARS** *Apple PCTC 254*	1	29 wks
17 Apr 76	● **WINGS AT THE SPEED OF SOUND** *Apple PAS 10010*	2	35 wks
15 Jan 77	● **WINGS OVER AMERICA** *Parlophone PAS 720*	8	22 wks
15 Apr 78	● **LONDON TOWN** *Parlophone PAS 10012*	4	23 wks
16 Dec 78	● **WINGS GREATEST** *Parlophone PCTC 256*	5	32 wks
23 Jun 79	● **BACK TO THE EGG** *Parlophone PCTC 257*	6	15 wks

Red Rose Speedway *and* Band On The Run *credited to Paul McCartney and Wings. Between its initial chart run and later runs* Wings At The Speed Of Sound *changed its label number to Parlophone PAS 10010. Group UK/US from* Venus & Mars *to* Wings Greatest.

Johnny WINTER

US, male vocal/instrumental group

16 May 70	**SECOND WINTER** *CBS 66321*	59	2 wks
31 Oct 70	**JOHNNY WINTER AND...** *CBS 64117*	29	4 wks
15 May 71	**JOHNNY WINTER AND LIVE** *CBS 64289*	20	6 wks

Ruby WINTERS

US, female vocalist

10 Jun 78	**RUBY WINTERS** *Creole CRLP 512*	27	7 wks
23 Jun 79	**SONGBIRD** *K-Tel NE 1045*	31	9 wks

Steve WINWOOD

UK, male vocalist

9 Jul 77	**STEVE WINWOOD** *Island ILPS 9494*	12	9 wks
10 Jan 81	**ARC OF A DIVER** *Island ILPS 9576*	13	10 wks
14 Aug 82	● **TALKING BACK TO THE NIGHT** *Island ILPS 9777*	6	13 wks

WIRE

UK, male vocal/instrumental group

7 Oct 78	**CHAIRS MISSING** *Harvest SHSP 4093*	48	1 wk
13 Oct 79	**154** *Harvest SHSP 4105*	39	1 wk

WISHBONE ASH

UK, male vocal/instrumental group

23 Jan 71	**WISHBONE ASH** *MCA MKPS 2014*	34	2 wks
9 Oct 71	**PILGRIMAGE** *MCA MDKS 8004*	14	9 wks
20 May 72	● **ARGUS** *MCA MDKS 8006*	3	20 wks
26 May 73	**WISHBONE FOUR** *MCA MDKS 8011*	12	10 wks
30 Nov 74	**THERE'S A RUB** *MCA MCF 2585*	16	5 wks
3 Apr 76	**LOCKED IN** *MCA MCF 2750*	36	2 wks
27 Nov 76	**NEW ENGLAND** *MCA MCG 3523*	22	3 wks
29 Oct 77	**FRONT PAGE NEWS** *MCA MCG 3524*	31	4 wks
28 Oct 78	**NO SMOKE WITHOUT FIRE** *MCA MCG 3528*	43	3 wks
2 Feb 80	**JUST TESTING** *MCA MCF 3052*	41	4 wks
1 Nov 80	**LIVE DATES II** *MCA MCG 4012*	40	3 wks
25 Apr 81	**NUMBER THE BRAVE** *MCA MCS 3103*	62	1 wk
16 Oct 82	**BOTH BARRELS BURNING** *AUM ASH 1*	22	5 wks

Bill WITHERS

US, male vocalist

11 Feb 78	**MENAGERIE** *CBS 82265*	27	5 wks

WIZZARD

UK, male vocal/instrumental group

19 May 73	**WIZZARD BREW** *Harvest SHSP 4025*	29	7 wks
17 Aug 74	**INTRODUCING EDDY AND THE FALCONS** *Warner Bros. K 52029*	19	4 wks

WOMBLES

UK, Mike Batt, male vocalist, arranger and producer under

group name

2 Mar 74	**WOMBLING SONGS** *CBS 65803*	**19**	17 wks
13 Jul 74	**REMEMBER YOU'RE A WOMBLE** *CBS 80191*	**18**	31 wks
21 Dec 74	**KEEP ON WOMBLING** *CBS 80526*	**17**	6 wks
8 Jan 77	**20 WOMBLING GREATS** *Warwick PR 5022*	**29**	1 wk

Stevie WONDER

US, male vocalist/multi-instrumentalist

7 Sep 68	**STEVIE WONDER'S GREATEST HITS** *Tamla Motown STML 11075*	**25**	10 wks
13 Dec 69	**MY CHERIE AMOUR** *Tamla Motown STML 11128*	**17**	2 wks
12 Feb 72	**GREATEST HITS VOL.2** *Tamla Motown STML 11196*	**30**	4 wks
3 Feb 73	**TALKING BOOK** *Tamla Motown STMA 8007*	**16**	48 wks
1 Sep 73	● **INNERVISIONS** *Tamla Motown STMA 8011*	**8**	55 wks
17 Aug 74	● **FULFILLINGNESS' FIRST FINALE** *Tamla Motown STMA 8019*	**5**	16 wks
16 Oct 76	● **SONGS IN THE KEY OF LIFE** *Tamla Motown TMSP 6002*	**2**	54 wks
10 Nov 79	● **JOURNEY THROUGH THE SECRET LIFE OF PLANTS** *Motown TMSP 6009*	**8**	15 wks
8 Nov 80	● **HOTTER THAN JULY** *Motown STMA 8035*	**2**	55 wks
22 May 82	● **ORIGINAL MUSIQUARIUM 1** *Motown TMSP 6012*	**8**	17 wks

Roy WOOD

UK, male vocalist/multi-instrumentalist

| 18 Aug 73 | **BOULDERS** *Harvest SHVL 803* | **15** | 8 wks |
| 24 Jul 82 | **THE SINGLES** *Speed SPEED 1000* | **37** | 6 wks |

Edward WOODWARD

UK, male vocalist

| 6 Jun 70 | **THIS MAN ALONE** *DJM DJLPS 405* | **53** | 2 wks |
| 19 Aug 72 | **THE EDWARD WOODWARD ALBUM** *Jam JAL 103* | **20** | 10 wks |

WRECKLESS ERIC

UK, male vocalist

| 1 Apr 78 | **WRECKLESS ERIC** *Stiff SEEZ 6* | **46** | 1 wk |
| 8 Mar 80 | **BIG SMASH** *Stiff SEEZ 21* | **30** | 4 wks |

Klaus WUNDERLICH

Germany, male instrumentalist - organ

30 Aug 75	**THE HIT WORLD OF KLAUS WUNDERLICH** *Decca SPA 434*	**27**	8 wks
20 May 78	**THE UNIQUE KLAUS WUNDERLICH SOUND** *Decca DBC 5/6*	**28**	4 wks
26 May 79	**THE FANTASTIC SOUND OF KLAUS WUNDERLICH** *Lotus LH 5013*	**43**	5 wks

WURZELS

UK, male vocal/instrumental group

| 3 Jul 76 | **COMBINE HARVESTER** *One-Up OU 2138* | **15** | 20 wks |
| 2 Apr 77 | **GOLDEN DELICIOUS** *EMI Note NTS 122* | **32** | 5 wks |

Bill WYMAN

UK, male vocalist

| 8 Jun 74 | **MONKEY GRIP** *Rolling Stones COC 59102* | **39** | 1 wk |
| 10 Apr 82 | **BILL WYMAN** *A&M AMLH 68540* | **55** | 6 wks |

Tammy WYNETTE

US, female vocalist

17 May 75	● **THE BEST OF TAMMY WYNETTE** *Epic EPC 63578*	**4**	23 wks
21 Jun 75	**STAND BY YOUR MAN** *Epic EPC 69141*	**13**	7 wks
17 Dec 77	● **20 COUNTRY CLASSICS** *CBS PR 5040*	**3**	11 wks
4 Feb 78	**COUNTRY GIRL MEETS COUNTRY BOY** *Warwick PR 5039*	**43**	3 wks

X-RAY SPEX

UK, male/female vocal instrumental group

| 9 Dec 78 | **GERM FREE ADOLESCENTS** *EMI International INS 3023* | **30** | 14 wks |

XTC

UK, male vocal/instrumental group

| 11 Feb 78 | **WHITE MUSIC** *Virgin V 2095* | **38** | 4 wks |
| 28 Oct 78 | **GO 2** *Virgin V 2108* | **21** | 3 wks |

NEIL YOUNG The most successful soloist to emerge from the Crosby, Stills, Nash and Young outfit.

YARDBIRDS
They failed to chart with highly regarded albums like 'Five Live Yardbirds' and 'Roger The Engineer'.

Right **FRANK ZAPPA** Francis Vincent Zappa Jr's first musical foray was at Antilope Valley High School in California with an eight piece called The Blackouts.

Above **Z.Z. TOP** The 'tres hombres' who have been a Texas blues/rock/R&B outfit since 1970 are Billy Gibbons, Dusty Hill and Frank Bearol.

174

Date	Title Label Number	Position	
1 Sep 79	DRUMS AND WIRES *Virgin V 2129*	34	7 wks
20 Sep 80	BLACK SEA *Virgin V 2173*	16	7 wks
20 Feb 82	● ENGLISH SETTLEMENT *Virgin V2223*	5	11 wks
13 Nov 82	WAXWORKS-SOME SINGLES (1977-82) *Virgin V 2251*	54	3 wks

Y

YARDBIRDS

UK, male vocal/instrumental group

Date	Title Label Number	Position	
23 Jul 66	YARDBIRDS *Columbia SX 6063*	20	8 wks

YAZOO

UK, female/male vocal/instrumental duo

Date	Title Label Number	Position	
4 Sep 82	● UPSTAIRS AT ERIC'S *Mute STUMM 7*	2†	17 wks

YES

UK, male vocal/instrumental group

Date	Title Label Number	Position	
1 Aug 70	TIME AND A WORD *Atlantic 2400-006*	45	3 wks
3 Apr 71	● THE YES ALBUM *Atlantic 2400-101*	7	29 wks
4 Dec 71	● FRAGILE *Atlantic 2409-019*	7	17 wks
23 Sep 72	● CLOSE TO THE EDGE *Atlantic K 50012*	4	13 wks
26 May 73	● YESSONGS *Atlantic K 60045*	7	13 wks
22 Dec 73	★ TALES FROM TOPOGRAPHIC OCEAN *Atlantic K 80001*	1	15 wks
21 Dec 74	● RELAYER *Atlantic K 50096*	4	11 wks
29 Mar 75	YESTERDAYS *Atlantic K 50048*	27	7 wks
30 Jul 77	★ GOING FOR THE ONE *Atlantic K 50379*	1	28 wks
7 Oct 78	● TORMATO *Atlantic K 50518*	8	11 wks
30 Aug 80	● DRAMA *Atlantic K 50736*	2	8 wks
10 Jan 81	YESSHOWS *Atlantic K 60142*	22	9 wks

Faron YOUNG

US, male vocalist

Date	Title Label Number	Position	
28 Oct 72	IT'S FOUR IN THE MORNING *Mercury 6338 095*	27	5 wks

Neil YOUNG

Canada, male vocalist

Date	Title Label Number	Position	
31 Oct 70	● AFTER THE GOLDRUSH *Reprise RSLP 6383*	7	68 wks
4 Mar 72	★ HARVEST *Reprise K 54005*	1	33 wks
27 Oct 73	TIME FADES AWAY *Warner Bros. K 54010*	20	2 wks
10 Aug 74	ON THE BEACH *Reprise K 54014*	42	2 wks
5 Jul 75	TONIGHT'S THE NIGHT *Reprise K 54040*	48	1 wk
27 Dec 75	ZUMA *Reprise K 54057*	44	2 wks
9 Jul 77	AMERICAN STARS 'N' BARS *Reprise K 54088*	17	8 wks
17 Dec 77	DECADE *Reprise K 64037*	46	4 wks
28 Oct 78	COMES A TIME *Reprise K 54099*	42	3 wks
14 Jul 79	RUST NEVER SLEEPS *Reprise K 54105*	13	13 wks
1 Dec 79	LIVE RUST *Reprise K 64041*	55	3 wks
15 Nov 80	HAWKS AND DOVES *Reprise K 54109*	34	3 wks
14 Nov 81	RE-AC-TOR *Reprise K 54116*	69	3 wks

Rust Never Sleeps, Live Rust and Re-ac-tor *credited to Neil Young and Crazy Horse. See also Stills-Young Band, and Crosby, Stills, Nash and Young.*

Y&T

US, male vocal/instrumental group

Date	Title Label Number	Position	
11 Sep 82	BLACK TIGER *A & M AMLH 64910*	53	8 wks

Z

Frank ZAPPA

US, male vocalist

Date	Title Label Number	Position	
28 Feb 70	● HOT RATS *Reprise RSLP 6356*	9	27 wks
19 Dec 70	CHUNGA'S REVENGE *Reprise RSLP 2030*	43	1 wk
6 May 78	ZAPPA IN NEW YORK *Discreet K 69204*	55	1 wk
10 Mar 79	SHEIK YERBOUTI *CBS 88339*	32	7 wks
13 Oct 79	JOE'S GARAGE ACT 1 *CBS 86101*	62	3 wks
19 Jan 80	JOE'S GARAGE ACTS 2 & 3 *CBS 88475*	75	1 wk
16 May 81	TINSEL TOWN REBELLION *CBS 88516*	55	4 wks
24 Oct 81	YOU ARE WHAT YOU IS *CBS 88560*	51	2 wks
19 Jun 82	SHIP ARRIVING TOO LATE TO SAVE A DROWNING WITCH *CBS 85804*	61	4 wks

See also Mothers of Invention.

Lena ZAVARONI

UK, female vocalist

Date	Title Label Number	Position	
23 Mar 74	● MA *Philips 6308 201*	8	5 wks

Z.Z.TOP

US, male vocal/instrumental group

Date	Title Label Number	Position	
12 Jul 75	FANDANGO *London SHU 8482*	60	1 wk
8 Aug 81	EL LOCO *Warner Bros. K 56929*	88	2 wks

VARIOUS ARTISTS

ANONYMOUS COVER VERSIONS

Date	Title *Label Number*	Position	
29 Feb 64	**BEATLEMANIA** *Top Six TSL 1*	19	2 wks
7 Aug 71	**HOT HITS 5** *MFP 5208*	48	1 wk
7 Aug 71	★ **HOT HITS 6** *MFP 5214*	1	7 wks
7 Aug 71	**TOP OF THE POPS VOL.17** *Hallmark SHM 740*	16	3 wks
7 Aug 71	★ **TOP OF THE POPS VOL. 18** *Hallmark SHM 745*	1	12 wks
7 Aug 71	**MILLION SELLER HITS** *MFP 5203*	46	2 wks
21 Aug 71	**SMASH HIT SUPREMES STYLE** *MFP 5184*	36	3 wks
2 Oct 71	● **TOP OF THE POPS VOL.19** *Hallmark SHM 750*	3	9 wks
23 Oct 71	**HOT HITS 7** *MFP 5236*	3	9 wks
6 Nov 71	**SMASH HITS COUNTRY STYLE** *MFP 5228*	38	1 wk
13 Nov 71	★ **TOP OF THE POPS VOL.20** *Hallmark SHM 739*	1	8 wks
27 Nov 71	**NON STOP 20 VOL.4** *Plexium PXMS 1006*	35	2 wks
4 Dec 71	**SMASH HITS 71** *MFP 5229*	21	3 wks
11 Dec 71	● **HOT HITS 8** *MFP 5243*	2	4 wks
27 Sep 75	**40 SINGALONG PUB SONGS** *K-Tel NE 509*	21	7 wks
6 Nov 76	**FORTY MANIA** *Ronco RDT 2018*	21	6 wks

COMPILATIONS

Date	Title *Label Number*	Position	
9 May 59	● **CURTAIN UP** *Pye Nixa BRTH 0059*	4	13 wks
10 Mar 62	**GREAT MOTION PICTURE THEMES** *HMV CLP 1508*	19	1 wk
23 Jun 62	**HONEY HIT PARADE** *Pye Golden Guinea GGL 0129*	13	7 wks
30 Nov 62	**ALL THE HITS BY ALL THE STARS** *Pye Golden Guinea GGL 0162*	19	2 wks
9 Mar 63	● **ALL STAR FESTIVAL** *Philips DL 99500*	4	19 wks
24 Aug 63	**THE MERSEY BEAT VOL.1** *Oriole PS 40047*	17	5 wks
7 Sep 63	**HITSVILLE** *Pye Golden Guinea GGL 0202*	11	6 wks
14 Sep 63	**THE BEST OF RADIO LUXEMBOURG** *Pye Golden Guinea GGL 0208*	14	2 wks
23 Nov 63	**HITSVILLE VOL.2** *Pye Golden Guinea GGL 0233*	20	1 wk
4 Jan 64	**THE BLUES VOL.1** *Pye NPL 28030*	15	3 wks
8 Feb 64	**READY STEADY GO** *Decca LK 4577*	20	1 wk
22 Feb 64	**FOLK FESTIVAL OF THE BLUES (LIVE RECORDING)** *Pye NPL 28033*	16	4 wks
16 May 64	**OUT CAME THE BLUES** *Ace Of Hearts AH 72*	19	1 wk
30 May 64	**THE BLUES VOL.2** *Pye NPL 28035*	16	3 wks
3 Apr 65	**A COLLECTION OF TAMLA MOTOWN HITS** *Tamla Motown TML 11043*	16	4 wks
2 Apr 66	**SOLID GOLD SOUL** *Atlantic ATL 5048*	12	27 wks
11 Sep 66	● **STARS CHARITY FANTASIA SAVE THE CHILDREN FUND** *SCF PL 145*	6	16 wks
5 Nov 66	**MIDNIGHT SOUL** *Atlantic 587-021*	22	19 wks
10 Dec 66	**STEREO MUSICALE SHOWCASE** *Polydor 104-450*	26	2 wks
4 Mar 67	**16 ORIGINAL BIG HITS - VOL.4** *Tamla Motown TML 11043*	33	3 wks

Date	Title *Label Number*	Position	
8 Apr 67	● **HIT THE ROAD STAX** *Stax 589-005*	10	16 wks
20 May 67	**THRILL TO THE SENSATIONAL SOUNDS OF SUPER STEREO** *CBS PR 5*	20	30 wks
17 Jun 67	**TAMLA MOTOWN HITS VOL.5** *Tamla Motown TML 11050*	11	40 wks
26 Aug 67	**CLUB SKA '67** *Island ILP 956*	37	19 wks
21 Oct 67	● **BREAKTHROUGH** *Studio Two STWO 1*	2	11 wks
21 Oct 67	● **BRITISH MOTOWN CHARTBUSTERS** *Tamla Motown TML 11055*	2	54 wks
10 Feb 68	**MOTOWN MEMORIES** *Tamla Motown TML 11064*	21	13 wks
10 Feb 68	**STARS OF '68** *Marble Arch MAL 762*	23	3 wks
11 May 68	**BLUES ANYTIME** *Immediate IMLP 014*	40	1 wk
24 Aug 68	**TAMLA MOTOWN HITS VOL.6** *Tamla Motown STML 11074*	32	2 wks
30 Nov 68	● **BRITISH MOTOWN CHARTBUSTERS VOL.2** *Tamla Motown STML 11082*	8	11 wks
14 Jun 69	**THIS IS SOUL** *Atlantic 643-301*	16	15 wks
14 Jun 69	**YOU CAN ALL JOIN IN** *Island IWPS 2*	18	10 wks
21 Jun 69	**IMPACT** *EMI STWO 2*	15	14 wks
28 Jun 69	**THE ROCK MACHINE TURNS YOU ON** *CBS SPR 22*	18	7 wks
28 Jun 69	**THE WORLD OF BLUES POWER** *Decca SPA 14*	24	6 wks
28 Jun 69	**ROCK MACHINE I LOVE YOU** *CBS SPR 26*	15	5 wks
5 Jul 69	**THE WORLD OF BRASS BANDS** *Decca SPA 20*	13	11 wks
6 Sep 69	● **THE WORLD OF HITS VOL.2** *Decca SPA 35*	7	5 wks
20 Sep 69	**THE WORLD OF PROGRESSIVE MUSIC (WOWIE ZOWIE)** *Decca SPA 34*	17	2 wks
20 Sep 69	**THE WORLD OF PHASE 4 STEREO** *Decca SPA 32*	29	2 wks
25 Oct 69	★ **BRITISH MOTOWN CHARTBUSTERS VOL.3** *Tamla Motown STML 11121*	1	93 wks
21 Feb 70	**COLLECTION OF BIG HITS VOL.8** *Tamla Motown STML 11130*	56	1 wk
24 Oct 70	★ **MOTOWN CHARTBUSTERS VOL.4** *Tamla Motown STML 11162*	1	40 wks
17 Apr 71	★ **MOTOWN CHARTBUSTERS VOL.5** *Tamla Motown STML 11181*	1	36 wks
7 Aug 71	● **THE WORLD OF YOUR 100 BEST TUNES** *Decca SPA 112*	10	22 wks
7 Aug 71	**TIGHTEN UP VOL.4** *Trojan TBL 163*	20	7 wks
21 Aug 71	**CLUB REGGAE** *Trojan TBL 159*	25	4 wks
4 Sep 71	**TOTAL SOUND** *Studio Two STWO 4*	39	4 wks
9 Oct 71	● **THE WORLD OF YOUR 100 BEST TUNES VOL.2** *Decca SPA 155*	9	13 wks
9 Oct 71	**THE A-Z OF EASY LISTENING** *Polydor 2661-005*	24	4 wks
16 Oct 71	**PYE CHARTBUSTERS VOL.6** *Pye PCB 15000*	36	1 wk
23 Oct 71	● **MOTOWN CHARTBUSTERS VOL.6** *Tamla Motown STML 11191*	2	36 wks
30 Oct 71	**STUDIO TWO CLASSICS** *Studio Two STWO 6*	16	4 wks
4 Dec 71	**BREAKTHROUGH** *MFP 1334*	49	1 wk

Date	Title Label Number	Position		Date	Title Label Number	Position	
18 Dec 71	PYE CHARTBUSTERS VOL.2 *Pye PCB 15001*	29	3 wks	15 May 76	● HIT MACHINE *K-Tel TE 713*	4	10 wks
22 Jan 72	★ CONCERT FOR BANGLADESH (RECORDED LIVE) *Apple STCX 3385*	1	13 wks	22 May 76	● A TOUCH OF COUNTRY *Topaz TOC 1976*	7	7 wks
26 Feb 72	MOTOWN MEMORIES *Tamla Motown STML 11200*	22	4 wks	29 May 76	HAMILTON'S HOT SHOTS *Warwick WW 5014*	15	5 wks
18 Mar 72	MOTOWN STORY *Tamla Motown TMSP 1130*	21	4 wks	3 Jul 76	GOLDEN FIDDLE AWARDS 1976 *Mountain TOPC 5002*	45	2 wks
25 Mar 72	THE NEW AGE OF ATLANTIC *Atlantic K 20024*	25	1 wk	3 Jul 76	A TOUCH OF CLASS *Topaz TOC 1976*	57	1 wk
20 May 72	● THE MUSIC PEOPLE *CBS 66315*	10	9 wks	2 Oct 76	SUMMER CRUISING *K-Tel NE 918*	30	1 wk
10 Jun 72	★ 20 DYNAMIC HITS *K-Tel TE 292*	1	28 wks	16 Oct 76	● COUNTRY COMFORT *K-Tel NE 294*	8	12 wks
29 Jul 72	● 20 FANTASTIC HITS *Arcade 2891 001*	1	24 wks	16 Oct 76	★ SOUL MOTION *K-Tel NE 930*	1	14 wks
7 Oct 72	★ 20 ALL TIME HITS OF THE 50'S *K-Tel NE 490*	1	22 wks	27 Nov 76	ALL THIS AND WORLD WAR II *Riva RVLP 2*	23	7 wks
21 Oct 72	● 20 STAR TRACKS *Ronco PP 2001*	2	13 wks	4 Dec 76	● DISCO ROCKET *K-Tel NE 948*	3	14 wks
29 Nov 72	● 25 DYNAMIC HITS VOL.2 *K-Tel TE 291*	2	12 wks	11 Dec 76	● 44 SUPERSTARS *K-Tel NE 939*	14	10 wks
29 Nov 72	● 20 FANTASTIC HITS VOL.2 *Arcade 2891 002*	2	14 wks	8 Jan 77	SONGS OF PRAISE *Warwick WW 5020*	31	2 wks
29 Nov 72	● MOTOWN CHARTBUSTERS VOL.7 *Tamla Motown STML 11215*	9	16 wks	8 Jan 77	CLASSICAL GOLD *Ronco RTD 42020*	24	12 wks
2 Dec 72	★ 25 ROCKIN' & ROLLIN' GREATS *K-Tel NE 493*	1	18 wks	29 Jan 77	HIT SCENE *Warwick PR 5023*	19	5 wks
23 Dec 72	PHIL SPECTOR'S CHRISTMAS ALBUM *Apple SAPCOR 24*	21	3 wks	12 Feb 77	● HEARTBREAKERS *K-Tel NE 954*	2	18 wks
31 Mar 73	★ 20 FLASHBACK GREATS OF THE SIXTIES *K-Tel NE 494*	1	11 wks	19 Feb 77	● DANCE TO THE MUSIC *K-Tel NE 957*	5	9 wks
7 Apr 73	● 40 FANTASTICS HITS FROM THE 50'S AND 60'S *Arcade ADEP 3/4*	2	15 wks	26 Mar 77	ROCK ON *Arcade ADEP 27*	16	10 wks
21 Apr 73	● BELIEVE IN MUSIC *K-Tel TE 294*	2	8 wks	7 May 77	HIT ACTION *K-Tel NE 993*	15	9 wks
26 May 73	● 20 FANTASTIC HITS VOL.3 *Arcade ADEP 5*	3	8 wks	7 May 77	THE MOTOWN STORY *Motown MS 5726*	36	4 wks
2 Jun 73	★ PURE GOLD *EMI EMK 251*	1	11 wks	2 Jun 77	RULE BRITANNIA *Arcade ADEP 29*	56	1 wk
2 Jun 73	● 20 ORIGINAL CHART HITS *Philips TV 1*	9	11 wks	16 Jul 77	THE ROXY LONDON WC2 *Harvest SHSP 4069*	24	5 wks
2 Jun 73	NICE 'N' EASY *Philips 6441 076*	36	1 wk	16 Jul 77	SUPERGROUPS *Ronco RTL 2023*	57	1 wk
23 Jun 73	★ THAT'LL BE THE DAY *Ronco MR 2002/3*	1	8 wks	6 Aug 77	NEW WAVE *Philips 6300 902*	11	12 wks
3 Nov 73	● MOTOWN CHARTBUSTERS VOL.8 *Tamla Motown STML 11246*	9	15 wks	15 Oct 77	PHIL SPECTOR'S ECHOES OF THE 60'S *Phil Spector International 2307 013*	21	10 wks
27 Apr 74	AMERICAN GRAFFITI *MCA MCSP 253*	37	1 wk	22 Oct 77	10 YEARS OF HITS-RADIO ONE *Super Beeb BEDP 002*	39	3 wks
22 Jun 74	ATLANTIC BLACK GOLD *Atlantic K 40550*	23	7 wks	29 Oct 77	SOUL CITY *K-Tel NE 1003*	12	7 wks
26 Oct 74	MOTOWN CHARTBUSTERS VOL.9 *Tamla Motown STML 11270*	14	15 wks	5 Nov 77	MOTOWN GOLD VOL.2 *Motown STML 12070*	28	4 wks
4 Jan 75	BBC TV'S BEST OF TOP OF THE POPS *Super Beeb BELP 001*	21	5 wks	12 Nov 77	● FEELINGS *K-Tel NE 1006*	3	24 wks
15 Mar 75	SOLID SOUL SENSATIONS *Disco Demand DDLP 5001*	30	1 wk	26 Nov 77	★ DISCO FEVER *K-Tel NE 1014*	1	20 wks
16 Aug 75	NEVER TOO YOUNG TO ROCK *GTO GTLP 004*	30	5 wks	26 Nov 77	BLACK JOY *Ronco RTL 2025*	26	13 wks
27 Sep 75	THE WORLD OF YOUR 100 BEST TUNES VOL.10 *Decca SPA 400*	41	4 wks	21 Jan 78	40 NUMBER ONE HITS *K-Tel NE 1008*	15	7 wks
1 Nov 75	● MOTOWN GOLD *Tamla Motown STML 12003*	8	35 wks	4 Mar 78	● DISCO STARS *K-Tel NE 1022*	6	8 wks
8 Nov 75	BLAZING BULLETS *Ronco RTI 2012*	17	8 wks	11 Mar 78	FONZIE'S FAVOURITES *Warwick WW 5037*	8	16 wks
8 Nov 75	GOOFY GREATS *K-Tel NE 707*	19	7 wks	11 Mar 78	STIFF'S LIVE STIFFS *Stiff GET 1*	28	7 wks
15 Nov 75	● DISCO HITS '75 *Arcade ADEP 18*	5	11 wks	18 Mar 78	● BOOGIE NIGHTS *Ronco RTL 2027*	5	7 wks
29 Nov 75	ALL-TIME PARTY HITS *Warwick WW 5001*	21	8 wks	25 Mar 78	HOPE AND ANCHOR FRONT ROW FESTIVAL *Warner Bros. K 66077*	28	3 wks
6 Dec 75	SUPERSONIC *Stallion SSM 001*	21	6 wks	10 Jun 78	● DISCO DOUBLE *K-Tel NE 1024*	10	6 wks
6 Dec 75	GREATEST HITS OF WALT DISNEY *Ronco RTD 2013*	11	12 wks	17 Jun 78	WHITE MANSIONS *A & M AMLX 64691*	51	3 wks
13 Dec 75	● 40 SUPER GREATS *K-Tel NE 708*	9	8 wks	8 Jul 78	THE WORLD'S WORST RECORD SHOW *Yuk/K-Tel NE 1023*	47	2 wks
13 Dec 75	A CHRISTMAS GIFT *Ronco P 12430*	39	5 wks	8 Jul 78	ROCK RULES *K-Tel RL 001*	12	11 wks
13 Dec 75	THE TOP 25 FROM YOUR 100 BEST TUNES *Decca HBT 1112*	21	5 wks	19 Aug 78	● STAR PARTY *K-Tel NE 1034*	4	9 wks
24 Jan 76	● STAR TRACKIN' 76 *Ronco RTL 2014*	9	5 wks	7 Oct 78	● BIG WHEELS OF MOTOWN *Motown EMTV 12*	2	18 wks
31 Jan 76	● MUSIC EXPRESS *K-Tel TE 702*	3	10 wks	21 Oct 78	SATIN CITY *CBS 10010*	10	11 wks
31 Jan 76	REGGAE CHARTBUSTERS 75 *Cactus CTLP 114*	53	1 wk	28 Oct 78	ECSTACY *Lotus WH 5003*	24	6 wks
3 Apr 76	BY INVITATION ONLY *Atlantic K 60112*	17	6 wks	4 Nov 78	● EMOTIONS *K-Tel NE 1035*	2	17 wks
10 Apr 76	● JUKE BOX JIVE *K-Tel NE 709*	3	13 wks	18 Nov 78	★ DON'T WALK BOOGIE *EMI EMTV 13*	1	23 wks
17 Apr 76	● INSTRUMENTAL GOLD *Warwick WW 5012*	3	24 wks	18 Nov 78	BOOGIE FEVER *Ronco RTL 2034*	15	11 wks
17 Apr 76	GREAT ITALIAN LOVE SONGS *K-Tel NE 303*	17	14 wks	25 Nov 78	● MIDNIGHT HUSTLE *K-Tel NE 1037*	2	13 wks
				25 Nov 78	LOVE SONGS *Warwick WW 5046*	47	7 wks
				2 Dec 78	BLACK VELVET *Warwick WW 5047*	72	3 wks
				9 Dec 78	STARS ON SUNDAY BY REQUEST *Curzon Sounds CSL 0081*	65	3 wks
				20 Jan 79	★ ACTION REPLAY *K-Tel NE 1040*	1	14 wks
				24 Feb 79	20 OF ANOTHER KIND *Polydor POLS 1006*	45	3 wks
				31 Mar 79	LEMON POPSICLE *Warwick WW 5050*	42	6 wks
				7 Apr 79	COUNTRY PORTRAITS *Warwick WW 5057*	14	10 wks

Date	Title *Label Number*	Position	
7 Apr 79	DISCO INFERNO *K-Tel NE 1043*	11	9 wks
21 Apr 79 ●	COUNTRY LIFE *EMI EMTV 16*	2	14 wks
5 May 79	HI ENERGY *K-Tel NE 1044*	17	7 wks
19 May 79	BOOGIE BUS *Polystar 9198 174*	23	11 wks
26 May 79	A MONUMENT TO BRITISH ROCK *Harvest EMTV 17*	13	12 wks
2 Jun 79 ●	THIS IS IT *CBS 10014*	6	12 wks
2 Jun 79	KNUCKLE SANDWICH *EMI International EMYV 18*	19	6 wks
9 Jun 79	THAT SUMMER *Arista SPART 1088*	36	8 wks
9 Jun 79	ROCK LEGENDS *Ronco RTL 2037*	54	3 wks
21 Jul 79 ★	THE BEST DISCO ALBUM IN THE WORLD *Warner Bros. K 58062*	1	17 wks
22 Sep 79	HOT TRACKS *K-Tel NE 1049*	31	8 wks
3 Nov 79 ●	ROCK 'N' ROLLER DISCO *Ronco RTL 2040*	3	11 wks
3 Nov 79	MODS MAYDAY 79 *Arista FOUR 1*	75	1 wk
10 Nov 79	20 SMASH DISCO HITS (THE BITCH) *Warwick WW 5061*	42	5 wks
24 Nov 79 ●	NIGHT MOVES *K-Tel NE 1065*	10	10 wks
24 Nov 79	TOGETHER *K-Tel NE 1053*	35	8 wks
8 Dec 79 ●	PEACE IN THE VALLEY *Ronco RTL 2043*	6	18 wks
15 Dec 79	ALL ABOARD *EMI EMTX 101*	13	8 wks
22 Dec 79	MILITARY GOLD *Ronco RTD 42042*	62	3 wks
12 Jan 80 ●	VIDEO STARS *K-Tel NE 1066*	5	10 wks
26 Jan 80	THE SUMMIT *K-Tel NE 1067*	17	5 wks
2 Feb 80 ★	THE LAST DANCE *Motown EMTV 20*	1	23 wks
9 Feb 80	CAPTAIN BEAKY AND HIS BAND *Polydor 238 3462*	28	12 wks
16 Feb 80	COUNTRY GUITAR *Warwick WW 5070*	46	7 wks
23 Feb 80	METAL FOR MUTHAS *EMI EMC 3318*	16	2 wks
23 Feb 80	FIRST LOVE *Arcade ADEP 41*	58	1 wk
8 Mar 80	THE WANDERERS *Gem GEMLP 103*	48	8 wks
29 Mar 80 ●	STAR TRACKS *K-Tel NE 1070*	6	6 wks
29 Mar 80	CLUB SKA '67 (re-issue) *Island IRSP 4*	53	6 wks
19 Apr 80	FIRST LADIES OF COUNTRY *CBS 10018*	37	3 wks
26 Apr 80	GOOD MORNING AMERICA *K-Tel NE 1072*	15	12 wks
3 May 80 ●	CHAMPAGNE AND ROSES *Polydor ROSTV 1*	7	14 wks
17 May 80	HAPPY DAYS *K-Tel ONE 1076*	32	6 wks
17 May 80 ●	MAGIC REGGAE *K-Tel NE 1074*	9	17 wks
24 May 80	PRECIOUS METAL *MCA MCF 3069*	60	2 wks
14 Jun 80 ●	HOT WAX *K-Tel NE 1082*	3	10 wks
14 Jun 80	METAL FOR MUTHAS VOL.2 *EMI EMC 3337*	58	1 wk
21 Jun 80	KILLER WATTS *CBS KW1*	27	6 wks
2 Aug 80	THE 20TH ANNIVERSARY ALBUM *Motown TMSP 6010*	53	2 wks
30 Aug 80	I AM WOMAN *Polydor WOMTV 1*	11	13 wks
27 Sep 80 ●	MOUNTING EXCITEMENT *K-Tel NE 1091*	2	8 wks
11 Oct 80 ●	THE LOVE ALBUM *K-Tel NE 1062*	6	16 wks
11 Oct 80	COUNTRY ROUND UP *Polydor KOWTV 1*	64	3 wks
18 Oct 80	MONSTERS OF ROCK *Polydor 2488 810*	16	5 wks
25 Oct 80	STREET LEVEL *Ronco RTL 2048*	29	5 wks
25 Oct 80	AXE ATTACK *K-Tel NE 1100*	15	18 wks
8 Nov 80 ●	COUNTRY LEGENDS *Ronco RTL 2050*	9	12 wks
15 Nov 80	RADIOACTIVE *Ronco RTL 2049*	13	9 wks
15 Nov 80 ●	CHART EXPLOSION *K-Tel NE 1103*	6	17 wks
22 Nov 80	CASH COWS *Virgin MILK 1*	49	1 wk
29 Nov 80	SPACE INVADERS *Ronco RTL 2051*	47	3 wks
6 Dec 80	THE LEGENDARY BIG BANDS *Ronco RTL 2047*	24	6 wks
6 Dec 80	THE HITMAKERS *Polydor HOPTV 1*	45	10 wks
3 Jan 81	NIGHTLIFE *K-Tel NE 1107*	25	9 wks
14 Feb 81	HIT MACHINE *K-Tel NE 1113*	17	6 wks
14 Mar 81	SOME BIZARRE ALBUM *Some Bizarre BZLP 1*	58	1 wk
21 Mar 81	RHYTHM 'N' REGGAE *K-Tel NE 1115*	42	4 wks
4 Apr 81 ●	ROLL ON *Polystar REDTV 1*	3	13 wks
4 Apr 81	REMIXTURE *Champagne CHAMP 1*	32	5 wks
4 Apr 81	BITTER SUITE *CBS 22082*	55	3 wks
11 Apr 81	CONCERTS FOR THE PEOPLE OF KAMPUCHEA *Atlantic K 60153*	39	2 wks
25 Apr 81 ●	CHARTBUSTERS 81 *K-Tel NE 1118*	3	9 wks
2 May 81	AXE ATTACK 2 *K-Tel NE -120*	31	6 wks
9 May 81 ★	DISCO DAZE AND DISCO NITES *Ronco RTL 2056 A/B*	1	23 wks
23 May 81 ●	THEMES *K-Tel NE 1122*	6	15 wks
30 May 81	STRENGTH THROUGH OI! *SKIN 1*	51	5 wks
8 Aug 81	ROYAL ROMANCE *Windsor WIN 001*	84	1 wk
29 Aug 81	CALIFORNIA DREAMING *K-Tel NE 1126*	27	11 wks
19 Sep 81 ●	SUPER HITS 1 & 2 *Ronco RTL 2058 A/B*	2	17 wks
19 Sep 81	DANCE DANCE DANCE *K-Tel NE 1143*	29	4 wks
3 Oct 81	THE PLATINUM ALBUM *K-Tel NE 1134*	32	11 wks
10 Oct 81 ●	LOVE IS.... *K-Tel NE 1129*	10	15 wks
17 Oct 81	MONSTER TRACKS *Polystar HOPTV 2*	20	8 wks
24 Oct 81	COUNTRY SUNRISE/COUNTRY SUNSET *Ronco RTL 2059 A/B*	27	11 wks
31 Oct 81	CARRY ON OI *Secret SEC 2*	60	4 wks
14 Nov 81	ROCK HOUSE *Ronco RTL 2061*	44	4 wks
14 Nov 81	DISCO EROTICA *Warwick WW 5108*	35	8 wks
21 Nov 81 ★	CHART HITS 81 *NE 1142*	1	17 wks
21 Nov 81	SLIP STREAM *Beggars Banquet BEGA 31*	72	3 wks
12 Dec 81	THE SECRET POLICEMAN'S OTHER BALL *Springtime HAHA 6003*	69	4 wks
12 Dec 81	MISTY MORNINGS *Ronco RTL 2066*	44	5 wks
12 Dec 81	MEMORIES ARE MADE OF THIS *Ronco RTL 2062*	84	4 wks
12 Dec 81	LIVE AND HEAVY *Nems NEL 6020*	100	2 wks
19 Dec 81	WE ARE MOST AMUSED *Ronco/Charisma 2067*	30	9 wks
26 Dec 81 ●	HITS HITS HITS *Ronco RTL 2063*	2	10 wks
26 Dec 81	MINI POPS *K-Tel NE 1102*	63	7 wks
9 Jan 82 ●	MODERN DANCE *K-Tel NE 1156*	6	10 wks
6 Feb 82 ●	DREAMING *K-Tel NE 1159*	2	12 wks
6 Mar 82 ●	ACTION TRAX *K-Tel NE 1162*	2	12 wks
13 Mar 82	20 WITH A BULLET *EMI EMTV 32*	11	8 wks
20 Mar 82 ●	KEEP FIT AND DANCE *K-Tel NE 1167*	9	13 wks
27 Mar 82 ●	JAMES BOND'S GREATEST HITS *Liberty EMTV 007*	4	13 wks
27 Mar 82	PUNK AND DISORDERLY *Abstract AABT 100*	48	8 wks
10 Apr 82	PS I LOVE YOU *Warwick WW 5121*	68	3 wks
17 Apr 82	MUSIC OF QUALITY AND DISTINCTION VOL 1 *Virgin V 2219*	25	6 wks
17 Apr 82 ●	SHAPE UP AND DANCE VOL 2 *Lifestyle LEG 2*	8	20 wks
24 Apr 82 ●	DISCO UK & DISCO USA *Ronco RTL 2073*	7	10 wks
1 May 82	MIDNIGHT HOUR *K-Tel NE 1157*	98	1 wk
15 May 82 ●	CHARTBUSTERS *Ronco RTL 2074*	3	10 wks
15 May 82	SEX SWEAT AND BLOOD *Beggars Banquet BEGA 34*	88	1 wk
3 Jul 82	TURBO TRAX *K-Tel NE 1176*	17	7 wks
3 Jul 82 ●	OVERLOAD *Ronco RTL 2074*	10	8 wks
14 Aug 82	SONETO *Rough Trade ROUGH 37*	66	3 wks
28 Aug 82	SOUL DAZE/SOUL NITES *Ronco RTL 2080*	25	10 wks
4 Sep 82	THE NO 1 SOUNDS OF THE SEVENTIES *K-Tel NE 1172*	83	1 wk
4 Sep 82	PUNK AND DISORDERLY (FURTHER CHARGES) *Anagram GRAM 001*	91	2 wks

Date	Title Label Number	Position	
11 Sep 82	● BREAKOUT *Ronco RTL 2081*	4	8 wks
11 Sep 82	THE BEST OF BRITISH JAZZ FUNK VOL 2 *Beggars Banquet BEGA 41*	44	4 wks
11 Sep 82	● CHARTBEAT/CHARTBEAT *K-Tel NE 1180*	2	14 wks
25 Sep 82	OI OI THAT'S YER LOT *Secret SEC 5*	54	4 wks
2 Oct 82	MODERN HEROES *TV Records TVA 1*	24	7 wks
9 Oct 82	ENDLESS LOVE *TV Records TVA 2*	26†	8 wks
16 Oct 82	● REFLECTIONS *CBS 10034*	4	11 wks
16 Oct 82	● CHART ATTACK *Telstar STAR 2221*	7	6 wks
16 Oct 82	BEST FRIENDS *Impression LP IMP 1*	29	11 wks
23 Oct 82	STREETPOISE VOL I *Epic/Streetware STR 32234*	51	4 wks
23 Oct 82	ON THE AIR - 60 YEARS OF BBC THEME MUSIC *BBC REF 454*	85	3 wks
30 Oct 82	MUSIC FOR THE SEASONS *Ronco RTL 2075*	41	8 wks
30 Oct 82	THE LOVE SONGS ALBUM *K-Tel NE 1179*	28†	7 wks
6 Nov 82	HITS OF THE SCREAMING 60'S *Warwick WW 5124*	24†	8 wks
6 Nov 82	FLASH TRACKS *Records PTVL 1*	19	7 wks
6 Nov 82	DISCO DANCER *K-Tel NE 1190*	26	7 wks
6 Nov 82	MIDNIGHT IN MOTOWN *Telstar STAR 2224*	34†	8 wks
6 Nov 82	CHART HITS '82 *NE 1195*	11†	8 wks
27 Nov 82	CHART WARS *Ronco RTL 2086*	30†	5 wks
27 Nov 82	THE GREAT COUNTRY MUSIC SHOW *Ronco RTD 2083*	38†	5 wks
18 Dec 82	THE COMPOSERS *Ronco RTL 2084*	49†	2 wks
18 Dec 82	STREETSCENE *K-Tel NE 1183*	52†	2 wks
18 Dec 82	DIRECT HITS *Telstar STAR 2224*	41†	2 wks
25 Dec 82	RAIDERS OF THE POP CHARTS *Ronco RTL 2088*	40†	1 wk
25 Dec 82	PARTY FEVER/DISCO MANIA *TV Records TVA 5*	93†	1 wk
25 Dec 82	PHIL SPECTOR'S CHRISTMAS ALBUM (re-issue) *Phil Spec.Int/Polydor 2307 005*	96†	1 wk

FILM SOUNDTRACKS

Date	Title Label Number	Position	
8 Nov 58	★ SOUTH PACIFIC *RCA RB 16065*	1	286 wks
8 Nov 58	● THE KING AND I *Capitol LCT 6108*	4	103 wks
8 Nov 58	● OKLAHOMA *Capitol LCT 6100*	4	90 wks
6 Dec 58	● CAROUSEL *Capitol LCT 6105*	8	15 wks
31 Jan 59	● GIGI *MGM C 770*	2	88 wks
10 Oct 59	● PORGY AND BESS *Philips ABL 3282*	7	5 wks
23 Jan 60	● THE FIVE PENNIES *London HAU 2189*	2	15 wks
7 May 60	● CAN CAN *Capitol W 1301*	2	31 wks
28 May 60	PAL JOEY *Capitol LCT 6148*	20	1 wk
23 Jul 60	HIGH SOCIETY *Capitol LCT 6116*	16	1 wk
5 Nov 60	BEN-HUR *MGM C 802*	15	3 wks
21 Jan 61	NEVER ON SUNDAY *London HAT 2309*	17	1 wk
18 Feb 61	● SONG WITHOUT END *Pye GGL 30169*	9	10 wks
29 Apr 61	● SEVEN BRIDES FOR SEVEN BROTHERS *MGM C 853*	6	22 wks
3 Jun 61	EXODUS *RCA RD 27210*	17	1 wk
11 Nov 61	GLEN MILLER STORY *Ace Of Hearts AH 12*	12	7 wks
24 Mar 62	★ WEST SIDE STORY *Philips BBL 7530*	1	175 wks
28 Apr 62	● IT'S TRAD DAD *Columbia 33SX 1412*	3	21 wks
22 Sep 62	THE MUSIC MAN *Warner Bros. WB 4066*	14	9 wks
3 Nov 62	PORGY AND BESS *CBS APG 60002*	14	7 wks
15 Jun 63	JUST FOR FUN *Decca LK 4524*	20	2 wks
31 Oct 64	● MY FAIR LADY *CBS BPG 72237*	9	51 wks

Date	Title Label Number	Position	
31 Oct 64	GOLDFINGER *United Artists ULP 1076*	14	5 wks
16 Jan 65	● MARY POPPINS *HMV CLP 1794*	2	82 wks
10 Apr 65	★ SOUND OF MUSIC *RCA RB 6616*	1	381 wks
30 Apr 66	FUNNY GIRL *Capitol W 2059*	19	3 wks
11 Sep 66	● DR ZHIVAGO *MGM C 8007*	3	106 wks
22 Jul 67	CASINO ROYALE *RCA Victor SF 7874*	35	1 wk
29 Jul 67	A MAN AND A WOMAN *United Artists SULP 1155*	31	11 wks
28 Oct 67	● THOROUGHLY MODERN MILLIE *Brunswick STA 8685*	9	19 wks
9 Mar 68	● THE JUNGLE BOOK *Disney ST 3948*	5	51 wks
21 Sep 68	STAR *Stateside SSL 10233*	36	1 wk
12 Oct 68	● THE GOOD, THE BAD AND THE UGLY *United Artists SULP 1197*	2	18 wks
23 Nov 68	● OLIVER *RCA Victor SB 6777*	4	107 wks
23 Nov 68	CAMELOT *Warner Bros. WS 1712*	37	1 wk
8 Feb 69	● CHITTY CHITTY BANG BANG *United Artists SULP 1200*	10	5 wks
10 May 69	FUNNY GIRL *CBS 70044*	11	22 wks
14 Jun 69	● 2001 - A SPACE ODYSSEY *MGMCS 8078*	3	67 wks
20 Dec 69	EASY RIDER *Stateside SSL 5018*	11	24 wks
24 Jan 70	JUNGLE BOOK (re-issue) *Disney BVS 4041*	25	26 wks
7 Feb 70	● PAINT YOUR WAGON *Paramount SPFL 257*	2	102 wks
14 Mar 70	HELLO DOLLY *Stateside SSL 10292*	45	2 wks
18 Jul 70	WOODSTOCK *Atlantic 2662 001*	35	19 wks
24 Apr 71	● LOVE STORY *Paramount SPFL 267*	10	33 wks
12 Feb 72	● CLOCKWORK ORANGE *Warner Bros. K 46127*	4	46 wks
8 Apr 72	FIDDLER ON THE ROOF *United Artists UAD 60011/2*	26	2 wks
13 May 72	2001 - A SPACE ODYSSEY (re-issue) *MGM 2315 034*	20	2 wks
29 Nov 72	SOUTH PACIFIC (re-issue) *RCA Victor SB 2011*	25	2 wks
31 Mar 73	CABARET *Probe SPB 1052*	13	22 wks
14 Apr 73	LOST HORIZON *Bell SYBEL 8000*	36	3 wks
22 Sep 73	JESUS CHRIST SUPERSTAR *MCA MDKS 8012/3*	23	18 wks
23 Mar 74	● THE STING *MCA MCF 2537*	7	35 wks
8 Jun 74	A TOUCH OF CLASS *Philips 6612 040*	32	1 wk
5 Oct 74	SUNSHINE *MCA MCF 2566*	47	3 wks
5 Apr 75	TOMMY *Polydor 2657 014*	21	9 wks
31 Jan 76	JAWS *MCA MCF 2716*	55	1 wk
5 Mar 77	MOSES *Pye NSPH*	43	2 wks
9 Apr 77	★ A STAR IS BORN *CBS 86021*	1	54 wks
2 Jul 77	THE BEST OF CAR WASH *MCA MCF 2799*	59	1 wk
11 Mar 78	★ SATURDAY NIGHT FEVER *RSO 2658 123*	1	65 wks
22 Apr 78	● THE STUD *Ronco RTD 2029*	2	19 wks
29 Apr 78	CLOSE ENCOUNTERS OF THE THIRD KIND *Arista DLART 2001*	40	6 wks
20 May 78	THANK GOD IT'S FRIDAY *Casablanca TGIF 100*	40	5 wks
27 May 78	FM *MCA MCSP 284*	37	7 wks
8 Jul 78	★ GREASE *RSO RSD 2001*	1	47 wks
12 Aug 78	SGT PEPPER'S LONELY HEARTS CLUB BAND *A & M AMLZ 66600*	38	2 wks
7 Oct 78	CONVOY *Capitol EST 24590*	52	1 wk
30 Jun 79	THE WORLD IS FULL OF MARRIED MEN *Ronco RTD 2038*	25	9 wks
14 Jul 79	THE WARRIORS *A & M AMLH 64761*	53	7 wks
6 Oct 79	QUADROPHENIA *Polydor 2625 037*	23	16 wks
5 Jan 80	THE SECRET POLICEMAN'S BALL *Island ILPS 9601*	33	6 wks

Date	Title Label Number	Position	
9 Feb 80	**SUNBURN** *Warwick RTL 2044*	45	7 wks
16 Feb 80	**GOING STEADY** *Warwick WW 5078*	25	10 wks
8 Mar 80	**THE ROSE** *Atlantic K 50681*	68	1 wk
7 Jun 80	**THE GREAT ROCK 'N' ROLL SWINDLE** *Virgin V 2168*	16	11 wks
19 Jul 80	● **XANADU** *Jet JET LX 526*	2	17 wks
16 Aug 80	● **CAN'T STOP THE MUSIC** *Mercury 6399 051*	9	8 wks
14 Feb 81	● **DANCE CRAZE** *2-Tone CHRTT 5004*	5	15 wks
6 Feb 82	**FAME** *RSO 2479 253*	21	25 wks
20 Mar 82	**THE SECRET POLICEMAN'S OTHER BALL (THE MUSIC)** *Springtime Ha-Ha 6004*	29	5 wks
17 Jul 82	**THE SOUND OF MUSIC** (re-issue) *RCA Ints 5134*	98	1 wk
4 Sep 82	**ROCKY III** *Liberty LBG 30351*	42	7 wks
4 Sep 82	**ANNIE** *CBS 70219*	83	2 wks
11 Sep 82	**BRIMSTONE AND TREACLE** *A & M AMLH 64915*	67	3 wks

The West Side Story album on Phillips BBL 7530 during its chart run changed label and number to CBS BPG 62058.

STAGE CAST RECORDINGS

Date	Title Label Number	Position	
8 Nov 58	● **MY FAIR LADY (BROADWAY)** *Philips RBL 1000*	2	129 wks
24 Jan 59	● **WEST SIDE STORY (BROADWAY)** *Philips BBL 7277*	3	27 wks
26 Mar 60	● **AT THE DROP OF A HAT (LONDON)** *Parlophone PMC 1033*	9	1 wk
26 Mar 60	● **FINGS AIN'T WOT THEY USED TO BE (LONDON)** *Decca LK 4346*	5	11 wks
2 Apr 60	● **FLOWER DRUM SONG (BROADWAY)** *Philips ABL 3302*	2	27 wks
7 May 60	● **FOLLOW THAT GIRL (LONDON)** *HMV CLP 1366*	5	9 wks
21 May 60	● **MOST HAPPY FELLA (BROADWAY)** *Philips BBL 7374*	6	13 wks
21 May 60	**MAKE ME AN OFFER (LONDON)** *HMV CLP 1333*	18	1 wk
28 May 60	● **FLOWER DRUM SONG (LONDON)** *HMV CLP 1359*	10	3 wks
9 Jul 60	**MOST HAPPY FELLA (LONDON)** *HMV CLP 1365*	19	1 wk
30 Jul 60	**WEST SIDE STORY (BROADWAY)** *Philips SBBL 504*	14	1 wk
10 Sep 60	● **OLIVER (LONDON)** *Decca LK 4359*	4	91 wks
11 Mar 61	**KING KONG (SOUTH AFRICA)** *Decca LK 4392*	12	8 wks
6 May 61	● **MUSIC MAN (LONDON)** *HMV CLP 1444*	8	13 wks
24 Jun 61	● **SOUND OF MUSIC (BROADWAY)** *Philips ABL 3370*	4	19 wks
22 Jul 61	**BYE-BYE BIRDIE** *Philips ABL 3385*	17	3 wks
22 Jul 61	**BEYOND THE FRINGE (LONDON)** *Parlophone PMC 1145*	13	17 wks
29 Jul 61	● **SOUND OF MUSIC (LONDON)** *HMV CLP 1453*	4	68 wks
9 Sep 61	● **STOP THE WORLD I WANT TO GET OFF (LONDON)** *Decca LK 4408*	8	14 wks
14 Jul 62	● **BLITZ (LONDON)** *HMV CLP 1569*	7	21 wks
18 May 63	**HALF A SIXPENCE (LONDON)** *Decca LK 4521*	20	2 wks
3 Aug 63	**PICKWICK (LONDON)** *Philips AL 3431*	12	10 wks
4 Jan 64	**MY FAIR LADY (BROADWAY)** *CBS BPG 68001*	19	1 wk
22 Feb 64	**AT THE DROP OF ANOTHER HAT (LONDON)** *Parlophone PMC 1216*	12	11 wks

Date	Title Label Number	Position	
3 Oct 64	● **CAMELOT (BROADWAY)** *CBS APG 60001*	10	12 wks
16 Jan 65	**CAMELOT (LONDON)** *HMV CLP 1756*	19	1 wk
11 Mar 67	● **FIDDLER ON THE ROOF (LONDON)** *CBS SBPG 70030*	4	50 wks
28 Dec 68	● **HAIR (LONDON)** *Polydor 583-043*	3	94 wks
30 Aug 69	**THE WORLD OF OLIVER (ORIG. LONDON CAST ALBUM)** (re-issue) *Decca SPA 30*	23	4 wks
6 Sep 69	**HAIR (BROADWAY)** *RCA SF 7959*	58	2 wks
19 Feb 72	**GODSPELL (LONDON)** *Bell BELLS 203*	25	17 wks
18 Nov 78	**EVITA (LONDON)** *MCA MCG 3257*	24	18 wks
1 Aug 81	● **CATS (LONDON)** *Polydor CATX 001*	6	26 wks
6 Nov 82	**MACK AND MABLE** *MCA MCL 1728*	38	6 wks

STUDIO CAST RECORDINGS

Date	Title Label Number	Position	
25 Jun 60	**SHOWBOAT** *HMV CLP 1310*	12	1 wk
8 Feb 72	● **JESUS CHRIST SUPERSTAR** *MCA MKPS 2011/2*	6	20 wks
22 Jan 77	● **EVITA** *MCA MCX 503*	4	35 wks

TV and RADIO SOUNDTRACKS and SPIN-OFFS

Date	Title Label Number	Position	
13 Dec 58	● **OH BOY!** *Parlophone PMC 1072*	9	14 wks
4 Mar 61	● **HUCKLEBERRY HOUND** *Pye GGL 004*	10	12 wks
30 Feb 63	**THAT WAS THE WEEK THAT WAS** *Parlophone PMC 1197*	11	9 wks
28 Mar 64	**STARS FROM STARS AND GARTERS** *Pye GGL 0252*	17	2 wks
10 Apr 76	★ **ROCK FOLLIES** *Island ILPS 9362*	1	15 wks
8 Apr 78	● **PENNIES FROM HEAVEN** *World Records SH 266*	10	17 wks
1 Jul 78	**MORE PENNIES FROM HEAVEN** *World Records SH 267*	31	4 wks
15 Dec 79	**FAWLTY TOWERS** *BBC REB 377*	25	10 wks
14 Feb 81	**HITCHHIKERS GUIDE TO THE GALAXY VOL.2** *Original ORA 54*	47	4 wks
1 Aug 81	**THE MUSIC OF COSMOS** *RCA RCALP 5032*	43	10 wks
21 Nov 81	**BRIDESHEAD REVISITED** *Chrysalis CDL 1367*	50	12 wks

MISCELLANEOUS

Date	Title Label Number	Position	
12 Sep 70	**EDINBURGH MILITARY TATTOO 1970** *Waverley SZLP 2121*	34	4 wks
18 Sep 71	**EDINBURGH MILITARY TATTOO 1971** *Waverley SZLP 2128*	44	1 wk
11 Dec 71	**ELECTRONIC ORGANS TODAY** *Ad-Rhythm ADBS 1*	48	1 wk
4 Nov 72	**THE BBC 1922-1972 (TV AND RADIO EXTRACTS)** *BBC 50*	16	7 wks
8 Dec 73	● **MUSIC FOR A ROYAL WEDDING** *BBC REW 163*	7	6 wks
27 Dec 75	**STRINGS OF SCOTLAND** *Philips 6382 108*	50	1 wk
8 Aug 81	★ **THE ROYAL WEDDING** *BBC REP 413*	1	11 wks

Part Two: HIT ALBUMS
Facts & Feats

Most Weeks on Chart

The following table lists all the recording acts that spent 100 weeks or more on the British albums chart from the first chart on 8 November 1958 up to and including the chart of 25 December 1982. It is of course possible for an act to be credited with 2 or more chart weeks in the same week via simultaneous hits.   **Weeks**

BEATLES.....................1000
SIMON AND GARFUNKEL
  (Paul Simon a further 106 weeks solo, Art Garfunkel a further 45 weeks solo).........977
ELVIS PRESLEY.............973
PINK FLOYD...............660
ROLLING STONES...........592
FRANK SINATRA *(Plus a further 23 weeks with Count Basie)*......588
CLIFF RICHARD..............570
DAVID BOWIE..............554
BOB DYLAN...............516
BEACH BOYS..............505
ABBA 471
ELTON JOHN..............462
ROD STEWART *(Plus 56 weeks with The Faces)*.............448
ANDY WILLIAMS..........429
CARPENTERS 427
FLEETWOOD MAC...........421
LED ZEPPELIN.............407
NEIL DIAMOND.............394
TOM JONES...............392
JIM REEVES.............381
'THE SOUND OF MUSIC' Cast
  from the film...........381
MIKE OLDFIELD...........377
QUEEN....................345
SHADOWS 342
ELECTRIC LIGHT ORCHESTRA 318
STATUS QUO...............315
HERB ALPERT.............312
BUDDY HOLLY............307
PAUL McCARTNEY/WINGS
  (Paul McCartney a further 105 weeks solo).............305

MEATLOAF 292
MOODY BLUES...............288
'SOUTH PACIFIC' *Cast from the film*.....................287
JOHNNY CASH...............285
JAMES LAST................281
DIANA ROSS *(Plus 50 weeks with Supremes)*................279
STEVIE WONDER............276
BARRY MANILOW...........275
SEEKERS...................269
BLONDIE..................249
CAT STEVENS................243
DEEP PURPLE..............240
JOHN LENNON *(and Yoko Ono Plastic Ono Band etc.)*........239
SHIRLEY BASSEY 235
ROXY MUSIC..............234
FOUR TOPS *(Plus 11 weeks with The Temptations)*..............233
GENESIS 231
GEORGE MITCHELL
  MINSTRELS 230
POLICE 228
EAGLES 223
DIRE STRAITS..............218
ENGELBERT HUMPERDINCK..214
LEO SAYER................214
BARBRA STREISAND..........212
JETHRO TULL..............201
JEFF WAYNE'S WAR OF THE
  WORLDS 200
MADNESS 195
10 CC 195
THIN LIZZY 195
OTIS REDDING *(Plus a further 17 weeks with Carla Thomas)*...192
GILBERT O'SULLIVAN.......191
JOHNNY MATHIS *(Plus a further 11 weeks with Deniece Williams)*...................190
NANA MOUSKOURI..........190
SUPREMES *(Plus a further 31 weeks with the Temptations and 11 weeks with the Four Tops)* 186
SANTANA.................185
PERRY COMO...............185
JIMI HENDRIX.............183
CREAM...................182

BLACK SABBATH............180
GLEN CAMPBELL 179
JOHN DENVER *(Plus a further 21 weeks with Placido Domingo)*.................178
SLADE 177
WHO 177
BREAD 176
WEST SIDE STORY *Cast from the film* 175
AC/DC 173
JACKSONS/JACKSON FIVE....173
PETERS AND LEE...........166
TYRANNOSAURUS/T.REX.....166
VAL DOONICAN.............164
YES 164
SKY 154
RAINBOW 153
MAX BYGRAVES.............151
DONNA SUMMER............151
BEE GEES 150
MANTOVANI 148
NEIL YOUNG *(Plus a further 79 weeks with Crosby, Stills Nash and Young, 5 weeks with the Stills-Young Band)*........*145*
BOB MARLEY..............143
DEMIS ROUSSOS...........143
ROY ORBISON.............142
STYLISTICS 139
KATE BUSH 138
SUPERTRAMP 136
EMERSON, LAKE AND PALMER
  (Plus Greg Lake a further 3 weeks solo).................135
EARTH WIND AND FIRE......134
HOLLIES 133
UB 40....................132
DR HOOK 130
MY FAIR LADY *(Broadway Cast)* 129
BAY CITY ROLLERS.........127
HUMAN LEAGUE.............127
ADAM AND THE ANTS.......126
BONEY M 125
SHOWADDYWADDY..........125
LEONARD COHEN...........123
RICK WAKEMAN...........122
STRANGLERS 121
MICHAEL JACKSON 119
LINDISFARNE 119

LED ZEPPELIN

John Bonham, John Paul-Jones, Jimmy Page and Robert Plant got higher than the airships of the same name and tended to stay up longer.

John +
Paul +
George +
Ringo = 1000

PERRY COMO
The man who caused a split between Jimi Hendrix and Santana (in our list).

Most Weeks On Chart Each Year

Year	Weeks
1958—ELVIS PRESLEY	16
1959—FRANK SINATRA	56
1960—ELVIS PRESLEY	51
1961—ELVIS PRESLEY	91
1962—GEORGE MITCHELL MINSTRELS	109
1963—CLIFF RICHARD	72
1964—JIM REEVES	115
1965—BOB DYLAN	112
1966—BEACH BOYS	95
1967—HERB ALPERT	101
1968—TOM JONES	135
1969—SEEKERS	66
1970—SIMON and GARFUNKEL	167
1971—ANDY WILLIAMS	111
1972—CAT STEVENS	89
1973—DAVID BOWIE	182
1974—DAVID BOWIE	107
1975—ELTON JOHN	105
1976—DEMIS ROUSSOS	84
1977—PINK FLOYD	108
1978—ABBA	112
1979—ELECTRIC LIGHT ORCHESTRA	112
1980—POLICE	116
1981—BARRY MANILOW	92
1982—JAPAN	85

Soundtrack albums are not included in this section.

Most Weeks On Chart In A Year

Year	Weeks
1973—DAVID BOWIE	182
1970—SIMON and GARFUNKEL	167
1968—TOM JONES	135
1970—JOHNNY CASH	125
1970—BEATLES	122
1968—OTIS REDDING	121
1980—POLICE	116
1970—MOODY BLUES	115
1964—JIM REEVES	115
1978—ABBA	112
1965—BOB DYLAN	112
1979—ELECTRIC LIGHT ORCHESTRA	112
1971—ANDY WILLIAMS	111
1968—BEACH BOYS	110
1962—GEORGE MITCHELL MINSTRELS	109
1977—PINK FLOYD	108
1974—DAVID BOWIE	107
1977—ABBA	106
1974—CARPENTERS	106
1975—ELTON JOHN	105
1964—BEATLES	104
1974—BEATLES	104
1973—SIMON and GARFUNKEL	104
1968—FOUR TOPS	103
1970—LED ZEPPELIN	102
1971—SIMON and GARFUNKEL	102
1967—HERB ALPERT	101
1974—SIMON and GARFUNKEL	101
1979—BLONDIE	100
1975—SIMON and GARFUNKEL	100

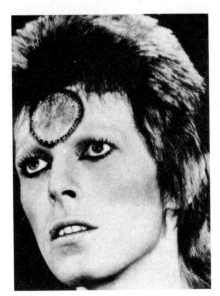

During 1973 the perennial David Bowie spent more weeks on the chart than any other artist in one year.

Most Hit Albums

Double, Treble and Quadruple albums count as only one album for the purposes of this table. Re-issues do not count as a new hit.

82	Elvis Presley
46	Frank Sinatra
43	James Last
39	Cliff Richard
31	Rolling Stones
27	Shirley Bassey
26	Bob Dylan
26	Jim Reeves
23	Beach Boys
23	Beatles
23	Johnny Mathis
23	Andy Williams
22	Elton John
21	Diana Ross
20	Neil Diamond
18	David Bowie
18	Tom Jones
17	Jethro Tull
17	Status Quo
16	Johnny Cash
16	Jimi Hendrix
16	Shadows
15	Deep Purple
15	Hawkwind
15	Who
14	Herb Alpert
14	Santana
14	Rod Stewart
14	Tyrannosaurus/T. Rex
13	Roy Orbison
13	Pink Floyd
13	Wishbone Ash
13	Neil Young
12	Black Sabbath
12	Carpenters
12	Fleetwood Mac
12	Genesis
12	John Mayall
12	Tangerine Dream
12	Yes
12	Queen
11	Eric Clapton
11	Ray Conniff

11	David Essex
11	Hollies
11	Buddy Holly
11	Moody Blues
11	Mantovani
11	Temptations
11	Don Williams
10	Abba
10	Max Bygraves
10	Byrds
10	Alice Cooper
10	Val Doonican
10	Rory Gallagher
10	Bert Kaempfert
10	Led Zeppelin
10	George Mitchell Minstrels
10	Joni Mitchell
10	Roxy Music
10	Leo Sayer
10	Slade
10	Barbra Streisand
10	Donna Summer
10	10 CC
10	Uriah Heep

STATUS QUO
Equal with Jethro Tull, the third
most number of hit albums for
a British group.

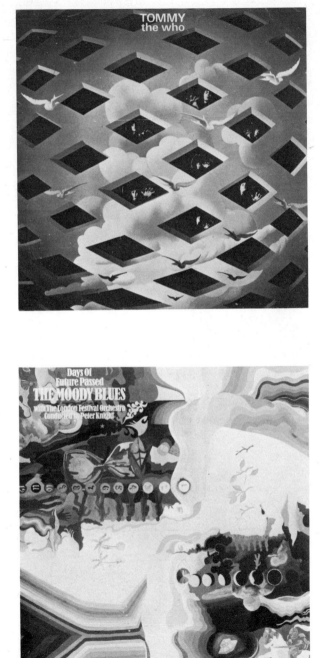

Most Top Ten Hit Albums

The rules for this category are the same as for Most Hit Albums except that the album must have made the Top Ten for at least 1 week.

35	Elvis Presley	6	Jethro Tull
27	Frank Sinatra	6	Diana Ross
24	Cliff Richard	6	Leo Sayer
23	Rolling Stones	6	Simon and Garfunkel
22	Bob Dylan	6	Stranglers
18	Beatles	6	Thin Lizzy
15	David Bowie	6	Stevie Wonder
14	Status Quo	6	John Lennon
12	Beach Boys	6	Mantovani
12	Elton John	5	Carpenters
12	Jim Reeves	5	Johnny Cash
12	Who	5	John Denver
11	Rod Stewart	5	Val Doonican
11	Tom Jones	5	Duane Eddy
11	Pink Floyd	5	Electric Light Orchestra
10	Genesis	5	Free
10	Led Zeppelin	5	Jam
10	Queen	5	Kinks
10	Andy Williams	5	Barry Manilow
9	Joni Mitchell	5	Santana
9	Roxy Music	5	Slade
9	Yes	5	Herb Alpert
9	Shadows	5	Rainbow
8	Abba	5	Tyrannosaurus/T. Rex
8	Black Sabbath		
8	Moody Blues		
8	Jimi Hendrix		
8	Wings		
7	Emerson, Lake and Palmer		
7	Cream		
7	Buddy Holly		
7	Johnny Mathis		
7	10 CC		
7	Deep Purple		
6	Shirley Bassey		
6	Elvis Costello		
6	Bee Gees		
6	Blondie		
6	Fleetwood Mac		
6	Hollies		
6	Engelbert Humperdinck		

The only album ever to spend more than 100 weeks at the top of the chart — even providing Captain Sensible with a number one single 'Happy Talk', in 1982.

Most Weeks At Number One By Album: Total

115	**South Pacific**—FILM SOUNDTRACK
70	**Sound Of Music**—FILM SOUNDTRACK
41	**Bridge Over Troubled Water**—SIMON AND GARFUNKEL
30	**Please Please Me**—BEATLES
27	**Sergeant Pepper's Lonely Hearts Club Band**—BEATLES
22	**GI Blues**—ELVIS PRESLEY
21	**With The Beatles**—BEATLES
21	**Hard Day's Night**—BEATLES
18	**Blue Hawaii**—ELVIS PRESLEY
18	**Saturday Night Fever**—FILM SOUNDTRACK
17	**Abbey Road**—BEATLES
17	**The Singles 1969–73**—CARPENTERS
14	**Summer Holiday**—CLIFF RICHARD
13	**West Side Story**—FILM SOUNDTRACK
13	**John Wesley Harding**—BOB DYLAN
13	**Grease**—FILM SOUNDTRACK
12	**Rolling Stones**—ROLLING STONES
12	**Kings Of The Wild Frontier**—ADAM AND THE ANTS
12	**Kids From Fame**—KIDS FROM FAME
11	**Beatles For Sale**—BEATLES
11	**20 All Time Hits Of The Fifties**—VARIOUS ARTISTS
11	**Elton John's Greatest Hits**—ELTON JOHN
11	**Greatest Hits**—ABBA
10	**Rolling Stones No 2**—ROLLING STONES
10	**20 Golden Greats**—BEACH BOYS
10	**Arrival**—ABBA

Most Weeks At Number One By Album: Consecutive

70 **South Pacific—FILM SOUNDTRACK**
30 **Please Please Me—BEATLES**
23 **Sergeant Pepper's Lonely Hearts Club Band—BEATLES**
21 **With The Beatles—BEATLES**
21 **Hard Day's Night—BEATLES**
19 **South Pacific—FILM SOUNDTRACK**
18 **Sound Of Music—FILM SOUNDTRACK**
18 **Saturday Night Fever—FILM SOUNDTRACK**
17 **Blue Hawaii—ELVIS PRESLEY**
14 **Summer Holiday—CLIFF RICHARD**
13 **South Pacific—FILM SOUNDTRACK**
13 **Bridge Over Troubled Water— SIMON and GARFUNKEL**
13 **Grease—FILM SOUNDTRACK**
12 **GI Blues—ELVIS PRESLEY**
12 **Rolling Stones—ROLLING STONES**
11 **Abbey Road—BEATLES**
11 **Bridge Over Troubled Water— SIMON and GARFUNKEL**
11 **The Singles 1969–73— CARPENTERS**
11 **Elton John's Greatest Hits— ELTON JOHN**
10 **Sound Of Music—FILM SOUNDTRACK**
10 **Sound Of Music—FILM SOUNDTRACK**
10 **Sound Of Music—FILM SOUNDTRACK**
    (Three seperate runs at number one of 10 weeks each)
10 **John Wesley Harding—BOB DYLAN**
10 **20 Golden Greats—BEACH BOYS**
10 **Kings Of The Wild Frontier— ADAM and the ANTS**

Most Weeks At Number One By Artist

164	Beatles
49	Abba
49	Elvis Presley
48	Simon and Garfunkel
43	Rolling Stones
27	Rod Stewart
22	Cliff Richard
22	Carpenters
22	Bob Dylan
21	Elton John
21	Shadows
19	George Mitchell Minstrels
16	David Bowie
15	Barbra Streisand
14	Led Zeppelin
12	Adam and the Ants
12	T. Rex
11	Police
11	Queen
10	Beach Boys
10	Stylistics
10	Supremes
10	Slim Whitman

Most Number One Albums

12	Beatles	3	Paul McCartney
9	Rolling Stones	3	George Mitchell Minstrels
8	Abba	3	Moody Blues
8	Led Zeppelin	3	Roxy Music
7	Rod Stewart	3	Slade
6	Bob Dylan	3	Barbra Streisand
6	Elvis Presley	3	T. Rex
5	Cliff Richard	3	Andy Williams
4	David Bowie	3	Boney M
4	Elton John		
4	Queen		
4	Shadows		
4	Status Quo		
3	Deep Purple		

Most Weeks on Chart by an Album in Total

The following table lists all the albums that have spent 100 weeks or more on the chart in total. Re-issues of an album do not count in this total.

Sound Of Music—FILM SOUNDTRACK...................................381
Bridge Over Troubled Water—SIMON and GARFUNKEL....................303
Dark Side Of The Moon—PINK FLOYD.................................292
South Pacific—FILM SOUNDTRACK....................................287
Greatest Hits—SIMON and GARFUNKEL................................281
Rumours—FLEETWOOD MAC..271
Tubular Bells—MIKE OLDFIELD......................................247
Bat Out Of Hell—MEATLOAF...246
Jeff Wayne's War Of The Worlds...................................200
West Side Story—FILM SOUNDTRACK..................................175
Buddy Holly Story—BUDDY HOLLY....................................156
Manilow Magic—BARRY MANILOW......................................151
Sergeant Pepper's Lonely Hearts Club Band—BEATLES................148
The Beatles 1962–66—BEATLES......................................148
Best Of The Beach Boys—BEACH BOYS................................142
Going Places—HERB ALPERT...138
Led Zeppelin 2—LED ZEPPELIN......................................138
Greatest Hits—ABBA...130
My Fair Lady—BROADWAY CAST.......................................129
Best Of The Seekers—SEEKERS......................................125
Band On The Run—WINGS..124
Greatest Hits—ANDY WILLIAMS......................................116
Johnny Cash At San Quentin—JOHNNY CASH...........................115
Singles 1969–73—CARPENTERS.......................................115
The Beatles 1967–70—BEATLES......................................113
Greatest Hits—GLEN CAMPBELL......................................113
And I Love You So—PERRY COMO.....................................109
Makin' Movies—DIRE STRAITS.......................................108
Out Of The Blue—ELECTRIC LIGHT ORCHESTRA.........................108
Oliver—FILM SOUNDTRACK...107
Dr Zhivago—FILM SOUNDTRACK.......................................106
The Rise And Fall Of Ziggy Stardust—DAVID BOWIE..................106
Over And Over—NANA MOUSKOURI.....................................105
Parallel Lines—BLONDIE...105
Sounds Of Silence—SIMON and GARFUNKEL............................104
The King And I—FILM SOUNDTRACK...................................103
Paint Your Wagon—FILM SOUNDTRACK.................................102
Imagine—JOHN LENNON/PLASTIC ONO BAND.............................101
Best Of Bread—BREAD..100
A New World Record—ELECTRIC LIGHT ORCHESTRA......................100

First Album Chart

8 Nov 1958

1	South Pacific	Film Soundtrack
2	Come Fly With Me	Frank Sinatra
3	Elvis' Golden Records	Elvis Presley
4	King Creole	Elvis Presley
5	My Fair Lady	Broadway Stage Cast
6	Warm	Johnny Mathis
7	The King And I	Film Soundtrack
8	Dear Perry	Perry Como
9	Oklahoma	Film Soundtrack
10	Songs By Tom Lehrer	Tom Lehrer

Number One Albums
8 Nov 1958—25 Dec 1982

8 Nov 58	**SOUTH PACIFIC**—SOUNDTRACK (RCA)	70
12 Mar 60	**THE EXPLOSIVE FREDDY CANNON**—FREDDY CANNON (TOP RANK)	1
19 Mar 60	**SOUTH PACIFIC**—SOUNDTRACK (RCA)	19
30 Jul 60	**ELVIS IS BACK**—ELVIS PRESLEY (RCA)	1
6 Aug 60	**SOUTH PACIFIC**—SOUNDTRACK (RCA)	5
10 Sep 60	**DOWN DRURY LANE TO MEMORY LANE**—101 STRINGS (PYE)	5
15 Oct 60	**SOUTH PACIFIC**—SOUNDTRACK (RCA)	13
14 Jan 61	**GI BLUES**—ELVIS PRESLEY (RCA)	7
4 Mar 61	**SOUTH PACIFIC**—SOUNDTRACK (RCA)	1
11 Mar 61	**GI BLUES**—ELVIS PRESLEY (RCA)	3
1 Apr 61	**SOUTH PACIFIC**—SOUNDTRACK (RCA)	1
8 Apr 61	**GI BLUES**—ELVIS PRESLEY (RCA)	12
1 Jul 61	**SOUTH PACIFIC**—SOUNDTRACK (RCA)	4
29 Jul 61	**BLACK AND WHITE MINSTREL SHOW**—GEORGE MITCHELL MINSTRELS (HMV)	4
26 Aug 61	**SOUTH PACIFIC**—SOUNDTRACK (RCA)	1
2 Sep 61	**BLACK AND WHITE MINSTREL SHOW**—GEORGE MITCHELL MINSTRELS (HMV)	1
9 Sep 61	**SOUTH PACIFIC**—SOUNDTRACK (RCA)	1
16 Sep 61	**BLACK AND WHITE MINSTREL SHOW**—GEORGE MITCHELL MINSTRELS (HMV)	1
23 Sep 61	**THE SHADOWS**—THE SHADOWS (COLUMBIA)	4
21 Oct 61	**BLACK AND WHITE MINSTREL SHOW**—GEORGE MITCHELL MINSTRELS (HMV)	1
28 Oct 61	**THE SHADOWS**—THE SHADOWS (COLUMBIA)	1
4 Nov 61	**I'M 21 TODAY**—CLIFF RICHARD (COLUMBIA)	1
11 Nov 61	**ANOTHER BLACK AND WHITE MINSTREL SHOW**—GEORGE MITCHELL MINSTRELS (HMV)	8
6 Jan 62	**BLUE HAWAII**—ELVIS PRESLEY (RCA)	1
13 Jan 62	**THE YOUNG ONES**—CLIFF RICHARD (COLUMBIA)	6
24 Feb 62	**BLUE HAWAII**—ELVIS PRESLEY (RCA)	17
23 Jun 62	**WEST SIDE STORY**—SOUNDTRACK (PHILIPS)*	5
28 Jul 62	**POT LUCK**—ELVIS PRESLEY (RCA)	5
2 Sep 62	**WEST SIDE STORY**—SOUNDTRACK (CBS)*	1
8 Sep 62	**POT LUCK**—ELVIS PRESLEY (RCA)	1
	* During its chart run West Side Story changed label to CBS.	
15 Sep 62	**WEST SIDE STORY**—SOUNDTRACK (CBS)	
22 Sep 62	**THE BEST OF BALL, BARBER AND BILK**—KENNY BALL, CHRIS BARBER, ACKER BILK (PYE)	1
29 Sep 62	**WEST SIDE STORY**—SOUNDTRACK (CBS)	3
20 Oct 62	**THE BEST OF BALL, BARBER AND BILK**—KENNY BALL, CHRIS BARBER, ACKER BILK (PYE)	1
27 Oct 62	**OUT OF THE SHADOWS**—SHADOWS (COLUMBIA)	3
17 Nov 62	**WEST SIDE STORY**—SOUNDTRACK (CBS)	1
24 Nov 62	**OUT OF THE SHADOWS**—SHADOWS (COLUMBIA)	1
1 Dec 62	**ON STAGE WITH THE BLACK AND WHITE MINSTRELS**—GEORGE MITCHELL MINSTRELS (HMV)	2
15 Dec 62	**WEST SIDE STORY**—SOUNDTRACK (CBS)	1
22 Dec 62	**OUT OF THE SHADOWS**—SHADOWS (COLUMBIA)	1
29 Dec 62	**BLACK AND WHITE MINSTREL SHOW**—GEORGE MITCHELL MINSTRELS (HMV)	2
12 Jan 63	**WEST SIDE STORY**—SOUNDTRACK (CBS)	1
19 Jan 63	**OUT OF THE SHADOWS**—SHADOWS (COLUMBIA)	2
2 Feb 63	**SUMMER HOLIDAY**—CLIFF RICHARD/SHADOWS (COLUMBIA)	14
11 May 63	**PLEASE PLEASE ME**—BEATLES (PARLOPHONE)	30
7 Dec 63	**WITH THE BEATLES**—BEATLES (PARLOPHONE)	21
2 May 64	**ROLLING STONES**—ROLLING STONES (DECCA)	12
25 Jul 64	**A HARD DAY'S NIGHT**—BEATLES (PARLOPHONE)	21
19 Dec 64	**BEATLES FOR SALE**—BEATLES (PARLOPHONE)	7

Right Acker Bilk. His trademarks were his liquorice stick, striped waistcoat and bowler hat. *Below* Kenny Ball. Blew his own trumpet to the top of the chart. *Bottom* The Black and White Minstrels. George Mitchell's team was helped to the top by the popular TV series of the same name.

Date Reached Top	Title/Artist/Label	Weeks at Top
6 Feb 65	**ROLLING STONES No 2**—ROLLING STONES (DECCA)	3
27 Feb 65	**BEATLES FOR SALE**—BEATLES (PARLOPHONE)	1
6 Mar 65	**ROLLING STONES No 2**—ROLLING STONES (DECCA)	6
17 Apr 65	**FREEWHEELIN' BOB DYLAN**—BOB DYLAN (CBS)	1
24 Apr 65	**ROLLING STONES No 2**—ROLLING STONES (DECCA)	1
1 May 65	**BEATLES FOR SALE**—BEATLES (PARLOPHONE)	3
22 May 65	**FREEWHEELIN'BOB DYLAN**—BOB DYLAN (CBS)	1
29 May 65	**BRINGING IT ALL BACK HOME**—BOB DYLAN (CBS)	1
5 Jun 65	**SOUND OF MUSIC**—SOUNDTRACK (RCA)	10
14 Aug 65	**HELP**—BEATLES (PARLOPHONE)	9
16 Oct 65	**SOUND OF MUSIC**—SOUNDTRACK (RCA)	10
25 Dec 65	**RUBBER SOUL**—BEATLES (PARLOPHONE)	9
19 Feb 66	**SOUND OF MUSIC**—SOUNDTRACK (RCA)	10
30 Apr 66	**AFTERMATH**—ROLLING STONES (DECCA)	8
25 Jun 66	**SOUND OF MUSIC**—SOUNDTRACK (RCA)	7
13 Aug 66	**REVOLVER**—BEATLES (PARLOPHONE)	7
1 Oct 66	**SOUND OF MUSIC**—SOUNDTRACK (RCA)	18
4 Feb 67	**MONKEES**—MONKEES (RCA)	7
25 Mar 67	**SOUND OF MUSIC**—SOUNDTRACK (RCA)	7
13 May 67	**MORE OF THE MONKEES**—MONKEES (RCA)	1
20 May 67	**SOUND OF MUSIC**—SOUNDTRACK (RCA)	1
27 May 67	**MORE OF THE MONKEES**—MONKEES (RCA)	1
3 Jun 67	**SOUND OF MUSIC**—SOUNDTRACK (RCA)	1
10 Jun 67	**SERGEANT PEPPER'S LONELY HEARTS CLUB BAND**—BEATLES (PARLOPHONE)	23
18 Nov 67	**SOUND OF MUSIC**—SOUNDTRACK (RCA)	1
25 Nov 67	**SERGEANT PEPPER'S LONELY HEARTS CLUB BAND**—BEATLES (PARLOPHONE)	1
2 Dec 67	**SOUND OF MUSIC**—SOUNDTRACK (RCA)	3
23 Dec 67	**SERGEANT PEPPER'S LONELY HEARTS CLUB BAND**—BEATLES (PARLOPHONE)	2
6 Jan 68	**VAL DOONICAN ROCKS BUT GENTLY**—VAL DOONICAN (PYE)	3
27 Jan 68	**SOUND OF MUSIC**—SOUNDTRACK (RCA)	1
3 Feb 68	**SERGEANT PEPPER'S LONELY HEARTS CLUB BAND**—BEATLES (PARLOPHONE)	1
10 Feb 68	**GREATEST HITS**—FOUR TOPS (TAMLA MOTOWN)	1
17 Feb 68	**GREATEST HITS**—DIANA ROSS AND THE SUPREMES (TAMLA MOTOWN)	3
9 Mar 68	**JOHN WESLEY HARDING**—BOB DYLAN (CBS)	10
18 May 68	**SCOTT 2**—SCOTT WALKER (PHILIPS)	1
25 May 68	**JOHN WESLEY HARDING**—BOB DYLAN (CBS)	3
15 Jun 68	**LOVE ANDY**—ANDY WILLIAMS (CBS)	1
22 Jun 68	**DOCK OF THE BAY**—OTIS REDDING (STAX)	1
29 Jun 68	**OGDEN'S NUT GONE FLAKE**—SMALL FACES (IMMEDIATE)	6
10 Aug 68	**DELILAH**—TOM JONES (DECCA)	1
17 Aug 68	**BOOKENDS**—SIMON AND GARFUNKEL (CBS)	5
21 Sep 68	**DELILAH**—TOM JONES (DECCA)	1
28 Sep 68	**BOOKENDS**—SIMON AND GARFUNKEL (CBS)	2
12 Oct 68	**GREATEST HITS**—HOLLIES (PARLOPHONE)	6
23 Nov 68	**SOUND OF MUSIC**—SOUNDTRACK (RCA)	1
30 Nov 68	**GREATEST HITS**—HOLLIES (PARLOPHONE)	1
7 Dec 68	**THE BEATLES** BEATLES (APPLE)	7
25 Jan 69	**BEST OF THE SEEKERS**—SEEKERS (COLUMBIA)	1
1 Feb 69	**THE BEATLES** BEATLES (APPLE)	1
8 Feb 69	**BEST OF THE SEEKERS**—SEEKERS (COLUMBIA)	1
15 Feb 69	**DIANA ROSS AND THE SUPREMES JOIN THE TEMPTATIONS**—DIANA ROSS/SUPREMES/TEMPTATIONS (TAMLA MOTOWN)	4
15 Mar 69	**GOODBYE**—CREAM (POLYDOR)	2
29 Mar 69	**BEST OF THE SEEKERS**—SEEKERS (COLUMBIA)	2
12 Apr 69	**GOODBYE**—CREAM (POLYDOR)	1
19 Apr 69	**BEST OF THE SEEKERS**—SEEKERS (COLUMBIA)	1
26 Apr 69	**GOODBYE**—CREAM (POLYDOR)	1
3 May 69	**BEST OF THE SEEKERS**—SEEKERS (COLUMBIA)	1
10 May 69	**ON THE THRESHOLD OF A DREAM**—MOODY BLUES (DERAM)	2
24 May 69	**NASHVILLE SKYLINE**—BOB DYLAN (CBS)	4
21 Jun 69	**HIS ORCHESTRA, HIS CHORUS, HIS SINGERS, HIS SOUND**—RAY CONNIFF (CBS)	3
12 Jul 69	**ACCORDING TO MY HEART**—JIM REEVES (RCA INTERNATIONAL)	4

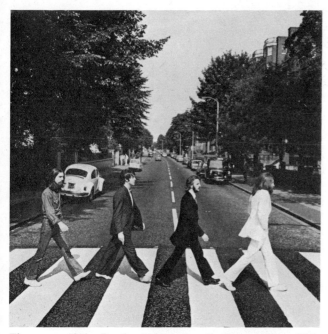

The cover of the Beatles 'Abbey Road' Album with a fifth "Beetle" parked outside the world's most famous studios.

Date Reached Top	Title/Artist/Label	Weeks at Top
9 Aug 69	**STAND UP**—JETHRO TULL (ISLAND)	3
30 Aug 69	**FROM ELVIS IN MEMPHIS**—ELVIS PRESLEY (RCA)	1
6 Sep 69	**STAND UP**—JETHRO TULL (ISLAND)	2
20 Sep 69	**BLIND FAITH**—BLIND FAITH (POLYDOR)	2
4 Oct 69	**ABBEY ROAD**—BEATLES (APPLE)	11
20 Dec 69	**LET IT BLEED**—ROLLING STONES (DECCA)	1
27 Dec 69	**ABBEY ROAD**—BEATLES (APPLE)	6
7 Feb 70	**LED ZEPPELIN 2**—LED ZEPPELIN (ATLANTIC)	1
14 Feb 70	**MOTOWN CHARTBUSTERS VOL 3**—VARIOUS (TAMLA MOTOWN)	1
21 Feb 70	**BRIDGE OVER TROUBLED WATER**—SIMON AND GARFUNKEL (CBS)	13
23 May 70	**LET IT BE**—BEATLES (PARLOPHONE)	3
13 Jun 70	**BRIDGE OVER TROUBLED WATER**—SIMON AND GARFUNKEL (CBS)	4

Date Reached Top	Title/Artist/Label	Weeks at Top
11 Jul 70	**SELF PORTRAIT**—BOB DYLAN (CBS)	1
18 Jul 70	**BRIDGE OVER TROUBLED WATER**—SIMON AND GARFUNKEL (CBS)	5
22 Aug 70	**QUESTION OF BALANCE**—MOODY BLUES (THRESHOLD)	3
12 Sep 70	**COSMO'S FACTORY**—CREEDENCE CLEARWATER REVIVAL (LIBERTY)	1
19 Sep 70	**GET YOUR YA YAS OUT**—ROLLING STONES (DECCA)	2
3 Oct 70	**BRIDGE OVER TROUBLED WATER**—SIMON AND GARFUNKEL (CBS)	1
10 Oct 70	**PARANOID**—BLACK SABBATH (VERTIGO)	1
17 Oct 70	**BRIDGE OVER TROUBLED WATER**—SIMON AND GARFUNKEL (CBS)	1
24 Oct 70	**ATOM HEART MOTHER**—PINK FLOYD (HARVEST)	1
31 Oct 70	**MOTOWN CHARTBUSTERS VOL 4**—VARIOUS (TAMLA MOTOWN)	1
7 Nov 70	**LED ZEPPELIN 3**—LED ZEPPELIN (ATLANTIC)	3
28 Nov 70	**NEW MORNING**—BOB DYLAN (CBS)	1
5 Dec 70	**GREATEST HITS**—ANDY WILLIAMS (CBS)	1
12 Dec 70	**LED ZEPPELIN 3**—LED ZEPPELIN (ATLANTIC)	1
19 Dec 70	**GREATEST HITS**—ANDY WILLIAMS (CBS)	4
16 Jan 71*	**BRIDGE OVER TROUBLED WATER**—SIMON AND GARFUNKEL (CBS)	11
3 Apr 71	**HOME LOVING MAN**—ANDY WILLIAMS (CBS)	2
17 Apr 71	**MOTOWN CHARTBUSTERS VOL 5**—VARIOUS (TAMLA MOTOWN)	3
8 May 71	**STICKY FINGERS**—ROLLING STONES (ROLLING STONES)	4
5 Jun 71	**RAM**—PAUL AND LINDA MCCARTNEY (APPLE)	2
19 June 71	**STICKY FINGERS**—ROLLING STONES (ROLLING STONES)	1
26 Jun 71	**TARKUS**—EMERSON, LAKE AND PALMER (ISLAND)	1
3 Jul 71	**BRIDGE OVER TROUBLED WATER**—SIMON AND GARFUNKEL (CBS)	5
7 Aug 71	**HOT HITS 6**—VARIOUS (MFP)	1
14 Aug 71	**EVERY GOOD BOY DESERVES FAVOUR**—MOODY BLUES (THRESHOLD)	1
21 Aug 71	**TOP OF THE POPS VOL 18**—VARIOUS (HALLMARK)	3

* This includes 8 weeks at number one when charts were not published due to a strike.

Art Garfunkel (left) had the number one hit singles after the duo split but it was Paul Simon who made the top with his self titled solo album. As a team they achieved two number one LP's in Britain; 'Bookends' in 1968 and the outstanding 'Bridge Over Troubled Water' in 1970. To the end of 1982 'Bridge Over Troubled Water' has spent just 9 weeks short of 6 years in the album chart.

Date Reached Top	Title/Artist/Label	Weeks at Top
11 Sep 71	**BRIDGE OVER TROUBLED WATER**—SIMON AND GARFUNKEL (CBS)	1
18 Sep 71	**WHO'S NEXT**—WHO (TRACK)	1
25 Sep 71	**FIREBALL**—DEEP PURPLE (HARVEST)	1
2 Oct 71	**EVERY PICTURE TELLS A STORY**—ROD STEWART (MERCURY)	4
30 Oct 71	**IMAGINE**—JOHN LENNON/PLASTIC ONO BAND (APPLE)	2
13 Nov 71	**EVERY PICTURE TELLS A STORY**—ROD STEWART (MERCURY)	2
27 Nov 71	**TOP OF THE POPS VOL 20**—VARIOUS (HALLMARK)	1
4 Dec 71	**FOUR SYMBOLS**—LED ZEPPELIN (ATLANTIC)	2
18 Dec 71	**ELECTRIC WARRIOR**—T. REX (FLY)	6
29 Jan 72	**CONCERT FOR BANGLADESH**—VARIOUS (APPLE)	1
5 Feb 72	**ELECTRIC WARRIOR**—T. REX (FLY)	2
19 Feb 72	**NEIL REID**—NEIL REID (DECCA)	3
11 Mar 72	**HARVEST**—NEIL YOUNG (REPRISE)	1
18 Mar 72	**PAUL SIMON**—PAUL SIMON (CBS)	1
25 Mar 72	**FOG ON THE TYNE**—LINDISFARNE (CHARISMA)	4
22 Apr 72	**MACHINE HEAD**—DEEP PURPLE (PURPLE)	2
6 May 72	**PROPHETS, SEERS AND SAGES AND THE ANGELS OF THE AGES/MY PEOPLE WERE FAIR AND HAD SKY IN THEIR HAIR . . . BUT NOW THEY'RE CONTENT TO WEAR STARS ON THEIR BROWS**—TYRANNOSAURUS REX (FLY DOUBLE BACK)	1
13 May 72	**MACHINE HEAD**—DEEP PURPLE (PURPLE)	1
20 May 72	**BOLAN BOOGIE**—T. REX (FLY)	3
10 Jun 72	**EXILE ON MAIN STREET**—ROLLING STONES (ROLLING STONES)	1
17 Jun 72	**20 DYNAMIC HITS**—VARIOUS (K-TEL)	8
12 Aug 72	**20 FANTASTIC HITS**—VARIOUS (ARCADE)	5
16 Sep 72	**NEVER A DULL MOMENT**—ROD STEWART (PHILIPS)	2
30 Sep 72	**20 FANTASTIC HITS**—VARIOUS (ARCADE)	1
7 Oct 72	**20 ALLTIME HITS OF THE FIFTIES**—VARIOUS (K-TEL)	8
2 Dec 72	**25 ROCKIN' AND ROLLIN' GREATS**—VARIOUS (K-TEL)	3
23 Dec 72	**20 ALLTIME HITS OF THE FIFTIES**—VARIOUS (K-TEL)	3

Date Reached Top	Title/Artist/Label	Weeks at Top
13 Jan 73	**SLAYED**—SLADE (POLYDOR)	1
20 Jan 73	**BACK TO FRONT**—GILBERT O'SULLIVAN (MAM)	1
27 Jan 73	**SLAYED**—SLADE (POLYDOR)	2
10 Feb 73	**DON'T SHOOT ME, I'M ONLY THE PIANO PLAYER**—ELTON JOHN (DJM)	6
24 Mar 73	**BILLION DOLLAR BABIES**—ALICE COOPER (WARNER BROS.)	1
31 Mar 73	**20 FLASHBACK GREAT HITS OF THE SIXTIES**—VARIOUS (K-TEL)	2
14 Apr 73	**HOUSES OF THE HOLY**—LED ZEPPELIN (ATLANTIC)	2
28 Apr 73	**OOH LA LA**—FACES (WARNER BROS.)	1
5 May 73	**ALADDIN SANE**—DAVID BOWIE (RCA VICTOR)	5

Gilbert O'Sullivan's 'Back to Front' Album took him in front of the chart for a week but he never went back.

A musical interpretation of Jules Verne novel gave Rick Wakeman his only solo number one LP.

Date Reached Top	Title/Artist/Label	Weeks at Top
8 Feb 75	**HIS GREATEST HITS**—ENGELBERT HUMPERDINCK (DECCA)	3
1 Mar 75	**ON THE LEVEL**—STATUS QUO (VERTIGO)	2
15 Mar 75	**PHYSICAL GRAFFITI**—LED ZEPPELIN (SWANSONG)	1
22 Mar 75	**20 GREATEST HITS**—TOM JONES (DECCA)	4
19 Apr 75	**THE BEST OF THE STYLISTICS**—STYLISTICS (AVCO)	2
3 May 75	**ONCE UPON A STAR**—BAY CITY ROLLERS (BELL)	3
24 May 75	**THE BEST OF THE STYLISTICS**—STYLISTICS (AVCO)	5
28 Jun 75	**VENUS AND MARS**—WINGS (APPLE)	1
5 Jul 75	**HORIZON**—CARPENTERS (A&M)	2
19 Jul 75	**VENUS AND MARS**—WINGS (APPLE)	1
26 Jul 75	**HORIZON**—CARPENTERS (A&M)	3
16 Aug 75	**THE BEST OF THE STYLISTICS**—STYLISTICS (AVCO)	2
30 Aug 75	**ATLANTIC CROSSING**—ROD STEWART (WARNER BROS.)	5
4 Oct 75	**WISH YOU WERE HERE**—PINK FLOYD (HARVEST)	1
11 Oct 75	**ATLANTIC CROSSING**—ROD STEWART (WARNER BROS.)	2
25 Oct 75	**40 GOLDEN GREATS**—JIM REEVES (ARCADE)	3
15 Nov 75	**WE ALL HAD DOCTORS' PAPERS**—MAX BOYCE (EMI)	1
22 Nov 75	**40 GREATEST HITS**—PERRY COMO (K-TEL)	5
27 Dec 75	**A NIGHT AT THE OPERA**—QUEEN (EMI)	2
10 Jan 76	**40 GREATEST HITS**—PERRY COMO (K-TEL)	1
17 Jan 76	**A NIGHT AT THE OPERA**—QUEEN (EMI)	2
31 Jan 76	**THE BEST OF ROY ORBISON**—ROY ORBISON (ARCADE)	1
7 Feb 76	**THE VERY BEST OF SLIM WHITMAN**—SLIM WHITMAN (UNITED ARTISTS)	6
20 Mar 76	**BLUE FOR YOU**—STATUS QUO (VERTIGO)	3
10 Apr 76	**ROCK FOLLIES**—TV SOUNDTRACK (ISLAND)	2
24 Apr 76	**PRESENCE**—LED ZEPPELIN (SWANSONG)	1
1 May 76	**ROCK FOLLIES**—TV SOUNDTRACK (ISLAND)	1
8 May 76	**GREATEST HITS**—ABBA (EPIC)	9
10 Jul 76	**A NIGHT ON THE TOWN**—ROD STEWART (RIVA)	2
24 Jul 76	**20 GOLDEN GREATS**—BEACH BOYS (CAPITOL)	10

Date Reached Top	Title/Artist/Label	Weeks at Top
2 Oct 76	**BEST OF THE STYLISTICS VOL. 2**—STYLISTICS (H&L)	1
9 Oct 76	**STUPIDITY**—DR FEELGOOD (UNITED ARTISTS)	1
16 Oct 76	**GREATEST HITS**—ABBA (EPIC)	2
30 Oct 76	**SOUL MOTION**—VARIOUS (K-TEL)	2
13 Nov 76	**THE SONG REMAINS THE SAME**—LED ZEPPELIN (SWANSONG)	1
20 Nov 76	**22 GOLDEN GUITAR GREATS**—BERT WEEDON (WARWICK)	
27 Nov 76	**20 GOLDEN GREATS**—GLEN CAMPBELL (CAPITOL)	6
8 Jan 77	**DAY AT THE RACES**—QUEEN (EMI)	1
15 Jan 77	**ARRIVAL**—ABBA (EPIC)	1
22 Jan 77	**RED RIVER VALLEY**—SLIM WHITMAN (UNITED ARTISTS)	4
19 Feb 77	**20 GOLDEN GREATS**—SHADOWS (EMI)	6
2 Apr 77	**PORTRAIT**—FRANK SINATRA (REPRISE)	2
16 Apr 77	**ARRIVAL**—ABBA (EPIC)	9
18 Jun 77	**LIVE AT THE HOLLYWOOD BOWL**—BEATLES (PARLOPHONE)	1
25 Jun 77	**MUPPETS**—MUPPETS (PYE)	1
2 Jul 77	**A STAR IS BORN**—SOUNDTRACK (CBS)	2
16 Jul 77	**JOHNNY MATHIS COLLECTION**—JOHNNY MATHIS (CBS)	4
13 Aug 77	**GOING FOR THE ONE**—YES (ATLANTIC)	2
27 Aug 77	**20 ALL TIME GREATS**—CONNIE FRANCIS (POLYDOR)	2
10 Sep 77	**ELVIS PRESLEY'S 40 GREATEST HITS**—ELVIS PRESLEY (ARCADE)	1
17 Sep 77	**20 GOLDEN GREATS**—DIANA ROSS AND THE SUPREMES (TAMLA MOTOWN)	7
5 Nov 77	**40 GOLDEN GREATS**—CLIFF RICHARD (EMI)	1
12 Nov 77	**NEVER MIND THE BOLLOCKS HERE'S THE SEX PISTOLS**—SEX PISTOLS (VIRGIN)	2
26 Nov 77	**SOUND OF BREAD**—BREAD (ELEKTRA)	2
10 Dec 77	**DISCO FEVER**—VARIOUS (K-TEL)	6
21 Jan 78	**THE SOUND OF BREAD**—BREAD (ELEKTRA)	1
28 Jan 78	**RUMOURS**—FLEETWOOD MAC (WARNER BROS.)	1
4 Feb 78	**THE ALBUM**—ABBA (EPIC)	7
25 Mar 78	**20 GOLDEN GREATS**—BUDDY HOLLY/CRICKETS (MCA)	3
15 Apr 78	**20 GOLDEN GREATS**—NAT KING COLE (CAPITOL)	3

202

Date Reached Top	Title/Artist/Label	Weeks at Top
6 May 78	**SATURDAY NIGHT FEVER**—VARIOUS (RSO)	18
9 Sep 78	**NIGHT FLIGHT TO VENUS**—BONEY M (ATLANTIC/HANSA)	4
7 Oct 78	**GREASE**—SOUNDTRACK (RSO)	13
6 Jan 79	**GREATEST HITS**—SHOWADDYWADDY (ARISTA)	2
26 Jan 79	**DONT WALK—BOOGIE**—VARIOUS (EMI)	3
10 Feb 79	**ACTION REPLAY**—VARIOUS (K-TEL)	1
17 Feb 79	**PARALLEL LINES**—BLONDIE (CHRYSALIS)	4
17 Mar 79	**SPIRITS HAVING FLOWN**—BEE GEES (RSO)	2
31 Mar 79	**GREATEST HITS VOL 2**—BARBRA STREISAND (CBS)	4
28 Apr 79	**THE VERY BEST OF LEO SAYER**—LEO SAYER (CHRYSALIS)	3
19 May 79	**VOULEZ—VOUS**—ABBA (EPIC)	4
16 Jun 79	**DISCOVERY**—ELECTRIC LIGHT ORCHESTRA (JET)	5
21 Jul 79	**REPLICAS**—TUBEWAY ARMY (BEGGARS BANQUET)	1
28 Jul 79	**THE BEST DISCO ALBUM IN THE WORLD**—VARIOUS (WARNER BROS.)	6
8 Sep 79	**IN THROUGH THE OUT DOOR**—LED ZEPPELIN (SWANSONG)	2
22 Sep 79	**THE PLEASURE PRINCIPLE**—GARY NUMAN (BEGGARS BANQUET)	1
29 Sep 79	**OCEANS OF FANTASY**—BONEY M (ATLANTIC/HANSA)	1
6 Oct 79	**THE PLEASURE PRINCIPLE**—GARY NUMAN (BEGGARS BANQUET)	1
13 Oct 79*	**EAT TO THE BEAT** BLONDIE (CHRYSALIS)	1
13 Oct 79*	**REGGATTA DE BLANC**—POLICE (A&M)	4
10 Nov 79	**TUSK**—FLEETWOOD MAC (WARNER BROS.)	1
17 Nov 79	**GREATEST HITS VOL 2**—ABBA (EPIC)	3
8 Dec 79	**GREATEST HITS**—ROD STEWART (RIVA)	5
12 Jan 80	**GREATEST HITS VOL 2**—ABBA (EPIC)	1
19 Jan 80	**PRETENDERS**—PRETENDERS (REAL)	4
16 Feb 80	**THE LAST DANCE**—VARIOUS (MOTOWN)	2
1 Mar 80	**STRING OF HITS**—SHADOWS (EMI)	3
22 Mar 80	**TEARS AND LAUGHTER**—JOHNNY MATHIS (CBS)	2
5 Apr 80	**DUKE**—GENESIS (CHARISMA)	2
19 Apr 80	**GREATEST HITS**—ROSE ROYCE (WINFIELD)	2
3 May 80	**SKY 2**—SKY (ARIOLA)	2

Date Reached Top	Title/Artist/Label	Weeks at Top
17 May 80	**THE MAGIC OF BONEY M**—BONEY M (ATLANTIC/HANSA)	2
31 May 80	**McCARTNEY II**—PAUL McCARTNEY (PARLOPHONE)	2
14 Jun 80	**PETER GABRIEL**—PETER GABRIEL (CHARISMA)	2
28 Jun 80	**FLESH AND BLOOD**—ROXY MUSIC (POLYDOR)	1
5 Jul 80	**EMOTIONAL RESCUE**—ROLLING STONES (ROLLING STONES)	2
19 Jul 80	**THE GAME**—QUEEN (EMI)	2
2 Aug 80	**DEEPEST PURPLE**—DEEP PURPLE (HARVEST)	1
9 Aug 80	**BACK IN BLACK**—AC/DC (ATLANTIC)	2
23 Aug 80	**FLESH AND BLOOD**—ROXY MUSIC (POLYDOR)	3
13 Sep 80	**TELEKON**—GARY NUMAN (BEGGARS BANQUET)	1
20 Sep 80	**NEVER FOR EVER**—KATE BUSH (EMI)	1
27 Sep 80	**SCAREY MONSTERS AND SUPERCREEPS**—DAVID BOWIE (RCA)	2
11 Oct 80	**ZENYATTA MONDATTA**—POLICE (A&M)	4
8 Nov 80	**GUILTY**—BARBRA STREISAND (CBS)	2
22 Nov 80	**SUPER TROUPER**—ABBA (EPIC)	9
24 Jan 81	**KINGS OF THE WILD FRONTIER**—ADAM AND THE ANTS (CBS)	2
7 Feb 81	**DOUBLE FANTASY**—JOHN LENNON (GEFFEN)	2
21 Feb 81	**FACE VALUE**—PHIL COLLINS (VIRGIN)	3
14 Mar 81	**KINGS OF THE WILD FRONTIER**—ADAM AND THE ANTS (CBS)	10
23 May 81	**STARS ON 45**—STARSOUND (CBS)	5
27 Jun 81	**NO SLEEP TIL HAMMERSMITH**—MOTORHEAD (BRONZE)	1
4 Jul 81	**DISCO DAZE & DISCO NITES**—VARIOUS (RONCO)	1
11 Jul 81	**LOVE SONGS**—CLIFF RICHARD (EMI)	5
15 Aug 81	**THE OFFICIAL BBC ALBUM OF THE ROYAL WEDDING**—SOUNDTRACK (BBC)	2
29 Aug 81	**TIME**—ELECTRIC LIGHT ORCHESTRA (JET)	2
12 Sep 81	**DEADRINGER**—MEATLOAF (EPIC)	2
26 Sep 81	**ABACAB**—GENESIS (CHARISMA)	2
10 Oct 81	**GHOST IN THE MACHINE**—POLICE (A&M)	3
31 Oct 81	**DARE**—HUMAN LEAGUE (VIRGIN)	1
7 Nov 81	**SHAKY**—SHAKIN' STEVENS (EPIC)	1
14 Nov 81	**GREATEST HITS**—QUEEN (EMI)	4
12 Dec 81	**CHART HITS '81**—VARIOUS (K-TEL)	1
19 Dec 81	**THE VISITORS**—ABBA (EPIC)	3

* Two charts published this week due to a change in chart collation.

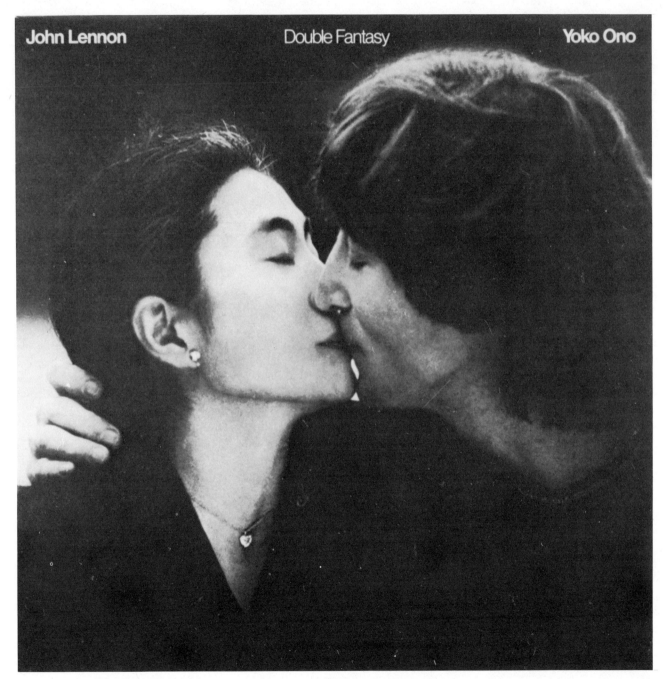

John Lennon   Double Fantasy   Yoko Ono

204

Date Reached Top	Title/Artist/Label	Weeks at Top
9 Jan 82	**DARE**—HUMAN LEAGUE (VIRGIN)	3
30 Jan 82	**LOVE SONGS**—BARBRA STREISAND (CBS)	7
20 Mar 82	**THE GIFT**—JAM (POLYDOR)	1
27 Mar 82	**LOVE SONGS**—BARBRA STREISAND (CBS)	2
10 Apr 82	**THE NUMBER OF THE BEAST**—IRON MAIDEN (EMI)	2
24 Apr 82	**1982**—STATUS QUO (VERTIGO/ PHONOGRAM)	1
1 May 82	**TUG OF WAR**—PAUL McCARTNEY (PARLOPHONE)	2
22 May 82	**COMPLETE MADNESS**—MADNESS (STIFF)	2
5 Jun 82	**AVALON**—ROXY MUSIC (POLYDOR)	1
12 Jun 82	**COMPLETE MADNESS**—MADNESS (STIFF)	1
19 Jun 82	**AVALON**—ROXY MUSIC (POLYDOR)	2

Date Reached Top	Title/Artist/Label	Weeks at Top
3 Jul 82	**THE LEXICON OF LOVE**—ABC (NEUTRON/PHONOGRAM)	3
24 Jul 82 =	**THE LEXICON OF LOVE**—ABC (NEUTRON/PHONOGRAM)	1
=	**FAME**—ORIGINAL SOUNDTRACK (RSO)	1
31 Jul 82	**FAME**—ORIGINAL SOUNDTRACK (RSO)	1
7 Aug 82	**KIDS FROM FAME**—KIDS FROM FAME (BBC)	8
2 Oct 82	**LOVE OVER GOLD**—DIRE STRAITS (VERTIGO/PHONOGRAM)	4
30 Oct 82	**KIDS FROM FAME**—KIDS FROM FAME (BBC)	4
27 Nov 82	**THE SINGLES, THE FIRST TEN YEARS**—ABBA (EPIC)	1
4 Dec 82	**THE JOHN LENNON COLLECTION**—JOHN LENNON (PARLOPHONE)	4†

The film *Fame* made little impression in Britain when it first appeared in 1980, but a TV serial based on the film sparked a period of 'Fame Fever'; Irene Cara's renditioning of the film's title track reached the top of the singles chart in July 82, a week later the original soundtrack album hit the peak of the LP chart and it was replaced at the top spot by an album 'The Kids From Fame', taken from the TV show.

1958 The American inventor Peter Goldmark was inspired to devise the long playing record while listening to classical music at a party. He realised he was always annoyed having to get up and change several 78s just to hear a complete piece. He thought there had to be a market for a single disc that could contain an entire symphony or sonata.

The eighteen albums that hit the chart in the last 8 weeks of 1958, the first weeks of *Melody Maker*'s Top Ten chart, demonstrated that Goldmark's invention also had other applications. None of the eighteen best-sellers was a classical orchestral performance! Thirteen were by adult male performers with wide audience appeal and five were of show business origin – that is, stage, screen or television.

The soundtrack to *South Pacific* was number one for each of the 8 weeks, a prelude to its equally total domination of the 1959 lists. The man with the most LPs to chart was Frank Sinatra, who touched the Top Ten four times. Elvis Presley had the most total weeks on chart, that is to say a sum of the runs of each of his hit LPs. Both 'Elvis Golden Records' and 'King Creole' were on every one of the eight charts.

The other artists who contributed to the all-male domain were Perry Como, Russ Conway, Mario Lanza, the American satirist Tom Lehrer, and Johnny Mathis. Perhaps Lanza was the closest to what Peter Goldmark had in mind: one side of his disc was the soundtrack to the film about the classical tenor Enrico Caruso, *The Great Caruso*.

1959 It can be whispered in reverent awe or shouted from the rooftops, but the achievement is so great it can not be conveyed in casual conversation: the original soundtrack to the film *South Pacific* was at number one for the entire year 1959. It led the list for every one of the 52 weeks, a feat which has never been matched. 'Here In My Heart' by Al Martino was on top of the singles scene for every chart in 1952, but the important qualification here is that there were no tables until 14 November.

'South Pacific' truly stands alone as the statistical star of the LP charts, though later discs would surpass it in sales. This family favourite boasted a wide range of memorable music, from the love ballad 'Some Enchanted Evening' (an American number one for Perry Como) to the novelty tune 'Happy Talk' (eventually a UK number one for Captain Sensible).

Film soundtracks were still the leading money-spinners in the LP market of 1959. The form was only a decade old, and soundtracks, Broadway cast performances and classical works were the most logical initial uses of Peter Goldmark's invention, requiring the additional space a long player could provide. The movie versions of *Gigi* and *The King and I* were notable winners in 1959, as was the New York stage production of *West Side Story*.

Rock-and-roll vocalists, previously content with singles, made further inroads into the album field, but Frank Sinatra still scored the most weeks on chart for a solo singer. Elvis Presley was a close second, registering an impressive success with 'Elvis' Golden Records'. The chart appearance of two LPs by Cliff Richard was the best 1959 showing by a young Briton.

'Curtain Up!', a compilation of stars from the London Palladium hosted by Bruce Forsyth, enjoyed a 13-week run, but the most impressive performance by a show business star was that of Peter Sellers, who spent 32 weeks in the Top Ten with two solo LPs and a further 5 with his colleagues the Goons.

1960 'South Pacific' dominated the album charts one more time in 1960, though not to the extent it had in 1959. It was in the best-sellers for every one of the 53 charts of the year, the only title to achieve that run, but it did occasionally let other discs take the top spot. Number one on the very first *Record Retailer* album chart, that of 10 March, was 'The Explosive Freddy Cannon', which fell in fragments the following week after giving Cannon the distinction of being the first rock-and-roll singer to have a number one LP. The second, Elvis Presley, may be a more predictable choice, but even he only managed 1 week at the summit, scoring with 'Elvis Is Back'. The other disc to interrupt 'South Pacific's streak was 'Down Drury Lane To Memory Lane', a nostalgic effort by the studio group 101 Strings.

Rock-and-roll made great progress in the long playing market in 1960. The previous year only four rockers had charted in the entire 12 months. This time five of the top six acts were rock stars, though the majority of chart artists were still not of this nature. Presley pipped Peter Sellers as the individual with most weeks on the chart, though Sellers would have ranked above Presley if the computation included his additional appearances with the Goons and Sophia Loren, not, one must add, on the same disc.

American guitarist Duane Eddy's surprisingly strong showing in fourth place should not be overlooked. The Shadows would be the only other rock instrumentalists to do well in a year-end tally.

1961

Commercial success does not guarantee artistic immortality, as the George Mitchell Minstrels have proved their *Black and White Minstrel Show* was an enormous success on television, record and stage, but an entire generation has grown up in, shall we say, the dark, about their achievements.

'The Black and White Minstrel Show' was the only album to stay in the chart for the whole of 1961. It accumulated 7 weeks at number one in four separate visits, while 'Another Black and White Minstrel Show' had a single mighty 8-week run at the top. Mass audiences loved the old-time performances of The Minstrels, many of whom blacked up to sing vintage popular songs. It was the dated nature of their material, as well as increased sophistication concerning racial matters, which spelled an end to large scale interest in the group in the late sixties.

Elvis Presley was the outstanding album artist for the second consecutive year, enjoying 22 weeks at number one with the soundtrack to 'GI Blues'. The granddaddy of film favourites, 'South Pacific', put in a final 9 weeks at the peak before retiring. It was a bumper year for original cast recordings of stage musicals, with a strong emphasis on the London stage. 'Oliver', 'Sound of Music' and 'Stop the World I Want to Get Off' all had lengthy runs with

207

British rosters. 1961 saw hit honours for the well-remembered 'Beyond the Fringe' and the completely forgotten 'King Kong'. Even the London cast of 'Bye Bye Birdie' flew out of the wings and into the charts.

Frank Sinatra continued his series of fine years, entering the Top Twenty with seven titles on four different labels. Cliff Richard had three new top two successes and one happy hangover from 1960, 'Me and My Shadows'. 'I'm 21 Today' was his first number one, though his mates beat him to the top by 6 weeks with their debut disc 'The Shadows'.

1962

Elvis Presley and the George Mitchell Minstrels overachieved again in 1962. The King of rock-and-roll notched up 18 weeks at number one with his 'Blue Hawaii' soundtrack, more time at the top than any other long player that year, and he ruled the roost for 6 more weeks with 'Pot Luck'. The Minstrels led the list with their new release, 'On Stage With the George Mitchell Minstrels', and then encored with their 1960 issue, the original 'Black and White Minstrel Show'. Their three albums tallied a total of 109 weeks in the chart, the first time any act had hit the century.

Compared to these two artists the rest of the field failed to flame, though 'South Pacific' again managed to appear in every one of the fifty-two charts. The new film sensation was 'West Side Story', surpassing its significant stage sales to pace the pack for 12 weeks. Four unusual multi-media successes were the soundtrack to 'It's Trad Dad', the original cast album of the London production *Blitz,* and two Dorothy Provine sets inspired by her television series *The Roaring 20's*. Further evidence of the taste for trad was the appearance of a budget album at number one for a week, 'The Best of Kenny Ball, Chris Barber and Acker Bilk'. Barber and Bilk had appeared together on two fast-selling packages in 1961.

The Shadows achieved the fabulous feat of nabbing their second number one with their second effort, 'Out of the Shadows'. They shared credit on Cliff Richard's table-topping 'The Young Ones'. Cliff managed to top the Shads in weeks on chart thanks to his subsequent release, the literally timed and titled '32 Minutes and 17 Seconds'.

1963

Beatlemania spread like a flash fire in 1963, and the album chart showed its effects. The Fab Four's 'Please Please Me' seized the top spot on 11 May and held it for 30 consecutive weeks, to be replaced only by 'With the Beatles', which kept clear for a further 21. The Liverpudlians had come from nowhere to hold the premier position for 1 week shy of a full year. It was nothing short of a musical

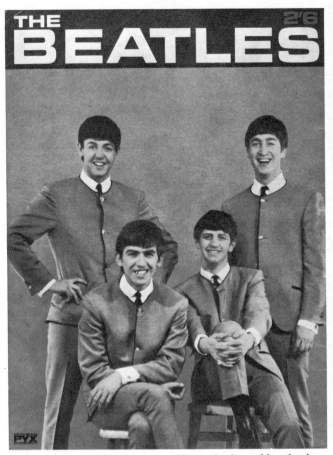

Between 11 May 1963 and 2 May 1964 nobody could make the Beatles relinquish their grip on the number one position.

revolution: from their arrival until 1968, only one non-rock album would have a look at number one. A field that had been the domain of the soundtrack and cast album overnight became ruled by rock. It was hard to believe that 1963 had begun with 'Black and White Minstrel Show' still in the lead.

With a couple of notable exceptions, the film and stage market dried up overnight. It is not surprising that they died in tandem, since the movie tracks were invariably Broadway shows adapted to the cinema. When the Great White Way stopped producing many memorable musicals, album sales dwindled accordingly. 'West Side Story' was a survivor in 1963, charting through the entire year.

Cliff Richard was the weeks on chart champ this time, his total fed by three new successes. No one could have predicted that the second highest figures would be achieved equally by Elvis Presley and Buddy Holly. The Pelvis began twitching in anxiety as the soundtracks to three bad films did progressively worse. Holly, dead for 4 years, had always been a strong album seller, but really surged in 1963 when the poignantly-titled collection 'Reminiscing' joined the list of his other posthumous best-sellers.

Frank Ifield proved a one-year though not a one-hit wonder, reaching number three with two releases. He never came close again. Frank Sinatra rebounded with three top tenners, including a team-up with Count Basie that went to number two.

1964

The Beatles and Rolling Stones monopolized the number one position during 1964, making it the purest year for rock music in terms of holding the star spot. The only 12 weeks John, Paul, George and Ringo were not ahead with either 'With the Beatles', 'A Hard Day's Night' or 'Beatles For Sale', their chief competition was in front with the debut disc 'The Rolling Stones'. The fresh triumphs of 'A Hard Day's Night' and 'Beatles For Sale' gave the Beatles four number ones in four releases, a 100 per cent success ratio they maintained through all of their eleven official outings, though two other issues, a compilation and the 'Yellow Submarine' soundtrack on which they played only a part, fell short of the top. No other act has hit number one every time with as many records.

The Fab Four's quartet of hit LPs gave them 104 weeks on chart, the second time a century had been achieved. But even they were outdistanced in this regard by Jim Reeves. The American country singer had enjoyed two big albums to accompany his two strong singles in the first half of the year. After he died in a plane crash in July, nine further packages made the chart, six in a 4-week period. Gentleman Jim accumulated 115 weeks on chart in all, a record that would stand until 1968.

Third in the weeks on chart category was Roy Orbison, who enjoyed the distinction of seeing his 'In Dreams' set on every chart of the year, a feat attained for the second consecutive year by 'West Side Story'. Cliff Richard had only one new album, below average for his early years, and Elvis Presley definitely slipped as none of his three long players reached the top three.

1965

For the three middle years of the sixties only the Beatles, Rolling Stones, Bob Dylan and 'The Sound of Music' reached number one, trading off in a seemingly endless sequence. The first three were the rock artists who came to represent the spirit of the decade, while the last was a show business phenomenon that came, saw, conquered, and wouldn't go away.

The Beatles began the year on top with 'Beatles For Sale' and ended it there with 'Rubber Soul', having spent much of the summer there as well with 'Help'. Bob Dylan had the second highest total of chart-toppers, two, succeeding 'The Freewheelin' Bob Dylan' with his own 'Bringing It All Back Home', but his most impressive statistic was his 112 weeks on chart. Much of his back catalogue charted in late 1964 and 1965. Though primarily considered an album artist, he also logged five top thirty singles in 1965, his peak year.

Dylan's dear friend Joan Baez shared his success, with three charters to follow her 1964 debut. Infuriatingly for chartists, her winners confusingly included not just 'Joan Baez' but 'Joan Baez No. 5' and 'Farewell Angelina'. She taught Chicago all they knew about titles.

Though Miss Baez was the front-running credited female vocalist, Julie Andrews accounted for the greatest grosses with her soundtracks. 'Mary Poppins' spent the most weeks on chart of any 1965 title, 50, and 'The Sound of Music' began a run to rival that of 'South Pacific', accumulating its first 20 weeks at number one.

Sir Winston Churchill had a posthumous Top Ten LP, 'The Voice of Sir Winston Churchill'.

The charts were alive with the sound of Julie.

1966

Cash register tills came alive to 'The Sound of Music' in 1966. If the Beatles or Rolling Stones didn't have a new album, the star soundtrack of the sixties kept the number one position warm. It followed 'Rubber Soul' and preceded 'Aftermath'; it moved back in the aftermath of 'Aftermath' and before 'Revolver'. When the latter Beatles album had shot its shot, Julie Andrews and company skipped back to the top for the last 3 months of the year.

'The Sound of Music' was the only album to spend all of 1966 in the best sellers. It was as big an international phenomenon as a UK success. *Time* reported that it had sold seven million copies by Christmas, outmoving all other stage or screen sets, even the legendary 'South Pacific'.

The musical version of the Von Trapp family story was a timely purchase in any season, not linked to fad or fashion. The Beatles' unprecedented popularity, on the other hand, had made every one of their new discs an immediate must purchase. A short period of colossal concentrated sale would now be followed by a chart decline. Hence 'Revolver', a summer number one, was almost gone by Christmas. Parlophone, wanting Beatles product for the major marketing month of the year, issued 'A Collection of Beatles Oldies' in December. The fans weren't fooled. It peaked at seven, a commercial miscalculation.

The Beach Boys spent more weeks on the chart than anyone in 1966, with five long players accumulating 95 weeks between them. This success reflected their four consecutive top three singles. One album, the classic 'Pet Sounds', did better in Britain than America, reaching number two.

The other album artist of note was Herb Alpert, who garnered 89 weeks, but while his Tijuana Brass LPs loitered on the list they did not reach the highest chart positions.

1967

History remembers 1967 as the year of flower power and psychedelia. The only real evidence of this in the upper echelons of the LP charts was the tremendous success of the Beatles' land-mark 'Sergeant Pepper's Lonely Hearts Club Band' and the considerable achievement of 'Are You Experienced?' by the Jimi Hendrix Experience.

'Sergeant Pepper', chosen the best rock album of all-time in an international critics' poll in 1977, spent exactly half the year at number one. The other 26 weeks were divided between the recurrent 'The Sound of Music' and the two debut sets by the distinctly unpsychedelic Monkees. In a year when they had six hit singles and a cult television show, the 'fabricated four' reached the top with both 'The Monkees' and 'More of the Monkees'.

With only those four albums going all the way in 1967, it was a major achievement to get to number two. Hendrix and band did. Cream did respectably but not quite as well, earning Top Ten placings with their first two cartons of 'Fresh Cream' and 'Disraeli Gears'. The Rolling Stones surprisingly peaked at three with 'Between The Buttons'.

It was a fine year for easy listening and soul. In addition to 'Best Of The Beach Boys', records that rode the roster for all 52 weeks included the soundtracks of *The Sound of Music* and *Dr. Zhivago* and *'Going Places'* by Herb Alpert and the Tijuana Brass. Alpert paced the pack with 101 weeks on chart, though the Beach Boys were a close second with 97. Tom Jones had three top ten issues and the Dubliners, Irish singers enjoying a year of British popularity, had two.

1967 was the best year on record for Geno Washington, an outstanding live soul attraction. Otis Redding and the Four Tops also had strong chart performances, but they would do even better in 1968.

1968

The album chart lost its sense of discipline in 1968. In previous years the number of different artists who had reached number one, not counting performers on film soundtracks, could be counted on the fingers of one hand. This time no fewer than a dozen different acts went all the way, with occasional further appearances by 'The Sound of Music'.

The nature of the chart-toppers changed, too. Recently the number one spot had been the property of the world's outstanding rock talents. In 1968 Val Doonican, Tom Jones and Andy Williams managed to head the hordes. The Small Faces and Scott Walker enjoyed their only number one LPs, and Simon and Garfunkel tallied their first. The Four Tops, Otis Redding, and Diana Ross and the Supremes broke the all-white stranglehold on the top spot. The only black faces to have been there before were the made up ones of the George Mitchell Minstrels. Sadly, Redding's number one was achieved posthumously. Four albums charted after his death, two studio sets, a compilation, and a live LP.

For the fifth time in six seasons, the Fab Four had the Christmas number one, this year with the double disc 'The Beatles', often referred to as 'The White Album'. The Rolling Stones could reach no higher than three for the second straight year. Bob Dylan, on the other hand, had a marvellous comeback from his motorcycle mishap, spending 13 weeks at number one with 'John Wesley Harding'.

Tom Jones had 135 weeks on the chart, the highest total yet achieved in any calendar year. Otis Redding also broke the previous high, set by another aeroplane casualty, Jim Reeves, by tallying

121 weeks. In the How Great Thou Were department, Elvis Presley only had 1 week on the chart in 1968, as did the George Mitchell Minstrels. The Mothers of Invention did better than both of them put together.

1969

For the third time the Beatles began and ended a year with different albums at number one. Their double LP 'The Beatles' ushered 1969 in and 'Abbey Road' showed it out. The 11 straight weeks the latter disc spent on top just before Christmas was the longest consecutive stint by any record since 'Sergeant Pepper'. 'Abbey Road's' return to the summit the last week of the year marked the fifth occasion in 1969 when a former number one encored at that position. This statistic demonstrates the instability of the chart during these 12 months.

Familiar faces pacing the pack including Bob Dylan, who successfully flirted with country music in 'Nashville Skyline', the Rolling Stones, who managed a week out front with 'Let It Bleed', and Elvis Presley, who scored a glorious comeback with 'From Elvis In Memphis'. Other rock luminaries who led the list included Cream, whose farewell set 'Goodbye' had three separate appearances at number one, the Moody Blues, who scored the first of their three toppers, and Jethro Tull, making their only standout stint with 'Stand Up'.

But one cannot overlook the achievement of the easy listening mogul Ray Conniff, who spent 3 weeks ahead of the herd without the benefit of a hit single. Jim Reeves astonished all by registering the only number one of his career 5 years after his death. It should be noted, however, that his 'According to My Heart' was a budget album, as was 'Four and Only Seekers', one of two sets by the Seekers to go all the way in 1969. The other, 'Best of the Seekers', got there on five separate occasions. The Australians had the most weeks on chart with a fairly feeble total of 66, three ahead of Simon and Garfunkel, who tallied their total without the benefit of a new release.

One LP most chartologists might not have thought of as a number one which did get there was 'Diana Ross and the Supremes Join the Temptations'. One LP most chartologists might have thought of as a number one which did not get there was the Who's rock opera 'Tommy', which had to settle for the second spot.

1970

Simon and Garfunkel were the mighty men of the new decade's first year. Britain's best-selling album of the seventies, 'Bridge Over Troubled Water,' dominated the chart, spending 23 weeks at number one. The closest competitors, 'Abbey Road' and 'Led Zeppelin III', managed 5 weeks each. The S&G catalogue also sold handsomely

in the wake of 'Water', giving the duo an astonishing 167 weeks on the chart in a single year, easily smashing Tom Jones' record of 135.

With the exception of the compilations 'Motown Chartbusters Vol 3 & 4' and the Christmas number one, 'Andy Williams Greatest Hits', every chart-topper was by a rock artist. The Beatles began their break-up year with 'Abbey Road' and parted with their spring smash 'Let It Be'. Fab Four fans obviously didn't want to say goodbye, buying enough various Beatle albums to give the group 122 weeks in the chart, the highest total of any year in their career. In parallel fashion, the greatest American star of the sixties, Bob Dylan, also had his last two number one LPs in 1970, those being 'Self Portrait' and 'New Morning'.

It was a banner year for what was then called progressive music. The Moody Blues had a number one and an admirable 115 weeks on the chart. Led Zeppelin flew over all followers with both 'II' and 'III'. Pink Floyd exploded with a real mother, 'Atom Heart Mother', and Black Sabbath won hosannas for heavy metal with their powerful 'Paranoid'.

The outstanding performance by an artist in a supporting role was by Johnny Cash. Though he did not get to number one the former Sun star did notch up 125 weeks on the chart as four albums entered on the heels of his phenomenally successful 'Johnny Cash at San Quentin'.

1971

'Bridge Over Troubled Water' was the outstanding album of yet another year, accumulating 17 weeks at number one, more than any other titleist. It was the only LP to appear on every one of the year's weekly tabulations.

Simon and Garfunkel works spent a total of 102 weeks on the chart during 1971, a sum exceeded only by the product of the prolific Andy Williams. The long-time hitmaker was at the peak of his career courtesy of his popular television series, and two different titles, 'Greatest Hits' and 'Home Loving Man', reached number one for him during the 12-month period. No other artist had more than one chart-topper this year, although three lots of uncredited session singers and instrumentalists did go all the way with budget compilations of cover versions. If anyone was involved with more than one of these productions, they have wisely remained silent.

Two ex-Beatles led the list with solo albums, Paul McCartney with 'Ram' and John Lennon with 'Imagine', though additional credits were given to Linda McCartney and the Plastic Ono Band, respectively. The Rolling Stones' first effort on their eponymous label, 'Sticky Fingers', gave them a one-for-one record. They continued their 100 per cent performance until their 1974 issue, 'It's Only

One line-up of Deep Purple. The group had a total of 15 hit albums from 1970 onwards.

Rock and Roll', only hit number two. The Stones' competitors for the title of the World's Greatest Live Rock and Roll Band, the Who, scored their only chart topper ever, 'Who's Next', while after a year of dominating the singles scene T. Rex managed an album number one in 'Electric Warrior'. Other acts enjoying outstanding years included Led Zeppelin, Rod Stewart, James Taylor, and the veteran Frank Sinatra. Only the 'My Way' man and Elvis Presley were still going strong from the original crew of 1958.

1972 Marc Bolan and a load of other people dominated the album charts in 1972. The T. Rex phenomenon was merely one aspect of genuine fan fervour. The appearance of five Various Artist LPs at number one was a triumph of marketing.

The year began with 'Electric Warrior' retaining the top spot. In May a double re-issue, 'My People Were Fair'/'Prophets Seers and Sages', grabbed the glory for a week, bearing the original label credit of Tyrannosaurus Rex. That an artist's old material released under an obsolete name could get to number one indicated the frenzied following T. Rex had at the time. The following set, 'Bolan Boogie', also went all the way. T. Rex were the first act to have three number one albums in 1 year.

Bolan's boys were one of four attractions to spend between 80 and 90 weeks on the chart in 1972. Cat Stevens did best with 89 in a year when no one hit the century.

Rod Stewart had his second good year as 'Never a Dull Moment' went to number one and 'Every Picture Tells a Story' continued a long run. These were the first two of six consecutive toppers by the leader of the Faces. That group's 'A Nod's as Good as a Wink' reached the second slot in 1972, narrowly missing an unusual double for Stewart. No artist had ever scored number ones as a soloist and a group member in the same year, though Cliff Richard had made it on his own and with the Shadows backing him. Paul Simon came close, touching the top with his eponymous solo debut in 1972, but 'Bridge Over Troubled Water' had just stopped making occasional appearances at number one.

Outside of the 'Concert for Bangladesh' triple album, the Various Artists compilations that led the list for 27 weeks, over half the year, were assembled by marketing firms for television advertising. This innovation in merchandising started a packaging trend that lasted for over a decade. Sales of this type of disc generally offered no indication of how popular taste in music was changing, as success was attributable to the impact of the commercial rather than the music itself.

1973

David Bowie and Max Bygraves have never shared the concert stage, but they certainly were together in the 1973 album charts. The innovatory space rocker had six hit LPs that year, the singalong star five. Two of Bowie's efforts, 'Aladdin Sane' and 'Pin Ups', were number ones, while the resuscitated 'Hunky Dory' soared to three. Bygraves scored three Top Ten entries with his everybody-join-in approach to medleys of old favourites. One of his charters boasted perhaps the most ludicrous title of all-time, '100 Golden Greats'.

'The Rise and Fall of Ziggy Stardust and the Spiders From Mars' had broken Bowie big in '72. Now he ruled the album chart, accumulating an unprecedented 182 weeks on the list during '73 with the six different titles. This sum shattered the mark of 167 weeks set by Simon and Garfunkel in 1970. Ironically, the defunct duo still managed to total 104 weeks in 1973, 3 years after their break-up, with the potent pairing of 'Greatest Hits' and 'Bridge Over Troubled Water'.

The siblings from the States, the Carpenters, managed 88 weeks in the list to tie Max Bygraves for third, though the positions reached were less impressive. Elton John and Slade both achieved two number ones, Gilbert O'Sullivan his only one and Roxy Music their first. Rod Stewart nabbed one as a soloist and another as a member of the Faces, completing the odd double that had eluded him in 1971.

Perhaps the most telling statistic of the year is that twenty different albums reached number one. This new high suggested that even the outstanding artists were not dominating the charts as firmly as in the sixties, and that marketing departments had learned how to achieve great sales in a limited time period.

1974

Two artists who were already strong in 1973, the Carpenters and Elton John, surged in 1974. Richard and Karen accumulated 17 weeks at number one in four summit visits with 'The Singles 1969–73', the highest total since 'Bridge Over Troubled Water'. The bespectacled pianist, who had scored two number ones the previous 12 months, bagged another brace this time, reigning with 'Caribou' and the Christmas number one 'Elton John's Greatest Hits'.

Another keyboard wizard did a double. For the second successive year the previously unknown feat of hitting the heights both as a soloist and a group member was achieved. Rick Wakeman's last album with Yes, 'Tales From Topographic Ocean', was the year's first number one. That spring the synthesiser star topped the table again with his own 'Journey to the Centre of the Earth'.

Dramatic evidence that the album and singles charts had grown far apart was offered in September. Mike Oldfield held the first two long player places with his new release, 'Hergest Ridge', and his 1973 classic, 'Tubular Bells'. The Osmonds were at one and two in the seven-inch stakes with their own 'Love Me For a Reason' and Donny and Marie's 'I'm Leaving It (All) Up to You'. Oldfield and Osmonds – two more different artists could hardly be imagined.

David Bowie narrowly nudged the Carpenters in the weeks on chart table in 1974, 107 to 106. In the process he picked up his third career number one, 'Diamond Dogs'.

The Beatles were close behind with 104, thanks to the year-long persistence of their 1973 compilations '1962–66' and '1967–70'. Paul McCartney was doubtlessly more pleased by the 7-week tenure at the top of Wings' 'Band on the Run'.

1975

The album and singles charts showed greater similarities in 1975 than in the immediate past. The three best-selling singles of the year were by the Bay City Rollers, Rod Stewart and the Stylistics, and all three artists also achieved number one LPs. 'Best of the Stylistics' spent more weeks in the Top Ten than any other disc, a statistic that startles until one recalls it benefited from a mighty marketing campaign that included considerable television advertising.

Other greatest hits albums that went to the summit courtesy of blurbs on the box included anthologies by Perry Como, Engelbert Humperdinck, Tom Jones and Jim Reeves; mass appeal singers logically benefited most from mass advertising. The one collection that went to number one naturally as a result of the artist's current popularity rather than artificial stimulus was 'Elton John's Greatest Hits'. By leading the list for the last 5 weeks of 1974 and the first 5 of 1975, the Pinner prodigy matched the Stylistics' 10 weeks over

2 calendar years. Elton was out front on his own with his total of 105 weeks on the chart, approached only by the slow-to-fade Simon and Garfunkel, whose back catalogue stayed around for one hundred more 7-day spells.

The year ended with 'Night at the Opera' pacing the pack. It included the Christmas number one single, 'Bohemian Rhapsody'. Status Quo, Led Zeppelin and Pink Floyd all lent the number one spot a heavier touch during the course of '75. Max Boyce translated his Welsh superstardom into disc sales with the first comedy number one ever, disregarding Bay City Rollers records.

1976

Beware of Greeks bearing gift tokens. There must have been a lot of them about in 1976, because Demis Roussos came from out of the Aegean blue to spend more weeks in the album chart than any other artist. The man-mountain scaled the survey with two top five entries, 'Happy to Be' and 'Forever and Ever', in reaching his total of 84 weeks, 1 more than Queen, 2 more than John Denver, and 3 more than Pink Floyd. Roussos also topped the singles chart with his 'Roussos Phenomenon' EP, the first time an Extended Play disc triumphed in that table.

The low magnitude of the leading weeks on chart total suggests that no artist dominated the field as David Bowie had only recently. This was indeed the case, as only Led Zeppelin zapped two number ones in 1976, both of which stayed on top for only 1 week. Were there a trend it would appear to have been in greatest hits compilations, with number one packages coming from Perry Como, Roy Orbison, Slim Whitman, Abba, the Beach Boys, and Glen Campbell. The legendary guitar star Bert Weedon actually made it all the way with a set of other people's hits. This information should not suggest that Weedon, Whitman, Como, Campbell or even the Beach Boys were enjoying a renaissance in singles sales, merely that television marketing of the greatest hits LP had reached the peak of its success. Only the 11 weeks spent at the summit by 'Abba's Greatest Hits', the highest sum of list leading weeks in 1976, reflected fame on forty-five. Indeed, the SuperSwedes were enjoying their best year on the singles chart.

'Rock Follies' and 'Stupidity' (by Dr. Feelgood) both reached the top without benefit of a hit single. For 'Rock Follies' the feat was doubly distinctive: the Andy Mackay-Howard Schuman score was the first television soundtrack to ever top the album chart.

1977

Marketing was the main matter when it came to getting to number one in 1977. Clever campaigns, with a heavy emphasis on television advertising, succeeded in helping several artists who had gone cold back to glory.

Slim Whitman, who had registered one hit single in 20 years, was once again brilliantly promoted to the premier long player position by United Artists promotion. The Beatles had their first summit scaler since 'Let It Be' with an extremely after-the-fact live album. Connie Francis and Bread, both of whom had fallen flat lately, had number one compilations. The role call of artists who vaulted to Valhalla with TV anthologies reads like a Hall of Fame: Johnny Mathis, Elvis Presley, Cliff Richard, Diana Ross and the Supremes, the Shadows, and Frank Sinatra. By its very nature this plethora of platters could only be issued once, so 1977 was the peak of this kind of catalogue culling.

The only number one greatest hits album that was part of the natural flow of an artist's output was Abba's. The SuperSwedes were on top for a total of 10 weeks, more than any other act or compilation. The Sex Pistols made history with their debut disc, 'Never Mind the Bollocks Here's the Sex Pistols', number one for 2 weeks in November despite some retail reluctance to display the provocative title. It was the first New Wave number one.

Pink Floyd bested Abba for most weeks on chart, 108 to 106, on the basis of their new number two, 'Animals', and their still-selling back list. In the year of his death Elvis Presley accumulated 95 weeks with an unprecedented eighteen titles, almost all re-entries.

1978

Two film soundtracks proved it was still possible for albums to achieve lengthy runs at number one, television advertising campaigns and a diverging market notwithstanding. 'Saturday Night Fever' stayed on top for 18 weeks, the longest uninterrupted reign since that of 'Sergeant Pepper's Lonely Hearts Club Band', and indeed there were fewer number one LPs in 1978, eight, than in any year since 1967, the time of the Beatle classic's release.

'Grease' was the other movie megahit, spending 13 weeks at the head of the hits. Since John Travolta starred in both films, one might assume he was the number one for 31 weeks of the year, the most by any artist since the cast of 'The Sound of Music' achieved the same figure in 1966. But though Travolta was shown on the cover of 'Fever', earning a royalty, he did not figure in the music. The Bee Gees, whose tunes dominated the motion picture, did not appear on the screen.

The real winner was the Robert Stigwood Organisation, which issued both films and both discs. The phenomenal sales these RSO albums and the singles from them enjoyed encouraged the music business to expand, an inflation of overheads that proved financially ill-advised when no similar sellers followed in the next few years.

Boney M., who shocked the system by scoring a pair of chart

topping singles in the same year, also enjoyed their most successful LP, 'Nightflight to Venus'. Abba earned 7 more number one weeks with 'The Album' and managed 112 weeks on chart during the year, clearly outdistancing all competition. Fleetwood Mac's 'Rumours', America's top record of 1977, finally managed 7 days at the summit in Britain.

1979 Nineteen different albums played musical chairs with the number one position in 1979, more than twice the total of toppers the previous year. No piece of product could compete with RSO's 1978 soundtracks in terms of length of stay at the summit. 'The Best Disco Album in the World', a Warner Brothers compilation released at the height of the disco craze and supported by television advertising, managed the longest stint, 6 weeks. Indeed, Warners as a company may have been the sales star of the year, managing to place three consecutive number ones at the top in their first week of release. Certainly the

artists involved – Led Zeppelin, Gary Numan and Boney M – could not have been appealing to the same buyers.

The real star performers of 1979 were Abba, Blondie and the Electric Light Orchestra. The first two named each achieved two number ones, spending totals of 7 and 5 weeks ahead respectively. Gary Numan did nab one winner under his own name and another in his group Tubeway Army, but each of those only lasted in the lead for 1 week.

ELO's mark of merit was the 112 weeks spent on the chart by their various albums, including the number one 'Discovery'. The Jeff Lynne-led ensemble had their finest 12 months, enjoying four Top Ten singles as well. The only act to approach ELO in weeks on chart was Blondie with an exact century; Earth Wind and Fire trailed in third with 68.

'Bat Out of Hell' by Meatloaf and Jeff Wayne's 'War of the Worlds' each spent the entire year on the chart as they headed for two of the longest runs in recent times. Neither album ever reached number one, but both ultimately outsold almost every disc that did in 1979.

1980 Twenty-three different albums led the list at some point during 1980, the most in any single year to date. The number one position was like New England's fabled weather: if you didn't like it, you could stick around for an hour and it might change. Johnny Mathis, Genesis and Rose Royce appeared in quick succession, and if the rapid variation from easy listening to rock to soul wasn't enough for the catholic consumer Sky followed with a kind of classical and pop hybrid that was impossible to categorise.

With more number one albums in a year than David Bowie has had images in a career, staying in front for even a month was an achievement. The Pretenders made it with their eponymous debut disc, and Roxy Music found 4 weeks in two stints with 'Flesh and Blood'. The star performers of the year were Police and Abba. The Bleach Boys had their second number one LP, 'Zenyatta Mondatta', and scored 116 on chart in total, far in front of the 70-week sum of runner-up AC/DC. The SuperSwedes once again had charttoppers early and late in a year, registering in January with 'Greatest Hits Volume 2' and beginning a 9-week rule in November with 'Super Trouper'.

An extremely odd circumstance characterised the spring. For the entire season, albums had 2-week runs at number one and were then replaced. Seven LPs were in the spring string. The previous record for consecutive 2-week reigns had been a mere two, so this development was certainly curious if ultimately unimportant.

1981 To find the top album artists of 1981 one didn't have to look far beyond the letter 'A' in alphabetical browser bins. Abba began and ended the year at number one with 'Super Trouper' and 'The Visitors', extending their string of charttopping LPs to 7. Adam and the Ants were the breakout act of the year, accumulating 12 weeks at the summit with 'Kings of the Wild Frontier', the longest leading stint. 'Kings' was also one of five long players to stay the course for the entire year. It was joined by previous Adam material and the end-of-year release 'Prince Charming' to give the Ants 87 weeks on the chart, a total topped only by Barry Manilow. The American balladeer bettered the Ant total by 5 weeks. Personal appearances and heavy promotion gave him a career peak in Britain several years after he had done his best at home.

One had to look hard to find evidence of the growth of technopop, the synthesised sound making great inroads in the singles market. 'Dare' by the Human League was the nation's best-seller for 1

week, but this was before the fourth single from the set, 'Don't You Want Me', became the year's Christmas number one and propelled its parent back up the chart in 1982. Ultravox, important pioneers of technopop, re-entered for another 48 weeks with 'Vienna' on the strength of the single of the same name.

There were oddities, as always. 'The Royal Wedding' of Prince Charles to Lady Diana Spencer was number one for a fortnight, twice as long as Motorhead managed with their equally live 'No Sleep Till Hammersmith', but the Royals never challenged the heavy metal merchants to a battle of the bands.

1982 'Remember my name', Irene Cara advised in the title tune of the film *Fame*, 'I'm gonna live forever'. Well, almost. *Fame* itself proved to be more enduring than any of the young people in it.

When the BBC began broadcasting the American television series 'Fame', a spin-off from the Alan Parker movie, Cara's original version of the theme song zoomed to the top of the singles chart. The US label for her solo efforts, Network, did not have a UK distribution deal at the time, so the RSO soundtrack was the only LP available containing the hit. 'Fame' went to number one, and it seemed as if a quaint resuscitation of a former American hit had peaked quickly. It was actually only the beginning of a phenomenon.

BBC Records' 'The Kids From Fame' television cast collection, number two while the movie melodies were ahead, proceeded to lead the list itself. Fuelled by two Top Ten singles, this album sold over 850,000 copies by December, surpassing even the previous year's 'Royal Wedding' to become the BBC's best-selling long player.

RCA had leased the album because BBC–1 could only plug vinyl with the BBC label, and they needed to establish the singing actors as a recording act. Mission accomplished, they issued a second TV platter, 'The Kids From Fame Again', and this also made the top three.

The sales success of the 'Kids From Fame' was peculiar to Britain. In contrast, the only LP that outsold theirs in the UK in 1982 was by a worldwide star. 'Love Songs' by Barbra Streisand was the year's best seller. That it did so well was mildly surprising, since it was a make-do collection with only two new songs assembled in lieu of new product by The Nose from New York.

ABC distinguished themselves by spending their first-ever week on the chart at number one with 'The Lexicon of Love'. The debut marked another first, the initial joint number one on the album chart. 'The Lexicon of Love' shared the spotlight with – yes – 'Fame'.